CLASSICS IN THE HISTORY OF POLITICAL THOUGHT

D0315127

CLASSICS IN THE HISTORY OF POLITICAL THOUGHT

AN ANTHOLOGY
SECOND EDITION

VOLUME I

DOME ACADEMIC PUBLISHERS

Published by Dome Academic Publishers
359 20th Avenue, Suite 304, San Francisco, CA 94121
DomeAcademicPublishers@gmail.com

Editorial matter copyright 2008 © Dome Academic Publishers. All rights reserved.

1st edition published 2007
Printed in the United States of America
Typeface Times 10pt

Classics in the History of Political Thought: An Anthology – 2nd ed.
Volumes I and II
1. Political Science- Political Theory.   2. Political Philosophy
I. Title. II. Title: Anthology, Volumes I and II

ISBN-10: 0-9798174-2-0
ISBN-13: 978-0-9798174-2-7

Front cover illustration: from the 1651 edition of *Leviathan* by Thomas Hobbes

Contents

Editors' Note

The present revised 2-volume edition brings together key classic texts in the history of political thought. The editors sought to minimize the reliance on excerpts in favor of giving the readers access to the entire texts. Thus, all readings except Plato's *Republic*, Aristotle's *Politics*, Hobbes' *Leviathan*, and Adam Smith's *On the Wealth of Nations* are reprinted in their entirety.

The versions of texts in the present edition draw on the following translations: Plato, *The Republic*, trans. Benjamin Jowett; Aristotle, *Politics*, trans. Benjamin Jowett; Machiavelli, *The Prince*, trans. W. K. Marriott; Locke, *A Letter Concerning Toleration*, trans. William Popple; Rousseau, *Discourse on the Origin of Inequality* and *The Social Contract*, both trans. G. D. H. Cole; and Marx and Engels' *Manifesto of the Communist Party*, trans. Samuel Moore with Friedrich Engels. Marx's *Critique of the Gotha Program* follows the first English edition of 1900.

Plato

Plato (b. 424 BC, Athens, d. 347 BC Athens) was one of the greatest Ancient Greek philosophers and scientists. He was a student of Socrates, who appears as the main interlocutor in many of his works, which are written in the form of dialogues with various disciples and critics. Plato was highly influenced by Socrates' ideas, which are difficult to separate from Plato's own, given the form of Plato's writings and the fact that Socrates left no independent written work of his own. Plato was also profoundly affected by what he saw as Socrates' unjust death in the hands of his unenlightened critics.

Plato established in Athens one of the first institutions of higher education, the Academy, and counted as one of his many students there the young Aristotle. Plato's most important contributions to political philosophy include two of his longest dialogues, *The Republic* and *The Laws*.

Plato's theory of the nature of things (their "ideal forms") has been largely determinative of the way scientists and mathematicians have thought about their subjects all the way into the 20th century, when it was challenged in the work of Ludwig Wittgenstein, Kurt Gödel, and others. A parallel conflict of ideas has occurred in moral and political philosophy, largely under the influence of the work of Friedrich Nietzsche, Martin Heidegger, Michel Foucault, and others.

*****

BOOK VI

SOCRATES, GLAUCON.

And thus, Glaucon, after the argument has gone a weary way, the true and the false philosophers have at length appeared in view.

5   I do not think, he said, that the way could have been shortened.

I suppose not, I said; and yet I believe that we might have had a better view of both of them if the discussion could have been confined to this one subject and if there were not many other questions awaiting us, which he who desires to see in what respect the life of the just differs from that of the unjust must
10   consider.

And what is the next question? he asked.

Surely, I said, the one which follows next in order. Inasmuch as philosophers only are able to grasp the eternal and unchangeable, and those who wander in the region of the many and variable are not philosophers, I must ask
15   you which of the two classes should be the rulers of our State?

And how can we rightly answer that question?

Whichever of the two are best able to guard the laws and institutions of our State — let them be our guardians.

Very good.

20   Neither, I said, can there be any question that the guardian who is to keep anything should have eyes rather than no eyes?

There can be no question of that.

And are not those who are verily and indeed wanting in the knowledge of
the true being of each thing, and who have in their souls no clear pattern, and are
unable as with a painter's eye to look at the absolute truth and to that original to
5   repair, and having perfect vision of the other world to order the laws about
beauty, goodness, justice in this, if not already ordered, and to guard and
preserve the order of them — are not such persons, I ask, simply blind?

Truly, he replied, they are much in that condition.

And shall they be our guardians when there are others who, besides being
10   their equals in experience and falling short of them in no particular of virtue,
also know the very truth of each thing?

There can be no reason, he said, for rejecting those who have this greatest of
all great qualities; they must always have the first place unless they fail in some
other respect.

15   Suppose then, I said, that we determine how far they can unite this and the
other excellences.

By all means.

In the first place, as we began by observing, the nature of the philosopher
has to be ascertained. We must come to an understanding about him, and, when
20   we have done so, then, if I am not mistaken, we shall also acknowledge that
such an union of qualities is possible, and that those in whom they are united,
and those only, should be rulers in the State.

What do you mean?

Let us suppose that philosophical minds always love knowledge of a sort
25   which shows them the eternal nature not varying from generation and
corruption.

Agreed.

And further, I said, let us agree that they are lovers of all true being; there is no part whether greater or less, or more or less honourable, which they are willing to renounce; as we said before of the lover and the man of ambition.

True.

5   And if they are to be what we were describing, is there not another quality which they should also possess?

What quality?

Truthfulness: they will never intentionally receive into their mind falsehood, which is their detestation, and they will love the truth.

10   Yes, that may be safely affirmed of them.

"May be," my friend, I replied, is not the word; say rather "must be affirmed:" for he whose nature is amorous of anything cannot help loving all that belongs or is akin to the object of his affections.

Right, he said.

15   And is there anything more akin to wisdom than truth?

How can there be?

Can the same nature be a lover of wisdom and a lover of falsehood? Never.

The true lover of learning then must from his earliest youth, as far as in him lies, desire all truth?

20   Assuredly.

But then again, as we know by experience, he whose desires are strong in one direction will have them weaker in others; they will be like a stream which has been drawn off into another channel.

True.

He whose desires are drawn towards knowledge in every form will be absorbed in the pleasures of the soul, and will hardly feel bodily pleasure — I mean, if he be a true philosopher and not a sham one.

That is most certain.

5   Such an one is sure to be temperate and the reverse of covetous; for the motives which make another man desirous of having and spending, have no place in his character.

Very true.

Another criterion of the philosophical nature has also to be considered.
10   What is that?

There should be no secret corner of illiberality; nothing can more antagonistic than meanness to a soul which is ever longing after the whole of things both divine and human.

Most true, he replied.

15   Then how can he who has magnificence of mind and is the spectator of all time and all existence, think much of human life?

He cannot.

Or can such an one account death fearful?

No indeed.

20   Then the cowardly and mean nature has no part in true philosophy?
Certainly not.

Or again: can he who is harmoniously constituted, who is not covetous or mean, or a boaster, or a coward — can he, I say, ever be unjust or hard in his dealings?

25   Impossible.

Then you will soon observe whether a man is just and gentle, or rude and unsociable; these are the signs which distinguish even in youth the philosophical nature from the unphilosophical.

True.

5   There is another point which should be remarked.

What point?

Whether he has or has not a pleasure in learning; for no one will love that which gives him pain, and in which after much toil he makes little progress.

Certainly not.

10   And again, if he is forgetful and retains nothing of what he learns, will he not be an empty vessel?

That is certain.

Labouring in vain, he must end in hating himself and his fruitless occupation?

15   Yes.

Then a soul which forgets cannot be ranked among genuine philosophic natures; we must insist that the philosopher should have a good memory?

Certainly.

And once more, the inharmonious and unseemly nature can only tend to
20   disproportion?

Undoubtedly.

And do you consider truth to be akin to proportion or to disproportion? To proportion.

Then, besides other qualities, we must try to find a naturally well-proportioned and gracious mind, which will move spontaneously towards the true being of everything.

Certainly.

5 Well, and do not all these qualities, which we have been enumerating, go together, and are they not, in a manner, necessary to a soul, which is to have a full and perfect participation of being?

They are absolutely necessary, he replied.

And must not that be a blameless study which he only can pursue who has the gift of a good memory, and is quick to learn, — noble, gracious, the friend of
10 truth, justice, courage, temperance, who are his kindred?

The god of jealousy himself, he said, could find no fault with such a study.

And to men like him, I said, when perfected by years and education, and to these only you will entrust the State.

Here Adeimantus interposed and said: To these statements, Socrates, no one
15 can offer a reply; but when you talk in this way, a strange feeling passes over the minds of your hearers: They fancy that they are led astray a little at each step in the argument, owing to their own want of skill in asking and answering questions; these littles accumulate, and at the end of the discussion they are found to have sustained a mighty overthrow and all their former notions appear
20 to be turned upside down. And as unskilful players of draughts are at last shut up by their more skilful adversaries and have no piece to move, so they too find themselves shut up at last; for they have nothing to say in this new game of which words are the counters; and yet all the time they are in the right. The observation is suggested to me by what is now occurring. For any one of us
25 might say, that although in words he is not able to meet you at each step of the argument, he sees as a fact that the votaries of philosophy, when they carry on the study, not only in youth as a part of education, but as the pursuit of their maturer years, most of them become strange monsters, not to say utter rogues, and that those who may be considered the best of them are made useless to the
30 world by the very study which you extol.

Well, and do you think that those who say so are wrong? I cannot tell, he replied; but I should like to know what is your opinion.

Hear my answer; I am of opinion that they are quite right.

Then how can you be justified in saying that cities will not cease from evil
5   until philosophers rule in them, when philosophers are acknowledged by us to be of no use to them?

You ask a question, I said, to which a reply can only be given in a parable.

Yes, Socrates; and that is a way of speaking to which you are not at all accustomed, I suppose.

10   I perceive, I said, that you are vastly amused at having plunged me into such a hopeless discussion; but now hear the parable, and then you will be still more amused at the meagreness of my imagination: for the manner in which the best men are treated in their own States is so grievous that no single thing on earth is comparable to it; and therefore, if I am to plead their cause, I must have
15   recourse to fiction, and put together a figure made up of many things, like the fabulous unions of goats and stags which are found in pictures. Imagine then a fleet or a ship in which there is a captain who is taller and stronger than any of the crew, but he is a little deaf and has a similar infirmity in sight, and his knowledge of navigation is not much better. The sailors are quarrelling with one
20   another about the steering — every one is of opinion that he has a right to steer, though he has never learned the art of navigation and cannot tell who taught him or when he learned, and will further assert that it cannot be taught, and they are ready to cut in pieces any one who says the contrary. They throng about the captain, begging and praying him to commit the helm to them; and if at any time
25   they do not prevail, but others are preferred to them, they kill the others or throw them overboard, and having first chained up the noble captain's senses with drink or some narcotic drug, they mutiny and take possession of the ship and make free with the stores; thus, eating and drinking, they proceed on their voyage in such a manner as might be expected of them. Him who is their
30   partisan and cleverly aids them in their plot for getting the ship out of the captain's hands into their own whether by force or persuasion, they compliment with the name of sailor, pilot, able seaman, and abuse the other sort of man, whom they call a good-for-nothing; but that the true pilot must pay attention to the year and seasons and sky and stars and winds, and whatever else belongs to
35   his art, if he intends to be really qualified for the command of a ship, and that he

must and will be the steerer, whether other people like or not — the possibility
of this union of authority with the steerer's art has never seriously entered into
their thoughts or been made part of their calling. Now in vessels which are in a
state of mutiny and by sailors who are mutineers, how will the true pilot be
5   regarded? Will he not be called by them a prater, a star-gazer, a good-for-
nothing?

   Of course, said Adeimantus.

   Then you will hardly need, I said, to hear the interpretation of the figure,
which describes the true philosopher in his relation to the State; for you
10   understand already.

   Certainly.

   Then suppose you now take this parable to the gentleman who is surprised
at finding that philosophers have no honour in their cities; explain it to him and
try to convince him that their having honour would be far more extraordinary.

15   I will.

   Say to him, that, in deeming the best votaries of philosophy to be useless to
the rest of the world, he is right; but also tell him to attribute their uselessness to
the fault of those who will not use them, and not to themselves. The pilot should
not humbly beg the sailors to be commanded by him — that is not the order of
20   nature; neither are "the wise to go to the doors of the rich" — the ingenious
author of this saying told a lie — but the truth is, that, when a man is ill, whether
he be rich or poor, to the physician he must go, and he who wants to be
governed, to him who is able to govern. The ruler who is good for anything
ought not to beg his subjects to be ruled by him; although the present governors
25   of mankind are of a different stamp; they may be justly compared to the
mutinous sailors, and the true helmsmen to those who are called by them good-
for-nothings and star-gazers.

   Precisely so, he said.

   For these reasons, and among men like these, philosophy, the noblest
30   pursuit of all, is not likely to be much esteemed by those of the opposite faction;
not that the greatest and most lasting injury is done to her by her opponents, but

by her own professing followers, the same of whom you suppose the accuser to say, that the greater number of them are arrant rogues, and the best are useless; in which opinion I agreed.

Yes.

5   And the reason why the good are useless has now been explained?

True.

Then shall we proceed to show that the corruption of the majority is also unavoidable, and that this is not to be laid to the charge of philosophy any more than the other?

10   By all means.

And let us ask and answer in turn, first going back to the description of the gentle and noble nature. Truth, as you will remember, was his leader, whom he followed always and in all things; failing in this, he was an impostor, and had no part or lot in true philosophy.

15   Yes, that was said.

Well, and is not this one quality, to mention no others, greatly at variance with present notions of him?

Certainly, he said.

And have we not a right to say in his defence, that the true lover of
20   knowledge is always striving after being — that is his nature; he will not rest in the multiplicity of individuals which is an appearance only, but will go on — the keen edge will not be blunted, nor the force of his desire abate until he have attained the knowledge of the true nature of every essence by a sympathetic and kindred power in the soul, and by that power drawing near and mingling and
25   becoming incorporate with very being, having begotten mind and truth, he will have knowledge and will live and grow truly, and then, and not till then, will he cease from his travail.

Nothing, he said, can be more just than such a description of him.

And will the love of a lie be any part of a philosopher's nature? Will he not utterly hate a lie?

He will.

5   And when truth is the captain, we cannot suspect any evil of the band which he leads?

Impossible.

Justice and health of mind will be of the company, and temperance will follow after?

10   True, he replied.

Neither is there any reason why I should again set in array the philosopher's virtues, as you will doubtless remember that courage, magnificence, apprehension, memory, were his natural gifts. And you objected that, although no one could deny what I then said, still, if you leave words and look at facts,
15   the persons who are thus described are some of them manifestly useless, and the greater number utterly depraved; we were then led to enquire into the grounds of these accusations, and have now arrived at the point of asking why are the majority bad, which question of necessity brought us back to the examination and definition of the true philosopher.

20   Exactly.

And we have next to consider the of the philosophic nature, why so many are spoiled and so few escape spoiling — I am speaking of those who were said to be useless but not wicked — and, when we have done with them, we will speak of the imitators of philosophy, what manner of men are they who aspire
25   after a profession which is above them and of which they are unworthy, and then, by their manifold inconsistencies, bring upon philosophy, and upon all philosophers, that universal reprobation of which we speak.

What are these corruptions? he said.

11

I will see if I can explain them to you. Every one will admit that a nature having in perfection all the qualities which we required in a philosopher, is a rare plant which is seldom seen among men.

Rare indeed.

5   And what numberless and powerful causes tend to destroy these rare natures!

What causes?

In the first place there are their own virtues, their courage, temperance, and the rest of them, every one of which praise worthy qualities (and this is a most
10   singular circumstance) destroys and distracts from philosophy the soul which is the possessor of them.

That is very singular, he replied.

Then there are all the ordinary goods of life — beauty, wealth, strength, rank, and great connections in the State — you understand the sort of things —
15   these also have a corrupting and distracting effect.

I understand; but I should like to know more precisely what you mean about them.

Grasp the truth as a whole, I said, and in the right way; you will then have no difficulty in apprehending the preceding remarks, and they will no longer
20   appear strange to you.

And how am I to do so? he asked.

Why, I said, we know that all germs or seeds, whether vegetable or animal, when they fail to meet with proper nutriment or climate or soil, in proportion to their vigour, are all the more sensitive to the want of a suitable environment, for
25   evil is a greater enemy to what is good than what is not.

Very true.

There is reason in supposing that the finest natures, when under alien

12

conditions, receive more injury than the inferior, because the contrast is greater.

Certainly.

And may we not say, Adeimantus, that the most gifted minds, when they are ill-educated, become pre-eminently bad? Do not great crimes and the spirit
5   of pure evil spring out of a fulness of nature ruined by education rather than from any inferiority, whereas weak natures are scarcely capable of any very great good or very great evil?

There I think that you are right.

And our philosopher follows the same analogy — he is like a plant which,
10   having proper nurture, must necessarily grow and mature into all virtue, but, if sown and planted in an alien soil, becomes the most noxious of all weeds, unless he be preserved by some divine power. Do you really think, as people so often say, that our youth are corrupted by Sophists, or that private teachers of the art corrupt them in any degree worth speaking of? Are not the public who say these
15   things the greatest of all Sophists? And do they not educate to perfection young and old, men and women alike, and fashion them after their own hearts?

When is this accomplished? he said.

When they meet together, and the world sits down at an assembly, or in a court of law, or a theatre, or a camp, or in any other popular resort, and there is a
20   great uproar, and they praise some things which are being said or done, and blame other things, equally exaggerating both, shouting and clapping their hands, and the echo of the rocks and the place in which they are assembled redoubles the sound of the praise or blame — at such a time will not a young man's heart, as they say, leap within him? Will any private training enable him
25   to stand firm against the overwhelming flood of popular opinion? or will he be carried away by the stream? Will he not have the notions of good and evil which the public in general have — he will do as they do, and as they are, such will he be?

Yes, Socrates; necessity will compel him.

30   And yet, I said, there is a still greater necessity, which has not been mentioned.

What is that?

The gentle force of attainder or confiscation or death which, as you are aware, these new Sophists and educators who are the public, apply when their words are powerless.

5   Indeed they do; and in right good earnest.

Now what opinion of any other Sophist, or of any private person, can be expected to overcome in such an unequal contest?

None, he replied.

No, indeed, I said, even to make the attempt is a great piece of folly; there
10   neither is, nor has been, nor is ever likely to be, any different type of character which has had no other training in virtue but that which is supplied by public opinion — I speak, my friend, of human virtue only; what is more than human, as the proverb says, is not included: for I would not have you ignorant that, in the present evil state of governments, whatever is saved and comes to good is
15   saved by the power of God, as we may truly say.

I quite assent, he replied.

Then let me crave your assent also to a further observation.

What are you going to say?

Why, that all those mercenary individuals, whom the many call Sophists
20   and whom they deem to be their adversaries, do, in fact, teach nothing but the opinion of the many, that is to say, the opinions of their assemblies; and this is their wisdom. I might compare them to a man who should study the tempers and desires of a mighty strong beast who is fed by him — he would learn how to approach and handle him, also at what times and from what causes he is
25   dangerous or the reverse, and what is the meaning of his several cries, and by what sounds, when another utters them, he is soothed or infuriated; and you may suppose further, that when, by continually attending upon him, he has become perfect in all this, he calls his knowledge wisdom, and makes of it a system or art, which he proceeds to teach, although he has no real notion of what he means
30   by the principles or passions of which he is speaking, but calls this honourable

and that dishonourable, or good or evil, or just or unjust, all in accordance with the tastes and tempers of the great brute. Good he pronounces to be that in which the beast delights and evil to be that which he dislikes; and he can give no other account of them except that the just and noble are the necessary, having never
5   himself seen, and having no power of explaining to others the nature of either, or the difference between them, which is immense. By heaven, would not such an one be a rare educator?

Indeed, he would.

And in what way does he who thinks that wisdom is the discernment of the
10   tempers and tastes of the motley multitude, whether in painting or music, or, finally, in politics, differ from him whom I have been describing For when a man consorts with the many, and exhibits to them his poem or other work of art or the service which he has done the State, making them his judges when he is not obliged, the so-called necessity of Diomede will oblige him to produce
15   whatever they praise. And yet the reasons are utterly ludicrous which they give in confirmation of their own notions about the honourable and good. Did you ever hear any of them which were not?

No, nor am I likely to hear.

You recognise the truth of what I have been saying? Then let me ask you to
20   consider further whether the world will ever be induced to believe in the existence of absolute beauty rather than of the many beautiful, or of the absolute in each kind rather than of the many in each kind?

Certainly not.

Then the world cannot possibly be a philosopher?

25   Impossible.

And therefore philosophers must inevitably fall under the censure of the world?

They must.

And of individuals who consort with the mob and seek to please them? That is evident.

Then, do you see any way in which the philosopher can be preserved in his calling to the end? and remember what we were saying of him, that he was to have quickness and memory and courage and magnificence — these were admitted by us to be the true philosopher's gifts.

Yes.

Will not such an one from his early childhood be in all things first among all, especially if his bodily endowments are like his mental ones?

Certainly, he said.

And his friends and fellow-citizens will want to use him as he gets older for their own purposes?

No question.

Falling at his feet, they will make requests to him and do him honour and flatter him, because they want to get into their hands now, the power which he will one day possess.

That often happens, he said.

And what will a man such as he be likely to do under such circumstances, especially if he be a citizen of a great city, rich and noble, and a tall proper youth? Will he not be full of boundless aspirations, and fancy himself able to manage the affairs of Hellenes and of barbarians, and having got such notions into his head will he not dilate and elevate himself in the fulness of vain pomp and senseless pride?

To be sure he will.

Now, when he is in this state of mind, if some one gently comes to him and tells him that he is a fool and must get understanding, which can only be got by slaving for it, do you think that, under such adverse circumstances, he will be easily induced to listen?

Far otherwise.

And even if there be some one who through inherent goodness or natural reasonableness has had his eyes opened a little and is humbled and taken captive
5   by philosophy, how will his friends behave when they think that they are likely to lose the advantage which they were hoping to reap from his companionship? Will they not do and say anything to prevent him from yielding to his better nature and to render his teacher powerless, using to this end private intrigues as well as public prosecutions?

10   There can be no doubt of it.

And how can one who is thus circumstanced ever become a philosopher? Impossible.

Then were we not right in saying that even the very qualities which make a man a philosopher may, if he be ill-educated, divert him from philosophy, no
15   less than riches and their accompaniments and the other so-called goods of life?

We were quite right.

Thus, my excellent friend, is brought about all that ruin and failure which I have been describing of the natures best adapted to the best of all pursuits; they are natures which we maintain to be rare at any time; this being the class out of
20   which come the men who are the authors of the greatest evil to States and individuals; and also of the greatest good when the tide carries them in that direction; but a small man never was the doer of any great thing either to individuals or to States.

That is most true, he said.

25   And so philosophy is left desolate, with her marriage rite incomplete: for her own have fallen away and forsaken her, and while they are leading a false and unbecoming life, other unworthy persons, seeing that she has no kinsmen to be her protectors, enter in and dishonour her; and fasten upon her the reproaches which, as you say, her reprovers utter, who affirm of her votaries that some are
30   good for nothing, and that the greater number deserve the severest punishment.

That is certainly what people say.

Yes; and what else would you expect, I said, when you think of the puny
creatures who, seeing this land open to them — a land well stocked with fair
names and showy titles — like prisoners running out of prison into a sanctuary,
5   take a leap out of their trades into philosophy; those who do so being probably
the cleverest hands at their own miserable crafts? For, although philosophy be in
this evil case, still there remains a dignity about her which is not to be found in
the arts. And many are thus attracted by her whose natures are imperfect and
whose souls are maimed and disfigured by their meannesses, as their bodies are
10   by their trades and crafts. Is not this unavoidable?

Yes.

Are they not exactly like a bald little tinker who has just got out of durance
and come into a fortune; he takes a bath and puts on a new coat, and is decked
out as a bridegroom going to marry his master's daughter, who is left poor and
15   desolate?

A most exact parallel.

What will be the issue of such marriages? Will they not be vile and bastard?

There can be no question of it.

And when persons who are unworthy of education approach philosophy and
20   make an alliance with her who is a rank above them what sort of ideas and
opinions are likely to be generated? Will they not be sophisms captivating to the
ear, having nothing in them genuine, or worthy of or akin to true wisdom?

No doubt, he said.

Then, Adeimantus, I said, the worthy disciples of philosophy will be but a
25   small remnant: perchance some noble and well-educated person, detained by
exile in her service, who in the absence of corrupting influences remains
devoted to her; or some lofty soul born in a mean city, the politics of which he
contemns and neglects; and there may be a gifted few who leave the arts, which
they justly despise, and come to her; — or peradventure there are some who are
30   restrained by our friend Theages' bridle; for everything in the life of Theages

18

conspired to divert him from philosophy; but ill-health kept him away from politics. My own case of the internal sign is hardly worth mentioning, for rarely, if ever, has such a monitor been given to any other man. Those who belong to this small class have tasted how sweet and blessed a possession philosophy is,
5   and have also seen enough of the madness of the multitude; and they know that no politician is honest, nor is there any champion of justice at whose side they may fight and be saved. Such an one may be compared to a man who has fallen among wild beasts — he will not join in the wickedness of his fellows, but neither is he able singly to resist all their fierce natures, and therefore seeing that
10 he would be of no use to the State or to his friends, and reflecting that he would have to throw away his life without doing any good either to himself or others, he holds his peace, and goes his own way. He is like one who, in the storm of dust and sleet which the driving wind hurries along, retires under the shelter of a wall; and seeing the rest of mankind full of wickedness, he is content, if only he
15 can live his own life and be pure from evil or unrighteousness, and depart in peace and good-will, with bright hopes.

Yes, he said, and he will have done a great work before he departs.

A great work — yes; but not the greatest, unless he find a State suitable to him; for in a State which is suitable to him, he will have a larger growth and be
20 the saviour of his country, as well as of himself.

The causes why philosophy is in such an evil name have now been sufficiently explained: the injustice of the charges against her has been shown — is there anything more which you wish to say?

Nothing more on that subject, he replied; but I should like to know which of
25 the governments now existing is in your opinion the one adapted to her.

Not any of them, I said; and that is precisely the accusation which I bring against them — not one of them is worthy of the philosophic nature, and hence that nature is warped and estranged; — as the exotic seed which is sown in a foreign land becomes denaturalized, and is wont to be overpowered and to lose
30 itself in the new soil, even so this growth of philosophy, instead of persisting, degenerates and receives another character. But if philosophy ever finds in the State that perfection which she herself is, then will be seen that she is in truth divine, and that all other things, whether natures of men or institutions, are but human; — and now, I know that you are going to ask, what that State is.

No, he said; there you are wrong, for I was going to ask another question —
whether it is the State of which. we are the founders and inventors, or some
other?

Yes, I replied, ours in most respects; but you may remember my saying
5   before, that some living authority would always be required in the State having
the same idea of the constitution which guided you when as legislator you were
laying down the laws.

That was said, he replied.

Yes, but not in a satisfactory manner; you frightened us by interposing
10   objections, which certainly showed that the discussion would be long and
difficult; and what still remains is the reverse of easy.

What is there remaining?

The question how the study of philosophy may be so ordered as not to be
the ruin of the State: All great attempts are attended with risk; "hard is the
15   good," as men say.

Still, he said, let the point be cleared up, and the enquiry will then be
complete.

I shall not be hindered, I said, by any want of will, but, if at all, by a want of
power: my zeal you may see for yourselves; and please to remark in what I am
20   about to say how boldly and unhesitatingly I declare that States should pursue
philosophy, not as they do now, but in a different spirit.

In what manner?

At present, I said, the students of philosophy are quite young; beginning
when they are hardly past childhood, they devote only the time saved from
25   moneymaking and housekeeping to such pursuits; and even those of them who
are reputed to have most of the philosophic spirit, when they come within sight
of the great difficulty of the subject, I mean dialectic, take themselves off. In
after life when invited by some one else, they may, perhaps, go and hear a
lecture, and about this they make much ado, for philosophy is not considered by
30   them to be their proper business: at last, when they grow old, in most cases they

20

are extinguished more truly than Heracleitus' sun, inasmuch as they never light up again.

But what ought to be their course?

Just the opposite. In childhood and youth their study, and what philosophy
5 they learn, should be suited to their tender years: during this period while they are growing up towards manhood, the chief and special care should be given to their bodies that they may have them to use in the service of philosophy; as life advances and the intellect begins to mature, let them increase the gymnastics of the soul; but when the strength of our citizens fails and is past civil and military
10 duties, then let them range at will and engage in no serious labour, as we intend them to live happily here, and to crown this life with a similar happiness in another.

How truly in earnest you are, Socrates! he said; I am sure of that; and yet most of your hearers, if I am not mistaken, are likely to be still more earnest in
15 their opposition to you, and will never be convinced; Thrasymachus least of all.

Do not make a quarrel, I said, between Thrasymachus and me, who have recently become friends, although, indeed, we were never enemies; for I shall go on striving to the utmost until I either convert him and other men, or do something which may profit them against the day when they live again, and hold
20 the like discourse in another state of existence.

You are speaking of a time which is not very near.

Rather, I replied, of a time which is as nothing in comparison with eternity. Nevertheless, I do not wonder that the many refuse to believe; for they have never seen that of which we are now speaking realised; they have seen only a
25 conventional imitation of philosophy, consisting of words artificially brought together, not like these of ours having a natural unity. But a human being who in word and work is perfectly moulded, as far as he can be, into the proportion and likeness of virtue — such a man ruling in a city which bears the same image, they have never yet seen, neither one nor many of them — do you think that
30 they ever did?

No indeed.

No, my friend, and they have seldom, if ever, heard free and noble sentiments; such as men utter when they are earnestly and by every means in their power seeking after truth for the sake of knowledge, while they look coldly on the subtleties of controversy, of which the end is opinion and strife, whether
5   they meet with them in the courts of law or in society.

They are strangers, he said, to the words of which you speak.

And this was what we foresaw, and this was the reason why truth forced us to admit, not without fear and hesitation, that neither cities nor States nor individuals will ever attain perfection until the small class of philosophers whom
10 we termed useless but not corrupt are providentially compelled, whether they will or not, to take care of the State, and until a like necessity be laid on the State to obey them; or until kings, or if not kings, the sons of kings or princes, are divinely inspired with a true love of true philosophy. That either or both of these alternatives are impossible, I see no reason to affirm: if they were so, we might
15 indeed be justly ridiculed as dreamers and visionaries. Am I not right?

Quite right.

If then, in the countless ages of the past, or at the present hour in some foreign clime which is far away and beyond our ken, the perfected philosopher is or has been or hereafter shall be compelled by a superior power to have the
20 charge of the State, we are ready to assert to the death, that this our constitution has been, and is — yea, and will be whenever the Muse of Philosophy is queen. There is no impossibility in all this; that there is a difficulty, we acknowledge ourselves.

My opinion agrees with yours, he said.

25 But do you mean to say that this is not the opinion of the multitude?

I should imagine not, he replied.

O my friend, I said, do not attack the multitude: they will change their minds, if, not in an aggressive spirit, but gently and with the view of soothing them and removing their dislike of over-education, you show them your
30 philosophers as they really are and describe as you were just now doing their character and profession, and then mankind will see that he of whom you are

speaking is not such as they supposed — if they view him in this new light, they will surely change their notion of him, and answer in another strain. Who can be at enmity with one who loves them, who that is himself gentle and free from envy will be jealous of one in whom there is no jealousy? Nay, let me answer
5   for you, that in a few this harsh temper may be found but not in the majority of mankind.

I quite agree with you, he said.

And do you not also think, as I do, that the harsh feeling which the many entertain towards philosophy originates in the pretenders, who rush in uninvited,
10   and are always abusing them, and finding fault with them, who make persons instead of things the theme of their conversation? and nothing can be more unbecoming in philosophers than this.

It is most unbecoming.

For he, Adeimantus, whose mind is fixed upon true being, has surely no
15   time to look down upon the affairs of earth, or to be filled with malice and envy, contending against men; his eye is ever directed towards things fixed and immutable, which he sees neither injuring nor injured by one another, but all in order moving according to reason; these he imitates, and to these he will, as far as he can, conform himself. Can a man help imitating that with which he holds
20   reverential converse?

Impossible.

And the philosopher holding converse with the divine order, becomes orderly and divine, as far as the nature of man allows; but like every one else, he will suffer from detraction.

25   Of course.

And if a necessity be laid upon him of fashioning, not only himself, but human nature generally, whether in States or individuals, into that which he beholds elsewhere, will he, think you, be an unskilful artificer of justice, temperance, and every civil virtue?

30   Anything but unskilful.

And if the world perceives that what we are saying about him is the truth, will they be angry with philosophy? Will they disbelieve us, when we tell them that no State can be happy which is not designed by artists who imitate the heavenly pattern?

5   They will not be angry if they understand, he said. But how will they draw out the plan of which you are speaking?

They will begin by taking the State and the manners of men, from which, as from a tablet, they will rub out the picture, and leave a clean surface. This is no easy task. But whether easy or not, herein will lie the difference between them
10   and every other legislator, — they will have nothing to do either with individual or State, and will inscribe no laws, until they have either found, or themselves made, a clean surface.

They will be very right, he said.

Having effected this, they will proceed to trace an outline of the
15   constitution?

No doubt.

And when they are filling in the work, as I conceive, they will often turn their eyes upwards and downwards: I mean that they will first look at absolute justice and beauty and temperance, and again at the human copy; and will
20   mingle and temper the various elements of life into the image of a man; and thus they will conceive according to that other image, which, when existing among men, Homer calls the form and likeness of God.

Very true, he said.

And one feature they will erase, and another they will put in, they have
25   made the ways of men, as far as possible, agreeable to the ways of God?

Indeed, he said, in no way could they make a fairer picture.

And now, I said, are we beginning to persuade those whom you described as rushing at us with might and main, that the painter of constitutions is such an one as we are praising; at whom they were so very indignant because to his hands we committed the State; and are they growing a little calmer at what they have just heard?

Much calmer, if there is any sense in them.

Why, where can they still find any ground for objection? Will they doubt
5   that the philosopher is a lover of truth and being?

They would not be so unreasonable.

Or that his nature, being such as we have delineated, is akin to the highest good?

Neither can they doubt this.

10   But again, will they tell us that such a nature, placed under favourable circumstances, will not be perfectly good and wise if any ever was? Or will they prefer those whom we have rejected?

Surely not.

Then will they still be angry at our saying, that, until philosophers bear rule,
15   States and individuals will have no rest from evil, nor will this our imaginary State ever be realised?

I think that they will be less angry.

Shall we assume that they are not only less angry but quite gentle, and that they have been converted and for very shame, if for no other reason, cannot
20   refuse to come to terms?

By all means, he said.

Then let us suppose that the reconciliation has been effected. Will any one deny the other point, that there may be sons of kings or princes who are by nature philosophers?

25   Surely no man, he said.

And when they have come into being will any one say that they must of
necessity be destroyed; that they can hardly be saved is not denied even by us;
but that in the whole course of ages no single one of them can escape — who
will venture to affirm this?

5   Who indeed!

But, said I, one is enough; let there be one man who has a city obedient to
his will, and he might bring into existence the ideal polity about which the world
is so incredulous.

Yes, one is enough.

10   The ruler may impose the laws and institutions which we have been
describing, and the citizens may possibly be willing to obey them?

Certainly.

And that others should approve of what we approve, is no miracle or
impossibility?

15   I think not.

But we have sufficiently shown, in what has preceded, that all this, if only
possible, is assuredly for the best.

We have.

And now we say not only that our laws, if they could be enacted, would be
20   for the best, but also that the enactment of them, though difficult, is not
impossible.

Very good.

And so with pain and toil we have reached the end of one subject, but more
remains to be discussed; — how and by what studies and pursuits will the
25   saviours of the constitution be created, and at what ages are they to apply
themselves to their several studies?

Certainly.

I omitted the troublesome business of the possession of women, and the procreation of children, and the appointment of the rulers, because I knew that the perfect State would be eyed with jealousy and was difficult of attainment;
5   but that piece of cleverness was not of much service to me, for I had to discuss them all the same. The women and children are now disposed of, but the other question of the rulers must be investigated from the very beginning. We were saying, as you will remember, that they were to be lovers of their country, tried by the test of pleasures and pains, and neither in hardships, nor in dangers, nor at
10 any other critical moment were to lose their patriotism — he was to be rejected who failed, but he who always came forth pure, like gold tried in the refiner's fire, was to be made a ruler, and to receive honours and rewards in life and after death. This was the sort of thing which was being said, and then the argument turned aside and veiled her face; not liking to stir the question which has now
15 arisen.

I perfectly remember, he said.

Yes, my friend, I said, and I then shrank from hazarding the bold word; but now let me dare to say — that the perfect guardian must be a philosopher.

Yes, he said, let that be affirmed.

20 And do not suppose that there will be many of them; for the gifts which were deemed by us to be essential rarely grow together; they are mostly found in shreds and patches.

What do you mean? he said.

You are aware, I replied, that quick intelligence, memory, sagacity,
25 cleverness, and similar qualities, do not often grow together, and that persons who possess them and are at the same time high-spirited and magnanimous are not so constituted by nature as to live orderly and in a peaceful and settled manner; they are driven any way by their impulses, and all solid principle goes out of them.

30 Very true, he said.

On the other hand, those steadfast natures which can better be depended upon, which in a battle are impregnable to fear and immovable, are equally immovable when there is anything to be learned; they are always in a torpid state, and are apt to yawn and go to sleep over any intellectual toil.

5   Quite true.

And yet we were saying that both qualities were necessary in those to whom the higher education is to be imparted, and who are to share in any office or command.

Certainly, he said.

10   And will they be a class which is rarely found?

Yes, indeed.

Then the aspirant must not only be tested in those labours and dangers and pleasures which we mentioned before, but there is another kind of probation which we did not mention — he must be exercised also in many kinds of
15   knowledge, to see whether the soul will be able to endure the highest of all, will faint under them, as in any other studies and exercises.

Yes, he said, you are quite right in testing him. But what do you mean by the highest of all knowledge?

You may remember, I said, that we divided the soul into three parts; and
20   distinguished the several natures of justice, temperance, courage, and wisdom?

Indeed, he said, if I had forgotten, I should not deserve to hear more.

And do you remember the word of caution which preceded the discussion . of them?

To what do you refer?

25   We were saying, if I am not mistaken, that he who wanted to see them in their perfect beauty must take a longer and more circuitous way, at the end of which they would appear; but that we could add on a popular exposition of them

on a level with the discussion which had preceded. And you replied that such an
exposition would be enough for you, and so the enquiry was continued in what
to me seemed to be a very inaccurate manner; whether you were satisfied or not,
it is for you to say.

5   Yes, he said, I thought and the others thought that you gave us a fair
measure of truth.

But, my friend, I said, a measure of such things Which in any degree falls
short of the whole truth is not fair measure; for nothing imperfect is the measure
of anything, although persons are too apt to be contented and think that they
10   need search no further.

Not an uncommon case when people are indolent.

Yes, I said; and there cannot be any worse fault in a guardian of the State
and of the laws.

True.

15   The guardian then, I said, must be required to take the longer circuit, and
toll at learning as well as at gymnastics, or he will never reach the highest
knowledge of all which, as we were just now saying, is his proper calling.

What, he said, is there a knowledge still higher than this — higher than
justice and the other virtues?

20   Yes, I said, there is. And of the virtues too we must behold not the outline
merely, as at present — nothing short of the most finished picture should satisfy
us. When little things are elaborated with an infinity of pains, in order that they
may appear in their full beauty and utmost clearness, how ridiculous that we
should not think the highest truths worthy of attaining the highest accuracy!

25   A right noble thought; but do you suppose that we shall refrain from asking
you what is this highest knowledge?

Nay, I said, ask if you will; but I am certain that you have heard the answer
many times, and now you either do not understand me or, as I rather think, you
are disposed to be troublesome; for you have of been told that the idea of good is

the highest knowledge, and that all other things become useful and advantageous only by their use of this. You can hardly be ignorant that of this I was about to speak, concerning which, as you have often heard me say, we know so little; and, without which, any other knowledge or possession of any kind will profit
5   us nothing. Do you think that the possession of all other things is of any value if we do not possess the good? or the knowledge of all other things if we have no knowledge of beauty and goodness?

Assuredly not.

You are further aware that most people affirm pleasure to be the good, but
10 the finer sort of wits say it is knowledge?

Yes.

And you are aware too that the latter cannot explain what they mean by knowledge, but are obliged after all to say knowledge of the good?

How ridiculous!

15 Yes, I said, that they should begin by reproaching us with our ignorance of the good, and then presume our knowledge of it — for the good they define to be knowledge of the good, just as if we understood them when they use the term "good" — this is of course ridiculous.

Most true, he said.

20 And those who make pleasure their good are in equal perplexity; for they are compelled to admit that there are bad pleasures as well as good.

Certainly.

And therefore to acknowledge that bad and good are the same?

True.

25 There can be no doubt about the numerous difficulties in which this question is involved.

There can be none.

Further, do we not see that many are willing to do or to have or to seem to be what is just and honourable without the reality; but no one is satisfied with the appearance of good — the reality is what they seek; in the case of the good,
5   appearance is despised by every one.

Very true, he said.

Of this then, which every soul of man pursues and makes the end of all his actions, having a presentiment that there is such an end, and yet hesitating because neither knowing the nature nor having the same assurance of this as of
10   other things, and therefore losing whatever good there is in other things, — of a principle such and so great as this ought the best men in our State, to whom everything is entrusted, to be in the darkness of ignorance?

Certainly not, he said.

I am sure, I said, that he who does not know now the beautiful and the just
15   are likewise good will be but a sorry guardian of them; and I suspect that no one who is ignorant of the good will have a true knowledge of them.

That, he said, is a shrewd suspicion of yours.

And if we only have a guardian who has this knowledge our State will be perfectly ordered?

20   Of course, he replied; but I wish that you would tell me whether you conceive this supreme principle of the good to be knowledge or pleasure, or different from either.

Aye, I said, I knew all along that a fastidious gentleman like you would not be contented with the thoughts of other people about these matters.

25   True, Socrates; but I must say that one who like you has passed a lifetime in the study of philosophy should not be always repeating the opinions of others, and never telling his own.

Well, but has any one a right to say positively what he does not know?

31

Not, he said, with the assurance of positive certainty; he has no right to do that: but he may say what he thinks, as a matter of opinion.

And do you not know, I said, that all mere opinions are bad, and the best of them blind? You would not deny that those who have any true notion without
5   intelligence are only like blind men who feel their way along the road?

Very true.

And do you wish to behold what is blind and crooked and base, when others will tell you of brightness and beauty?

Still, I must implore you, Socrates, said Glaucon, not to turn away just as
10 you are reaching the goal; if you will only give such an explanation of the good as you have already given of justice and temperance and the other virtues, we shall be satisfied.

Yes, my friend, and I shall be at least equally satisfied, but I cannot help fearing that I shall fall, and that my indiscreet zeal will bring ridicule upon me.
15 No, sweet sirs, let us not at present ask what is the actual nature of the good, for to reach what is now in my thoughts would be an effort too great for me. But of the child of the good who is likest him, I would fain speak, if I could be sure that you wished to hear — otherwise, not.

By all means, he said, tell us about the child, and you shall remain in our
20 debt for the account of the parent.

I do indeed wish, I replied, that I could pay, and you receive, the account of the parent, and not, as now, of the offspring only; take, however, this latter by way of interest,[1] and at the same time have a care that i do not render a false account, although I have no intention of deceiving you.

25 Yes, we will take all the care that we can: proceed.

Yes, I said, but I must first come to an understanding with you, and remind you of what I have mentioned in the course of this discussion, and at many other times.

What?

The old story, that there is a many beautiful and a many good, and so of other things which we describe and define; to all of them "many" is applied.

True, he said.

5   And there is an absolute beauty and an absolute good, and of other things to which the term "many" is applied there is an absolute; for they may be brought under a single idea, which is called the essence of each.

Very true.

The many, as we say, are seen but not known, and the ideas are known but 10   not seen.

Exactly.

And what is the organ with which we see the visible things?

The sight, he said.

And with the hearing, I said, we hear, and with the other senses perceive the 15   other objects of sense?

True.

But have you remarked that sight is by far the most costly and complex piece of workmanship which the artificer of the senses ever contrived?

No, I never have, he said.

20   Then reflect; has the ear or voice need of any third or additional nature in order that the one may be able to hear and the other to be heard?

Nothing of the sort.

No, indeed, I replied; and the same is true of most, if not all, the other senses — you would not say that any of them requires such an addition?

Certainly not.

But you see that without the addition of some other nature there is no seeing or being seen?

How do you mean?

5   Sight being, as I conceive, in the eyes, and he who has eyes wanting to see; colour being also present in them, still unless there be a third nature specially adapted to the purpose, the owner of the eyes will see nothing and the colours will be invisible.

Of what nature are you speaking?

10   Of that which you term light, I replied.

True, he said.

Noble, then, is the bond which links together sight and visibility, and great beyond other bonds by no small difference of nature; for light is their bond, and light is no ignoble thing?

15   Nay, he said, the reverse of ignoble.

And which, I said, of the gods in heaven would you say was the lord of this element? Whose is that light which makes the eye to see perfectly and the visible to appear?

You mean the sun, as you and all mankind say.

20   May not the relation of sight to this deity be described as follows? How?

Neither sight nor the eye in which sight resides is the sun?

No.

Yet of all the organs of sense the eye is the most like the sun?

By far the most like.

And the power which the eye possesses is a sort of effluence which is dispensed from the sun?

Exactly.

5   Then the sun is not sight, but the author of sight who is recognised by sight.

True, he said.

And this is he whom I call the child of the good, whom the good begat in his own likeness, to be in the visible world, in relation to sight and the things of sight, what the good is in the intellectual world in relation to mind and the things
10   of mind.

Will you be a little more explicit? he said.

Why, you know, I said, that the eyes, when a person directs them towards objects on which the light of day is no longer shining, but the moon and stars only, see dimly, and are nearly blind; they seem to have no clearness of vision in
15   them?

Very true.

But when they are directed towards objects on which the sun shines, they see clearly and there is sight in them?

Certainly.

20   And the soul is like the eye: when resting upon that on which truth and being shine, the soul perceives and understands and is radiant with intelligence; but when turned towards the twilight of becoming and perishing, then she has opinion only, and goes blinking about, and is first of one opinion and then of another, and seems to have no intelligence?

25   Just so.

Now, that which imparts truth to the known and the power of knowing to the knower is what I would have you term the idea of good, and this you will deem to be the cause of science, and of truth in so far as the latter becomes the subject of knowledge; beautiful too, as are both truth and knowledge, you will
5   be right in esteeming this other nature as more beautiful than either; and, as in the previous instance, light and sight may be truly said to be like the sun, and yet not to be the sun, so in this other sphere, science and truth may be deemed to be like the good, but not the good; the good has a place of honour yet higher.

What a wonder of beauty that must be, he said, which is the author of
10   science and truth, and yet surpasses them in beauty; for you surely cannot mean to say that pleasure is the good?

God forbid, I replied; but may I ask you to consider the image in another point of view?

In what point of view?

15   You would say, would you not, that the sun is only the author of visibility in all visible things, but of generation and nourishment and growth, though he himself is not generation?

Certainly.

In like manner the good may be said to be not only the author of knowledge
20   to all things known, but of their being and essence, and yet the good is not essence, but far exceeds essence in dignity and power.

Glaucon said, with a ludicrous earnestness: By the light of heaven, how amazing!

Yes, I said, and the exaggeration may be set down to you; for you made me
25   utter my fancies.

And pray continue to utter them; at any rate let us hear if there is anything more to be said about the similitude of the sun.

Yes, I said, there is a great deal more.

Then omit nothing, however slight.

I will do my best, I said; but I should think that a great deal will have to be omitted.

5   You have to imagine, then, that there are two ruling powers, and that one of them is set over the intellectual world, the other over the visible. I do not say heaven, lest you should fancy that I am playing upon the name ("ourhanoz, orhatoz"). May I suppose that you have this distinction of the visible and intelligible fixed in your mind?

I have.

10   Now take a line which has been cut into two unequal parts, and divide each of them again in the same proportion, and suppose the two main divisions to answer, one to the visible and the other to the intelligible, and then compare the subdivisions in respect of their clearness and want of clearness, and you will find that the first section in the sphere of the visible consists of images. And by
15   images I mean, in the first place, shadows, and in the second place, reflections in water and in solid, smooth and polished bodies and the like: Do you understand?

Yes, I understand.

Imagine, now, the other section, of which this is only the resemblance, to include the animals which we see, and everything that grows or is made.

20   Very good.

Would you not admit that both the sections of this division have different degrees of truth, and that the copy is to the original as the sphere of opinion is to the sphere of knowledge?

Most undoubtedly.

25   Next proceed to consider the manner in which the sphere of the intellectual is to be divided.

In what manner?

Thus: — There are two subdivisions, in the lower or which the soul uses the figures given by the former division as images; the enquiry can only be hypothetical, and instead of going upwards to a principle descends to the other end; in the higher of the two, the soul passes out of hypotheses, and goes up to a

5 principle which is above hypotheses, making no use of images as in the former case, but proceeding only in and through the ideas themselves.

I do not quite understand your meaning, he said.

Then I will try again; you will understand me better when I have made some preliminary remarks. You are aware that students of geometry, arithmetic,

10 and the kindred sciences assume the odd and the even and the figures and three kinds of angles and the like in their several branches of science; these are their hypotheses, which they and everybody are supposed to know, and therefore they do not deign to give any account of them either to themselves or others; but they begin with them, and go on until they arrive at last, and in a consistent manner,

15 at their conclusion?

Yes, he said, I know.

And do you not know also that although they make use of the visible forms and reason about them, they are thinking not of these, but of the ideals which they resemble; not of the figures which they draw, but of the absolute square and

20 the absolute diameter, and so on — the forms which they draw or make, and which have shadows and reflections in water of their own, are converted by them into images, but they are really seeking to behold the things themselves, which can only be seen with the eye of the mind?

That is true.

25 And of this kind I spoke as the intelligible, although in the search after it the soul is compelled to use hypotheses; not ascending to a first principle, because she is unable to rise above the region of hypothesis, but employing the objects of which the shadows below are resemblances in their turn as images, they having in relation to the shadows and reflections of them a greater distinctness, and

30 therefore a higher value.

I understand, he said, that you are speaking of the province of geometry and the sister arts.

And when I speak of the other division of the intelligible, you will understand me to speak of that other sort of knowledge which reason herself attains by the power of dialectic, using the hypotheses not as first principles, but
5   only as hypotheses — that is to say, as steps and points of departure into a world which is above hypotheses, in order that she may soar beyond them to the first principle of the whole; and clinging to this and then to that which depends on this, by successive steps she descends again without the aid of any sensible object, from ideas, through ideas, and in ideas she ends.

10   I understand you, he replied; not perfectly, for you seem to me to be describing a task which is really tremendous; but, at any rate, I understand you to say that knowledge and being, which the science of dialectic contemplates, are clearer than the notions of the arts, as they are termed, which proceed from hypotheses only: these are also contemplated by the understanding, and not by
15   the senses: yet, because they start from hypotheses and do not ascend to a principle, those who contemplate them appear to you not to exercise the higher reason upon them, although when a first principle is added to them they are cognizable by the higher reason. And the habit which is concerned with geometry and the cognate sciences I suppose that you would term understanding
20   and not reason, as being intermediate between opinion and reason.

You have quite conceived my meaning, I said; and now, corresponding to these four divisions, let there be four faculties in the soul — reason answering to the highest, understanding to the second, faith (or conviction) to the third, and perception of shadows to the last — and let there be a scale of them, and let us
25   suppose that the several faculties have clearness in the same degree that their objects have truth.

I understand, he replied, and give my assent, and accept your arrangement.

---

[1] A play upon *tokos*, which means both "offspring" and "interest."

Aristotle

Aristotle (b. 384 BC, Stageira, d. 322 BC, Euboea) was one of the most influential Ancient Greek philosophers. He was a student of Plato and a tutor of Alexander the Great. Aristotle spent most of his adult life in Athens, where he founded and directed the Lyceum – a philosophical academy that was the place of education and scholarship for a number of notable Ancient Greek philosophers and politicians.

Aristotle was a prolific writer, but the bulk of his work has not survived. What remains is estimated to be about one fifth of his full scholarly output. His most important surviving works include *Nicmachean Ethics*, *Politics*, *De Anima*, *Metaphysics*, *Poetics*, and *Physics*.

Aristotle contributed to a number of fields of knowledge, including physics, biology, logic, rhetoric, politics, and others, and his contributions to philosophy and rhetoric remain very influential to this day. His work has had a fundamental impact on the development of the Western philosophical tradition, directly influencing such diverse thinkers as Thomas Aquinas, Friedrich Nietzsche, and Martha Nussbaum.

BOOK ONE

I

Every state is a community of some kind, and every community is established with a view to some good; for mankind always act in order to obtain that which they think good. But, if all communities aim at some good, the state
5 or political community, which is the highest of all, and which embraces all the rest, aims at good in a greater degree than any other, and at the highest good.

Some people think that the qualifications of a statesman, king, householder, and master are the same, and that they differ, not in kind, but only in the number of their subjects. For example, the ruler over a few is called a master; over more,
10 the manager of a household; over a still larger number, a statesman or king, as if there were no difference between a great household and a small state. The distinction which is made between the king and the statesman is as follows: When the government is personal, the ruler is a king; when, according to the rules of the political science, the citizens rule and are ruled in turn, then he is
15 called a statesman.

But all this is a mistake; for governments differ in kind, as will be evident to any one who considers the matter according to the method which has hitherto guided us. As in other departments of science, so in politics, the compound should always be resolved into the simple elements or least parts of the whole. We must therefore look at the elements of which the state is composed, in order that we may see in what the different kinds of rule differ from one another, and whether any scientific result can be attained about each one of them.

II

He who thus considers things in their first growth and origin, whether a state or anything else, will obtain the clearest view of them. In the first place there must be a union of those who cannot exist without each other; namely, of male and female, that the race may continue (and this is a union which is
20 formed, not of deliberate purpose, but because, in common with other animals and with plants, mankind have a natural desire to leave behind them an image of themselves), and of natural ruler and subject, that both may be preserved. For that which can foresee by the exercise of mind is by nature intended to be lord and master, and that which can with its body give effect to such foresight is a

42

subject, and by nature a slave; hence master and slave have the same interest. Now nature has distinguished between the female and the slave. For she is not niggardly, like the smith who fashions the Delphian knife for many uses; she makes each thing for a single use, and every instrument is best made when
5 intended for one and not for many uses. But among barbarians no distinction is made between women and slaves, because there is no natural ruler among them: they are a community of slaves, male and female. Wherefore the poets say, "It is meet that Hellenes should rule over barbarians;" as if they thought that the barbarian and the slave were by nature one.
10 Out of these two relationships between man and woman, master and slave, the first thing to arise is the family, and Hesiod is right when he says, "First house and wife and an ox for the plough," for the ox is the poor man's slave. The family is the association established by nature for the supply of men's everyday wants, and the members of it are called by Charondas 'companions of
15 the cupboard,' and by Epimenides the Cretan, 'companions of the manger.' But when several families are united, and the association aims at something more than the supply of daily needs, the first society to be formed is the village. And the most natural form of the village appears to be that of a colony from the family, composed of the children and grandchildren, who are said to be suckled
20 'with the same milk.' And this is the reason why Hellenic states were originally governed by kings; because the Hellenes were under royal rule before they came together, as the barbarians still are. Every family is ruled by the eldest, and therefore in the colonies of the family the kingly form of government prevailed because they were of the same blood. As Homer says: "Each one gives law to
25 his children and to his wives."
For they lived dispersedly, as was the manner in ancient times. Wherefore men say that the Gods have a king, because they themselves either are or were in ancient times under the rule of a king. For they imagine, not only the forms of the Gods, but their ways of life to be like their own.
30 When several villages are united in a single complete community, large enough to be nearly or quite self-sufficing, the state comes into existence, originating in the bare needs of life, and continuing in existence for the sake of a good life. And therefore, if the earlier forms of society are natural, so is the state, for it is the end of them, and the nature of a thing is its end. For what each
35 thing is when fully developed, we call its nature, whether we are speaking of a man, a horse, or a family. Besides, the final cause and end of a thing is the best, and to be self-sufficing is the end and the best.
Hence it is evident that the state is a creation of nature, and that man is by nature a political animal. And he who by nature and not by mere accident is
40 without a state, is either a bad man or above humanity; he is like the "Tribeless,

lawless, heartless one," whom Homer denounces- the natural outcast is forthwith a lover of war; he may be compared to an isolated piece at draughts.

Now, that man is more of a political animal than bees or any other gregarious animals is evident. Nature, as we often say, makes nothing in vain, and man is the only animal whom she has endowed with the gift of speech. And whereas mere voice is but an indication of pleasure or pain, and is therefore found in other animals (for their nature attains to the perception of pleasure and pain and the intimation of them to one another, and no further), the power of speech is intended to set forth the expedient and inexpedient, and therefore likewise the just and the unjust. And it is a characteristic of man that he alone has any sense of good and evil, of just and unjust, and the like, and the association of living beings who have this sense makes a family and a state.

Further, the state is by nature clearly prior to the family and to the individual, since the whole is of necessity prior to the part; for example, if the whole body be destroyed, there will be no foot or hand, except in an equivocal sense, as we might speak of a stone hand; for when destroyed the hand will be no better than that. But things are defined by their working and power; and we ought not to say that they are the same when they no longer have their proper quality, but only that they have the same name. The proof that the state is a creation of nature and prior to the individual is that the individual, when isolated, is not self-sufficing; and therefore he is like a part in relation to the whole. But he who is unable to live in society, or who has no need because he is sufficient for himself, must be either a beast or a god: he is no part of a state. A social instinct is implanted in all men by nature, and yet he who first founded the state was the greatest of benefactors. For man, when perfected, is the best of animals, but, when separated from law and justice, he is the worst of all; since armed injustice is the more dangerous, and he is equipped at birth with arms, meant to be used by intelligence and virtue, which he may use for the worst ends. Wherefore, if he have not virtue, he is the most unholy and the most savage of animals, and the most full of lust and gluttony. But justice is the bond of men in states, for the administration of justice, which is the determination of what is just, is the principle of order in political society.

III

Seeing then that the state is made up of households, before speaking of the state we must speak of the management of the household. The parts of household management correspond to the persons who compose the household, and a complete household consists of slaves and freemen. Now we should begin by examining everything in its fewest possible elements; and the first and fewest possible parts of a family are master and slave, husband and wife, father and children. We have therefore to consider what each of these three relations is and ought to be: I mean the relation of master and servant, the marriage relation (the conjunction of man and wife has no name of its own), and thirdly, the procreative relation (this also has no proper name). And there is another element

5 of a household, the so-called art of getting wealth, which, according to some, is identical with household management, according to others, a principal part of it; the nature of this art will also have to be considered by us.

Let us first speak of master and slave, looking to the needs of practical life and also seeking to attain some better theory of their relation than exists at present. For some are of opinion that the rule of a master is a science, and that the management of a household, and the mastership of slaves, and the political and royal rule, as I was saying at the outset, are all the same. Others affirm that the rule of a master over slaves is contrary to nature, and that the distinction between slave and freeman exists by law only, and not by nature; and being an interference with nature is therefore unjust.

IV

Property is a part of the household, and the art of acquiring property is a part of the art of managing the household; for no man can live well, or indeed

10 live at all, unless he be provided with necessaries. And as in the arts which have a definite sphere the workers must have their own proper instruments for the accomplishment of their work, so it is in the management of a household. Now instruments are of various sorts; some are living, others lifeless; in the rudder, the pilot of a ship has a lifeless, in the look-out man, a living instrument; for in

15 the arts the servant is a kind of instrument. Thus, too, a possession is an instrument for maintaining life. And so, in the arrangement of the family, a slave is a living possession, and property a number of such instruments; and the servant is himself an instrument which takes precedence of all other instruments. For if every instrument could accomplish its own work, obeying or anticipating

20 the will of others, like the statues of Daedalus, or the tripods of Hephaestus, which, says the poet, "of their own accord entered the assembly of the Gods;" if, in like manner, the shuttle would weave and the plectrum touch the lyre without a hand to guide them, chief workmen would not want servants, nor masters slaves. Here, however, another distinction must be drawn; the instruments

25 commonly so called are instruments of production, whilst a possession is an instrument of action. The shuttle, for example, is not only of use; but something else is made by it, whereas of a garment or of a bed there is only the use. Further, as production and action are different in kind, and both require instruments, the instruments which they employ must likewise differ in kind.

30 But life is action and not production, and therefore the slave is the minister of

action. Again, a possession is spoken of as a part is spoken of; for the part is not only a part of something else, but wholly belongs to it; and this is also true of a possession. The master is only the master of the slave; he does not belong to him, whereas the slave is not only the slave of his master, but wholly belongs to

5   him. Hence we see what is the nature and office of a slave; he who is by nature not his own but another's man, is by nature a slave; and he may be said to be another's man who, being a human being, is also a possession. And a possession may be defined as an instrument of action, separable from the possessor.

V

But is there any one thus intended by nature to be a slave, and for whom
10   such a condition is expedient and right, or rather is not all slavery a violation of nature?

There is no difficulty in answering this question, on grounds both of reason and of fact. For that some should rule and others be ruled is a thing not only necessary, but expedient; from the hour of their birth, some are marked out for
15   subjection, others for rule.

And there are many kinds both of rulers and subjects (and that rule is the better which is exercised over better subjects- for example, to rule over men is better than to rule over wild beasts; for the work is better which is executed by better workmen, and where one man rules and another is ruled, they may be said
20   to have a work); for in all things which form a composite whole and which are made up of parts, whether continuous or discrete, a distinction between the ruling and the subject element comes to fight. Such a duality exists in living creatures, but not in them only; it originates in the constitution of the universe; even in things which have no life there is a ruling principle, as in a musical
25   mode. But we are wandering from the subject. We will therefore restrict ourselves to the living creature, which, in the first place, consists of soul and body: and of these two, the one is by nature the ruler, and the other the subject. But then we must look for the intentions of nature in things which retain their nature, and not in things which are corrupted. And therefore we must study the
30   man who is in the most perfect state both of body and soul, for in him we shall see the true relation of the two; although in bad or corrupted natures the body will often appear to rule over the soul, because they are in an evil and unnatural condition. At all events we may firstly observe in living creatures both a despotical and a constitutional rule; for the soul rules the body with a despotical
35   rule, whereas the intellect rules the appetites with a constitutional and royal rule. And it is clear that the rule of the soul over the body, and of the mind and the rational element over the passionate, is natural and expedient; whereas the equality of the two or the rule of the inferior is always hurtful. The same holds

46

good of animals in relation to men; for tame animals have a better nature than wild, and all tame animals are better off when they are ruled by man; for then they are preserved. Again, the male is by nature superior, and the female inferior; and the one rules, and the other is ruled; this principle, of necessity,
5   extends to all mankind.

     Where then there is such a difference as that between soul and body, or between men and animals (as in the case of those whose business is to use their body, and who can do nothing better), the lower sort are by nature slaves, and it is better for them as for all inferiors that they should be under the rule of a
10   master. For he who can be, and therefore is, another's and he who participates in rational principle enough to apprehend, but not to have, such a principle, is a slave by nature. Whereas the lower animals cannot even apprehend a principle; they obey their instincts. And indeed the use made of slaves and of tame animals is not very different; for both with their bodies minister to the needs of life.
15   Nature would like to distinguish between the bodies of freemen and slaves, making the one strong for servile labor, the other upright, and although useless for such services, useful for political life in the arts both of war and peace. But the opposite often happens- that some have the souls and others have the bodies of freemen. And doubtless if men differed from one another in the mere forms
20   of their bodies as much as the statues of the Gods do from men, all would acknowledge that the inferior class should be slaves of the superior. And if this is true of the body, how much more just that a similar distinction should exist in the soul? but the beauty of the body is seen, whereas the beauty of the soul is not seen. It is clear, then, that some men are by nature free, and others slaves, and
25   that for these latter slavery is both expedient and right.

VI

     But that those who take the opposite view have in a certain way right on their side, may be easily seen. For the words slavery and slave are used in two senses. There is a slave or slavery by law as well as by nature. The law of which I speak is a sort of convention- the law by which whatever is taken in war is
30   supposed to belong to the victors. But this right many jurists impeach, as they would an orator who brought forward an unconstitutional measure: they detest the notion that, because one man has the power of doing violence and is superior in brute strength, another shall be his slave and subject. Even among philosophers there is a difference of opinion. The origin of the dispute, and what
35   makes the views invade each other's territory, is as follows: in some sense virtue, when furnished with means, has actually the greatest power of exercising force; and as superior power is only found where there is superior excellence of some kind, power seems to imply virtue, and the dispute to be simply one about

justice (for it is due to one party identifying justice with goodwill while the other identifies it with the mere rule of the stronger). If these views are thus set out separately, the other views have no force or plausibility against the view that the superior in virtue ought to rule, or be master. Others, clinging, as they think,

5   simply to a principle of justice (for law and custom are a sort of justice), assume that slavery in accordance with the custom of war is justified by law, but at the same moment they deny this. For what if the cause of the war be unjust? And again, no one would ever say he is a slave who is unworthy to be a slave. Were this the case, men of the highest rank would be slaves and the children of slaves

10 if they or their parents chance to have been taken captive and sold. Wherefore Hellenes do not like to call Hellenes slaves, but confine the term to barbarians. Yet, in using this language, they really mean the natural slave of whom we spoke at first; for it must be admitted that some are slaves everywhere, others nowhere. The same principle applies to nobility. Hellenes regard themselves as

15 noble everywhere, and not only in their own country, but they deem the barbarians noble only when at home, thereby implying that there are two sorts of nobility and freedom, the one absolute, the other relative. The Helen of Theodectes says: "Who would presume to call me servant who am on both sides sprung from the stem of the Gods?"

20 What does this mean but that they distinguish freedom and slavery, noble and humble birth, by the two principles of good and evil? They think that as men and animals beget men and animals, so from good men a good man springs. But this is what nature, though she may intend it, cannot always accomplish.

We see then that there is some foundation for this difference of opinion, and

25 that all are not either slaves by nature or freemen by nature, and also that there is in some cases a marked distinction between the two classes, rendering it expedient and right for the one to be slaves and the others to be masters: the one practicing obedience, the others exercising the authority and lordship which nature intended them to have. The abuse of this authority is injurious to both; for

30 the interests of part and whole, of body and soul, are the same, and the slave is a part of the master, a living but separated part of his bodily frame. Hence, where the relation of master and slave between them is natural they are friends and have a common interest, but where it rests merely on law and force the reverse is true.

VII

35 The previous remarks are quite enough to show that the rule of a master is not a constitutional rule, and that all the different kinds of rule are not, as some affirm, the same with each other. For there is one rule exercised over subjects who are by nature free, another over subjects who are by nature slaves. The rule

of a household is a monarchy, for every house is under one head: whereas constitutional rule is a government of freemen and equals. The master is not called a master because he has science, but because he is of a certain character, and the same remark applies to the slave and the freeman. Still there may be a

5 science for the master and science for the slave. The science of the slave would be such as the man of Syracuse taught, who made money by instructing slaves in their ordinary duties. And such a knowledge may be carried further, so as to include cookery and similar menial arts. For some duties are of the more necessary, others of the more honorable sort; as the proverb says, 'slave before

10 slave, master before master.' But all such branches of knowledge are servile. There is likewise a science of the master, which teaches the use of slaves; for the master as such is concerned, not with the acquisition, but with the use of them. Yet this so-called science is not anything great or wonderful; for the master need only know how to order that which the slave must know how to execute. Hence

15 those who are in a position which places them above toil have stewards who attend to their households while they occupy themselves with philosophy or with politics. But the art of acquiring slaves, I mean of justly acquiring them, differs both from the art of the master and the art of the slave, being a species of hunting or war. Enough of the distinction between master and slave.

BOOK THREE

I

20 He who would inquire into the essence and attributes of various kinds of governments must first of all determine 'What is a state?' At present this is a disputed question. Some say that the state has done a certain act; others, no, not the state, but the oligarchy or the tyrant. And the legislator or statesman is concerned entirely with the state; a constitution or government being an

25 arrangement of the inhabitants of a state. But a state is composite, like any other whole made up of many parts; these are the citizens, who compose it. It is evident, therefore, that we must begin by asking, Who is the citizen, and what is the meaning of the term? For here again there may be a difference of opinion. He who is a citizen in a democracy will often not be a citizen in an oligarchy.

30 Leaving out of consideration those who have been made citizens, or who have obtained the name of citizen any other accidental manner, we may say, first, that a citizen is not a citizen because he lives in a certain place, for resident aliens and slaves share in the place; nor is he a citizen who has no legal right except that of suing and being sued; for this right may be enjoyed under the provisions

35 of a treaty. Nay, resident aliens in many places do not possess even such rights

completely, for they are obliged to have a patron, so that they do but imperfectly participate in citizenship, and we call them citizens only in a qualified sense, as we might apply the term to children who are too young to be on the register, or to old men who have been relieved from state duties. Of these we do not say
5 quite simply that they are citizens, but add in the one case that they are not of age, and in the other, that they are past the age, or something of that sort; the precise expression is immaterial, for our meaning is clear. Similar difficulties to those which I have mentioned may be raised and answered about deprived citizens and about exiles. But the citizen whom we are seeking to define is a
10 citizen in the strictest sense, against whom no such exception can be taken, and his special characteristic is that he shares in the administration of justice, and in offices. Now of offices some are discontinuous, and the same persons are not allowed to hold them twice, or can only hold them after a fixed interval; others have no limit of time- for example, the office of a dicast or ecclesiast. It may,
15 indeed, be argued that these are not magistrates at all, and that their functions give them no share in the government. But surely it is ridiculous to say that those who have the power do not govern. Let us not dwell further upon this, which is a purely verbal question; what we want is a common term including both dicast and ecclesiast. Let us, for the sake of distinction, call it 'indefinite
20 office,' and we will assume that those who share in such office are citizens. This is the most comprehensive definition of a citizen, and best suits all those who are generally so called.

But we must not forget that things of which the underlying principles differ in kind, one of them being first, another second, another third, have, when
25 regarded in this relation, nothing, or hardly anything, worth mentioning in common. Now we see that governments differ in kind, and that some of them are prior and that others are posterior; those which are faulty or perverted are necessarily posterior to those which are perfect. (What we mean by perversion will be hereafter explained.) The citizen then of necessity differs under each
30 form of government; and our definition is best adapted to the citizen of a democracy; but not necessarily to other states. For in some states the people are not acknowledged, nor have they any regular assembly, but only extraordinary ones; and suits are distributed by sections among the magistrates. At Lacedaemon, for instance, the Ephors determine suits about contracts, which
35 they distribute among themselves, while the elders are judges of homicide, and other causes are decided by other magistrates. A similar principle prevails at Carthage; there certain magistrates decide all causes. We may, indeed, modify our definition of the citizen so as to include these states. In them it is the holder of a definite, not of an indefinite office, who legislates and judges, and to some
40 or all such holders of definite offices is reserved the right of deliberating or

50

judging about some things or about all things. The conception of the citizen now begins to clear up.

He who has the power to take part in the deliberative or judicial administration of any state is said by us to be a citizens of that state; and,
5 speaking generally, a state is a body of citizens sufficing for the purposes of life.

II

But in practice a citizen is defined to be one of whom both the parents are citizens; others insist on going further back; say to two or three or more ancestors. This is a short and practical definition but there are some who raise the further question: How this third or fourth ancestor came to be a citizen?
10 Gorgias of Leontini, partly because he was in a difficulty, partly in irony, said- 'Mortars are what is made by the mortar-makers, and the citizens of Larissa are those who are made by the magistrates; for it is their trade to make Larissaeans.' Yet the question is really simple, for, if according to the definition just given they shared in the government, they were citizens. This is a better definition than
15 the other. For the words, 'born of a father or mother who is a citizen,' cannot possibly apply to the first inhabitants or founders of a state.

There is a greater difficulty in the case of those who have been made citizens after a revolution, as by Cleisthenes at Athens after the expulsion of the tyrants, for he enrolled in tribes many metics, both strangers and slaves. The
20 doubt in these cases is, not who is, but whether he who is ought to be a citizen; and there will still be a furthering the state, whether a certain act is or is not an act of the state; for what ought not to be is what is false. Now, there are some who hold office, and yet ought not to hold office, whom we describe as ruling, but ruling unjustly. And the citizen was defined by the fact of his holding some
25 kind of rule or office- he who holds a judicial or legislative office fulfills our definition of a citizen. It is evident, therefore, that the citizens about whom the doubt has arisen must be called citizens.

III

Whether they ought to be so or not is a question which is bound up with the previous inquiry. For a parallel question is raised respecting the state, whether a
30 certain act is or is not an act of the state; for example, in the transition from an oligarchy or a tyranny to a democracy. In such cases persons refuse to fulfill their contracts or any other obligations, on the ground that the tyrant, and not the state, contracted them; they argue that some constitutions are established by force, and not for the sake of the common good. But this would apply equally to
35 democracies, for they too may be founded on violence, and then the acts of the democracy will be neither more nor less acts of the state in question than those

of an oligarchy or of a tyranny. This question runs up into another: on what principle shall we ever say that the state is the same, or different? It would be a very superficial view which considered only the place and the inhabitants (for the soil and the population may be separated, and some of the inhabitants may live in one place and some in another). This, however, is not a very serious difficulty; we need only remark that the word 'state' is ambiguous.

It is further asked: When are men, living in the same place, to be regarded as a single city- what is the limit? Certainly not the wall of the city, for you might surround all Peloponnesus with a wall. Like this, we may say, is Babylon, and every city that has the compass of a nation rather than a city; Babylon, they say, had been taken for three days before some part of the inhabitants became aware of the fact. This difficulty may, however, with advantage be deferred to another occasion; the statesman has to consider the size of the state, and whether it should consist of more than one nation or not.

Again, shall we say that while the race of inhabitants, as well as their place of abode, remain the same, the city is also the same, although the citizens are always dying and being born, as we call rivers and fountains the same, although the water is always flowing away and coming again Or shall we say that the generations of men, like the rivers, are the same, but that the state changes? For, since the state is a partnership, and is a partnership of citizens in a constitution, when the form of government changes, and becomes different, then it may be supposed that the state is no longer the same, just as a tragic differs from a comic chorus, although the members of both may be identical. And in this manner we speak of every union or composition of elements as different when the form of their composition alters; for example, a scale containing the same sounds is said to be different, accordingly as the Dorian or the Phrygian mode is employed. And if this is true it is evident that the sameness of the state consists chiefly in the sameness of the constitution, and it may be called or not called by the same name, whether the inhabitants are the same or entirely different. It is quite another question, whether a state ought or ought not to fulfill engagements when the form of government changes.

IV

There is a point nearly allied to the preceding: Whether the virtue of a good man and a good citizen is the same or not. But, before entering on this discussion, we must certainly first obtain some general notion of the virtue of the citizen. Like the sailor, the citizen is a member of a community. Now, sailors have different functions, for one of them is a rower, another a pilot, and a third a look-out man, a fourth is described by some similar term; and while the precise definition of each individual's virtue applies exclusively to him, there is, at the same time, a common definition applicable to them all. For they have all of them a common object, which is safety in navigation. Similarly, one citizen differs from another, but the salvation of the community is the common business of them all. This community is the constitution; the virtue of the citizen must

5   therefore be relative to the constitution of which he is a member. If, then, there are many forms of government, it is evident that there is not one single virtue of the good citizen which is perfect virtue. But we say that the good man is he who has one single virtue which is perfect virtue. Hence it is evident that the good citizen need not of necessity possess the virtue which makes a good man.

10   The same question may also be approached by another road, from a consideration of the best constitution. If the state cannot be entirely composed of good men, and yet each citizen is expected to do his own business well, and must therefore have virtue, still inasmuch as all the citizens cannot be alike, the virtue of the citizen and of the good man cannot coincide. All must have the

15   virtue of the good citizen- thus, and thus only, can the state be perfect; but they will not have the virtue of a good man, unless we assume that in the good state all the citizens must be good.

Again, the state, as composed of unlikes, may be compared to the living being: as the first elements into which a living being is resolved are soul and

20   body, as soul is made up of rational principle and appetite, the family of husband and wife, property of master and slave, so of all these, as well as other dissimilar elements, the state is composed; and, therefore, the virtue of all the citizens cannot possibly be the same, any more than the excellence of the leader of a chorus is the same as that of the performer who stands by his side. I have said

25   enough to show why the two kinds of virtue cannot be absolutely and always the same.

But will there then be no case in which the virtue of the good citizen and the virtue of the good man coincide? To this we answer that the good ruler is a good and wise man, and that he who would be a statesman must be a wise man. And

30   some persons say that even the education of the ruler should be of a special kind; for are not the children of kings instructed in riding and military exercises? As Euripides says: "No subtle arts for me, but what the state requires."

As though there were a special education needed by a ruler. If then the virtue of a good ruler is the same as that of a good man, and we assume further

35   that the subject is a citizen as well as the ruler, the virtue of the good citizen and the virtue of the good man cannot be absolutely the same, although in some cases they may; for the virtue of a ruler differs from that of a citizen. It was the sense of this difference which made Jason say that 'he felt hungry when he was not a tyrant,' meaning that he could not endure to live in a private station. But,

40   on the other hand, it may be argued that men are praised for knowing both how

to rule and how to obey, and he is said to be a citizen of approved virtue who is able to do both. Now if we suppose the virtue of a good man to be that which rules, and the virtue of the citizen to include ruling and obeying, it cannot be said that they are equally worthy of praise. Since, then, it is sometimes thought that the ruler and the ruled must learn different things and not the same, but that the citizen must know and share in them both, the inference is obvious. There is, indeed, the rule of a master, which is concerned with menial offices- the master need not know how to perform these, but may employ others in the execution of them: the other would be degrading; and by the other I mean the power actually to do menial duties, which vary much in character and are executed by various classes of slaves, such, for example, as handicraftsmen, who, as their name signifies, live by the labor of their hands: under these the mechanic is included. Hence in ancient times, and among some nations, the working classes had no share in the government- a privilege which they only acquired under the extreme democracy. Certainly the good man and the statesman and the good citizen ought not to learn the crafts of inferiors except for their own occasional use; if they habitually practice them, there will cease to be a distinction between master and slave.

This is not the rule of which we are speaking; but there is a rule of another kind, which is exercised over freemen and equals by birth -a constitutional rule, which the ruler must learn by obeying, as he would learn the duties of a general of cavalry by being under the orders of a general of cavalry, or the duties of a general of infantry by being under the orders of a general of infantry, and by having had the command of a regiment and of a company. It has been well said that 'he who has never learned to obey cannot be a good commander.' The two are not the same, but the good citizen ought to be capable of both; he should know how to govern like a freeman, and how to obey like a freeman- these are the virtues of a citizen. And, although the temperance and justice of a ruler are distinct from those of a subject, the virtue of a good man will include both; for the virtue of the good man who is free and also a subject, e.g., his justice, will not be one but will comprise distinct kinds, the one qualifying him to rule, the other to obey, and differing as the temperance and courage of men and women differ. For a man would be thought a coward if he had no more courage than a courageous woman, and a woman would be thought loquacious if she imposed no more restraint on her conversation than the good man; and indeed their part in the management of the household is different, for the duty of the one is to acquire, and of the other to preserve. Practical wisdom only is characteristic of the ruler: it would seem that all other virtues must equally belong to ruler and subject. The virtue of the subject is certainly not wisdom, but only true opinion; he may be compared to the maker of the flute, while his master is like the flute-player or user of the flute.

From these considerations may be gathered the answer to the question, whether the virtue of the good man is the same as that of the good citizen, or different, and how far the same, and how far different.

V

5   There still remains one more question about the citizen: Is he only a true citizen who has a share of office, or is the mechanic to be included? If they who hold no office are to be deemed citizens, not every citizen can have this virtue of ruling and obeying; for this man is a citizen And if none of the lower class are citizens, in which part of the state are they to be placed? For they are not
10   resident aliens, and they are not foreigners. May we not reply, that as far as this objection goes there is no more absurdity in excluding them than in excluding slaves and freedmen from any of the above-mentioned classes? It must be admitted that we cannot consider all those to be citizens who are necessary to the existence of the state; for example, children are not citizen equally with
15   grown-up men, who are citizens absolutely, but children, not being grown up, are only citizens on a certain assumption. Nay, in ancient times, and among some nations the artisan class were slaves or foreigners, and therefore the majority of them are so now. The best form of state will not admit them to citizenship; but if they are admitted, then our definition of the virtue of a citizen
20   will not apply to every citizen nor to every free man as such, but only to those who are freed from necessary services. The necessary people are either slaves who minister to the wants of individuals, or mechanics and laborers who are the servants of the community. These reflections carried a little further will explain their position; and indeed what has been said already is of itself, when
25   understood, explanation enough.

Since there are many forms of government there must be many varieties of citizen and especially of citizens who are subjects; so that under some governments the mechanic and the laborer will be citizens, but not in others, as, for example, in aristocracy or the so-called government of the best (if there be
30   such an one), in which honors are given according to virtue and merit; for no man can practice virtue who is living the life of a mechanic or laborer. In oligarchies the qualification for office is high, and therefore no laborer can ever be a citizen; but a mechanic may, for an actual majority of them are rich. At Thebes there was a law that no man could hold office who had not retired from
35   business for ten years. But in many states the law goes to the length of admitting aliens; for in some democracies a man is a citizen though his mother only be a citizen; and a similar principle is applied to illegitimate children; the law is relaxed when there is a dearth of population. But when the number of citizens

increases, first the children of a male or a female slave are excluded; then those whose mothers only are citizens; and at last the right of citizenship is confined to those whose fathers and mothers are both citizens.

Hence, as is evident, there are different kinds of citizens; and he is a citizen
5   in the highest sense who shares in the honors of the state. Compare Homer's words, 'like some dishonored stranger'; he who is excluded from the honors of the state is no better than an alien. But when his exclusion is concealed, then the object is that the privileged class may deceive their fellow inhabitants.

As to the question whether the virtue of the good man is the same as that of
10 the good citizen, the considerations already adduced prove that in some states the good man and the good citizen are the same, and in others different. When they are the same it is not every citizen who is a good man, but only the statesman and those who have or may have, alone or in conjunction with others, the conduct of public affairs.

VI

15   Having determined these questions, we have next to consider whether there is only one form of government or many, and if many, what they are, and how many, and what are the differences between them.

A constitution is the arrangement of magistracies in a state, especially of the highest of all. The government is everywhere sovereign in the state, and the
20 constitution is in fact the government. For example, in democracies the people are supreme, but in oligarchies, the few; and, therefore, we say that these two forms of government also are different: and so in other cases.

First, let us consider what is the purpose of a state, and how many forms of government there are by which human society is regulated. We have already
25 said, in the first part of this treatise, when discussing household management and the rule of a master, that man is by nature a political animal. And therefore, men, even when they do not require one another's help, desire to live together; not but that they are also brought together by their common interests in proportion as they severally attain to any measure of well-being. This is
30 certainly the chief end, both of individuals and of states. And also for the sake of mere life (in which there is possibly some noble element so long as the evils of existence do not greatly overbalance the good) mankind meet together and maintain the political community. And we all see that men cling to life even at the cost of enduring great misfortune, seeming to find in life a natural sweetness
35 and happiness.

There is no difficulty in distinguishing the various kinds of authority; they have been often defined already in discussions outside the school. The rule of a master, although the slave by nature and the master by nature have in reality the

same interests, is nevertheless exercised primarily with a view to the interest of the master, but accidentally considers the slave, since, if the slave perish, the rule of the master perishes with him. On the other hand, the government of a wife and children and of a household, which we have called household
5   management, is exercised in the first instance for the good of the governed or for the common good of both parties, but essentially for the good of the governed, as we see to be the case in medicine, gymnastic, and the arts in general, which are only accidentally concerned with the good of the artists themselves. For there is no reason why the trainer may not sometimes practice gymnastics, and
10   the helmsman is always one of the crew. The trainer or the helmsman considers the good of those committed to his care. But, when he is one of the persons taken care of, he accidentally participates in the advantage, for the helmsman is also a sailor, and the trainer becomes one of those in training. And so in politics: when the state is framed upon the principle of equality and likeness, the citizens
15   think that they ought to hold office by turns. Formerly, as is natural, every one would take his turn of service; and then again, somebody else would look after his interest, just as he, while in office, had looked after theirs. But nowadays, for the sake of the advantage which is to be gained from the public revenues and from office, men want to be always in office. One might imagine that the rulers,
20   being sickly, were only kept in health while they continued in office; in that case we may be sure that they would be hunting after places. The conclusion is evident: that governments which have a regard to the common interest are constituted in accordance with strict principles of justice, and are therefore true forms; but those which regard only the interest of the rulers are all defective and
25   perverted forms, for they are despotic, whereas a state is a community of freemen.

VII

Having determined these points, we have next to consider how many forms of government there are, and what they are; and in the first place what are the true forms, for when they are determined the perversions of them will at once be
30   apparent. The words constitution and government have the same meaning, and the government, which is the supreme authority in states, must be in the hands of one, or of a few, or of the many. The true forms of government, therefore, are those in which the one, or the few, or the many, govern with a view to the common interest; but governments which rule with a view to the private interest,
35   whether of the one or of the few, or of the many, are perversions. For the members of a state, if they are truly citizens, ought to participate in its advantages. Of forms of government in which one rules, we call that which regards the common interests, kingship or royalty; that in which more than one,

but not many, rule, aristocracy; and it is so called, either because the rulers are the best men, or because they have at heart the best interests of the state and of the citizens. But when the citizens at large administer the state for the common interest, the government is called by the generic name- a constitution. And there

5 is a reason for this use of language. One man or a few may excel in virtue; but as the number increases it becomes more difficult for them to attain perfection in every kind of virtue, though they may in military virtue, for this is found in the masses. Hence in a constitutional government the fighting-men have the supreme power, and those who possess arms are the citizens.

10 Of the above-mentioned forms, the perversions are as follows: of royalty, tyranny; of aristocracy, oligarchy; of constitutional government, democracy. For tyranny is a kind of monarchy which has in view the interest of the monarch only; oligarchy has in view the interest of the wealthy; democracy, of the needy: none of them the common good of all.

VIII

15 But there are difficulties about these forms of government, and it will therefore be necessary to state a little more at length the nature of each of them. For he who would make a philosophical study of the various sciences, and does not regard practice only, ought not to overlook or omit anything, but to set forth the truth in every particular. Tyranny, as I was saying, is monarchy exercising

20 the rule of a master over the political society; oligarchy is when men of property have the government in their hands; democracy, the opposite, when the indigent, and not the men of property, are the rulers. And here arises the first of our difficulties, and it relates to the distinction drawn. For democracy is said to be the government of the many. But what if the many are men of property and have

25 the power in their hands? In like manner oligarchy is said to be the government of the few; but what if the poor are fewer than the rich, and have the power in their hands because they are stronger? In these cases the distinction which we have drawn between these different forms of government would no longer hold good.

30 Suppose, once more, that we add wealth to the few and poverty to the many, and name the governments accordingly- an oligarchy is said to be that in which the few and the wealthy, and a democracy that in which the many and the poor are the rulers- there will still be a difficulty. For, if the only forms of government are the ones already mentioned, how shall we describe those other

35 governments also just mentioned by us, in which the rich are the more numerous and the poor are the fewer, and both govern in their respective states?

The argument seems to show that, whether in oligarchies or in democracies, the number of the governing body, whether the greater number, as in a

democracy, or the smaller number, as in an oligarchy, is an accident due to the fact that the rich everywhere are few, and the poor numerous. But if so, there is a misapprehension of the causes of the difference between them. For the real difference between democracy and oligarchy is poverty and wealth. Wherever
5 men rule by reason of their wealth, whether they be few or many, that is an oligarchy, and where the poor rule, that is a democracy. But as a fact the rich are few and the poor many; for few are well-to-do, whereas freedom is enjoyed by an, and wealth and freedom are the grounds on which the oligarchical and democratical parties respectively claim power in the state.

IX

10 Let us begin by considering the common definitions of oligarchy and democracy, and what is justice oligarchical and democratical. For all men cling to justice of some kind, but their conceptions are imperfect and they do not express the whole idea. For example, justice is thought by them to be, and is, equality, not. however, for however, for but only for equals. And inequality is
15 thought to be, and is, justice; neither is this for all, but only for unequals. When the persons are omitted, then men judge erroneously. The reason is that they are passing judgment on themselves, and most people are bad judges in their own case. And whereas justice implies a relation to persons as well as to things, and a just distribution, as I have already said in the Ethics, implies the same ratio
20 between the persons and between the things, they agree about the equality of the things, but dispute about the equality of the persons, chiefly for the reason which I have just given- because they are bad judges in their own affairs; and secondly, because both the parties to the argument are speaking of a limited and partial justice, but imagine themselves to be speaking of absolute justice. For the one
25 party, if they are unequal in one respect, for example wealth, consider themselves to be unequal in all; and the other party, if they are equal in one respect, for example free birth, consider themselves to be equal in all. But they leave out the capital point. For if men met and associated out of regard to wealth only, their share in the state would be proportioned to their property, and the
30 oligarchical doctrine would then seem to carry the day. It would not be just that he who paid one mina should have the same share of a hundred minae, whether of the principal or of the profits, as he who paid the remaining ninety-nine. But a state exists for the sake of a good life, and not for the sake of life only: if life only were the object, slaves and brute animals might form a state, but they
35 cannot, for they have no share in happiness or in a life of free choice. Nor does a state exist for the sake of alliance and security from injustice, nor yet for the sake of exchange and mutual intercourse; for then the Tyrrhenians and the Carthaginians, and all who have commercial treaties with one another, would be

the citizens of one state. True, they have agreements about imports, and engagements that they will do no wrong to one another, and written articles of alliance. But there are no magistrates common to the contracting parties who will enforce their engagements; different states have each their own
5   magistracies. Nor does one state take care that the citizens of the other are such as they ought to be, nor see that those who come under the terms of the treaty do no wrong or wickedness at an, but only that they do no injustice to one another. Whereas, those who care for good government take into consideration virtue and vice in states. Whence it may be further inferred that virtue must be the care of a
10 state which is truly so called, and not merely enjoys the name: for without this end the community becomes a mere alliance which differs only in place from alliances of which the members live apart; and law is only a convention, 'a surety to one another of justice,' as the sophist Lycophron says, and has no real power to make the citizens.
15   This is obvious; for suppose distinct places, such as Corinth and Megara, to be brought together so that their walls touched, still they would not be one city, not even if the citizens had the right to intermarry, which is one of the rights peculiarly characteristic of states. Again, if men dwelt at a distance from one another, but not so far off as to have no intercourse, and there were laws among
20 them that they should not wrong each other in their exchanges, neither would this be a state. Let us suppose that one man is a carpenter, another a husbandman, another a shoemaker, and so on, and that their number is ten thousand: nevertheless, if they have nothing in common but exchange, alliance, and the like, that would not constitute a state. Why is this? Surely not because
25 they are at a distance from one another: for even supposing that such a community were to meet in one place, but that each man had a house of his own, which was in a manner his state, and that they made alliance with one another, but only against evil-doers; still an accurate thinker would not deem this to be a state, if their intercourse with one another was of the same character after as
30 before their union. It is clear then that a state is not a mere society, having a common place, established for the prevention of mutual crime and for the sake of exchange. These are conditions without which a state cannot exist; but all of them together do not constitute a state, which is a community of families and aggregations of families in well-being, for the sake of a perfect and self-
35 sufficing life. Such a community can only be established among those who live in the same place and intermarry. Hence arise in cities family connections, brotherhoods, common sacrifices, amusements which draw men together. But these are created by friendship, for the will to live together is friendship. The end of the state is the good life, and these are the means towards it. And the state
40 is the union of families and villages in a perfect and self-sufficing life, by which

we mean a happy and honorable life.

Our conclusion, then, is that political society exists for the sake of noble actions, and not of mere companionship. Hence they who contribute most to such a society have a greater share in it than those who have the same or a
5   greater freedom or nobility of birth but are inferior to them in political virtue; or than those who exceed them in wealth but are surpassed by them in virtue.

From what has been said it will be clearly seen that all the partisans of different forms of government speak of a part of justice only.

X

There is also a doubt as to what is to be the supreme power in the state: Is it
10   the multitude? Or the wealthy? Or the good? Or the one best man? Or a tyrant? Any of these alternatives seems to involve disagreeable consequences. If the poor, for example, because they are more in number, divide among themselves the property of the rich- is not this unjust? No, by heaven (will be the reply), for the supreme authority justly willed it. But if this is not injustice, pray what is?
15   Again, when in the first division all has been taken, and the majority divide anew the property of the minority, is it not evident, if this goes on, that they will ruin the state? Yet surely, virtue is not the ruin of those who possess her, nor is justice destructive of a state; and therefore this law of confiscation clearly cannot be just. If it were, all the acts of a tyrant must of necessity be just; for he
20   only coerces other men by superior power, just as the multitude coerce the rich. But is it just then that the few and the wealthy should be the rulers? And what if they, in like manner, rob and plunder the people- is this just? if so, the other case will likewise be just. But there can be no doubt that all these things are wrong and unjust.
25   Then ought the good to rule and have supreme power? But in that case everybody else, being excluded from power, will be dishonored. For the offices of a state are posts of honor; and if one set of men always holds them, the rest must be deprived of them. Then will it be well that the one best man should rule? Nay, that is still more oligarchical, for the number of those who are
30   dishonored is thereby increased. Some one may say that it is bad in any case for a man, subject as he is to all the accidents of human passion, to have the supreme power, rather than the law. But what if the law itself be democratical or oligarchical, how will that help us out of our difficulties? Not at all; the same consequences will follow.

XI

35   Most of these questions may be reserved for another occasion. The principle that the multitude ought to be supreme rather than the few best is one that is

maintained, and, though not free from difficulty, yet seems to contain an element of truth. For the many, of whom each individual is but an ordinary person, when they meet together may very likely be better than the few good, if regarded not individually but collectively, just as a feast to which many
5   contribute is better than a dinner provided out of a single purse. For each individual among the many has a share of virtue and prudence, and when they meet together, they become in a manner one man, who has many feet, and hands, and senses; that is a figure of their mind and disposition. Hence the many are better judges than a single man of music and poetry; for some understand
10   one part, and some another, and among them they understand the whole. There is a similar combination of qualities in good men, who differ from any individual of the many, as the beautiful are said to differ from those who are not beautiful, and works of art from realities, because in them the scattered elements are combined, although, if taken separately, the eye of one person or some other
15   feature in another person would be fairer than in the picture. Whether this principle can apply to every democracy, and to all bodies of men, is not clear. Or rather, by heaven, in some cases it is impossible of application; for the argument would equally hold about brutes; and wherein, it will be asked, do some men differ from brutes? But there may be bodies of men about whom our statement is
20   nevertheless true. And if so, the difficulty which has been already raised, and also another which is akin to it -viz., what power should be assigned to the mass of freemen and citizens, who are not rich and have no personal merit- are both solved. There is still a danger in allowing them to share the great offices of state, for their folly will lead them into error, and their dishonesty into crime. But
25   there is a danger also in not letting them share, for a state in which many poor men are excluded from office will necessarily be full of enemies. The only way of escape is to assign to them some deliberative and judicial functions. For this reason Solon and certain other legislators give them the power of electing to offices, and of calling the magistrates to account, but they do not allow them to
30   hold office singly. When they meet together their perceptions are quite good enough, and combined with the better class they are useful to the state (just as impure food when mixed with what is pure sometimes makes the entire mass more wholesome than a small quantity of the pure would be), but each individual, left to himself, forms an imperfect judgment. On the other hand, the
35   popular form of government involves certain difficulties. In the first place, it might be objected that he who can judge of the healing of a sick man would be one who could himself heal his disease, and make him whole- that is, in other words, the physician; and so in all professions and arts. As, then, the physician ought to be called to account by physicians, so ought men in general to be called
40   to account by their peers. But physicians are of three kinds: there is the ordinary

practitioner, and there is the physician of the higher class, and thirdly the intelligent man who has studied the art: in all arts there is such a class; and we attribute the power of judging to them quite as much as to professors of the art. Secondly, does not the same principle apply to elections? For a right election

5 can only be made by those who have knowledge; those who know geometry, for example, will choose a geometrician rightly, and those who know how to steer, a pilot; and, even if there be some occupations and arts in which private persons share in the ability to choose, they certainly cannot choose better than those who know. So that, according to this argument, neither the election of magistrates,

10 nor the calling of them to account, should be entrusted to the many. Yet possibly these objections are to a great extent met by our old answer, that if the people are not utterly degraded, although individually they may be worse judges than those who have special knowledge- as a body they are as good or better. Moreover, there are some arts whose products are not judged of solely, or best,

15 by the artists themselves, namely those arts whose products are recognized even by those who do not possess the art; for example, the knowledge of the house is not limited to the builder only; the user, or, in other words, the master, of the house will be even a better judge than the builder, just as the pilot will judge better of a rudder than the carpenter, and the guest will judge better of a feast

20 than the cook.

This difficulty seems now to be sufficiently answered, but there is another akin to it. That inferior persons should have authority in greater matters than the good would appear to be a strange thing, yet the election and calling to account of the magistrates is the greatest of all. And these, as I was saying, are functions

25 which in some states are assigned to the people, for the assembly is supreme in all such matters. Yet persons of any age, and having but a small property qualification, sit in the assembly and deliberate and judge, although for the great officers of state, such as treasurers and generals, a high qualification is required. This difficulty may be solved in the same manner as the preceding, and the

30 present practice of democracies may be really defensible. For the power does not reside in the dicast, or senator, or ecclesiast, but in the court, and the senate, and the assembly, of which individual senators, or ecclesiasts, or dicasts, are only parts or members. And for this reason the many may claim to have a higher authority than the few; for the people, and the senate, and the courts consist of

35 many persons, and their property collectively is greater than the property of one or of a few individuals holding great offices. But enough of this.

The discussion of the first question shows nothing so clearly as that laws, when good, should be supreme; and that the magistrate or magistrates should regulate those matters only on which the laws are unable to speak with precision

40 owing to the difficulty of any general principle embracing all particulars. But

what are good laws has not yet been clearly explained; the old difficulty remains. The goodness or badness, justice or injustice, of laws varies of necessity with the constitutions of states. This, however, is clear, that the laws must be adapted to the constitutions. But if so, true forms of government will of
5   necessity have just laws, and perverted forms of government will have unjust laws.

XII

In all sciences and arts the end is a good, and the greatest good and in the highest degree a good in the most authoritative of all- this is the political science of which the good is justice, in other words, the common interest. All men think
10   justice to be a sort of equality; and to a certain extent they agree in the philosophical distinctions which have been laid down by us about Ethics. For they admit that justice is a thing and has a relation to persons, and that equals ought to have equality. But there still remains a question: equality or inequality of what? Here is a difficulty which calls for political speculation. For very likely
15   some persons will say that offices of state ought to be unequally distributed according to superior excellence, in whatever respect, of the citizen, although there is no other difference between him and the rest of the community; for that those who differ in any one respect have different rights and claims. But, surely, if this is true, the complexion or height of a man, or any other advantage, will be
20   a reason for his obtaining a greater share of political rights. The error here lies upon the surface, and may be illustrated from the other arts and sciences. When a number of flute players are equal in their art, there is no reason why those of them who are better born should have better flutes given to them; for they will not play any better on the flute, and the superior instrument should be reserved
25   for him who is the superior artist. If what I am saying is still obscure, it will be made clearer as we proceed. For if there were a superior flute-player who was far inferior in birth and beauty, although either of these may be a greater good than the art of flute-playing, and may excel flute-playing in a greater ratio than he excels the others in his art, still he ought to have the best flutes given to him,
30   unless the advantages of wealth and birth contribute to excellence in flute-playing, which they do not. Moreover, upon this principle any good may be compared with any other. For if a given height may be measured wealth and against freedom, height in general may be so measured. Thus if A excels in height more than B in virtue, even if virtue in general excels height still more,
35   all goods will be commensurable; for if a certain amount is better than some other, it is clear that some other will be equal. But since no such comparison can be made, it is evident that there is good reason why in politics men do not ground their claim to office on every sort of inequality any more than in the arts.

For if some be slow, and others swift, that is no reason why the one should have little and the others much; it is in gymnastics contests that such excellence is rewarded. Whereas the rival claims of candidates for office can only be based on the possession of elements which enter into the composition of a state. And

5   therefore the noble, or free-born, or rich, may with good reason claim office; for holders of offices must be freemen and taxpayers: a state can be no more composed entirely of poor men than entirely of slaves. But if wealth and freedom are necessary elements, justice and valor are equally so; for without the former qualities a state cannot exist at all, without the latter not well.

XIII

10   If the existence of the state is alone to be considered, then it would seem that all, or some at least, of these claims are just; but, if we take into account a good life, then, as I have already said, education and virtue have superior claims. As, however, those who are equal in one thing ought not to have an equal share in all, nor those who are unequal in one thing to have an unequal share in all, it

15   is certain that all forms of government which rest on either of these principles are perversions. All men have a claim in a certain sense, as I have already admitted, but all have not an absolute claim. The rich claim because they have a greater share in the land, and land is the common element of the state; also they are generally more trustworthy in contracts. The free claim under the same tide

20   as the noble; for they are nearly akin. For the noble are citizens in a truer sense than the ignoble, and good birth is always valued in a man's own home and country. Another reason is, that those who are sprung from better ancestors are likely to be better men, for nobility is excellence of race. Virtue, too, may be truly said to have a claim, for justice has been acknowledged by us to be a social

25   virtue, and it implies all others. Again, the many may urge their claim against the few; for, when taken collectively, and compared with the few, they are stronger and richer and better. But, what if the good, the rich, the noble, and the other classes who make up a state, are all living together in the same city, Will there, or will there not, be any doubt who shall rule? No doubt at all in

30   determining who ought to rule in each of the above-mentioned forms of government. For states are characterized by differences in their governing bodies-one of them has a government of the rich, another of the virtuous, and so on. But a difficulty arises when all these elements co-exist. How are we to decide? Suppose the virtuous to be very few in number: may we consider their

35   numbers in relation to their duties, and ask whether they are enough to administer the state, or so many as will make up a state? Objections may be urged against all the aspirants to political power. For those who found their claims on wealth or family might be thought to have no basis of justice; on this

principle, if any one person were richer than all the rest, it is clear that he ought to be ruler of them. In like manner he who is very distinguished by his birth ought to have the superiority over all those who claim on the ground that they are freeborn. In an aristocracy, or government of the best, a like difficulty occurs
5   about virtue; for if one citizen be better than the other members of the government, however good they may be, he too, upon the same principle of justice, should rule over them. And if the people are to be supreme because they are stronger than the few, then if one man, or more than one, but not a majority, is stronger than the many, they ought to rule, and not the many.
10   All these considerations appear to show that none of the principles on which men claim to rule and to hold all other men in subjection to them are strictly right. To those who claim to be masters of the government on the ground of their virtue or their wealth, the many might fairly answer that they themselves are often better and richer than the few- I do not say individually, but collectively.
15   And another ingenious objection which is sometimes put forward may be met in a similar manner. Some persons doubt whether the legislator who desires to make the justest laws ought to legislate with a view to the good of the higher classes or of the many, when the case which we have mentioned occurs. Now what is just or right is to be interpreted in the sense of 'what is equal'; and that
20   which is right in the sense of being equal is to be considered with reference to the advantage of the state, and the common good of the citizens. And a citizen is one who shares in governing and being governed. He differs under different forms of government, but in the best state he is one who is able and willing to be governed and to govern with a view to the life of virtue.
25   If, however, there be some one person, or more than one, although not enough to make up the full complement of a state, whose virtue is so pre-eminent that the virtues or the political capacity of all the rest admit of no comparison with his or theirs, he or they can be no longer regarded as part of a state; for justice will not be done to the superior, if he is reckoned only as the
30   equal of those who are so far inferior to him in virtue and in political capacity. Such an one may truly be deemed a God among men. Hence we see that legislation is necessarily concerned only with those who are equal in birth and in capacity; and that for men of pre-eminent virtue there is no law- they are themselves a law. Any would be ridiculous who attempted to make laws for
35   them: they would probably retort what, in the fable of Antisthenes, the lions said to the hares, when in the council of the beasts the latter began haranguing and claiming equality for all. And for this reason democratic states have instituted ostracism; equality is above all things their aim, and therefore they ostracized and banished from the city for a time those who seemed to predominate too
40   much through their wealth, or the number of their friends, or through any other

political influence. Mythology tells us that the Argonauts left Heracles behind for a similar reason; the ship Argo would not take him because she feared that he would have been too much for the rest of the crew. Wherefore those who denounce tyranny and blame the counsel which Periander gave to Thrasybulus

5 cannot be held altogether just in their censure. The story is that Periander, when the herald was sent to ask counsel of him, said nothing, but only cut off the tallest ears of corn till he had brought the field to a level. The herald did not know the meaning of the action, but came and reported what he had seen to Thrasybulus, who understood that he was to cut off the principal men in the

10 state; and this is a policy not only expedient for tyrants or in practice confined to them, but equally necessary in oligarchies and democracies. Ostracism is a measure of the same kind, which acts by disabling and banishing the most prominent citizens. Great powers do the same to whole cities and nations, as the Athenians did to the Samians, Chians, and Lesbians; no sooner had they

15 obtained a firm grasp of the empire, than they humbled their allies contrary to treaty; and the Persian king has repeatedly crushed the Medes, Babylonians, and other nations, when their spirit has been stirred by the recollection of their former greatness.

The problem is a universal one, and equally concerns all forms of

20 government, true as well as false; for, although perverted forms with a view to their own interests may adopt this policy, those which seek the common interest do so likewise. The same thing may be observed in the arts and sciences; for the painter will not allow the figure to have a foot which, however beautiful, is not in proportion, nor will the shipbuilder allow the stem or any other part of the

25 vessel to be unduly large, any more than the chorus-master will allow any one who sings louder or better than all the rest to sing in the choir. Monarchs, too, may practice compulsion and still live in harmony with their cities, if their own government is for the interest of the state. Hence where there is an acknowledged superiority the argument in favor of ostracism is based upon a

30 kind of political justice. It would certainly be better that the legislator should from the first so order his state as to have no need of such a remedy. But if the need arises, the next best thing is that he should endeavor to correct the evil by this or some similar measure. The principle, however, has not been fairly applied in states; for, instead of looking to the good of their own constitution,

35 they have used ostracism for factious purposes. It is true that under perverted forms of government, and from their special point of view, such a measure is just and expedient, but it is also clear that it is not absolutely just. In the perfect state there would be great doubts about the use of it, not when applied to excess in strength, wealth, popularity, or the like, but when used against some one who

40 is pre-eminent in virtue- what is to be done with him? Mankind will not say that

such an one is to be expelled and exiled; on the other hand, he ought not to be a subject- that would be as if mankind should claim to rule over Zeus, dividing his offices among them. The only alternative is that all should joyfully obey such a ruler, according to what seems to be the order of nature, and that men like him should be kings in their state for life.

5

XIV

The preceding discussion, by a natural transition, leads to the consideration of royalty, which we admit to be one of the true forms of government. Let us see whether in order to be well governed a state or country should be under the rule of a king or under some other form of government; and whether monarchy, although good for some, may not be bad for others. But first we must determine whether there is one species of royalty or many. It is easy to see that there are many, and that the manner of government is not the same in all of them.

10

Of royalties according to law, (1) the Lacedaemonian is thought to answer best to the true pattern; but there the royal power is not absolute, except when the kings go on an expedition, and then they take the command. Matters of religion are likewise committed to them. The kingly office is in truth a kind of generalship, irresponsible and perpetual. The king has not the power of life and death, except in a specified case, as for instance, in ancient times, he had it when upon a campaign, by right of force. This custom is described in Homer. For Agamemnon is patient when he is attacked in the assembly, but when the army goes out to battle he has the power even of life and death. Does he not say- 'When I find a man skulking apart from the battle, nothing shall save him from the dogs and vultures, for in my hands is death'?

15

20

This, then, is one form of royalty-a generalship for life: and of such royalties some are hereditary and others elective.

25

(2) There is another sort of monarchy not uncommon among the barbarians, which nearly resembles tyranny. But this is both legal and hereditary. For barbarians, being more servile in character than Hellenes, and Asiadics than Europeans, do not rebel against a despotic government. Such royalties have the nature of tyrannies because the people are by nature slaves; but there is no danger of their being overthrown, for they are hereditary and legal. Wherefore also their guards are such as a king and not such as a tyrant would employ, that is to say, they are composed of citizens, whereas the guards of tyrants are mercenaries. For kings rule according to law over voluntary subjects, but tyrants over involuntary; and the one are guarded by their fellow-citizens the others are guarded against them.

30

35

These are two forms of monarchy, and there was a third (3) which existed in ancient Hellas, called an Aesymnetia or dictatorship. This may be defined

generally as an elective tyranny, which, like the barbarian monarchy, is legal, but differs from it in not being hereditary. Sometimes the office was held for life, sometimes for a term of years, or until certain duties had been performed. For example, the Mytilenaeans elected Pittacus leader against the exiles, who
5   were headed by Antimenides and Alcaeus the poet. And Alcaeus himself shows in one of his banquet odes that they chose Pittacus tyrant, for he reproaches his fellow-citizens for 'having made the low-born Pittacus tyrant of the spiritless and ill-fated city, with one voice shouting his praises.'

These forms of government have always had the character of tyrannies,
10 because they possess despotic power; but inasmuch as they are elective and acquiesced in by their subjects, they are kingly.

(4) There is a fourth species of kingly rule- that of the heroic times- which was hereditary and legal, and was exercised over willing subjects. For the first chiefs were benefactors of the people in arts or arms; they either gathered them
15 into a community, or procured land for them; and thus they became kings of voluntary subjects, and their power was inherited by their descendants. They took the command in war and presided over the sacrifices, except those which required a priest. They also decided causes either with or without an oath; and when they swore, the form of the oath was the stretching out of their sceptre. In
20 ancient times their power extended continuously to all things whatsoever, in city and country, as well as in foreign parts; but at a later date they relinquished several of these privileges, and others the people took from them, until in some states nothing was left to them but the sacrifices; and where they retained more of the reality they had only the right of leadership in war beyond the border.
25 These, then, are the four kinds of royalty. First the monarchy of the heroic ages; this was exercised over voluntary subjects, but limited to certain functions; the king was a general and a judge, and had the control of religion The second is that of the barbarians, which is a hereditary despotic government in accordance with law. A third is the power of the so-called Aesynmete or Dictator; this is an
30 elective tyranny. The fourth is the Lacedaemonian, which is in fact a generalship, hereditary and perpetual. These four forms differ from one another in the manner which I have described.

(5) There is a fifth form of kingly rule in which one has the disposal of all, just as each nation or each state has the disposal of public matters; this form
35 corresponds to the control of a household. For as household management is the kingly rule of a house, so kingly rule is the household management of a city, or of a nation, or of many nations.

XV

Of these forms we need only consider two, the Lacedaemonian and the absolute royalty; for most of the others he in a region between them, having less power than the last, and more than the first. Thus the inquiry is reduced to two points: first, is it advantageous to the state that there should be a perpetual
5   general, and if so, should the office be confined to one family, or open to the citizens in turn? Secondly, is it well that a single man should have the supreme power in all things? The first question falls under the head of laws rather than of constitutions; for perpetual generalship might equally exist under any form of government, so that this matter may be dismissed for the present. The other kind
10   of royalty is a sort of constitution; this we have now to consider, and briefly to run over the difficulties involved in it. We will begin by inquiring whether it is more advantageous to be ruled by the best man or by the best laws.

The advocates of royalty maintain that the laws speak only in general terms, and cannot provide for circumstances; and that for any science to abide by
15   written rules is absurd. In Egypt the physician is allowed to alter his treatment after the fourth day, but if sooner, he takes the risk. Hence it is clear that a government acting according to written laws is plainly not the best. Yet surely the ruler cannot dispense with the general principle which exists in law; and this is a better ruler which is free from passion than that in which it is innate.
20   Whereas the law is passionless, passion must ever sway the heart of man. Yes, it may be replied, but then on the other hand an individual will be better able to deliberate in particular cases.

The best man, then, must legislate, and laws must be passed, but these laws will have no authority when they miss the mark, though in all other cases
25   retaining their authority. But when the law cannot determine a point at all, or not well, should the one best man or should all decide? According to our present practice assemblies meet, sit in judgment, deliberate, and decide, and their judgments an relate to individual cases. Now any member of the assembly, taken separately, is certainly inferior to the wise man. But the state is made up of
30   many individuals. And as a feast to which all the guests contribute is better than a banquet furnished by a single man, so a multitude is a better judge of many things than any individual.

Again, the many are more incorruptible than the few; they are like the greater quantity of water which is less easily corrupted than a little. The
35   individual is liable to be overcome by anger or by some other passion, and then his judgment is necessarily perverted; but it is hardly to be supposed that a great number of persons would all get into a passion and go wrong at the same moment. Let us assume that they are the freemen, and that they never act in violation of the law, but fill up the gaps which the law is obliged to leave. Or, if

such virtue is scarcely attainable by the multitude, we need only suppose that the majority are good men and good citizens, and ask which will be the more incorruptible, the one good ruler, or the many who are all good? Will not the many? But, you will say, there may be parties among them, whereas the one

5   man is not divided against himself. To which we may answer that their character is as good as his. If we call the rule of many men, who are all of them good, aristocracy, and the rule of one man royalty, then aristocracy will be better for states than royalty, whether the government is supported by force or not, provided only that a number of men equal in virtue can be found.

10   The first governments were kingships, probably for this reason, because of old, when cities were small, men of eminent virtue were few. Further, they were made kings because they were benefactors, and benefits can only be bestowed by good men. But when many persons equal in merit arose, no longer enduring the pre-eminence of one, they desired to have a commonwealth, and set up a

15   constitution. The ruling class soon deteriorated and enriched themselves out of the public treasury; riches became the path to honor, and so oligarchies naturally grew up. These passed into tyrannies and tyrannies into democracies; for love of gain in the ruling classes was always tending to diminish their number, and so to strengthen the masses, who in the end set upon their masters and established

20   democracies. Since cities have increased in size, no other form of government appears to be any longer even easy to establish.

        Even supposing the principle to be maintained that kingly power is the best thing for states, how about the family of the king? Are his children to succeed him? If they are no better than anybody else, that will be mischievous. But, says

25   the lover of royalty, the king, though he might, will not hand on his power to his children. That, however, is hardly to be expected, and is too much to ask of human nature. There is also a difficulty about the force which he is to employ; should a king have guards about him by whose aid he may be able to coerce the refractory? If not, how will he administer his kingdom? Even if he be the lawful

30   sovereign who does nothing arbitrarily or contrary to law, still he must have some force wherewith to maintain the law. In the case of a limited monarchy there is not much difficulty in answering this question; the king must have such force as will be more than a match for one or more individuals, but not so great as that of the people. The ancients observe this principle when they have guards

35   to any one whom they appointed dictator or tyrant. Thus, when Dionysius asked the Syracusans to allow him guards, somebody advised that they should give him only such a number.

XVI

At this place in the discussion there impends the inquiry respecting the king who acts solely according to his own will he has now to be considered. The so-called limited monarchy, or kingship according to law, as I have already remarked, is not a distinct form of government, for under all governments, as,
5 for example, in a democracy or aristocracy, there may be a general holding office for life, and one person is often made supreme over the administration of a state. A magistracy of this kind exists at Epidamnus, and also at Opus, but in the latter city has a more limited power. Now, absolute monarchy, or the arbitrary rule of a sovereign over an the citizens, in a city which consists of
10 equals, is thought by some to be quite contrary to nature; it is argued that those who are by nature equals must have the same natural right and worth, and that for unequals to have an equal share, or for equals to have an uneven share, in the offices of state, is as bad as for different bodily constitutions to have the same food and clothing. Wherefore it is thought to be just that among equals every
15 one be ruled as well as rule, and therefore that an should have their turn. We thus arrive at law; for an order of succession implies law. And the rule of the law, it is argued, is preferable to that of any individual. On the same principle, even if it be better for certain individuals to govern, they should be made only guardians and ministers of the law. For magistrates there must be- this is
20 admitted; but then men say that to give authority to any one man when all are equal is unjust. Nay, there may indeed be cases which the law seems unable to determine, but in such cases can a man? Nay, it will be replied, the law trains officers for this express purpose, and appoints them to determine matters which are left undecided by it, to the best of their judgment. Further, it permits them to
25 make any amendment of the existing laws which experience suggests. Therefore he who bids the law rule may be deemed to bid God and Reason alone rule, but he who bids man rule adds an element of the beast; for desire is a wild beast, and passion perverts the minds of rulers, even when they are the best of men. The law is reason unaffected by desire. We are told that a patient should call in a
30 physician; he will not get better if he is doctored out of a book. But the parallel of the arts is clearly not in point; for the physician does nothing contrary to rule from motives of friendship; he only cures a patient and takes a fee; whereas magistrates do many things from spite and partiality. And, indeed, if a man suspected the physician of being in league with his enemies to destroy him for a
35 bribe, he would rather have recourse to the book. But certainly physicians, when they are sick, call in other physicians, and training-masters, when they are in training, other training-masters, as if they could not judge judge truly about their own case and might be influenced by their feelings. Hence it is evident that in seeking for justice men seek for the mean or neutral, for the law is the mean.

Again, customary laws have more weight, and relate to more important matters, than written laws, and a man may be a safer ruler than the written law, but not safer than the customary law.

Again, it is by no means easy for one man to superintend many things; he will have to appoint a number of subordinates, and what difference does it make whether these subordinates always existed or were appointed by him because he needed theme If, as I said before, the good man has a right to rule because he is better, still two good men are better than one: this is the old saying, two going together, and the prayer of Agamemnon, "Would that I had ten such councillors!"

And at this day there are magistrates, for example judges, who have authority to decide some matters which the law is unable to determine, since no one doubts that the law would command and decide in the best manner whatever it could. But some things can, and other things cannot, be comprehended under the law, and this is the origin of the next question whether the best law or the best man should rule. For matters of detail about which men deliberate cannot be included in legislation. Nor does any one deny that the decision of such matters must be left to man, but it is argued that there should be many judges, and not one only. For every ruler who has been trained by the law judges well; and it would surely seem strange that a person should see better with two eyes, or hear better with two ears, or act better with two hands or feet, than many with many; indeed, it is already the practice of kings to make to themselves many eyes and ears and hands and feet. For they make colleagues of those who are the friends of themselves and their governments. They must be friends of the monarch and of his government; if not his friends, they will not do what he wants; but friendship implies likeness and equality; and, therefore, if he thinks that his friends ought to rule, he must think that those who are equal to himself and like himself ought to rule equally with himself. These are the principal controversies relating to monarchy.

XVII

But may not all this be true in some cases and not in others? for there is by nature both a justice and an advantage appropriate to the rule of a master, another to kingly rule, another to constitutional rule; but there is none naturally appropriate to tyranny, or to any other perverted form of government; for these come into being contrary to nature. Now, to judge at least from what has been said, it is manifest that, where men are alike and equal, it is neither expedient nor just that one man should be lord of all, whether there are laws, or whether there are no laws, but he himself is in the place of law. Neither should a good man be lord over good men, nor a bad man over bad; nor, even if he excels in virtue, should he have a right to rule, unless in a particular case, at which I have already hinted, and to which I will once more recur. But first of all, I must determine what natures are suited for government by a king, and what for an aristocracy, and what for a constitutional government.

5   A people who are by nature capable of producing a race superior in the virtue needed for political rule are fitted for kingly government; and a people submitting to be ruled as freemen by men whose virtue renders them capable of political command are adapted for an aristocracy; while the people who are suited for constitutional freedom are those among whom there naturally exists a
10   warlike multitude able to rule and to obey in turn by a law which gives office to the well-to-do according to their desert. But when a whole family or some individual, happens to be so pre-eminent in virtue as to surpass all others, then it is just that they should be the royal family and supreme over all, or that this one citizen should be king of the whole nation. For, as I said before, to give them
15   authority is not only agreeable to that ground of right which the founders of all states, whether aristocratical, or oligarchical, or again democratical, are accustomed to put forward (for these all recognize the claim of excellence, although not the same excellence), but accords with the principle already laid down. For surely it would not be right to kill, or ostracize, or exile such a
20   person, or require that he should take his turn in being governed. The whole is naturally superior to the part, and he who has this pre-eminence is in the relation of a whole to a part. But if so, the only alternative is that he should have the supreme power, and that mankind should obey him, not in turn, but always. These are the conclusions at which we arrive respecting royalty and its various
25   forms, and this is the answer to the question, whether it is or is not advantageous to states, and to which, and how.

XVIII

We maintain that the true forms of government are three, and that the best must be that which is administered by the best, and in which there is one man, or a whole family, or many persons, excelling all the others together in virtue, and
30   both rulers and subjects are fitted, the one to rule, the others to be ruled, in such a manner as to attain the most eligible life. We showed at the commencement of our inquiry that the virtue of the good man is necessarily the same as the virtue of the citizen of the perfect state. Clearly then in the same manner, and by the same means through which a man becomes truly good, he will frame a state that
35   is to be ruled by an aristocracy or by a king, and the same education and the same habits will be found to make a good man and a man fit to be a statesman or a king.

Having arrived at these conclusions, we must proceed to speak of the perfect state, and describe how it comes into being and is established.

BOOK FOUR

I

In all arts and sciences which embrace the whole of any subject, and do not come into being in a fragmentary way, it is the province of a single art or
5   science to consider all that appertains to a single subject. For example, the art of gymnastic considers not only the suitableness of different modes of training to different bodies (2), but what sort is absolutely the best (1); (for the absolutely best must suit that which is by nature best and best furnished with the means of life), and also what common form of training is adapted to the great majority of
10   men (4). And if a man does not desire the best habit of body, or the greatest skill in gymnastics, which might be attained by him, still the trainer or the teacher of gymnastic should be able to impart any lower degree of either (3). The same principle equally holds in medicine and shipbuilding, and the making of clothes, and in the arts generally.
15   Hence it is obvious that government too is the subject of a single science, which has to consider what government is best and of what sort it must be, to be most in accordance with our aspirations, if there were no external impediment, and also what kind of government is adapted to particular states. For the best is often unattainable, and therefore the true legislator and statesman ought to be
20   acquainted, not only with (1) that which is best in the abstract, but also with (2) that which is best relatively to circumstances. We should be able further to say how a state may be constituted under any given conditions (3); both how it is originally formed and, when formed, how it may be longest preserved; the supposed state being so far from having the best constitution that it is
25   unprovided even with the conditions necessary for the best; neither is it the best under the circumstances, but of an inferior type.

He ought, moreover, to know (4) the form of government which is best suited to states in general; for political writers, although they have excellent ideas, are often unpractical. We should consider, not only what form of
30   government is best, but also what is possible and what is easily attainable by all. There are some who would have none but the most perfect; for this many natural advantages are required. Others, again, speak of a more attainable form, and, although they reject the constitution under which they are living, they extol some one in particular, for example the Lacedaemonian. Any change of
35   government which has to be introduced should be one which men, starting from

their existing constitutions, will be both willing and able to adopt, since there is quite as much trouble in the reformation of an old constitution as in the establishment of a new one, just as to unlearn is as hard as to learn. And therefore, in addition to the qualifications of the statesman already mentioned,

5 he should be able to find remedies for the defects of existing constitutions, as has been said before. This he cannot do unless he knows how many forms of government there are. It is often supposed that there is only one kind of democracy and one of oligarchy. But this is a mistake; and, in order to avoid such mistakes, we must ascertain what differences there are in the constitutions

10 of states, and in how many ways they are combined. The same political insight will enable a man to know which laws are the best, and which are suited to different constitutions; for the laws are, and ought to be, relative to the constitution, and not the constitution to the laws. A constitution is the organization of offices in a state, and determines what is to be the governing

15 body, and what is the end of each community. But laws are not to be confounded with the principles of the constitution; they are the rules according to which the magistrates should administer the state, and proceed against offenders. So that we must know the varieties, and the number of varieties, of each form of government, if only with a view to making laws. For the same laws

20 cannot be equally suited to all oligarchies or to all democracies, since there is certainly more than one form both of democracy and of oligarchy.

II

In our original discussion about governments we divided them into three true forms: kingly rule, aristocracy, and constitutional government, and three corresponding perversions- tyranny, oligarchy, and democracy. Of kingly rule

25 and of aristocracy, we have already spoken, for the inquiry into the perfect state is the same thing with the discussion of the two forms thus named, since both imply a principle of virtue provided with external means. We have already determined in what aristocracy and kingly rule differ from one another, and when the latter should be established. In what follows we have to describe the

30 so-called constitutional government, which bears the common name of all constitutions, and the other forms, tyranny, oligarchy, and democracy.

It is obvious which of the three perversions is the worst, and which is the next in badness. That which is the perversion of the first and most divine is necessarily the worst. And just as a royal rule, if not a mere name, must exist by

35 virtue of some great personal superiority in the king, so tyranny, which is the worst of governments, is necessarily the farthest removed from a well-constituted form; oligarchy is little better, for it is a long way from aristocracy, and democracy is the most tolerable of the three.

A writer who preceded me has already made these distinctions, but his point of view is not the same as mine. For he lays down the principle that when all the constitutions are good (the oligarchy and the rest being virtuous), democracy is the worst, but the best when all are bad. Whereas we maintain that they are in
5   any case defective, and that one oligarchy is not to be accounted better than another, but only less bad.

Not to pursue this question further at present, let us begin by determining (1) how many varieties of constitution there are (since of democracy and oligarchy there are several): (2) what constitution is the most generally
10 acceptable, and what is eligible in the next degree after the perfect state; and besides this what other there is which is aristocratical and well-constituted, and at the same time adapted to states in general; (3) of the other forms of government to whom each is suited. For democracy may meet the needs of some better than oligarchy, and conversely. In the next place (4) we have to consider
15 in what manner a man ought to proceed who desires to establish some one among these various forms, whether of democracy or of oligarchy; and lastly, (5) having briefly discussed these subjects to the best of our power, we will endeavor to ascertain the modes of ruin and preservation both of constitutions generally and of each separately, and to what causes they are to be attributed.

III

20 The reason why there are many forms of government is that every state contains many elements. In the first place we see that all states are made up of families, and in the multitude of citizen there must be some rich and some poor, and some in a middle condition; the rich are heavy-armed, and the poor not. Of the common people, some are husbandmen, and some traders, and some
25 artisans. There are also among the notables differences of wealth and property-for example, in the number of horses which they keep, for they cannot afford to keep them unless they are rich. And therefore in old times the cities whose strength lay in their cavalry were oligarchies, and they used cavalry in wars against their neighbors; as was the practice of the Eretrians and Chalcidians, and
30 also of the Magnesians on the river Maeander, and of other peoples in Asia. Besides differences of wealth there are differences of rank and merit, and there are some other elements which were mentioned by us when in treating of aristocracy we enumerated the essentials of a state. Of these elements, sometimes all, sometimes the lesser and sometimes the greater number, have a
35 share in the government. It is evident then that there must be many forms of government, differing in kind, since the parts of which they are composed differ from each other in kind. For a constitution is an organization of offices, which all the citizens distribute among themselves, according to the power which

different classes possess, for example the rich or the poor, or according to some principle of equality which includes both. There must therefore be as many forms of government as there are modes of arranging the offices, according to the superiorities and differences of the parts of the state.

5   There are generally thought to be two principal forms: as men say of the winds that there are but two- north and south, and that the rest of them are only variations of these, so of governments there are said to be only two forms- democracy and oligarchy. For aristocracy is considered to be a kind of oligarchy, as being the rule of a few, and the so-called constitutional government
10   to be really a democracy, just as among the winds we make the west a variation of the north, and the east of the south wind. Similarly of musical modes there are said to be two kinds, the Dorian and the Phrygian; the other arrangements of the scale are comprehended under one or other of these two. About forms of government this is a very favorite notion. But in either case the better and more
15   exact way is to distinguish, as I have done, the one or two which are true forms, and to regard the others as perversions, whether of the most perfectly attempered mode or of the best form of government: we may compare the severer and more overpowering modes to the oligarchical forms, and the more relaxed and gentler ones to the democratic.

IV

20   It must not be assumed, as some are fond of saying, that democracy is simply that form of government in which the greater number are sovereign, for in oligarchies, and indeed in every government, the majority rules; nor again is oligarchy that form of government in which a few are sovereign. Suppose the whole population of a city to be 1300, and that of these 1000 are rich, and do not
25   allow the remaining 300 who are poor, but free, and in an other respects their equals, a share of the government- no one will say that this is a democracy. In like manner, if the poor were few and the masters of the rich who outnumber them, no one would ever call such a government, in which the rich majority have no share of office, an oligarchy. Therefore we should rather say that
30   democracy is the form of government in which the free are rulers, and oligarchy in which the rich; it is only an accident that the free are the many and the rich are the few. Otherwise a government in which the offices were given according to stature, as is said to be the case in Ethiopia, or according to beauty, would be an oligarchy; for the number of tall or good-looking men is small. And yet
35   oligarchy and democracy are not sufficiently distinguished merely by these two characteristics of wealth and freedom. Both of them contain many other elements, and therefore we must carry our analysis further, and say that the government is not a democracy in which the freemen, being few in number, rule

over the many who are not free, as at Apollonia, on the Ionian Gulf, and at
Thera; (for in each of these states the nobles, who were also the earliest settlers,
were held in chief honor, although they were but a few out of many). Neither is
it a democracy when the rich have the government because they exceed in
5   number; as was the case formerly at Colophon, where the bulk of the inhabitants
were possessed of large property before the Lydian War. But the form of
government is a democracy when the free, who are also poor and the majority,
govern, and an oligarchy when the rich and the noble govern, they being at the
same time few in number.

10   I have said that there are many forms of government, and have explained to
what causes the variety is due. Why there are more than those already
mentioned, and what they are, and whence they arise, I will now proceed to
consider, starting from the principle already admitted, which is that every state
consists, not of one, but of many parts. If we were going to speak of the different
15   species of animals, we should first of all determine the organs which are
indispensable to every animal, as for example some organs of sense and the
instruments of receiving and digesting food, such as the mouth and the stomach,
besides organs of locomotion. Assuming now that there are only so many kinds
of organs, but that there may be differences in them- I mean different kinds of
20   mouths, and stomachs, and perceptive and locomotive organs- the possible
combinations of these differences will necessarily furnish many variedes of
animals. (For animals cannot be the same which have different kinds of mouths
or of ears.) And when all the combinations are exhausted, there will be as many
sorts of animals as there are combinations of the necessary organs. The same,
25   then, is true of the forms of government which have been described; states, as I
have repeatedly said, are composed, not of one, but of many elements. One
element is the food-producing class, who are called husbandmen; a second, the
class of mechanics who practice the arts without which a city cannot exist; of
these arts some are absolutely necessary, others contribute to luxury or to the
30   grace of life. The third class is that of traders, and by traders I mean those who
are engaged in buying and selling, whether in commerce or in retail trade. A
fourth class is that of the serfs or laborers. The warriors make up the fifth class,
and they are as necessary as any of the others, if the country is not to be the
slave of every invader. For how can a state which has any title to the name be of
35   a slavish nature? The state is independent and self-sufficing, but a slave is the
reverse of independent. Hence we see that this subject, though ingeniously, has
not been satisfactorily treated in the Republic. Socrates says that a state is made
up of four sorts of people who are absolutely necessary; these are a weaver, a
husbandman, a shoemaker, and a builder; afterwards, finding that they are not
40   enough, he adds a smith, and again a herdsman, to look after the necessary

animals; then a merchant, and then a retail trader. All these together form the complement of the first state, as if a state were established merely to supply the necessaries of life, rather than for the sake of the good, or stood equally in need of shoemakers and of husbandmen. But he does not admit into the state a

5   military class until the country has increased in size, and is beginning to encroach on its neighbor's land, whereupon they go to war. Yet even amongst his four original citizens, or whatever be the number of those whom he associates in the state, there must be some one who will dispense justice and determine what is just. And as the soul may be said to be more truly part of an

10   animal than the body, so the higher parts of states, that is to say, the warrior class, the class engaged in the administration of justice, and that engaged in deliberation, which is the special business of political common sense-these are more essential to the state than the parts which minister to the necessaries of life. Whether their several functions are the functions of different citizens, or of the

15   same- for it may often happen that the same persons are both warriors and husbandmen- is immaterial to the argument. The higher as well as the lower elements are to be equally considered parts of the state, and if so, the military element at any rate must be included. There are also the wealthy who minister to the state with their property; these form the seventh class. The eighth class is

20   that of magistrates and of officers; for the state cannot exist without rulers. And therefore some must be able to take office and to serve the state, either always or in turn. There only remains the class of those who deliberate and who judge between disputants; we were just now distinguishing them. If presence of all these elements, and their fair and equitable organization, is necessary to states,

25   then there must also be persons who have the ability of statesmen. Different functions appear to be often combined in the same individual; for example, the warrior may also be a husbandman, or an artisan; or, again, the councillor a judge. And all claim to possess political ability, and think that they are quite competent to fill most offices. But the same persons cannot be rich and poor at

30   the same time. For this reason the rich and the poor are regarded in an especial sense as parts of a state. Again, because the rich are generally few in number, while the poor are many, they appear to be antagonistic, and as the one or the other prevails they form the government. Hence arises the common opinion that there are two kinds of government- democracy and oligarchy.

35   I have already explained that there are many forms of constitution, and to what causes the variety is due. Let me now show that there are different forms both of democracy and oligarchy, as will indeed be evident from what has preceded. For both in the common people and in the notables various classes are included; of the common people, one class are husbandmen, another artisans;

40   another traders, who are employed in buying and selling; another are the

seafaring class, whether engaged in war or in trade, as ferrymen or as fishermen.
(In many places any one of these classes forms quite a large population; for
example, fishermen at Tarentum and Byzantium, crews of triremes at Athens,
merchant seamen at Aegina and Chios, ferrymen at Tenedos.) To the classes
5   already mentioned may be added day-laborers, and those who, owing to their
needy circumstances, have no leisure, or those who are not of free birth on both
sides; and there may be other classes as well. The notables again may be divided
according to their wealth, birth, virtue, education, and similar differences.

Of forms of democracy first comes that which is said to be based strictly on
10   equality. In such a democracy the law says that it is just for the poor to have no
more advantage than the rich; and that neither should be masters, but both equal.
For if liberty and equality, as is thought by some, are chiefly to be found in
democracy, they will be best attained when all persons alike share in the
government to the utmost. And since the people are the majority, and the
15   opinion of the majority is decisive, such a government must necessarily be a
democracy. Here then is one sort of democracy. There is another, in which the
magistrates are elected according to a certain property qualification, but a low
one; he who has the required amount of property has a share in the government,
but he who loses his property loses his rights. Another kind is that in which all
20   the citizens who are under no disqualification share in the government, but still
the law is supreme. In another, everybody, if he be only a citizen, is admitted to
the government, but the law is supreme as before. A fifth form of democracy, in
other respects the same, is that in which, not the law, but the multitude, have the
supreme power, and supersede the law by their decrees. This is a state of affairs
25   brought about by the demagogues. For in democracies which are subject to the
law the best citizens hold the first place, and there are no demagogues; but
where the laws are not supreme, there demagogues spring up. For the people
becomes a monarch, and is many in one; and the many have the power in their
hands, not as individuals, but collectively. Homer says that 'it is not good to
30   have a rule of many,' but whether he means this corporate rule, or the rule of
many individuals, is uncertain. At all events this sort of democracy, which is
now a monarch, and no longer under the control of law, seeks to exercise
monarchical sway, and grows into a despot; the flatterer is held in honor; this
sort of democracy being relatively to other democracies what tyranny is to other
35   forms of monarchy. The spirit of both is the same, and they alike exercise a
despotic rule over the better citizens. The decrees of the demos correspond to the
edicts of the tyrant; and the demagogue is to the one what the flatterer is to the
other. Both have great power; the flatterer with the tyrant, the demagogue with
democracies of the kind which we are describing. The demagogues make the
40   decrees of the people override the laws, by referring all things to the popular

assembly. And therefore they grow great, because the people have an things in their hands, and they hold in their hands the votes of the people, who are too ready to listen to them. Further, those who have any complaint to bring against the magistrates say, 'Let the people be judges'; the people are too happy to
5   accept the invitation; and so the authority of every office is undermined. Such a democracy is fairly open to the objection that it is not a constitution at all; for where the laws have no authority, there is no constitution. The law ought to be supreme over all, and the magistracies should judge of particulars, and only this should be considered a constitution. So that if democracy be a real form of
10   government, the sort of system in which all things are regulated by decrees is clearly not even a democracy in the true sense of the word, for decrees relate only to particulars.

These then are the different kinds of democracy.

V

Of oligarchies, too, there are different kinds: one where the property
15   qualification for office is such that the poor, although they form the majority, have no share in the government, yet he who acquires a qualification may obtain a share. Another sort is when there is a qualification for office, but a high one, and the vacancies in the governing body are fired by co-optation. If the election is made out of all the qualified persons, a constitution of this kind inclines to an
20   aristocracy, if out of a privileged class, to an oligarchy. Another sort of oligarchy is when the son succeeds the father. There is a fourth form, likewise hereditary, in which the magistrates are supreme and not the law. Among oligarchies this is what tyranny is among monarchies, and the last-mentioned form of democracy among democracies; and in fact this sort of oligarchy
25   receives the name of a dynasty (or rule of powerful families).

These are the different sorts of oligarchies and democracies. It should, however, be remembered that in many states the constitution which is established by law, although not democratic, owing to the education and habits of the people may be administered democratically, and conversely in other states
30   the established constitution may incline to democracy, but may be administered in an oligarchical spirit. This most often happens after a revolution: for governments do not change at once; at first the dominant party are content with encroaching a little upon their opponents. The laws which existed previously continue in force, but the authors of the revolution have the power in their
35   hands.

VI

From what has been already said we may safely infer that there are so many different kinds of democracies and of oligarchies. For it is evident that either all the classes whom we mentioned must share in the government, or some only and not others. When the class of husbandmen and of those who possess moderate fortunes have the supreme power, the government is

5 administered according to law. For the citizens being compelled to live by their labor have no leisure; and so they set up the authority of the law, and attend assemblies only when necessary. They all obtain a share in the government when they have acquired the qualification which is fixed by the law- the absolute exclusion of any class would be a step towards oligarchy; hence all

10 who have acquired the property qualification are admitted to a share in the constitution. But leisure cannot be provided for them unless there are revenues to support them. This is one sort of democracy, and these are the causes which give birth to it. Another kind is based on the distinction which naturally comes next in order; in this, every one to whose birth there is no objection is eligible,

15 but actually shares in the government only if he can find leisure. Hence in such a democracy the supreme power is vested in the laws, because the state has no means of paying the citizens. A third kind is when all freemen have a right to share in the government, but do not actually share, for the reason which has been already given; so that in this form again the law must rule. A fourth kind of

20 democracy is that which comes latest in the history of states. In our own day, when cities have far outgrown their original size, and their revenues have increased, all the citizens have a place in the government, through the great preponderance of the multitude; and they all, including the poor who receive pay, and therefore have leisure to exercise their rights, share in the

25 administration. Indeed, when they are paid, the common people have the most leisure, for they are not hindered by the care of their property, which often fetters the rich, who are thereby prevented from taking part in the assembly or in the courts, and so the state is governed by the poor, who are a majority, and not by the laws.

30 So many kinds of democracies there are, and they grow out of these necessary causes.

Of oligarchies, one form is that in which the majority of the citizens have some property, but not very much; and this is the first form, which allows to any one who obtains the required amount the right of sharing in the government. The

35 sharers in the government being a numerous body, it follows that the law must govern, and not individuals. For in proportion as they are further removed from a monarchical form of government, and in respect of property have neither so much as to be able to live without attending to business, nor so little as to need state support, they must admit the rule of law and not claim to rule themselves.

40 But if the men of property in the state are fewer than in the former case, and own

more property, there arises a second form of oligarchy. For the stronger they are, the more power they claim, and having this object in view, they themselves select those of the other classes who are to be admitted to the government; but, not being as yet strong enough to rule without the law, they make the law
5   represent their wishes. When this power is intensified by a further diminution of their numbers and increase of their property, there arises a third and further stage of oligarchy, in which the governing class keep the offices in their own hands, and the law ordains that the son shall succeed the father. When, again, the rulers have great wealth and numerous friends, this sort of family despotism
10 approaches a monarchy; individuals rule and not the law. This is the fourth sort of oligarchy, and is analogous to the last sort of democracy.

VII

There are still two forms besides democracy and oligarchy; one of them is universally recognized and included among the four principal forms of government, which are said to be (1) monarchy, (2) oligarchy, (3) democracy,
15 and (4) the so-called aristocracy or government of the best. But there is also a fifth, which retains the generic name of polity or constitutional government; this is not common, and therefore has not been noticed by writers who attempt to enumerate the different kinds of government; like Plato, in their books about the state, they recognize four only. The term 'aristocracy' is rightly applied to the
20 form of government which is described in the first part of our treatise; for that only can be rightly called aristocracy which is a government formed of the best men absolutely, and not merely of men who are good when tried by any given standard. In the perfect state the good man is absolutely the same as the good citizen; whereas in other states the good citizen is only good relatively to his
25 own form of government. But there are some states differing from oligarchies and also differing from the so-called polity or constitutional government; these are termed aristocracies, and in them the magistrates are certainly chosen, both according to their wealth and according to their merit. Such a form of government differs from each of the two just now mentioned, and is termed an
30 aristocracy. For indeed in states which do not make virtue the aim of the community, men of merit and reputation for virtue may be found. And so where a government has regard to wealth, virtue, and numbers, as at Carthage, that is aristocracy; and also where it has regard only to two out of the three, as at Lacedaemon, to virtue and numbers, and the two principles of democracy and
35 virtue temper each other. There are these two forms of aristocracy in addition to the first and perfect state, and there is a third form, viz., the constitutions which incline more than the so-called polity towards oligarchy.

VIII

I have yet to speak of the so-called polity and of tyranny. I put them in this order, not because a polity or constitutional government is to be regarded as a perversion any more than the above mentioned aristocracies. The truth is, that they an fall short of the most perfect form of government, and so they are

5   reckoned among perversions, and the really perverted forms are perversions of these, as I said in the original discussion. Last of all I will speak of tyranny, which I place last in the series because I am inquiring into the constitutions of states, and this is the very reverse of a constitution.

Having explained why I have adopted this order, I will proceed to consider

10   constitutional government; of which the nature will be clearer now that oligarchy and democracy have been defined. For polity or constitutional government may be described generally as a fusion of oligarchy and democracy; but the term is usually applied to those forms of government which incline towards democracy, and the term aristocracy to those which incline towards

15   oligarchy, because birth and education are commonly the accompaniments of wealth. Moreover, the rich already possess the external advantages the want of which is a temptation to crime, and hence they are called noblemen and gentlemen. And inasmuch as aristocracy seeks to give predominance to the best of the citizens, people say also of oligarchies that they are composed of

20   noblemen and gentlemen. Now it appears to be an impossible thing that the state which is governed not by the best citizens but by the worst should be well-governed, and equally impossible that the state which is ill-governed should be governed by the best. But we must remember that good laws, if they are not obeyed, do not constitute good government. Hence there are two parts of good

25   government; one is the actual obedience of citizens to the laws, the other part is the goodness of the laws which they obey; they may obey bad laws as well as good. And there may be a further subdivision; they may obey either the best laws which are attainable to them, or the best absolutely.

The distribution of offices according to merit is a special characteristic of

30   aristocracy, for the principle of an aristocracy is virtue, as wealth is of an oligarchy, and freedom of a democracy. In all of them there of course exists the right of the majority, and whatever seems good to the majority of those who share in the government has authority. Now in most states the form called polity exists, for the fusion goes no further than the attempt to unite the freedom of the

35   poor and the wealth of the rich, who commonly take the place of the noble. But as there are three grounds on which men claim an equal share in the government, freedom, wealth, and virtue (for the fourth or good birth is the result of the two last, being only ancient wealth and virtue), it is clear that the admixture of the two elements, that is to say, of the rich and poor, is to be called

a polity or constitutional government; and the union of the three is to be called aristocracy or the government of the best, and more than any other form of government, except the true and ideal, has a right to this name.

Thus far I have shown the existence of forms of states other than monarchy, democracy, and oligarchy, and what they are, and in what aristocracies differ from one another, and polities from aristocracies- that the two latter are not very unlike is obvious.

IX

Next we have to consider how by the side of oligarchy and democracy the so-called polity or constitutional government springs up, and how it should be organized. The nature of it will be at once understood from a comparison of oligarchy and democracy; we must ascertain their different characteristics, and taking a portion from each, put the two together, like the parts of an indenture. Now there are three modes in which fusions of government may be affected. In the first mode we must combine the laws made by both governments, say concerning the administration of justice. In oligarchies they impose a fine on the rich if they do not serve as judges, and to the poor they give no pay; but in democracies they give pay to the poor and do not fine the rich. Now (1) the union of these two modes is a common or middle term between them, and is therefore characteristic of a constitutional government, for it is a combination of both. This is one mode of uniting the two elements. Or (2) a mean may be taken between the enactments of the two: thus democracies require no property qualification, or only a small one, from members of the assembly, oligarchies a high one; here neither of these is the common term, but a mean between them. (3) There is a third mode, in which something is borrowed from the oligarchical and something from the democratical principle. For example, the appointment of magistrates by lot is thought to be democratical, and the election of them oligarchical; democratical again when there is no property qualification, oligarchical when there is. In the aristocratical or constitutional state, one element will be taken from each- from oligarchy the principle of electing to offices, from democracy the disregard of qualification. Such are the various modes of combination.

There is a true union of oligarchy and democracy when the same state may be termed either a democracy or an oligarchy; those who use both names evidently feel that the fusion is complete. Such a fusion there is also in the mean; for both extremes appear in it. The Lacedaemonian constitution, for example, is often described as a democracy, because it has many democratical features. In the first place the youth receive a democratical education. For the sons of the poor are brought up with with the sons of the rich, who are educated in such a manner as to make it possible for the sons of the poor to be educated by them. A similar equality prevails in the following period of life, and when the citizens are grown up to manhood the same rule is observed; there is no distinction between the rich and poor. In like manner they all have the same

5 food at their public tables, and the rich wear only such clothing as any poor man can afford. Again, the people elect to one of the two greatest offices of state, and in the other they share; for they elect the Senators and share in the Ephoralty. By others the Spartan constitution is said to be an oligarchy, because it has many oligarchical elements. That all offices are filled by election and none by lot, is

10 one of these oligarchical characteristics; that the power of inflicting death or banishment rests with a few persons is another; and there are others. In a well attempted polity there should appear to be both elements and yet neither; also the government should rely on itself, and not on foreign aid, and on itself not through the good will of a majority- they might be equally well-disposed when

15 there is a vicious form of government- but through the general willingness of all classes in the state to maintain the constitution.

Enough of the manner in which a constitutional government, and in which the so-called aristocracies ought to be framed.

BOOK SEVEN

I

He who would duly inquire about the best form of a state ought first to
20 determine which is the most eligible life; while this remains uncertain the best form of the state must also be uncertain; for, in the natural order of things, those may be expected to lead the best life who are governed in the best manner of which their circumstances admit. We ought therefore to ascertain, first of all, which is the most generally eligible life, and then whether the same life is or is
25 not best for the state and for individuals.

Assuming that enough has been already said in discussions outside the school concerning the best life, we will now only repeat what is contained in them. Certainly no one will dispute the propriety of that partition of goods which separates them into three classes, viz., external goods, goods of the body, and
30 goods of the soul, or deny that the happy man must have all three. For no one would maintain that he is happy who has not in him a particle of courage or temperance or justice or prudence, who is afraid of every insect which flutters past him, and will commit any crime, however great, in order to gratify his lust of meat or drink, who will sacrifice his dearest friend for the sake of half-a-
35 farthing, and is as feeble and false in mind as a child or a madman. These

87

propositions are almost universally acknowledged as soon as they are uttered, but men differ about the degree or relative superiority of this or that good. Some think that a very moderate amount of virtue is enough, but set no limit to their desires of wealth, property, power, reputation, and the like. To whom we reply

5   by an appeal to facts, which easily prove that mankind do not acquire or preserve virtue by the help of external goods, but external goods by the help of virtue, and that happiness, whether consisting in pleasure or virtue, or both, is more often found with those who are most highly cultivated in their mind and in their character, and have only a moderate share of external goods, than among

10 those who possess external goods to a useless extent but are deficient in higher qualities; and this is not only matter of experience, but, if reflected upon, will easily appear to be in accordance with reason. For, whereas external goods have a limit, like any other instrument, and all things useful are of such a nature that where there is too much of them they must either do harm, or at any rate be of

15 no use, to their possessors, every good of the soul, the greater it is, is also of greater use, if the epithet useful as well as noble is appropriate to such subjects. No proof is required to show that the best state of one thing in relation to another corresponds in degree of excellence to the interval between the natures of which we say that these very states are states: so that, if the soul is more noble than our

20 possessions or our bodies, both absolutely and in relation to us, it must be admitted that the best state of either has a similar ratio to the other. Again, it is for the sake of the soul that goods external and goods of the body are eligible at all, and all wise men ought to choose them for the sake of the soul, and not the soul for the sake of them.

25   Let us acknowledge then that each one has just so much of happiness as he has of virtue and wisdom, and of virtuous and wise action. God is a witness to us of this truth, for he is happy and blessed, not by reason of any external good, but in himself and by reason of his own nature. And herein of necessity lies the difference between good fortune and happiness; for external goods come of

30 themselves, and chance is the author of them, but no one is just or temperate by or through chance. In like manner, and by a similar train of argument, the happy state may be shown to be that which is best and which acts rightly; and rightly it cannot act without doing right actions, and neither individual nor state can do right actions without virtue and wisdom. Thus the courage, justice, and wisdom

35 of a state have the same form and nature as the qualities which give the individual who possesses them the name of just, wise, or temperate.

Thus much may suffice by way of preface: for I could not avoid touching upon these questions, neither could I go through all the arguments affecting them; these are the business of another science.

40   Let us assume then that the best life, both for individuals and states, is the

life of virtue, when virtue has external goods enough for the performance of good actions. If there are any who controvert our assertion, we will in this treatise pass them over, and consider their objections hereafter.

II

There remains to be discussed the question whether the happiness of the
5   individual is the same as that of the state, or different. Here again there can be no doubt- no one denies that they are the same. For those who hold that the well-being of the individual consists in his wealth, also think that riches make the happiness of the whole state, and those who value most highly the life of a tyrant deem that city the happiest which rules over the greatest number; while they
10 who approve an individual for his virtue say that the more virtuous a city is, the happier it is. Two points here present themselves for consideration: first (1), which is the more eligible life, that of a citizen who is a member of a state, or that of an alien who has no political ties; and again (2), which is the best form of constitution or the best condition of a state, either on the supposition that
15 political privileges are desirable for all, or for a majority only? Since the good of the state and not of the individual is the proper subject of political thought and speculation, and we are engaged in a political discussion, while the first of these two points has a secondary interest for us, the latter will be the main subject of our inquiry.
20   Now it is evident that the form of government is best in which every man, whoever he is, can act best and live happily. But even those who agree in thinking that the life of virtue is the most eligible raise a question, whether the life of business and politics is or is not more eligible than one which is wholly independent of external goods, I mean than a contemplative life, which by some
25 is maintained to be the only one worthy of a philosopher. For these two lives-the life of the philosopher and the life of the statesman- appear to have been preferred by those who have been most keen in the pursuit of virtue, both in our own and in other ages. Which is the better is a question of no small moment; for the wise man, like the wise state, will necessarily regulate his life according to
30 the best end. There are some who think that while a despotic rule over others is the greatest injustice, to exercise a constitutional rule over them, even though not unjust, is a great impediment to a man's individual wellbeing. Others take an opposite view; they maintain that the true life of man is the practical and political, and that every virtue admits of being practiced, quite as much by
35 statesmen and rulers as by private individuals. Others, again, are of opinion that arbitrary and tyrannical rule alone consists with happiness; indeed, in some states the entire aim both of the laws and of the constitution is to give men despotic power over their neighbors. And, therefore, although in most cities the

laws may be said generally to be in a chaotic state, still, if they aim at anything, they aim at the maintenance of power: thus in Lacedaemon and Crete the system of education and the greater part of the of the laws are framed with a view to war. And in all nations which are able to gratify their ambition military power is
5   held in esteem, for example among the Scythians and Persians and Thracians and Celts.

   In some nations there are even laws tending to stimulate the warlike virtues, as at Carthage, where we are told that men obtain the honor of wearing as many armlets as they have served campaigns. There was once a law in Macedonia that
10   he who had not killed an enemy should wear a halter, and among the Scythians no one who had not slain his man was allowed to drink out of the cup which was handed round at a certain feast. Among the Iberians, a warlike nation, the number of enemies whom a man has slain is indicated by the number of obelisks which are fixed in the earth round his tomb; and there are numerous practices
15   among other nations of a like kind, some of them established by law and others by custom. Yet to a reflecting mind it must appear very strange that the statesman should be always considering how he can dominate and tyrannize over others, whether they will or not. How can that which is not even lawful be the business of the statesman or the legislator? Unlawful it certainly is to rule
20   without regard to justice, for there may be might where there is no right. The other arts and sciences offer no parallel a physician is not expected to persuade or coerce his patients, nor a pilot the passengers in his ship. Yet most men appear to think that the art of despotic government is statesmanship, and what men affirm to be unjust and inexpedient in their own case they are not ashamed
25   of practicing towards others; they demand just rule for themselves, but where other men are concerned they care nothing about it. Such behavior is irrational; unless the one party is, and the other is not, born to serve, in which case men have a right to command, not indeed all their fellows, but only those who are intended to be subjects; just as we ought not to hunt mankind, whether for food
30   or sacrifice, but only the animals which may be hunted for food or sacrifice, this is to say, such wild animals as are eatable. And surely there may be a city happy in isolation, which we will assume to be well-governed (for it is quite possible that a city thus isolated might be well-administered and have good laws); but such a city would not be constituted with any view to war or the conquest of
35   enemies- all that sort of thing must be excluded. Hence we see very plainly that warlike pursuits, although generally to be deemed honorable, are not the supreme end of all things, but only means. And the good lawgiver should inquire how states and races of men and communities may participate in a good life, and in the happiness which is attainable by them. His enactments will not be
40   always the same; and where there are neighbors he will have to see what sort of

studies should be practiced in relation to their several characters, or how the measures appropriate in relation to each are to be adopted. The end at which the best form of government should aim may be properly made a matter of future consideration.

III

5   Let us now address those who, while they agree that the life of virtue is the most eligible, differ about the manner of practicing it. For some renounce political power, and think that the life of the freeman is different from the life of the statesman and the best of all; but others think the life of the statesman best. The argument of the latter is that he who does nothing cannot do well, and that

10   virtuous activity is identical with happiness. To both we say: 'you are partly right and partly wrong.' first class are right in affirming that the life of the freeman is better than the life of the despot; for there is nothing grand or noble in having the use of a slave, in so far as he is a slave; or in issuing commands about necessary things. But it is an error to suppose that every sort of rule is

15   despotic like that of a master over slaves, for there is as great a difference between the rule over freemen and the rule over slaves as there is between slavery by nature and freedom by nature, about which I have said enough at the commencement of this treatise. And it is equally a mistake to place inactivity above action, for happiness is activity, and the actions of the just and wise are

20   the realization of much that is noble.

But perhaps some one, accepting these premises, may still maintain that supreme power is the best of all things, because the possessors of it are able to perform the greatest number of noble actions. if so, the man who is able to rule, instead of giving up anything to his neighbor, ought rather to take away his

25   power; and the father should make no account of his son, nor the son of his father, nor friend of friend; they should not bestow a thought on one another in comparison with this higher object, for the best is the most eligible and 'doing eligible' and 'doing well' is the best. There might be some truth in such a view if we assume that robbers and plunderers attain the chief good. But this can

30   never be; their hypothesis is false. For the actions of a ruler cannot really be honorable, unless he is as much superior to other men as a husband is to a wife, or a father to his children, or a master to his slaves. And therefore he who violates the law can never recover by any success, however great, what he has already lost in departing from virtue. For equals the honorable and the just

35   consist in sharing alike, as is just and equal. But that the unequal should be given to equals, and the unlike to those who are like, is contrary to nature, and nothing which is contrary to nature is good. If, therefore, there is any one

superior in virtue and in the power of performing the best actions, him we ought to follow and obey, but he must have the capacity for action as well as virtue.

If we are right in our view, and happiness is assumed to be virtuous activity, the active life will be the best, both for every city collectively, and for individuals. Not that a life of action must necessarily have relation to others, as some persons think, nor are those ideas only to be regarded as practical which are pursued for the sake of practical results, but much more the thoughts and contemplations which are independent and complete in themselves; since virtuous activity, and therefore a certain kind of action, is an end, and even in the case of external actions the directing mind is most truly said to act. Neither, again, is it necessary that states which are cut off from others and choose to live alone should be inactive; for activity, as well as other things, may take place by sections; there are many ways in which the sections of a state act upon one another. The same thing is equally true of every individual. If this were otherwise, God and the universe, who have no external actions over and above their own energies, would be far enough from perfection. Hence it is evident that the same life is best for each individual, and for states and for mankind collectively.

XIII

Returning to the constitution itself, let us seek to determine out of what and what sort of elements the state which is to be happy and well-governed should be composed. There are two things in which all which all well-being consists: one of them is the choice of a right end and aim of action, and the other the discovery of the actions which are means towards it; for the means and the end may agree or disagree. Sometimes the right end is set before men, but in practice they fail to attain it; in other cases they are successful in all the means, but they propose to themselves a bad end; and sometimes they fail in both. Take, for example, the art of medicine; physicians do not always understand the nature of health, and also the means which they use may not effect the desired end. In all arts and sciences both the end and the means should be equally within our control.

The happiness and well-being which all men manifestly desire, some have the power of attaining, but to others, from some accident or defect of nature, the attainment of them is not granted; for a good life requires a supply of external goods, in a less degree when men are in a good state, in a greater degree when they are in a lower state. Others again, who possess the conditions of happiness, go utterly wrong from the first in the pursuit of it. But since our object is to discover the best form of government, that, namely, under which a city will be best governed, and since the city is best governed which has the greatest opportunity of obtaining happiness, it is evident that we must clearly ascertain the nature of happiness.

We maintain, and have said in the Ethics, if the arguments there adduced are of any value, that happiness is the realization and perfect exercise of virtue,
5 and this not conditional, but absolute. And I used the term 'conditional' to express that which is indispensable, and 'absolute' to express that which is good in itself. Take the case of just actions; just punishments and chastisements do indeed spring from a good principle, but they are good only because we cannot do without them- it would be better that neither individuals nor states should
10 need anything of the sort- but actions which aim at honor and advantage are absolutely the best. The conditional action is only the choice of a lesser evil; whereas these are the foundation and creation of good. A good man may make the best even of poverty and disease, and the other ills of life; but he can only attain happiness under the opposite conditions (for this also has been determined
15 in accordance with ethical arguments, that the good man is he for whom, because he is virtuous, the things that are absolutely good are good; it is also plain that his use of these goods must be virtuous and in the absolute sense good). This makes men fancy that external goods are the cause of happiness, yet we might as well say that a brilliant performance on the lyre was to be attributed
20 to the instrument and not to the skill of the performer.

It follows then from what has been said that some things the legislator must find ready to his hand in a state, others he must provide. And therefore we can only say: May our state be constituted in such a manner as to be blessed with the goods of which fortune disposes (for we acknowledge her power): whereas
25 virtue and goodness in the state are not a matter of chance but the result of knowledge and purpose. A city can be virtuous only when the citizens who have a share in the government are virtuous, and in our state all the citizens share in the government; let us then inquire how a man becomes virtuous. For even if we could suppose the citizen body to be virtuous, without each of them being so, yet
30 the latter would be better, for in the virtue of each the virtue of all is involved.

There are three things which make men good and virtuous; these are nature, habit, rational principle. In the first place, every one must be born a man and not some other animal; so, too, he must have a certain character, both of body and soul. But some qualities there is no use in having at birth, for they are altered by
35 habit, and there are some gifts which by nature are made to be turned by habit to good or bad. Animals lead for the most part a life of nature, although in lesser particulars some are influenced by habit as well. Man has rational principle, in addition, and man only. Wherefore nature, habit, rational principle must be in harmony with one another; for they do not always agree; men do many things
40 against habit and nature, if rational principle persuades them that they ought. We

93

have already determined what natures are likely to be most easily molded by the hands of the legislator. An else is the work of education; we learn some things by habit and some by instruction.

XIV

Since every political society is composed of rulers and subjects let us
5   consider whether the relations of one to the other should interchange or be permanent. For the education of the citizens will necessarily vary with the answer given to this question. Now, if some men excelled others in the same degree in which gods and heroes are supposed to excel mankind in general (having in the first place a great advantage even in their bodies, and secondly in
10   their minds), so that the superiority of the governors was undisputed and patent to their subjects, it would clearly be better that once for an the one class should rule and the other serve. But since this is unattainable, and kings have no marked superiority over their subjects, such as Scylax affirms to be found among the Indians, it is obviously necessary on many grounds that all the citizens alike
15   should take their turn of governing and being governed. Equality consists in the same treatment of similar persons, and no government can stand which is not founded upon justice. For if the government be unjust every one in the country unites with the governed in the desire to have a revolution, and it is an impossibility that the members of the government can be so numerous as to be
20   stronger than all their enemies put together. Yet that governors should excel their subjects is undeniable. How all this is to be effected, and in what way they will respectively share in the government, the legislator has to consider. The subject has been already mentioned. Nature herself has provided the distinction when she made a difference between old and young within the same species, of
25   whom she fitted the one to govern and the other to be governed. No one takes offense at being governed when he is young, nor does he think himself better than his governors, especially if he will enjoy the same privilege when he reaches the required age.

We conclude that from one point of view governors and governed are
30   identical, and from another different. And therefore their education must be the same and also different. For he who would learn to command well must, as men say, first of all learn to obey. As I observed in the first part of this treatise, there is one rule which is for the sake of the rulers and another rule which is for the sake of the ruled; the former is a despotic, the latter a free government. Some
35   commands differ not in the thing commanded, but in the intention with which they are imposed. Wherefore, many apparently menial offices are an honor to the free youth by whom they are performed; for actions do not differ as honorable or dishonorable in themselves so much as in the end and intention of

them. But since we say that the virtue of the citizen and ruler is the same as that of the good man, and that the same person must first be a subject and then a ruler, the legislator has to see that they become good men, and by what means this may be accomplished, and what is the end of the perfect life.

5   Now the soul of man is divided into two parts, one of which has a rational principle in itself, and the other, not having a rational principle in itself, is able to obey such a principle. And we call a man in any way good because he has the virtues of these two parts. In which of them the end is more likely to be found is no matter of doubt to those who adopt our division; for in the world both of
10   nature and of art the inferior always exists for the sake of the better or superior, and the better or superior is that which has a rational principle. This principle, too, in our ordinary way of speaking, is divided into two kinds, for there is a practical and a speculative principle. This part, then, must evidently be similarly divided. And there must be a corresponding division of actions; the actions of
15   the naturally better part are to be preferred by those who have it in their power to attain to two out of the three or to all, for that is always to every one the most eligible which is the highest attainable by him. The whole of life is further divided into two parts, business and leisure, war and peace, and of actions some aim at what is necessary and useful, and some at what is honorable. And the
20   preference given to one or the other class of actions must necessarily be like the preference given to one or other part of the soul and its actions over the other; there must be war for the sake of peace, business for the sake of leisure, things useful and necessary for the sake of things honorable. All these points the statesman should keep in view when he frames his laws; he should consider the
25   parts of the soul and their functions, and above all the better and the end; he should also remember the diversities of human lives and actions. For men must be able to engage in business and go to war, but leisure and peace are better; they must do what is necessary and indeed what is useful, but what is honorable is better. On such principles children and persons of every age which requires
30   education should be trained. Whereas even the Hellenes of the present day who are reputed to be best governed, and the legislators who gave them their constitutions, do not appear to have framed their governments with a regard to the best end, or to have given them laws and education with a view to all the virtues, but in a vulgar spirit have fallen back on those which promised to be
35   more useful and profitable. Many modern writers have taken a similar view: they commend the Lacedaemonian constitution, and praise the legislator for making conquest and war his sole aim, a doctrine which may be refuted by argument and has long ago been refuted by facts. For most men desire empire in the hope of accumulating the goods of fortune; and on this ground Thibron and
40   all those who have written about the Lacedaemonian constitution have praised

their legislator, because the Lacedaemonians, by being trained to meet dangers, gained great power. But surely they are not a happy people now that their empire has passed away, nor was their legislator right. How ridiculous is the result, if, when they are continuing in the observance of his laws and no one
5 interferes with them, they have lost the better part of life! These writers further err about the sort of government which the legislator should approve, for the government of freemen is nobler and implies more virtue than despotic government. Neither is a city to be deemed happy or a legislator to be praised because he trains his citizens to conquer and obtain dominion over their
10 neighbors, for there is great evil in this. On a similar principle any citizen who could, should obviously try to obtain the power in his own state- the crime which the Lacedaemonians accuse king Pausanias of attempting, although he had so great honor already. No such principle and no law having this object is either statesmanlike or useful or right. For the same things are best both for
15 individuals and for states, and these are the things which the legislator ought to implant in the minds of his citizens.

Neither should men study war with a view to the enslavement of those who do not deserve to be enslaved; but first of all they should provide against their own enslavement, and in the second place obtain empire for the good of the
20 governed, and not for the sake of exercising a general despotism, and in the third place they should seek to be masters only over those who deserve to be slaves. Facts, as well as arguments, prove that the legislator should direct all his military and other measures to the provision of leisure and the establishment of peace. For most of these military states are safe only while they are at war, but
25 fall when they have acquired their empire; like unused iron they lose their temper in time of peace. And for this the legislator is to blame, he never having taught them how to lead the life of peace.

XV

Since the end of individuals and of states is the same, the end of the best man and of the best constitution must also be the same; it is therefore evident
30 that there ought to exist in both of them the virtues of leisure; for peace, as has been often repeated, is the end of war, and leisure of toil. But leisure and cultivation may be promoted, not only by those virtues which are practiced in leisure, but also by some of those which are useful to business. For many necessaries of life have to be supplied before we can have leisure. Therefore a
35 city must be temperate and brave, and able to endure: for truly, as the proverb says, 'There is no leisure for slaves,' and those who cannot face danger like men are the slaves of any invader. Courage and endurance are required for business and philosophy for leisure, temperance and justice for both, and more especially

in times of peace and leisure, for war compels men to be just and temperate, whereas the enjoyment of good fortune and the leisure which comes with peace tend to make them insolent. Those then who seem to be the best-off and to be in the possession of every good, have special need of justice and temperance- for
5   example, those (if such there be, as the poets say) who dwell in the Islands of the Blest; they above all will need philosophy and temperance and justice, and all the more the more leisure they have, living in the midst of abundance. There is no difficulty in seeing why the state that would be happy and good ought to have these virtues. If it be disgraceful in men not to be able to use the goods of life, it
10   is peculiarly disgraceful not to be able to use them in time of leisure- to show excellent qualities in action and war, and when they have peace and leisure to be no better than slaves. Wherefore we should not practice virtue after the manner of the Lacedaemonians. For they, while agreeing with other men in their conception of the highest goods, differ from the rest of mankind in thinking that
15   they are to be obtained by the practice of a single virtue. And since they think these goods and the enjoyment of them greater than the enjoyment derived from the virtues ... and that it should be practiced for its own sake, is evident from what has been said; we must now consider how and by what means it is to be attained.
20   We have already determined that nature and habit and rational principle are required, and, of these, the proper nature of the citizens has also been defined by us. But we have still to consider whether the training of early life is to be that of rational principle or habit, for these two must accord, and when in accord they will then form the best of harmonies. The rational principle may be mistaken
25   and fail in attaining the highest ideal of life, and there may be a like evil influence of habit. Thus much is clear in the first place, that, as in all other things, birth implies an antecedent beginning, and that there are beginnings whose end is relative to a further end. Now, in men rational principle and mind are the end towards which nature strives, so that the birth and moral discipline of
30   the citizens ought to be ordered with a view to them. In the second place, as the soul and body are two, we see also that there are two parts of the soul, the rational and the irrational, and two corresponding states- reason and appetite. And as the body is prior in order of generation to the soul, so the irrational is prior to the rational. The proof is that anger and wishing and desire are
35   implanted in children from their very birth, but reason and understanding are developed as they grow older. Wherefore, the care of the body ought to precede that of the soul, and the training of the appetitive part should follow: none the less our care of it must be for the sake of the reason, and our care of the body for the sake of the soul.

Niccolo Machiavelli

Niccolo Machiavelli (b. 1469, Val di Pesa, d. 1527, San Casciano) was a Florentine politician, political theorist, historian, and playwrite. He was educated in the humanist tradition and rose to become one of the political leaders of the Florentine Republic (serving as the head of the diplomatic service as well as of the militia defending the city) before it was defeated by the alliance of the Medici and Pope Julius II. When the Medici returned to Florence in 1513, Machiavelli was accused of an anti-Medici conspiracy and tortured on the rack. He denied his participation and upon release retired to his estate near Florence, where he spent the rest of his life, writing philosophical works and plays.

Machiavelli's key philosophical works are *The Prince* and *Discourses on Levy*, the latter of which is considered to be a passionate defense of republicanism in an apparent contrast with the monarchical tone of *The Prince*.

Machiavelli is generally regarded as one of the founders of the modernist tradition in the history of political thought. He influenced Thomas Hobbes and the philosophers of "the reason of state" such as Jean Bodin, as well as the contemporary development of republican political theory in the works of Quentin Skinner and Philip Pettit.

DEDICATION

To the Magnificent Lorenzo Di Piero De' Medici:

Those who strive to obtain the good graces of a prince are accustomed to
come before him with such things as they hold most precious, or in which they
see him take most delight; whence one often sees horses, arms, cloth of gold,
5   precious stones, and similar ornaments presented to princes, worthy of their
greatness.

Desiring therefore to present myself to your Magnificence with some
testimony of my devotion towards you, I have not found among my possessions
anything which I hold more dear than, or value so much as, the knowledge of
10 the actions of great men, acquired by long experience in contemporary affairs,
and a continual study of antiquity; which, having reflected upon it with great and
prolonged diligence, I now send, digested into a little volume, to your
Magnificence.

And although I may consider this work unworthy of your countenance,
15 nevertheless I trust much to your benignity that it may be acceptable, seeing that
it is not possible for me to make a better gift than to offer you the opportunity of
understanding in the shortest time all that I have learnt in so many years, and
with so many troubles and dangers; which work I have not embellished with
swelling or magnificent words, nor stuffed with rounded periods, nor with any
20 extrinsic allurements or adornments whatever, with which so many are
accustomed to embellish their works; for I have wished either that no honour
should be given it, or else that the truth of the matter and the weightiness of the
theme shall make it acceptable.

Nor do I hold with those who regard it as a presumption if a man of low and
25 humble condition dare to discuss and settle the concerns of princes; because, just
as those who draw landscapes place themselves below in the plain to
contemplate the nature of the mountains and of lofty places, and in order to
contemplate the plains place themselves upon high mountains, even so to
understand the nature of the people it needs to be a prince, and to understand
30 that of princes it needs to be of the people.

Take then, your Magnificence, this little gift in the spirit in which I send it;
wherein, if it be diligently read and considered by you, you will learn my

extreme desire that you should attain that greatness which fortune and your other attributes promise. And if your Magnificence from the summit of your greatness will sometimes turn your eyes to these lower regions, you will see how unmeritedly I suffer a great and continued malignity of fortune.

CHAPTER I:
How many kinds of principalities there are, and by what means they are acquired

5   All states, all powers, that have held and hold rule over men have been and are either republics or principalities.

Principalities are either hereditary, in which the family has been long established; or they are new.

The new are either entirely new, as was Milan to Francesco Sforza, or they
10   are, as it were, members annexed to the hereditary state of the prince who has acquired them, as was the kingdom of Naples to that of the King of Spain. Such dominions thus acquired are either accustomed to live under a prince, or to live in freedom; and are acquired either by the arms of the prince himself, or of others, or else by fortune or by ability.

CHAPTER II:
Concerning hereditary principalities

15   I will leave out all discussion on republics, inasmuch as in another place I have written of them at length, and will address myself only to principalities. In doing so I will keep to the order indicated above, and discuss how such principalities are to be ruled and preserved.

I say at once there are fewer difficulties in holding hereditary states, and
20   those long accustomed to the family of their prince, than new ones; for it is sufficient only not to transgress the customs of his ancestors, and to deal prudently with circumstances as they arise, for a prince of average powers to maintain himself in his state, unless he be deprived of it by some extraordinary and excessive force; and if he should be so deprived of it, whenever anything
25   sinister happens to the usurper, he will regain it.

We have in Italy, for example, the Duke of Ferrara, who could not have withstood the attacks of the Venetians in '84, nor those of Pope Julius in '10, unless he had been long established in his dominions. For the hereditary prince has less cause and less necessity to offend; hence it happens that he will be more
30   loved; and unless extraordinary vices cause him to be hated, it is reasonable to expect that his subjects will be naturally well disposed towards him; and in the

antiquity and duration of his rule the memories and motives that make for change are lost, for one change always leaves the toothing for another.

CHAPTER III:
Concerning mixed principalities

But the difficulties occur in a new principality. And firstly, if it be not entirely new, but is, as it were, a member of a state which, taken collectively,
5   may be called composite, the changes arise chiefly from an inherent difficulty which there is in all new principalities; for men change their rulers willingly, hoping to better themselves, and this hope induces them to take up arms against him who rules: wherein they are deceived, because they afterwards find by experience they have gone from bad to worse. This follows also on another
10   natural and common necessity, which always causes a new prince to burden those who have submitted to him with his soldiery and with infinite other hardships which he must put upon his new acquisition.

In this way you have enemies in all those whom you have injured in seizing that principality, and you are not able to keep those friends who put you there
15   because of your not being able to satisfy them in the way they expected, and you cannot take strong measures against them, feeling bound to them. For, although one may be very strong in armed forces, yet in entering a province one has always need of the goodwill of the natives.

For these reasons Louis the Twelfth, King of France, quickly occupied
20   Milan, and as quickly lost it; and to turn him out the first time it only needed Lodovico's own forces; because those who had opened the gates to him, finding themselves deceived in their hopes of future benefit, would not endure the ill-treatment of the new prince. It is very true that, after acquiring rebellious provinces a second time, they are not so lightly lost afterwards, because the
25   prince, with little reluctance, takes the opportunity of the rebellion to punish the delinquents, to clear out the suspects, and to strengthen himself in the weakest places. Thus to cause France to lose Milan the first time it was enough for the Duke Lodovico[1] to raise insurrections on the borders; but to cause him to lose it a second time it was necessary to bring the whole world against him, and that his
30   armies should be defeated and driven out of Italy; which followed from the causes above mentioned.

Nevertheless Milan was taken from France both the first and the second time. The general reasons for the first have been discussed; it remains to name those for the second, and to see what resources he had, and what any one in his
35   situation would have had for maintaining himself more securely in his acquisition than did the King of France.

Now I say that those dominions which, when acquired, are added to an ancient state by him who acquires them, are either of the same country and language, or they are not. When they are, it is easier to hold them, especially when they have not been accustomed to self-government; and to hold them
5   securely it is enough to have destroyed the family of the prince who was ruling them; because the two peoples, preserving in other things the old conditions, and not being unlike in customs, will live quietly together, as one has seen in Brittany, Burgundy, Gascony, and Normandy, which have been bound to France for so long a time: and, although there may be some difference in language,
10   nevertheless the customs are alike, and the people will easily be able to get on amongst themselves. He who has annexed them, if he wishes to hold them, has only to bear in mind two considerations: the one, that the family of their former lord is extinguished; the other, that neither their laws nor their taxes are altered, so that in a very short time they will become entirely one body with the old
15   principality.

But when states are acquired in a country differing in language, customs, or laws, there are difficulties, and good fortune and great energy are needed to hold them, and one of the greatest and most real helps would be that he who has acquired them should go and reside there. This would make his position more
20   secure and durable, as it has made that of the Turk in Greece, who, notwithstanding all the other measures taken by him for holding that state, if he had not settled there, would not have been able to keep it. Because, if one is on the spot, disorders are seen as they spring up, and one can quickly remedy them; but if one is not at hand, they are heard of only when they are great, and then
25   one can no longer remedy them. Besides this, the country is not pillaged by your officials; the subjects are satisfied by prompt recourse to the prince; thus, wishing to be good, they have more cause to love him, and wishing to be otherwise, to fear him. He who would attack that state from the outside must have the utmost caution; as long as the prince resides there it can only be
30   wrested from him with the greatest difficulty.

The other and better course is to send colonies to one or two places, which may be as keys to that state, for it is necessary either to do this or else to keep there a great number of cavalry and infantry. A prince does not spend much on colonies, for with little or no expense he can send them out and keep them there,
35   and he offends a minority only of the citizens from whom he takes lands and houses to give them to the new inhabitants; and those whom he offends, remaining poor and scattered, are never able to injure him; whilst the rest being uninjured are easily kept quiet, and at the same time are anxious not to err for fear it should happen to them as it has to those who have been despoiled. In
40   conclusion, I say that these colonies are not costly, they are more faithful, they

injure less, and the injured, as has been said, being poor and scattered, cannot hurt. Upon this, one has to remark that men ought either to be well treated or crushed, because they can avenge themselves of lighter injuries, of more serious ones they cannot; therefore the injury that is to be done to a man ought to be of
5 such a kind that one does not stand in fear of revenge.

But in maintaining armed men there in place of colonies one spends much more, having to consume on the garrison all the income from the state, so that the acquisition turns into a loss, and many more are exasperated, because the whole state is injured; through the shifting of the garrison up and down all
10 become acquainted with hardship, and all become hostile, and they are enemies who, whilst beaten on their own ground, are yet able to do hurt. For every reason, therefore, such guards are as useless as a colony is useful.

Again, the prince who holds a country differing in the above respects ought to make himself the head and defender of his less powerful neighbours, and to
15 weaken the more powerful amongst them, taking care that no foreigner as powerful as himself shall, by any accident, get a footing there; for it will always happen that such a one will be introduced by those who are discontented, either through excess of ambition or through fear, as one has seen already. The Romans were brought into Greece by the Aetolians; and in every other country
20 where they obtained a footing they were brought in by the inhabitants. And the usual course of affairs is that, as soon as a powerful foreigner enters a country, all the subject states are drawn to him, moved by the hatred which they feel against the ruling power. So that in respect to those subject states he has not to take any trouble to gain them over to himself, for the whole of them quickly
25 rally to the state which he has acquired there. He has only to take care that they do not get hold of too much power and too much authority, and then with his own forces, and with their goodwill, he can easily keep down the more powerful of them, so as to remain entirely master in the country. And he who does not properly manage this business will soon lose what he has acquired, and whilst he
30 does hold it he will have endless difficulties and troubles.

The Romans, in the countries which they annexed, observed closely these measures; they sent colonies and maintained friendly relations with the minor powers, without increasing their strength; they kept down the greater, and did not allow any strong foreign powers to gain authority. Greece appears to me
35 sufficient for an example. The Achaeans and Aetolians were kept friendly by them, the kingdom of Macedonia was humbled, Antiochus was driven out; yet the merits of the Achaeans and Aetolians never secured for them permission to increase their power, nor did the persuasions of Philip ever induce the Romans to be his friends without first humbling him, nor did the influence of Antiochus
40 make them agree that he should retain any lordship over the country. Because

the Romans did in these instances what all prudent princes ought to do, who
have to regard not only present troubles, but also future ones, for which they
must prepare with every energy, because, when foreseen, it is easy to remedy
them; but if you wait until they approach, the medicine is no longer in time
5   because the malady has become incurable; for it happens in this, as the
physicians say it happens in hectic fever, that in the beginning of the malady it is
easy to cure but difficult to detect, but in the course of time, not having been
either detected or treated in the beginning, it becomes easy to detect but difficult
to cure. This it happens in affairs of state, for when the evils that arise have been
10   foreseen (which it is only given to a wise man to see), they can be quickly
redressed, but when, through not having been foreseen, they have been
permitted to grow in a way that every one can see them, there is no longer a
remedy. Therefore, the Romans, foreseeing troubles, dealt with them at once,
and, even to avoid a war, would not let them come to a head, for they knew that
15   war is not to be avoided, but is only to be put off to the advantage of others;
moreover they wished to fight with Philip and Antiochus in Greece so as not to
have to do it in Italy; they could have avoided both, but this they did not wish;
nor did that ever please them which is for ever in the mouths of the wise ones of
our time:–Let us enjoy the benefits of the time–but rather the benefits of their
20   own valour and prudence, for time drives everything before it, and is able to
bring with it good as well as evil, and evil as well as good.

But let us turn to France and inquire whether she has done any of the things
mentioned. I will speak of Louis[2] (and not of Charles[3]) as the one whose
conduct is the better to be observed, he having held possession of Italy for the
25   longest period; and you will see that he has done the opposite to those things
which ought to be done to retain a state composed of divers elements.

King Louis was brought into Italy by the ambition of the Venetians, who
desired to obtain half the state of Lombardy by his intervention. I will not blame
the course taken by the king, because, wishing to get a foothold in Italy, and
30   having no friends there–seeing rather that every door was shut to him owing to
the conduct of Charles–he was forced to accept those friendships which he could
get, and he would have succeeded very quickly in his design if in other matters
he had not made some mistakes. The king, however, having acquired Lombardy,
regained at once the authority which Charles had lost: Genoa yielded; the
35   Florentines became his friends; the Marquess of Mantua, the Duke of Ferrara,
the Bentivogli, my lady of Forli, the Lords of Faenza, of Pesaro, of Rimini, of
Camerino, of Piombino, the Lucchese, the Pisans, the Sienese–everybody made
advances to him to become his friend. Then could the Venetians realize the
rashness of the course taken by them, which, in order that they might secure two
40   towns in Lombardy, had made the king master of two-thirds of Italy.

Let any one now consider with what little difficulty the king could have maintained his position in Italy had he observed the rules above laid down, and kept all his friends secure and protected; for although they were numerous they were both weak and timid, some afraid of the Church, some of the Venetians,

5　and thus they would always have been forced to stand in with him, and by their means he could easily have made himself secure against those who remained powerful. But he was no sooner in Milan than he did the contrary by assisting Pope Alexander to occupy the Romagna. It never occurred to him that by this action he was weakening himself, depriving himself of friends and of those who

10　had thrown themselves into his lap, whilst he aggrandized the Church by adding much temporal power to the spiritual, thus giving it greater authority. And having committed this prime error, he was obliged to follow it up, so much so that, to put an end to the ambition of Alexander, and to prevent his becoming the master of Tuscany, he was himself forced to come into Italy.

15　And as if it were not enough to have aggrandized the Church, and deprived himself of friends, he, wishing to have the kingdom of Naples, divides it with the King of Spain, and where he was the prime arbiter in Italy he takes an associate, so that the ambitious of that country and the malcontents of his own should have somewhere to shelter; and whereas he could have left in the

20　kingdom his own pensioner as king, he drove him out, to put one there who was able to drive him, Louis, out in turn.

The wish to acquire is in truth very natural and common, and men always do so when they can, and for this they will be praised not blamed; but when they cannot do so, yet wish to do so by any means, then there is folly and blame.

25　Therefore, if France could have attacked Naples with her own forces she ought to have done so; if she could not, then she ought not to have divided it. And if the partition which she made with the Venetians in Lombardy was justified by the excuse that by it she got a foothold in Italy, this other partition merited blame, for it had not the excuse of that necessity.

30　Therefore Louis made these five errors: he destroyed the minor powers, he increased the strength of one of the greater powers in Italy, he brought in a foreign power, he did not settle in the country, he did not send colonies. Which errors, had he lived, were not enough to injure him had he not made a sixth by taking away their dominions from the Venetians; because, had he not

35　aggrandized the Church, nor brought Spain into Italy, it would have been very reasonable and necessary to humble them; but having first taken these steps, he ought never to have consented to their ruin, for they, being powerful, would always have kept off others from designs on Lombardy, to which the Venetians would never have consented except to become masters themselves there; also

40　because the others would not wish to take Lombardy from France in order to give it to the Venetians, and to run counter to both they would not have had the courage.

And if any one should say: "King Louis yielded the Romagna to Alexander and the kingdom to Spain to avoid war," I answer for the reasons given above
5 that a blunder ought never to be perpetrated to avoid war, because it is not to be avoided, but is only deferred to your disadvantage. And if another should allege the pledge which the king had given to the Pope that he would assist him in the enterprise, in exchange for the dissolution of his marriage[4] and for the cap to Rouen,[5] to that I reply what I shall write later on concerning the faith of princes,
10 and how it ought to be kept.

Thus King Louis lost Lombardy by not having followed any of the conditions observed by those who have taken possession of countries and wished to retain them. Nor is there any miracle in this, but much that is reasonable and quite natural. And on these matters I spoke at Nantes with
15 Rouen, when Valentino, as Cesare Borgia, the son of Pope Alexander, was usually called, occupied the Romagna, and on Cardinal Rouen observing to me that the Italians did not understand war, I replied to him that the French did not understand statecraft, meaning that otherwise they would not have allowed the Church to reach such greatness. And in fact is has been seen that the greatness of
20 the Church and of Spain in Italy has been caused by France, and her ruin may be attributed to them. From this a general rule is drawn which never or rarely fails: that he who is the cause of another becoming powerful is ruined; because that predominancy has been brought about either by astuteness or else by force, and both are distrusted by him who has been raised to power.

CHAPTER IV:
Why the kingdom of Darius, conqured by Alexander, did not rebel against the successors of Alexander at his death

25 Considering the difficulties which men have had to hold to a newly acquired state, some might wonder how, seeing that Alexander the Great became the master of Asia in a few years, and died whilst it was scarcely settled (whence it might appear reasonable that the whole empire would have rebelled), nevertheless his successors maintained themselves, and had to meet no other
30 difficulty than that which arose among themselves from their own ambitions.

I answer that the principalities of which one has record are found to be governed in two different ways; either by a prince, with a body of servants, who assist him to govern the kingdom as ministers by his favour and permission; or by a prince and barons, who hold that dignity by antiquity of blood and not by
35 the grace of the prince. Such barons have states and their own subjects, who

recognize them as lords and hold them in natural affection. Those states that are governed by a prince and his servants hold their prince in more consideration, because in all the country there is no one who is recognized as superior to him, and if they yield obedience to another they do it as to a minister and official, and
5   they do not bear him any particular affection.

The examples of these two governments in our time are the Turk and the King of France. The entire monarchy of the Turk is governed by one lord, the others are his servants; and, dividing his kingdom into sanjaks, he sends there different administrators, and shifts and changes them as he chooses. But the
10   King of France is placed in the midst of an ancient body of lords, acknowledged by their own subjects, and beloved by them; they have their own prerogatives, nor can the king take these away except at his peril. Therefore, he who considers both of these states will recognize great difficulties in seizing the state of the Turk, but, once it is conquered, great ease in holding it. The causes of the
15   difficulties in seizing the kingdom of the Turk are that the usurper cannot be called in by the princes of the kingdom, nor can he hope to be assisted in his designs by the revolt of those whom the lord has around him. This arises from the reasons given above; for his ministers, being all slaves and bondmen, can only be corrupted with great difficulty, and one can expect little advantage from
20   them when they have been corrupted, as they cannot carry the people with them, for the reasons assigned. Hence, he who attacks the Turk must bear in mind that he will find him united, and he will have to rely more on his own strength than on the revolt of others; but, if once the Turk has been conquered, and routed in the field in such a way that he cannot replace his armies, there is nothing to fear
25   but the family of this prince, and, this being exterminated, there remains no one to fear, the others having no credit with the people; and as the conqueror did not rely on them before his victory, so he ought not to fear them after it.

The contrary happens in kingdoms governed like that of France, because one can easily enter there by gaining over some baron of the kingdom, for one
30   always finds malcontents and such as desire a change. Such men, for the reasons given, can open the way into the state and render the victory easy; but if you wish to hold it afterwards, you meet with infinite difficulties, both from those who have assisted you and from those you have crushed. Nor is it enough for you to have exterminated the family of the prince, because the lords that remain
35   make themselves the heads of fresh movements against you, and as you are unable either to satisfy or exterminate them, that state is lost whenever time brings the opportunity.

Now if you will consider what was the nature of the government of Darius, you will find it similar to the kingdom of the Turk, and therefore it was only
40   necessary for Alexander, first to overthrow him in the field, and then to take the

country from him. After which victory, Darius being killed, the state remained secure to Alexander, for the above reasons. And if his successors had been united they would have enjoyed it securely and at their ease, for there were no tumults raised in the kingdom except those they provoked themselves.

5 But it is impossible to hold with such tranquillity states constituted like that of France. Hence arose those frequent rebellions against the Romans in Spain, France, and Greece, owing to the many principalities there were in these states, of which, as long as the memory of them endured, the Romans always held an insecure possession; but with the power and long continuance of the empire the 10 memory of them passed away, and the Romans then became secure possessors. And when fighting afterwards amongst themselves, each one was able to attach to himself his own parts of the country, according to the authority he had assumed there; and the family of the former lord being exterminated, none other than the Romans were acknowledged.

15 When these things are remembered no one will marvel at the ease with which Alexander held the Empire of Asia, or at the difficulties which others have had to keep an acquisition, such as Pyrrhus and many more; this is not occasioned by the little or abundance of ability in the conqueror, but by the want of uniformity in the subject state.

CHAPTER V:
Concerning the way to govern cities or principalities which lived under their own laws before they were annexed

20 Whenever those states which have been acquired as stated have been accustomed to live under their own laws and in freedom, there are three courses for those who wish to hold them: the first is to ruin them, the next is to reside there in person, the third is to permit them to live under their own laws, drawing a tribute, and establishing within it an oligarchy which will keep it friendly to 25 you. Because such a government, being created by the prince, knows that it cannot stand without his friendship and interest, and does it utmost to support him; and therefore he who would keep a city accustomed to freedom will hold it more easily by the means of its own citizens than in any other way.

There are, for example, the Spartans and the Romans. The Spartans held 30 Athens and Thebes, establishing there an oligarchy, nevertheless they lost them. The Romans, in order to hold Capua, Carthage, and Numantia, dismantled them, and did not lose them. They wished to hold Greece as the Spartans held it, making it free and permitting its laws, and did not succeed. So to hold it they were compelled to dismantle many cities in the country, for in truth there is no 35 safe way to retain them otherwise than by ruining them. And he who becomes

master of a city accustomed to freedom and does not destroy it, may expect to be destroyed by it, for in rebellion it has always the watchword of liberty and its ancient privileges as a rallying point, which neither time nor benefits will ever cause it to forget. And whatever you may do or provide against, they never
5   forget that name or their privileges unless they are disunited or dispersed, but at every chance they immediately rally to them, as Pisa after the hundred years she had been held in bondage by the Florentines.

    But when cities or countries are accustomed to live under a prince, and his family is exterminated, they, being on the one hand accustomed to obey and on
10   the other hand not having the old prince, cannot agree in making one from amongst themselves, and they do not know how to govern themselves. For this reason they are very slow to take up arms, and a prince can gain them to himself and secure them much more easily. But in republics there is more vitality, greater hatred, and more desire for vengeance, which will never permit them to
15   allow the memory of their former liberty to rest; so that the safest way is to destroy them or to reside there.

CHAPTER VI:
Concerning new principalities which are acquired by one's own arms and ability

    Let no one be surprised if, in speaking of entirely new principalities as I shall do, I adduce the highest examples both of prince and of state; because men, walking almost always in paths beaten by others, and following by imitation
20   their deeds, are yet unable to keep entirely to the ways of others or attain to the power of those they imitate. A wise man ought always to follow the paths beaten by great men, and to imitate those who have been supreme, so that if his ability does not equal theirs, at least it will savour of it. Let him act like the clever archers who, designing to hit the mark which yet appears too far distant, and
25   knowing the limits to which the strength of their bow attains, take aim much higher than the mark, not to reach by their strength or arrow to so great a height, but to be able with the aid of so high an aim to hit the mark they wish to reach.

    I say, therefore, that in entirely new principalities, where there is a new prince, more or less difficulty is found in keeping them, accordingly as there is
30   more or less ability in him who has acquired the state. Now, as the fact of becoming a prince from a private station presupposes either ability or fortune, it is clear that one or other of these things will mitigate in some degree many difficulties. Nevertheless, he who has relied least on fortune is established the strongest. Further, it facilitates matters when the prince, having no other state, is
35   compelled to reside there in person.

But to come to those who, by their own ability and not through fortune, have risen to be princes, I say that Moses, Cyrus, Romulus, Theseus, and such like are the most excellent examples. And although one may not discuss Moses, he having been a mere executor of the will of God, yet he ought to be admired,
5 if only for that favour which made him worthy to speak with God. But in considering Cyrus and others who have acquired or founded kingdoms, all will be found admirable; and if their particular deeds and conduct shall be considered, they will not be found inferior to those of Moses, although he had so great a preceptor. And in examining their actions and lives one cannot see that
10 they owed anything to fortune beyond opportunity, which brought them the material to mould into the form which seemed best to them. Without that opportunity their powers of mind would have been extinguished, and without those powers the opportunity would have come in vain.

It was necessary, therefore, to Moses that he should find the people of Israel
15 in Egypt enslaved and oppressed by the Egyptians, in order that they should be disposed to follow him so as to be delivered out of bondage. It was necessary that Romulus should not remain in Alba, and that he should be abandoned at his birth, in order that he should become King of Rome and founder of the fatherland. It was necessary that Cyrus should find the Persians discontented
20 with the government of the Medes, and the Medes soft and effeminate through their long peace. Theseus could not have shown his ability had he not found the Athenians dispersed. These opportunities, therefore, made those men fortunate, and their high ability enabled them to recognize the opportunity whereby their country was ennobled and made famous.
25 Those who by valorous ways become princes, like these men, acquire a principality with difficulty, but they keep it with ease. The difficulties they have in acquiring it rise in part from the new rules and methods which they are forced to introduce to establish their government and its security. And it ought to be remembered that there is nothing more difficult to take in hand, more perilous to
30 conduct, or more uncertain in its success, then to take the lead in the introduction of a new order of things. Because the innovator has for enemies all those who have done well under the old conditions, and lukewarm defenders in those who may do well under the new. This coolness arises partly from fear of the opponents, who have the laws on their side, and partly from the incredulity
35 of men, who do not readily believe in new things until they have had a long experience of them. Thus it happens that whenever those who are hostile have the opportunity to attack they do it like partisans, whilst the others defend lukewarmly, in such wise that the prince is endangered along with them.

It is necessary, therefore, if we desire to discuss this matter thoroughly, to
40 inquire whether these innovators can rely on themselves or have to depend on

others: that is to say, whether, to consummate their enterprise, have they to use prayers or can they use force? In the first instance they always succeed badly, and never compass anything; but when they can rely on themselves and use force, then they are rarely endangered. Hence it is that all armed prophets have
5   conquered, and the unarmed ones have been destroyed. Besides the reasons mentioned, the nature of the people is variable, and whilst it is easy to persuade them, it is difficult to fix them in that persuasion. And thus it is necessary to take such measures that, when they believe no longer, it may be possible to make them believe by force.
10   If Moses, Cyrus, Theseus, and Romulus had been unarmed they could not have enforced their constitutions for long–as happened in our time to Fra Girolamo Savonarola, who was ruined with his new order of things immediately the multitude believed in him no longer, and he had no means of keeping steadfast those who believed or of making the unbelievers to believe. Therefore
15   such as these have great difficulties in consummating their enterprise, for all their dangers are in the ascent, yet with ability they will overcome them; but when these are overcome, and those who envied them their success are exterminated, they will begin to be respected, and they will continue afterwards powerful, secure, honoured, and happy.
20   To these great examples I wish to add a lesser one; still it bears some resemblance to them, and I wish it to suffice me for all of a like kind: it is Hiero the Syracusan.[6] This man rose from a private station to be Prince of Syracuse, nor did he, either, owe anything to fortune but opportunity; for the Syracusans, being oppressed, chose him for their captain, afterwards he was rewarded by
25   being made their prince. He was of so great ability, even as a private citizen, that one who writes of him says he wanted nothing but a kingdom to be a king. This man abolished the old soldiery, organized the new, gave up old alliances, made new ones; and as he had his own soldiers and allies, on such foundations he was able to build any edifice: thus, whilst he had endured much trouble in acquiring,
30   he had but little in keeping.

CHAPTER VII:
Concerning new principalities which are acquired either by the arms of others or by good fortune

Those who solely by good fortune become princes from being private citizens have little trouble in rising, but much in keeping atop; they have not any difficulties on the way up, because they fly, but they have many when they reach the summit. Such are those to whom some state is given either for money or by
35   the favour of him who bestows it; as happened to many in Greece, in the cities

of Ionia and of the Hellespont, where princes were made by Darius, in order that
they might hold the cities both for his security and his glory; as also were those
emperors who, by the corruption of the soldiers, from being citizens came to
empire. Such stand simply elevated upon the goodwill and the fortune of him
5   who has elevated them–two most inconstant and unstable things. Neither have
they the knowledge requisite for the position; because, unless they are men of
great worth and ability, it is not reasonable to expect that they should know how
to command, having always lived in a private condition; besides, they cannot
hold it because they have not forces which they can keep friendly and faithful.
10   States that rise unexpectedly, then, like all other things in nature which are
born and grow rapidly, cannot leave their foundations and correspondencies[7]
fixed in such a way that the first storm will not overthrow them; unless, as is
said, those who unexpectedly become princes are men of so much ability that
they know they have to be prepared at once to hold that which fortune has
15   thrown into their laps, and that those foundations, which others have laid
BEFORE they became princes, they must lay AFTERWARDS.
        Concerning these two methods of rising to be a prince by ability or fortune,
I wish to adduce two examples within our own recollection, and these are
Francesco Sforza[8] and Cesare Borgia. Francesco, by proper means and with
20   great ability, from being a private person rose to be Duke of Milan, and that
which he had acquired with a thousand anxieties he kept with little trouble. On
the other hand, Cesare Borgia, called by the people Duke Valentino, acquired
his state during the ascendancy of his father, and on its decline he lost it,
notwithstanding that he had taken every measure and done all that ought to be
25   done by a wise and able man to fix firmly his roots in the states which the arms
and fortunes of others had bestowed on him.
        Because, as is stated above, he who has not first laid his foundations may be
able with great ability to lay them afterwards, but they will be laid with trouble
to the architect and danger to the building. If, therefore, all the steps taken by the
30   duke be considered, it will be seen that he laid solid foundations for his future
power, and I do not consider it superfluous to discuss them, because I do not
know what better precepts to give a new prince than the example of his actions;
and if his dispositions were of no avail, that was not his fault, but the
extraordinary and extreme malignity of fortune.
35   Alexander the Sixth, in wishing to aggrandize the duke, his son, had many
immediate and prospective difficulties. Firstly, he did not see his way to make
him master of any state that was not a state of the Church; and if he was willing
to rob the Church he knew that the Duke of Milan and the Venetians would not
consent, because Faenza and Rimini were already under the protection of the
40   Venetians. Besides this, he saw the arms of Italy, especially those by which he

might have been assisted, in hands that would fear the aggrandizement of the Pope, namely, the Orsini and the Colonnesi and their following. It behoved him, therefore, to upset this state of affairs and embroil the powers, so as to make himself securely master of part of their states. This was easy for him to do, because he found the Venetians, moved by other reasons, inclined to bring back the French into Italy; he would not only not oppose this, but he would render it more easy by dissolving the former marriage of King Louis. Therefore the king came into Italy with the assistance of the Venetians and the consent of Alexander. He was no sooner in Milan than the Pope had soldiers from him for the attempt on the Romagna, which yielded to him on the reputation of the king. The duke, therefore, having acquired the Romagna and beaten the Colonnesi, while wishing to hold that and to advance further, was hindered by two things: the one, his forces did not appear loyal to him, the other, the goodwill of France: that is to say, he feared that the forces of the Orsini, which he was using, would not stand to him, that not only might they hinder him from winning more, but might themselves seize what he had won, and that the king might also do the same. Of the Orsini he had a warning when, after taking Faenza and attacking Bologna, he saw them go very unwillingly to that attack. And as to the king, he learned his mind when he himself, after taking the Duchy of Urbino, attacked Tuscany, and the king made him desist from that undertaking; hence the duke decided to depend no more upon the arms and the luck of others.

For the first thing he weakened the Orsini and Colonnesi parties in Rome, by gaining to himself all their adherents who were gentlemen, making them his gentlemen, giving them good pay, and, according to their rank, honouring them with office and command in such a way that in a few months all attachment to the factions was destroyed and turned entirely to the duke. After this he awaited an opportunity to crush the Orsini, having scattered the adherents of the Colonna house. This came to him soon and he used it well; for the Orsini, perceiving at length that the aggrandizement of the duke and the Church was ruin to them, called a meeting of the Magione in Perugia. From this sprung the rebellion at Urbino and the tumults in the Romagna, with endless dangers to the duke, all of which he overcame with the help of the French. Having restored his authority, not to leave it at risk by trusting either to the French or other outside forces, he had recourse to his wiles, and he knew so well how to conceal his mind that, by the mediation of Signor Pagolo–whom the duke did not fail to secure with all kinds of attention, giving him money, apparel, and horses–the Orsini were reconciled, so that their simplicity brought them into his power at Sinigalia.[9] Having exterminated the leaders, and turned their partisans into his friends, the duke laid sufficiently good foundations to his power, having all the Romagna and the Duchy of Urbino; and the people now beginning to appreciate their prosperity, he gained them all over to himself. And as this point is worthy of notice, and to be imitated by others, I am not willing to leave it out.

When the duke occupied the Romagna he found it under the rule of weak masters, who rather plundered their subjects than ruled them, and gave them
5   more cause for disunion than for union, so that the country was full of robbery, quarrels, and every kind of violence; and so, wishing to bring back peace and obedience to authority, he considered it necessary to give it a good governor. Thereupon he promoted Messer Ramiro d'Orco,[10] a swift and cruel man, to whom he gave the fullest power. This man in a short time restored peace and
10   unity with the greatest success. Afterwards the duke considered that it was not advisable to confer such excessive authority, for he had no doubt but that he would become odious, so he set up a court of judgment in the country, under a most excellent president, wherein all cities had their advocates. And because he knew that the past severity had caused some hatred against himself, so, to clear
15   himself in the minds of the people, and gain them entirely to himself, he desired to show that, if any cruelty had been practised, it had not originated with him, but in the natural sternness of the minister. Under this pretence he took Ramiro, and one morning caused him to be executed and left on the piazza at Cesena with the block and a bloody knife at his side. The barbarity of this spectacle
20   caused the people to be at once satisfied and dismayed.

But let us return whence we started. I say that the duke, finding himself now sufficiently powerful and partly secured from immediate dangers by having armed himself in his own way, and having in a great measure crushed those forces in his vicinity that could injure him if he wished to proceed with his
25   conquest, had next to consider France, for he knew that the king, who too late was aware of his mistake, would not support him. And from this time he began to seek new alliances and to temporize with France in the expedition which she was making towards the kingdom of Naples against the Spaniards who were besieging Gaeta. It was his intention to secure himself against them, and this he
30   would have quickly accomplished had Alexander lived.

Such was his line of action as to present affairs. But as to the future he had to fear, in the first place, that a new successor to the Church might not be friendly to him and might seek to take from him that which Alexander had given him, so he decided to act in four ways. Firstly, by exterminating the families of
35   those lords whom he had despoiled, so as to take away that pretext from the Pope. Secondly, by winning to himself all the gentlemen of Rome, so as to be able to curb the Pope with their aid, as has been observed. Thirdly, by converting the college more to himself. Fourthly, by acquiring so much power before the Pope should die that he could by his own measures resist the first
40   shock. Of these four things, at the death of Alexander, he had accomplished

three. For he had killed as many of the dispossessed lords as he could lay hands on, and few had escaped; he had won over the Roman gentlemen, and he had the most numerous party in the college. And as to any fresh acquisition, he intended to become master of Tuscany, for he already possessed Perugia and Piombino,

5 and Pisa was under his protection. And as he had no longer to study France (for the French were already driven out of the kingdom of Naples by the Spaniards, and in this way both were compelled to buy his goodwill), he pounced down upon Pisa. After this, Lucca and Siena yielded at once, partly through hatred and partly through fear of the Florentines; and the Florentines would have had no

10 remedy had he continued to prosper, as he was prospering the year that Alexander died, for he had acquired so much power and reputation that he would have stood by himself, and no longer have depended on the luck and the forces of others, but solely on his own power and ability.

But Alexander died five years after he had first drawn the sword. He left the

15 duke with the state of Romagna alone consolidated, with the rest in the air, between two most powerful hostile armies, and sick unto death. Yet there were in the duke such boldness and ability, and he knew so well how men are to be won or lost, and so firm were the foundations which in so short a time he had laid, that if he had not had those armies on his back, or if he had been in good

20 health, he would have overcome all difficulties. And it is seen that his foundations were good, for the Romagna awaited him for more than a month. In Rome, although but half alive, he remained secure; and whilst the Baglioni, the Vitelli, and the Orsini might come to Rome, they could not effect anything against him. If he could not have made Pope him whom he wished, at least the

25 one whom he did not wish would not have been elected. But if he had been in sound health at the death of Alexander,[11] everything would have been different to him. On the day that Julius the Second[12] was elected, he told me that he had thought of everything that might occur at the death of his father, and had provided a remedy for all, except that he had never anticipated that, when the

30 death did happen, he himself would be on the point to die. When all the actions of the duke are recalled, I do not know how to blame him, but rather it appears to be, as I have said, that I ought to offer him for imitation to all those who, by the fortune or the arms of others, are raised to government. Because he, having a lofty spirit and far-reaching aims, could not have regulated his conduct

35 otherwise, and only the shortness of the life of Alexander and his own sickness frustrated his designs. Therefore, he who considers it necessary to secure himself in his new principality, to win friends, to overcome either by force or fraud, to make himself beloved and feared by the people, to be followed and revered by the soldiers, to exterminate those who have power or reason to hurt

40 him, to change the old order of things for new, to be severe and gracious,

magnanimous and liberal, to destroy a disloyal soldiery and to create new, to
maintain friendship with kings and princes in such a way that they must help
him with zeal and offend with caution, cannot find a more lively example than
the actions of this man.

5   Only can he be blamed for the election of Julius the Second, in whom he
made a bad choice, because, as is said, not being able to elect a Pope to his own
mind, he could have hindered any other from being elected Pope; and he ought
never to have consented to the election of any cardinal whom he had injured or
who had cause to fear him if they became pontiffs. For men injure either from

10   fear or hatred. Those whom he had injured, amongst others, were San Pietro ad
Vincula, Colonna, San Giorgio, and Ascanio.[13] The rest, in becoming Pope, had
to fear him, Rouen and the Spaniards excepted; the latter from their relationship
and obligations, the former from his influence, the kingdom of France having
relations with him. Therefore, above everything, the duke ought to have created

15   a Spaniard Pope, and, failing him, he ought to have consented to Rouen and not
San Pietro ad Vincula. He who believes that new benefits will cause great
personages to forget old injuries is deceived. Therefore, the duke erred in his
choice, and it was the cause of his ultimate ruin.

<hr />

CHAPTER VIII:
Concerning those who have obtained a principality by wickedness

      Although a prince may rise from a private station in two ways, neither of

20   which can be entirely attributed to fortune or genius, yet it is manifest to me that
I must not be silent on them, although one could be more copiously treated when
I discuss republics. These methods are when, either by some wicked or nefarious
ways, one ascends to the principality, or when by the favour of his fellow-
citizens a private person becomes the prince of his country. And speaking of the

25   first method, it will be illustrated by two examples–one ancient, the other
modern–and without entering further into the subject, I consider these two
examples will suffice those who may be compelled to follow them.

      Agathocles, the Sicilian,[14] became King of Syracuse not only from a private
but from a low and abject position. This man, the son of a potter, through all the

30   changes in his fortunes always led an infamous life. Nevertheless, he
accompanied his infamies with so much ability of mind and body that, having
devoted himself to the military profession, he rose through its ranks to be
Praetor of Syracuse. Being established in that position, and having deliberately
resolved to make himself prince and to seize by violence, without obligation to

35   others, that which had been conceded to him by assent, he came to an
understanding for this purpose with Amilcar, the Carthaginian, who, with his

army, was fighting in Sicily. One morning he assembled the people and the
senate of Syracuse, as if he had to discuss with them things relating to the
Republic, and at a given signal the soldiers killed all the senators and the richest
of the people; these dead, he seized and held the princedom of that city without
5   any civil commotion. And although he was twice routed by the Carthaginians,
and ultimately besieged, yet not only was he able to defend his city, but leaving
part of his men for its defence, with the others he attacked Africa, and in a short
time raised the siege of Syracuse. The Carthaginians, reduced to extreme
necessity, were compelled to come to terms with Agathocles, and, leaving Sicily
10   to him, had to be content with the possession of Africa.

Therefore, he who considers the actions and the genius of this man will see
nothing, or little, which can be attributed to fortune, inasmuch as he attained pre-
eminence, as is shown above, not by the favour of any one, but step by step in
the military profession, which steps were gained with a thousand troubles and
15   perils, and were afterwards boldly held by him with many hazardous dangers.
Yet it cannot be called talent to slay fellow-citizens, to deceive friends, to be
without faith, without mercy, without religion; such methods may gain empire,
but not glory. Still, if the courage of Agathocles in entering into and extricating
himself from dangers be considered, together with his greatness of mind in
20   enduring and overcoming hardships, it cannot be seen why he should be
esteemed less than the most notable captain. Nevertheless, his barbarous cruelty
and inhumanity with infinite wickedness do not permit him to be celebrated
among the most excellent men. What he achieved cannot be attributed either to
fortune or genius.

25   In our times, during the rule of Alexander the Sixth, Oliverotto da Fermo,
having been left an orphan many years before, was brought up by his maternal
uncle, Giovanni Fogliani, and in the early days of his youth sent to fight under
Pagolo Vitelli, that, being trained under his discipline, he might attain some high
position in the military profession. After Pagolo died, he fought under his
30   brother Vitellozzo, and in a very short time, being endowed with wit and a
vigorous body and mind, he became the first man in his profession. But it
appearing a paltry thing to serve under others, he resolved, with the aid of some
citizens of Fermo, to whom the slavery of their country was dearer than its
liberty, and with the help of the Vitelleschi, to seize Fermo. So he wrote to
35   Giovanni Fogliani that, having been away from home for many years, he wished
to visit him and his city, and in some measure to look upon his patrimony; and
although he had not laboured to acquire anything except honour, yet, in order
that the citizens should see he had not spent his time in vain, he desired to come
honourably, so would be accompanied by one hundred horsemen, his friends
40   and retainers; and he entreated Giovanni to arrange that he should be received

118

honourably by the Fermians, all of which would be not only to his honour, but also to that of Giovanni himself, who had brought him up.

Giovanni, therefore, did not fail in any attentions due to his nephew, and he caused him to be honourably received by the Fermians, and he lodged him in his
5   own house, where, having passed some days, and having arranged what was necessary for his wicked designs, Oliverotto gave a solemn banquet to which he invited Giovanni Fogliani and the chiefs of Fermo. When the viands and all the other entertainments that are usual in such banquets were finished, Oliverotto artfully began certain grave discourses, speaking of the greatness of Pope
10 Alexander and his son Cesare, and of their enterprises, to which discourse Giovanni and others answered; but he rose at once, saying that such matters ought to be discussed in a more private place, and he betook himself to a chamber, whither Giovanni and the rest of the citizens went in after him. No sooner were they seated than soldiers issued from secret places and slaughtered
15 Giovanni and the rest. After these murders Oliverotto, mounted on horseback, rode up and down the town and besieged the chief magistrate in the palace, so that in fear the people were forced to obey him, and to form a government, of which he made himself the prince. He killed all the malcontents who were able to injure him, and strengthened himself with new civil and military ordinances,
20 in such a way that, in the year during which he held the principality, not only was he secure in the city of Fermo, but he had become formidable to all his neighbours. And his destruction would have been as difficult as that of Agathocles if he had not allowed himself to be overreached by Cesare Borgia, who took him with the Orsini and Vitelli at Sinigalia, as was stated above. Thus
25 one year after he had committed this parricide, he was strangled, together with Vitellozzo, whom he had made his leader in valour and wickedness.

Some may wonder how it can happen that Agathocles, and his like, after infinite treacheries and cruelties, should live for long secure in his country, and defend himself from external enemies, and never be conspired against by his
30 own citizens; seeing that many others, by means of cruelty, have never been able even in peaceful times to hold the state, still less in the doubtful times of war. I believe that this follows from severities[15] being badly or properly used. Those may be called properly used, if of evil it is possible to speak well, that are applied at one blow and are necessary to one's security, and that are not
35 persisted in afterwards unless they can be turned to the advantage of the subjects. The badly employed are those which, notwithstanding they may be few in the commencement, multiply with time rather than decrease. Those who practise the first system are able, by aid of God or man, to mitigate in some degree their rule, as Agathocles did. It is impossible for those who follow the
40 other to maintain themselves.

Hence it is to be remarked that, in seizing a state, the usurper ought to examine closely into all those injuries which it is necessary for him to inflict, and to do them all at one stroke so as not to have to repeat them daily; and thus by not unsettling men he will be able to reassure them, and win them to himself

5   by benefits. He who does otherwise, either from timidity or evil advice, is always compelled to keep the knife in his hand; neither can he rely on his subjects, nor can they attach themselves to him, owing to their continued and repeated wrongs. For injuries ought to be done all at one time, so that, being tasted less, they offend less; benefits ought to be given little by little, so that the

10   flavour of them may last longer.

And above all things, a prince ought to live amongst his people in such a way that no unexpected circumstances, whether of good or evil, shall make him change; because if the necessity for this comes in troubled times, you are too late for harsh measures; and mild ones will not help you, for they will be

15   considered as forced from you, and no one will be under any obligation to you for them.

CHAPTER IX:
Concerning a civil principality

But coming to the other point–where a leading citizen becomes the prince of his country, not by wickedness or any intolerable violence, but by the favour of his fellow citizens–this may be called a civil principality: nor is genius or

20   fortune altogether necessary to attain to it, but rather a happy shrewdness. I say then that such a principality is obtained either by the favour of the people or by the favour of the nobles. Because in all cities these two distinct parties are found, and from this it arises that the people do not wish to be ruled nor oppressed by the nobles, and the nobles wish to rule and oppress the people; and

25   from these two opposite desires there arises in cities one of three results, either a principality, self-government, or anarchy.

A principality is created either by the people or by the nobles, accordingly as one or other of them has the opportunity; for the nobles, seeing they cannot withstand the people, begin to cry up the reputation of one of themselves, and

30   they make him a prince, so that under his shadow they can give vent to their ambitions. The people, finding they cannot resist the nobles, also cry up the reputation of one of themselves, and make him a prince so as to be defended by his authority. He who obtains sovereignty by the assistance of the nobles maintains himself with more difficulty than he who comes to it by the aid of the

35   people, because the former finds himself with many around him who consider themselves his equals, and because of this he can neither rule nor manage them

to his liking. But he who reaches sovereignty by popular favour finds himself alone, and has none around him, or few, who are not prepared to obey him.

Besides this, one cannot by fair dealing, and without injury to others, satisfy the nobles, but you can satisfy the people, for their object is more righteous than that of the nobles, the latter wishing to oppress, while the former only desire not to be oppressed. It is to be added also that a prince can never secure himself against a hostile people, because of their being too many, whilst from the nobles he can secure himself, as they are few in number. The worst that a prince may expect from a hostile people is to be abandoned by them; but from hostile nobles he has not only to fear abandonment, but also that they will rise against him; for they, being in these affairs more far-seeing and astute, always come forward in time to save themselves, and to obtain favours from him whom they expect to prevail. Further, the prince is compelled to live always with the same people, but he can do well without the same nobles, being able to make and unmake them daily, and to give or take away authority when it pleases him.

Therefore, to make this point clearer, I say that the nobles ought to be looked at mainly in two ways: that is to say, they either shape their course in such a way as binds them entirely to your fortune, or they do not. Those who so bind themselves, and are not rapacious, ought to be honoured and loved; those who do not bind themselves may be dealt with in two ways; they may fail to do this through pusillanimity and a natural want of courage, in which case you ought to make use of them, especially of those who are of good counsel; and thus, whilst in prosperity you honour them, in adversity you do not have to fear them. But when for their own ambitious ends they shun binding themselves, it is a token that they are giving more thought to themselves than to you, and a prince ought to guard against such, and to fear them as if they were open enemies, because in adversity they always help to ruin him.

Therefore, one who becomes a prince through the favour of the people ought to keep them friendly, and this he can easily do seeing they only ask not to be oppressed by him. But one who, in opposition to the people, becomes a prince by the favour of the nobles, ought, above everything, to seek to win the people over to himself, and this he may easily do if he takes them under his protection. Because men, when they receive good from him of whom they were expecting evil, are bound more closely to their benefactor; thus the people quickly become more devoted to him than if he had been raised to the principality by their favours; and the prince can win their affections in many ways, but as these vary according to the circumstances one cannot give fixed rules, so I omit them; but, I repeat, it is necessary for a prince to have the people friendly, otherwise he has no security in adversity.

Nabis,[16] Prince of the Spartans, sustained the attack of all Greece, and of a victorious Roman army, and against them he defended his country and his government; and for the overcoming of this peril it was only necessary for him to make himself secure against a few, but this would not have been sufficient

5   had the people been hostile. And do not let any one impugn this statement with the trite proverb that "He who builds on the people, builds on the mud," for this is true when a private citizen makes a foundation there, and persuades himself that the people will free him when he is oppressed by his enemies or by the magistrates; wherein he would find himself very often deceived, as happened to

10   the Gracchi in Rome and to Messer Giorgio Scali[17] in Florence. But granted a prince who has established himself as above, who can command, and is a man of courage, undismayed in adversity, who does not fail in other qualifications, and who, by his resolution and energy, keeps the whole people encouraged–such a one will never find himself deceived in them, and it will be shown that he has

15   laid his foundations well.

These principalities are liable to danger when they are passing from the civil to the absolute order of government, for such princes either rule personally or through magistrates. In the latter case their government is weaker and more insecure, because it rests entirely on the goodwill of those citizens who are

20   raised to the magistracy, and who, especially in troubled times, can destroy the government with great ease, either by intrigue or open defiance; and the prince has not the chance amid tumults to exercise absolute authority, because the citizens and subjects, accustomed to receive orders from magistrates, are not of a mind to obey him amid these confusions, and there will always be in doubtful

25   times a scarcity of men whom he can trust. For such a prince cannot rely upon what he observes in quiet times, when citizens have need of the state, because then every one agrees with him; they all promise, and when death is far distant they all wish to die for him; but in troubled times, when the state has need of its citizens, then he finds but few. And so much the more is this experiment

30   dangerous, inasmuch as it can only be tried once. Therefore a wise prince ought to adopt such a course that his citizens will always in every sort and kind of circumstance have need of the state and of him, and then he will always find them faithful.

CHAPTER X:
Concerning the way in which the strength of all principalities ought to be measured

It is necessary to consider another point in examining the character of these

35   principalities: that is, whether a prince has such power that, in case of need, he

can support himself with his own resources, or whether he has always need of the assistance of others. And to make this quite clear I say that I consider those who are able to support themselves by their own resources who can, either by abundance of men or money, raise a sufficient army to join battle against any
5 one who comes to attack them; and I consider those always to have need of others who cannot show themselves against the enemy in the field, but are forced to defend themselves by sheltering behind walls. The first case has been discussed, but we will speak of it again should it recur. In the second case one can say nothing except to encourage such princes to provision and fortify their
10 towns, and not on any account to defend the country. And whoever shall fortify his town well, and shall have managed the other concerns of his subjects in the way stated above, and to be often repeated, will never be attacked without great caution, for men are always adverse to enterprises where difficulties can be seen, and it will be seen not to be an easy thing to attack one who has his town well
15 fortified, and is not hated by his people.

The cities of Germany are absolutely free, they own but little country around them, and they yield obedience to the emperor when it suits them, nor do they fear this or any other power they may have near them, because they are fortified in such a way that every one thinks the taking of them by assault would
20 be tedious and difficult, seeing they have proper ditches and walls, they have sufficient artillery, and they always keep in public depots enough for one year's eating, drinking, and firing. And beyond this, to keep the people quiet and without loss to the state, they always have the means of giving work to the community in those labours that are the life and strength of the city, and on the
25 pursuit of which the people are supported; they also hold military exercises in repute, and moreover have many ordinances to uphold them.

Therefore, a prince who has a strong city, and had not made himself odious, will not be attacked, or if any one should attack he will only be driven off with disgrace; again, because that the affairs of this world are so changeable, it is
30 almost impossible to keep an army a whole year in the field without being interfered with. And whoever should reply: If the people have property outside the city, and see it burnt, they will not remain patient, and the long siege and self-interest will make them forget their prince; to this I answer that a powerful and courageous prince will overcome all such difficulties by giving at one time
35 hope to his subjects that the evil will not be for long, at another time fear of the cruelty of the enemy, then preserving himself adroitly from those subjects who seem to him to be too bold.

Further, the enemy would naturally on his arrival at once burn and ruin the country at the time when the spirits of the people are still hot and ready for the
40 defence; and, therefore, so much the less ought the prince to hesitate; because

after a time, when spirits have cooled, the damage is already done, the ills are incurred, and there is no longer any remedy; and therefore they are so much the more ready to unite with their prince, he appearing to be under obligations to them now that their houses have been burnt and their possessions ruined in his
5 defence. For it is the nature of men to be bound by the benefits they confer as much as by those they receive. Therefore, if everything is well considered, it will not be difficult for a wise prince to keep the minds of his citizens steadfast from first to last, when he does not fail to support and defend them.

CHAPTER XI:
Concerning ecclesiastical principalities

It only remains now to speak of ecclesiastical principalities, touching which
10 all difficulties are prior to getting possession, because they are acquired either by capacity or good fortune, and they can be held without either; for they are sustained by the ancient ordinances of religion, which are so all-powerful, and of such a character that the principalities may be held no matter how their princes behave and live. These princes alone have states and do not defend them; and
15 they have subjects and do not rule them; and the states, although unguarded, are not taken from them, and the subjects, although not ruled, do not care, and they have neither the desire nor the ability to alienate themselves. Such principalities only are secure and happy. But being upheld by powers, to which the human mind cannot reach, I shall speak no more of them, because, being exalted and
20 maintained by God, it would be the act of a presumptuous and rash man to discuss them.

Nevertheless, if any one should ask of me how comes it that the Church has attained such greatness in temporal power, seeing that from Alexander backwards the Italian potentates (not only those who have been called
25 potentates, but every baron and lord, though the smallest) have valued the temporal power very slightly–yet now a king of France trembles before it, and it has been able to drive him from Italy, and to ruin the Venetians–although this may be very manifest, it does not appear to me superfluous to recall it in some measure to memory.

30 Before Charles, King of France, passed into Italy,[18] this country was under the dominion of the Pope, the Venetians, the King of Naples, the Duke of Milan, and the Florentines. These potentates had two principal anxieties: the one, that no foreigner should enter Italy under arms; the other, that none of themselves should seize more territory. Those about whom there was the most anxiety were
35 the Pope and the Venetians. To restrain the Venetians the union of all the others was necessary, as it was for the defence of Ferrara; and to keep down the Pope

they made use of the barons of Rome, who, being divided into two factions, Orsini and Colonnesi, had always a pretext for disorder, and, standing with arms in their hands under the eyes of the Pontiff, kept the pontificate weak and powerless. And although there might arise sometimes a courageous pope, such
5   as Sixtus, yet neither fortune nor wisdom could rid him of these annoyances. And the short life of a pope is also a cause of weakness; for in the ten years, which is the average life of a pope, he can with difficulty lower one of the factions; and if, so to speak, one people should almost destroy the Colonnesi, another would arise hostile to the Orsini, who would support their opponents,
10   and yet would not have time to ruin the Orsini. This was the reason why the temporal powers of the pope were little esteemed in Italy.

     Alexander the Sixth arose afterwards, who of all the pontiffs that have ever been showed how a pope with both money and arms was able to prevail; and through the instrumentality of the Duke Valentino, and by reason of the entry of
15   the French, he brought about all those things which I have discussed above in the actions of the duke. And although his intention was not to aggrandize the Church, but the duke, nevertheless, what he did contributed to the greatness of the Church, which, after his death and the ruin of the duke, became the heir to all his labours.

20   Pope Julius came afterwards and found the Church strong, possessing all the Romagna, the barons of Rome reduced to impotence, and, through the chastisements of Alexander, the factions wiped out; he also found the way open to accumulate money in a manner such as had never been practised before Alexander's time. Such things Julius not only followed, but improved upon, and
25   he intended to gain Bologna, to ruin the Venetians, and to drive the French out of Italy. All of these enterprises prospered with him, and so much the more to his credit, inasmuch as he did everything to strengthen the Church and not any private person. He kept also the Orsini and Colonnesi factions within the bounds in which he found them; and although there was among them some mind to
30   make disturbance, nevertheless he held two things firm: the one, the greatness of the Church, with which he terrified them; and the other, not allowing them to have their own cardinals, who caused the disorders among them. For whenever these factions have their cardinals they do not remain quiet for long, because cardinals foster the factions in Rome and out of it, and the barons are compelled
35   to support them, and thus from the ambitions of prelates arise disorders and tumults among the barons. For these reasons his Holiness Pope Leo[19] found the pontificate most powerful, and it is to be hoped that, if others made it great in arms, he will make it still greater and more venerated by his goodness and infinite other virtues.

CHAPTER XII:
How many kinds of soldiery there are, and concerning mercenaries

Having discoursed particularly on the characteristics of such principalities as in the beginning I proposed to discuss, and having considered in some degree the causes of their being good or bad, and having shown the methods by which many have sought to acquire them and to hold them, it now remains for me to
5   discuss generally the means of offence and defence which belong to each of them.

We have seen above how necessary it is for a prince to have his foundations well laid, otherwise it follows of necessity he will go to ruin. The chief foundations of all states, new as well as old or composite, are good laws and
10   good arms; and as there cannot be good laws where the state is not well armed, it follows that where they are well armed they have good laws. I shall leave the laws out of the discussion and shall speak of the arms.

I say, therefore, that the arms with which a prince defends his state are either his own, or they are mercenaries, auxiliaries, or mixed. Mercenaries and
15   auxiliaries are useless and dangerous; and if one holds his state based on these arms, he will stand neither firm nor safe; for they are disunited, ambitious, and without discipline, unfaithful, valiant before friends, cowardly before enemies; they have neither the fear of God nor fidelity to men, and destruction is deferred only so long as the attack is; for in peace one is robbed by them, and in war by
20   the enemy. The fact is, they have no other attraction or reason for keeping the field than a trifle of stipend, which is not sufficient to make them willing to die for you. They are ready enough to be your soldiers whilst you do not make war, but if war comes they take themselves off or run from the foe; which I should have little trouble to prove, for the ruin of Italy has been caused by nothing else
25   than by resting all her hopes for many years on mercenaries, and although they formerly made some display and appeared valiant amongst themselves, yet when the foreigners came they showed what they were. Thus it was that Charles, King of France, was allowed to seize Italy with chalk in hand;[20] and he who told us that our sins were the cause of it told the truth, but they were not the sins he
30   imagined, but those which I have related. And as they were the sins of princes, it is the princes who have also suffered the penalty.

I wish to demonstrate further the infelicity of these arms. The mercenary captains are either capable men or they are not; if they are, you cannot trust them, because they always aspire to their own greatness, either by oppressing
35   you, who are their master, or others contrary to your intentions; but if the captain is not skilful, you are ruined in the usual way.

And if it be urged that whoever is armed will act in the same way, whether mercenary or not, I reply that when arms have to be resorted to, either by a prince or a republic, then the prince ought to go in person and perform the duty of a captain; the republic has to send its citizens, and when one is sent who does
5 not turn out satisfactorily, it ought to recall him, and when one is worthy, to hold him by the laws so that he does not leave the command. And experience has shown princes and republics, single-handed, making the greatest progress, and mercenaries doing nothing except damage; and it is more difficult to bring a republic, armed with its own arms, under the sway of one of its citizens than it is
10 to bring one armed with foreign arms. Rome and Sparta stood for many ages armed and free. The Switzers are completely armed and quite free.

Of ancient mercenaries, for example, there are the Carthaginians, who were oppressed by their mercenary soldiers after the first war with the Romans, although the Carthaginians had their own citizens for captains. After the death of
15 Epaminondas, Philip of Macedon was made captain of their soldiers by the Thebans, and after victory he took away their liberty.

Duke Filippo being dead, the Milanese enlisted Francesco Sforza against the Venetians, and he, having overcome the enemy at Caravaggio,[21] allied himself with them to crush the Milanese, his masters. His father, Sforza, having
20 been engaged by Queen Johanna[22] of Naples, left her unprotected, so that she was forced to throw herself into the arms of the King of Aragon, in order to save her kingdom. And if the Venetians and Florentines formerly extended their dominions by these arms, and yet their captains did not make themselves princes, but have defended them, I reply that the Florentines in this case have
25 been favoured by chance, for of the able captains, of whom they might have stood in fear, some have not conquered, some have been opposed, and others have turned their ambitions elsewhere. One who did not conquer was Giovanni Acuto,[23] and since he did not conquer his fidelity cannot be proved; but every one will acknowledge that, had he conquered, the Florentines would have stood
30 at his discretion. Sforza had the Bracceschi always against him, so they watched each other. Francesco turned his ambition to Lombardy; Braccio against the Church and the kingdom of Naples. But let us come to that which happened a short while ago. The Florentines appointed as their captain Pagolo Vitelli, a most prudent man, who from a private position had risen to the greatest renown.
35 If this man had taken Pisa, nobody can deny that it would have been proper for the Florentines to keep in with him, for if he became the soldier of their enemies they had no means of resisting, and if they held to him they must obey him. The Venetians, if their achievements are considered, will be seen to have acted safely and gloriously so long as they sent to war their own men, when with armed
40 gentlemen and plebians they did valiantly. This was before they turned to

enterprises on land, but when they began to fight on land they forsook this virtue and followed the custom of Italy. And in the beginning of their expansion on land, through not having much territory, and because of their great reputation, they had not much to fear from their captains; but when they expanded, as under
5 Carmignuola,[24] they had a taste of this mistake; for, having found him a most valiant man (they beat the Duke of Milan under his leadership), and, on the other hand, knowing how lukewarm he was in the war, they feared they would no longer conquer under him, and for this reason they were not willing, nor were they able, to let him go; and so, not to lose again that which they had acquired,
10 they were compelled, in order to secure themselves, to murder him. They had afterwards for their captains Bartolomeo da Bergamo, Roberto da San Severino, the count of Pitigliano,[25] and the like, under whom they had to dread loss and not gain, as happened afterwards at Vaila,[26] where in one battle they lost that which in eight hundred years they had acquired with so much trouble. Because
15 from such arms conquests come but slowly, long delayed and inconsiderable, but the losses sudden and portentous.

And as with these examples I have reached Italy, which has been ruled for many years by mercenaries, I wish to discuss them more seriously, in order that, having seen their rise and progress, one may be better prepared to counteract
20 them. You must understand that the empire has recently come to be repudiated in Italy, that the Pope has acquired more temporal power, and that Italy has been divided up into more states, for the reason that many of the great cities took up arms against their nobles, who, formerly favoured by the emperor, were oppressing them, whilst the Church was favouring them so as to gain authority
25 in temporal power: in many others their citizens became princes. From this it came to pass that Italy fell partly into the hands of the Church and of republics, and, the Church consisting of priests and the republic of citizens unaccustomed to arms, both commenced to enlist foreigners.

The first who gave renown to this soldiery was Alberigo da Conio,[27] the
30 Romagnian. From the school of this man sprang, among others, Braccio and Sforza, who in their time were the arbiters of Italy. After these came all the other captains who till now have directed the arms of Italy; and the end of all their valour has been, that she has been overrun by Charles, robbed by Louis, ravaged by Ferdinand, and insulted by the Switzers. The principle that has guided them
35 has been, first, to lower the credit of infantry so that they might increase their own. They did this because, subsisting on their pay and without territory, they were unable to support many soldiers, and a few infantry did not give them any authority; so they were led to employ cavalry, with a moderate force of which they were maintained and honoured; and affairs were brought to such a pass
40 that, in an army of twenty thousand soldiers, there were not to be found two

thousand foot soldiers. They had, besides this, used every art to lessen fatigue
and danger to themselves and their soldiers, not killing in the fray, but taking
prisoners and liberating without ransom. They did not attack towns at night, nor
did the garrisons of the towns attack encampments at night; they did not
5   surround the camp either with stockade or ditch, nor did they campaign in the
winter. All these things were permitted by their military rules, and devised by
them to avoid, as I have said, both fatigue and dangers; thus they have brought
Italy to slavery and contempt.

CHAPTER XIII
Concerning auxiliaries, mixed soldiery, and one's own

Auxiliaries, which are the other useless arm, are employed when a prince is
10   called in with his forces to aid and defend, as was done by Pope Julius in the
most recent times; for he, having, in the enterprise against Ferrara, had poor
proof of his mercenaries, turned to auxiliaries, and stipulated with Ferdinand,
King of Spain,[28] for his assistance with men and arms. These arms may be
useful and good in themselves, but for him who calls them in they are always
15   disadvantageous; for losing, one is undone, and winning, one is their captive.

And although ancient histories may be full of examples, I do not wish to
leave this recent one of Pope Julius the Second, the peril of which cannot fail to
be perceived; for he, wishing to get Ferrara, threw himself entirely into the
hands of the foreigner. But his good fortune brought about a third event, so that
20   he did not reap the fruit of his rash choice; because, having his auxiliaries routed
at Ravenna, and the Switzers having risen and driven out the conquerors (against
all expectation, both his and others), it so came to pass that he did not become
prisoner to his enemies, they having fled, nor to his auxiliaries, he having
conquered by other arms than theirs.

25   The Florentines, being entirely without arms, sent ten thousand Frenchmen
to take Pisa, whereby they ran more danger than at any other time of their
troubles.

The Emperor of Constantinople,[29] to oppose his neighbours, sent ten
thousand Turks into Greece, who, on the war being finished, were not willing to
30   quit; this was the beginning of the servitude of Greece to the infidels.

Therefore, let him who has no desire to conquer make use of these arms, for
they are much more hazardous than mercenaries, because with them the ruin is
ready made; they are all united, all yield obedience to others; but with
mercenaries, when they have conquered, more time and better opportunities are
35   needed to injure you; they are not all of one community, they are found and paid
by you, and a third party, which you have made their head, is not able all at once

to assume enough authority to injure you. In conclusion, in mercenaries dastardy is most dangerous; in auxiliaries, valour. The wise prince, therefore, has always avoided these arms and turned to his own; and has been willing rather to lose with them than to conquer with the others, not deeming that a real victory which
5   is gained with the arms of others.

I shall never hesitate to cite Cesare Borgia and his actions. This duke entered the Romagna with auxiliaries, taking there only French soldiers, and with them he captured Imola and Forli; but afterwards, such forces not appearing to him reliable, he turned to mercenaries, discerning less danger in
10   them, and enlisted the Orsini and Vitelli; whom presently, on handling and finding them doubtful, unfaithful, and dangerous, he destroyed and turned to his own men. And the difference between one and the other of these forces can easily be seen when one considers the difference there was in the reputation of the duke, when he had the French, when he had the Orsini and Vitelli, and when
15   he relied on his own soldiers, on whose fidelity he could always count and found it ever increasing; he was never esteemed more highly than when every one saw that he was complete master of his own forces.

I was not intending to go beyond Italian and recent examples, but I am unwilling to leave out Hiero, the Syracusan, he being one of those I have named
20   above. This man, as I have said, made head of the army by the Syracusans, soon found out that a mercenary soldiery, constituted like our Italian condottieri, was of no use; and it appearing to him that he could neither keep them nor let them go, he had them all cut to pieces, and afterwards made war with his own forces and not with aliens.
25   I wish also to recall to memory an instance from the Old Testament applicable to this subject. David offered himself to Saul to fight with Goliath, the Philistine champion, and, to give him courage, Saul armed him with his own weapons; which David rejected as soon as he had them on his back, saying he could make no use of them, and that he wished to meet the enemy with his sling
30   and his knife. In conclusion, the arms of others either fall from your back, or they weigh you down, or they bind you fast.

Charles the Seventh,[30] the father of King Louis the Eleventh,[31] having by good fortune and valour liberated France from the English, recognized the necessity of being armed with forces of his own, and he established in his
35   kingdom ordinances concerning men-at-arms and infantry. Afterwards his son, King Louis, abolished the infantry and began to enlist the Switzers, which mistake, followed by others, is, as is now seen, a source of peril to that kingdom; because, having raised the reputation of the Switzers, he has entirely diminished the value of his own arms, for he has destroyed the infantry altogether; and his
40   men-at-arms he has subordinated to others, for, being as they are so accustomed

to fight along with Switzers, it does not appear that they can now conquer without them. Hence it arises that the French cannot stand against the Switzers, and without the Switzers they do not come off well against others. The armies of the French have thus become mixed, partly mercenary and partly national, both

5   of which arms together are much better than mercenaries alone or auxiliaries alone, but much inferior to one's own forces. And this example proves it, for the kingdom of France would be unconquerable if the ordinance of Charles had been enlarged or maintained.

But the scanty wisdom of man, on entering into an affair which looks well

10 at first, cannot discern the poison that is hidden in it, as I have said above of hectic fevers. Therefore, if he who rules a principality cannot recognize evils until they are upon him, he is not truly wise; and this insight is given to few. And if the first disaster to the Roman Empire[32] should be examined, it will be found to have commenced only with the enlisting of the Goths; because from

15 that time the vigour of the Roman Empire began to decline, and all that valour which had raised it passed away to others.

I conclude, therefore, that no principality is secure without having its own forces; on the contrary, it is entirely dependent on good fortune, not having the valour which in adversity would defend it. And it has always been the opinion

20 and judgment of wise men that nothing can be so uncertain or unstable as fame or power not founded on its own strength. And one's own forces are those which are composed either of subjects, citizens, or dependents; all others are mercenaries or auxiliaries. And the way to make ready one's own forces will be easily found if the rules suggested by me shall be reflected upon, and if one will

25 consider how Philip, the father of Alexander the Great, and many republics and princes have armed and organized themselves, to which rules I entirely commit myself.

CHAPTER XIV:
That which concerns a prince on the subject of the art of war

A prince ought to have no other aim or thought, nor select anything else for his study, than war and its rules and discipline; for this is the sole art that

30 belongs to him who rules, and it is of such force that it not only upholds those who are born princes, but it often enables men to rise from a private station to that rank. And, on the contrary, it is seen that when princes have thought more of ease than of arms they have lost their states. And the first cause of your losing it is to neglect this art; and what enables you to acquire a state is to be master of

35 the art. Francesco Sforza, through being martial, from a private person became Duke of Milan; and the sons, through avoiding the hardships and troubles of

arms, from dukes became private persons. For among other evils which being unarmed brings you, it causes you to be despised, and this is one of those ignominies against which a prince ought to guard himself, as is shown later on. Because there is nothing proportionate between the armed and the unarmed; and
5   it is not reasonable that he who is armed should yield obedience willingly to him who is unarmed, or that the unarmed man should be secure among armed servants. Because, there being in the one disdain and in the other suspicion, it is not possible for them to work well together. And therefore a prince who does not understand the art of war, over and above the other misfortunes already
10 mentioned, cannot be respected by his soldiers, nor can he rely on them. He ought never, therefore, to have out of his thoughts this subject of war, and in peace he should addict himself more to its exercise than in war; this he can do in two ways, the one by action, the other by study.

As regards action, he ought above all things to keep his men well organized
15 and drilled, to follow incessantly the chase, by which he accustoms his body to hardships, and learns something of the nature of localities, and gets to find out how the mountains rise, how the valleys open out, how the plains lie, and to understand the nature of rivers and marshes, and in all this to take the greatest care. Which knowledge is useful in two ways. Firstly, he learns to know his
20 country, and is better able to undertake its defence; afterwards, by means of the knowledge and observation of that locality, he understands with ease any other which it may be necessary for him to study hereafter; because the hills, valleys, and plains, and rivers and marshes that are, for instance, in Tuscany, have a certain resemblance to those of other countries, so that with a knowledge of the
25 aspect of one country one can easily arrive at a knowledge of others. And the prince that lacks this skill lacks the essential which it is desirable that a captain should possess, for it teaches him to surprise his enemy, to select quarters, to lead armies, to array the battle, to besiege towns to advantage.

Philopoemen,[33] Prince of the Achaeans, among other praises which writers
30 have bestowed on him, is commended because in time of peace he never had anything in his mind but the rules of war; and when he was in the country with friends, he often stopped and reasoned with them: "If the enemy should be upon that hill, and we should find ourselves here with our army, with whom would be the advantage? How should one best advance to meet him, keeping the ranks? If
35 we should wish to retreat, how ought we to pursue?" And he would set forth to them, as he went, all the chances that could befall an army; he would listen to their opinion and state his, confirming it with reasons, so that by these continual discussions there could never arise, in time of war, any unexpected circumstances that he could not deal with.

But to exercise the intellect the prince should read histories, and study there the actions of illustrious men, to see how they have borne themselves in war, to examine the causes of their victories and defeat, so as to avoid the latter and imitate the former; and above all do as an illustrious man did, who took as an
5   exemplar one who had been praised and famous before him, and whose achievements and deeds he always kept in his mind, as it is said Alexander the Great imitated Achilles, Caesar Alexander, Scipio Cyrus. And whoever reads the life of Cyrus, written by Xenophon, will recognize afterwards in the life of Scipio how that imitation was his glory, and how in chastity, affability,
10   humanity, and liberality Scipio conformed to those things which have been written of Cyrus by Xenophon. A wise prince ought to observe some such rules, and never in peaceful times stand idle, but increase his resources with industry in such a way that they may be available to him in adversity, so that if fortune chances it may find him prepared to resist her blows.

CHAPTER XV:
Concerning things for which men, and especially princes, are praised or blamed

15   It remains now to see what ought to be the rules of conduct for a prince towards subject and friends. And as I know that many have written on this point, I expect I shall be considered presumptuous in mentioning it again, especially as in discussing it I shall depart from the methods of other people. But, it being my intention to write a thing which shall be useful to him who apprehends it, it
20   appears to me more appropriate to follow up the real truth of the matter than the imagination of it; for many have pictured republics and principalities which in fact have never been known or seen, because how one lives is so far distant from how one ought to live, that he who neglects what is done for what ought to be done, sooner effects his ruin than his preservation; for a man who wishes to act
25   entirely up to his professions of virtue soon meets with what destroys him among so much that is evil.

Hence it is necessary for a prince wishing to hold his own to know how to do wrong, and to make use of it or not according to necessity. Therefore, putting on one side imaginary things concerning a prince, and discussing those which
30   are real, I say that all men when they are spoken of, and chiefly princes for being more highly placed, are remarkable for some of those qualities which bring them either blame or praise; and thus it is that one is reputed liberal, another miserly, using a Tuscan term (because an avaricious person in our language is still he who desires to possess by robbery, whilst we call one miserly who deprives
35   himself too much of the use of his own); one is reputed generous, one rapacious;

one cruel, one compassionate; one faithless, another faithful; one effeminate and cowardly, another bold and brave; one affable, another haughty; one lascivious, another chaste; one sincere, another cunning; one hard, another easy; one grave, another frivolous; one religious, another unbelieving, and the like. And I know
5   that every one will confess that it would be most praiseworthy in a prince to exhibit all the above qualities that are considered good; but because they can neither be entirely possessed nor observed, for human conditions do not permit it, it is necessary for him to be sufficiently prudent that he may know how to avoid the reproach of those vices which would lose him his state; and also to
10   keep himself, if it be possible, from those which would not lose him it; but this not being possible, he may with less hesitation abandon himself to them. And again, he need not make himself uneasy at incurring a reproach for those vices without which the state can only be saved with difficulty, for if everything is considered carefully, it will be found that something which looks like virtue, if
15   followed, would be his ruin; whilst something else, which looks like vice, yet followed brings him security and prosperity.

CHAPTER XVI:
Concerning liberality and meanness

Commencing then with the first of the above-named characteristics, I say that it would be well to be reputed liberal. Nevertheless, liberality exercised in a way that does not bring you the reputation for it, injures you; for if one exercises
20   it honestly and as it should be exercised, it may not become known, and you will not avoid the reproach of its opposite. Therefore, any one wishing to maintain among men the name of liberal is obliged to avoid no attribute of magnificence; so that a prince thus inclined will consume in such acts all his property, and will be compelled in the end, if he wish to maintain the name of liberal, to unduly
25   weigh down his people, and tax them, and do everything he can to get money. This will soon make him odious to his subjects, and becoming poor he will be little valued by any one; thus, with his liberality, having offended many and rewarded few, he is affected by the very first trouble and imperilled by whatever may be the first danger; recognizing this himself, and wishing to draw back from
30   it, he runs at once into the reproach of being miserly.

Therefore, a prince, not being able to exercise this virtue of liberality in such a way that it is recognized, except to his cost, if he is wise he ought not to fear the reputation of being mean, for in time he will come to be more considered than if liberal, seeing that with his economy his revenues are enough,
35   that he can defend himself against all attacks, and is able to engage in enterprises without burdening his people; thus it comes to pass that he exercises

liberality towards all from whom he does not take, who are numberless, and meanness towards those to whom he does not give, who are few.

We have not seen great things done in our time except by those who have been considered mean; the rest have failed. Pope Julius the Second was assisted
5 in reaching the papacy by a reputation for liberality, yet he did not strive afterwards to keep it up, when he made war on the King of France; and he made many wars without imposing any extraordinary tax on his subjects, for he supplied his additional expenses out of his long thriftiness. The present King of Spain would not have undertaken or conquered in so many enterprises if he had
10 been reputed liberal. A prince, therefore, provided that he has not to rob his subjects, that he can defend himself, that he does not become poor and abject, that he is not forced to become rapacious, ought to hold of little account a reputation for being mean, for it is one of those vices which will enable him to govern.
15 And if any one should say: Caesar obtained empire by liberality, and many others have reached the highest positions by having been liberal, and by being considered so, I answer: Either you are a prince in fact, or in a way to become one. In the first case this liberality is dangerous, in the second it is very necessary to be considered liberal; and Caesar was one of those who wished to
20 become pre-eminent in Rome; but if he had survived after becoming so, and had not moderated his expenses, he would have destroyed his government. And if any one should reply: Many have been princes, and have done great things with armies, who have been considered very liberal, I reply: Either a prince spends that which is his own or his subjects' or else that of others. In the first case he
25 ought to be sparing, in the second he ought not to neglect any opportunity for liberality. And to the prince who goes forth with his army, supporting it by pillage, sack, and extortion, handling that which belongs to others, this liberality is necessary, otherwise he would not be followed by soldiers. And of that which is neither yours nor your subjects' you can be a ready giver, as were Cyrus,
30 Caesar, and Alexander; because it does not take away your reputation if you squander that of others, but adds to it; it is only squandering your own that injures you.

And there is nothing wastes so rapidly as liberality, for even whilst you exercise it you lose the power to do so, and so become either poor or despised,
35 or else, in avoiding poverty, rapacious and hated. And a prince should guard himself, above all things, against being despised and hated; and liberality leads you to both. Therefore it is wiser to have a reputation for meanness which brings reproach without hatred, than to be compelled through seeking a reputation for liberality to incur a name for rapacity which begets reproach with hatred.

CHAPTER XVII:
Concerning cruelty and clemency, and whether it is better to be loved than feared

Coming now to the other qualities mentioned above, I say that every prince ought to desire to be considered clement and not cruel. Nevertheless he ought to take care not to misuse this clemency. Cesare Borgia was considered cruel; notwithstanding, his cruelty reconciled the Romagna, unified it, and restored it
5 to peace and loyalty. And if this be rightly considered, he will be seen to have been much more merciful than the Florentine people, who, to avoid a reputation for cruelty, permitted Pistoia to be destroyed.[34] Therefore a prince, so long as he keeps his subjects united and loyal, ought not to mind the reproach of cruelty; because with a few examples he will be more merciful than those who, through
10 too much mercy, allow disorders to arise, from which follow murders or robberies; for these are wont to injure the whole people, whilst those executions which originate with a prince offend the individual only.

And of all princes, it is impossible for the new prince to avoid the imputation of cruelty, owing to new states being full of dangers. Hence Virgil,
15 through the mouth of Dido, excuses the inhumanity of her reign owing to its being new, saying: "Res dura, et regni novitas me talia cogunt Moliri, et late fines custode tueri."[35]

Nevertheless he ought to be slow to believe and to act, nor should he himself show fear, but proceed in a temperate manner with prudence and
20 humanity, so that too much confidence may not make him incautious and too much distrust render him intolerable.

Upon this a question arises: whether it be better to be loved than feared or feared than loved? It may be answered that one should wish to be both, but, because it is difficult to unite them in one person, it is much safer to be feared
25 than loved, when, of the two, either must be dispensed with. Because this is to be asserted in general of men, that they are ungrateful, fickle, false, cowardly, covetous, and as long as you succeed they are yours entirely; they will offer you their blood, property, life, and children, as is said above, when the need is far distant; but when it approaches they turn against you. And that prince who,
30 relying entirely on their promises, has neglected other precautions, is ruined; because friendships that are obtained by payments, and not by greatness or nobility of mind, may indeed be earned, but they are not secured, and in time of need cannot be relied upon; and men have less scruple in offending one who is beloved than one who is feared, for love is preserved by the link of obligation
35 which, owing to the baseness of men, is broken at every opportunity for their advantage; but fear preserves you by a dread of punishment which never fails.

Nevertheless a prince ought to inspire fear in such a way that, if he does not win love, he avoids hatred; because he can endure very well being feared whilst he is not hated, which will always be as long as he abstains from the property of his citizens and subjects and from their women. But when it is necessary for him
5   to proceed against the life of someone, he must do it on proper justification and for manifest cause, but above all things he must keep his hands off the property of others, because men more quickly forget the death of their father than the loss of their patrimony. Besides, pretexts for taking away the property are never wanting; for he who has once begun to live by robbery will always find pretexts
10 for seizing what belongs to others; but reasons for taking life, on the contrary, are more difficult to find and sooner lapse. But when a prince is with his army, and has under control a multitude of soldiers, then it is quite necessary for him to disregard the reputation of cruelty, for without it he would never hold his army united or disposed to its duties.
15   Among the wonderful deeds of Hannibal this one is enumerated: that having led an enormous army, composed of many various races of men, to fight in foreign lands, no dissensions arose either among them or against the prince, whether in his bad or in his good fortune. This arose from nothing else than his inhuman cruelty, which, with his boundless valour, made him revered and
20 terrible in the sight of his soldiers, but without that cruelty, his other virtues were not sufficient to produce this effect. And short-sighted writers admire his deeds from one point of view and from another condemn the principal cause of them. That it is true his other virtues would not have been sufficient for him may be proved by the case of Scipio, that most excellent man, not only of his own
25 times but within the memory of man, against whom, nevertheless, his army rebelled in Spain; this arose from nothing but his too great forbearance, which gave his soldiers more license than is consistent with military discipline. For this he was upbraided in the Senate by Fabius Maximus, and called the corrupter of the Roman soldiery. The Locrians were laid waste by a legate of Scipio, yet they
30 were not avenged by him, nor was the insolence of the legate punished, owing entirely to his easy nature. Insomuch that someone in the Senate, wishing to excuse him, said there were many men who knew much better how not to err than to correct the errors of others. This disposition, if he had been continued in the command, would have destroyed in time the fame and glory of Scipio; but,
35 he being under the control of the Senate, this injurious characteristic not only concealed itself, but contributed to his glory.

Returning to the question of being feared or loved, I come to the conclusion that, men loving according to their own will and fearing according to that of the prince, a wise prince should establish himself on that which is in his own control and not in that of others; he must endeavour only to avoid hatred, as is noted.

CHAPTER XVIII:
Concerning the way in which princes should keep faith

5   Every one admits how praiseworthy it is in a prince to keep faith, and to live with integrity and not with craft. Nevertheless our experience has been that those princes who have done great things have held good faith of little account, and have known how to circumvent the intellect of men by craft, and in the end have overcome those who have relied on their word. You must know there are

10   two ways of contesting,[36] the one by the law, the other by force; the first method is proper to men, the second to beasts; but because the first is frequently not sufficient, it is necessary to have recourse to the second. Therefore it is necessary for a prince to understand how to avail himself of the beast and the man. This has been figuratively taught to princes by ancient writers, who

15   describe how Achilles and many other princes of old were given to the Centaur Chiron to nurse, who brought them up in his discipline; which means solely that, as they had for a teacher one who was half beast and half man, so it is necessary for a prince to know how to make use of both natures, and that one without the other is not durable. A prince, therefore, being compelled knowingly to adopt

20   the beast, ought to choose the fox and the lion; because the lion cannot defend himself against snares and the fox cannot defend himself against wolves. Therefore, it is necessary to be a fox to discover the snares and a lion to terrify the wolves. Those who rely simply on the lion do not understand what they are about. Therefore a wise lord cannot, nor ought he to, keep faith when such

25   observance may be turned against him, and when the reasons that caused him to pledge it exist no longer. If men were entirely good this precept would not hold, but because they are bad, and will not keep faith with you, you too are not bound to observe it with them. Nor will there ever be wanting to a prince legitimate reasons to excuse this non-observance. Of this endless modern examples could

30   be given, showing how many treaties and engagements have been made void and of no effect through the faithlessness of princes; and he who has known best how to employ the fox has succeeded best.

       But it is necessary to know well how to disguise this characteristic, and to be a great pretender and dissembler; and men are so simple, and so subject to

35   present necessities, that he who seeks to deceive will always find someone who will allow himself to be deceived. One recent example I cannot pass over in

138

silence. Alexander the Sixth did nothing else but deceive men, nor ever thought of doing otherwise, and he always found victims; for there never was a man who had greater power in asserting, or who with greater oaths would affirm a thing, yet would observe it less; nevertheless his deceits always succeeded according

5   to his wishes,[37] because he well understood this side of mankind.

Therefore it is unnecessary for a prince to have all the good qualities I have enumerated, but it is very necessary to appear to have them. And I shall dare to say this also, that to have them and always to observe them is injurious, and that to appear to have them is useful; to appear merciful, faithful, humane, religious,

10   upright, and to be so, but with a mind so framed that should you require not to be so, you may be able and know how to change to the opposite.

And you have to understand this, that a prince, especially a new one, cannot observe all those things for which men are esteemed, being often forced, in order to maintain the state, to act contrary to fidelity,[38] friendship, humanity,

15   and religion. Therefore it is necessary for him to have a mind ready to turn itself accordingly as the winds and variations of fortune force it, yet, as I have said above, not to diverge from the good if he can avoid doing so, but, if compelled, then to know how to set about it.

For this reason a prince ought to take care that he never lets anything slip

20   from his lips that is not replete with the above-named five qualities, that he may appear to him who sees and hears him altogether merciful, faithful, humane, upright, and religious. There is nothing more necessary to appear to have than this last quality, inasmuch as men judge generally more by the eye than by the hand, because it belongs to everybody to see you, to few to come in touch with

25   you. Every one sees what you appear to be, few really know what you are, and those few dare not oppose themselves to the opinion of the many, who have the majesty of the state to defend them; and in the actions of all men, and especially of princes, which it is not prudent to challenge, one judges by the result.

For that reason, let a prince have the credit of conquering and holding his

30   state, the means will always be considered honest, and he will be praised by everybody; because the vulgar are always taken by what a thing seems to be and by what comes of it; and in the world there are only the vulgar, for the few find a place there only when the many have no ground to rest on.

One prince[39] of the present time, whom it is not well to name, never

35   preaches anything else but peace and good faith, and to both he is most hostile, and either, if he had kept it, would have deprived him of reputation and kingdom many a time.

CHAPTER XIX:
That one should avoid being despised and hated

Now, concerning the characteristics of which mention is made above, I have spoken of the more important ones, the others I wish to discuss briefly under this generality, that the prince must consider, as has been in part said before, how to avoid those things which will make him hated or contemptible; and as often as he shall have succeeded he will have fulfilled his part, and he need not fear any danger in other reproaches.

It makes him hated above all things, as I have said, to be rapacious, and to be a violator of the property and women of his subjects, from both of which he must abstain. And when neither their property nor their honor is touched, the majority of men live content, and he has only to contend with the ambition of a few, whom he can curb with ease in many ways.

It makes him contemptible to be considered fickle, frivolous, effeminate, mean-spirited, irresolute, from all of which a prince should guard himself as from a rock; and he should endeavour to show in his actions greatness, courage, gravity, and fortitude; and in his private dealings with his subjects let him show that his judgments are irrevocable, and maintain himself in such reputation that no one can hope either to deceive him or to get round him.

That prince is highly esteemed who conveys this impression of himself, and he who is highly esteemed is not easily conspired against; for, provided it is well known that he is an excellent man and revered by his people, he can only be attacked with difficulty. For this reason a prince ought to have two fears, one from within, on account of his subjects, the other from without, on account of external powers. From the latter he is defended by being well armed and having good allies, and if he is well armed he will have good friends, and affairs will always remain quiet within when they are quiet without, unless they should have been already disturbed by conspiracy; and even should affairs outside be disturbed, if he has carried out his preparations and has lived as I have said, as long as he does not despair, he will resist every attack, as I said Nabis the Spartan did.

But concerning his subjects, when affairs outside are disturbed he has only to fear that they will conspire secretly, from which a prince can easily secure himself by avoiding being hated and despised, and by keeping the people satisfied with him, which it is most necessary for him to accomplish, as I said above at length. And one of the most efficacious remedies that a prince can have against conspiracies is not to be hated and despised by the people, for he who conspires against a prince always expects to please them by his removal; but when the conspirator can only look forward to offending them, he will not have the courage to take such a course, for the difficulties that confront a conspirator are infinite. And as experience shows, many have been the conspiracies, but few have been successful; because he who conspires cannot act alone, nor can he take a companion except from those whom he believes to be malcontents, and as soon as you have opened your mind to a malcontent you have given him the

5   material with which to content himself, for by denouncing you he can look for every advantage; so that, seeing the gain from this course to be assured, and seeing the other to be doubtful and full of dangers, he must be a very rare friend, or a thoroughly obstinate enemy of the prince, to keep faith with you.

        And, to reduce the matter into a small compass, I say that, on the side of the

10   conspirator, there is nothing but fear, jealousy, prospect of punishment to terrify him; but on the side of the prince there is the majesty of the principality, the laws, the protection of friends and the state to defend him; so that, adding to all these things the popular goodwill, it is impossible that any one should be so rash as to conspire. For whereas in general the conspirator has to fear before the

15   execution of his plot, in this case he has also to fear the sequel to the crime; because on account of it he has the people for an enemy, and thus cannot hope for any escape.

        Endless examples could be given on this subject, but I will be content with one, brought to pass within the memory of our fathers. Messer Annibale

20   Bentivogli, who was prince in Bologna (grandfather of the present Annibale), having been murdered by the Canneschi, who had conspired against him, not one of his family survived but Messer Giovanni,[40] who was in childhood: immediately after his assassination the people rose and murdered all the Canneschi. This sprung from the popular goodwill which the house of

25   Bentivogli enjoyed in those days in Bologna; which was so great that, although none remained there after the death of Annibale who was able to rule the state, the Bolognese, having information that there was one of the Bentivogli family in Florence, who up to that time had been considered the son of a blacksmith, sent to Florence for him and gave him the government of their city, and it was ruled

30   by him until Messer Giovanni came in due course to the government.

        For this reason I consider that a prince ought to reckon conspiracies of little account when his people hold him in esteem; but when it is hostile to him, and bears hatred towards him, he ought to fear everything and everybody. And well-ordered states and wise princes have taken every care not to drive the nobles to

35   desperation, and to keep the people satisfied and contented, for this is one of the most important objects a prince can have.

        Among the best ordered and governed kingdoms of our times is France, and in it are found many good institutions on which depend the liberty and security of the king; of these the first is the parliament and its authority, because he who

40   founded the kingdom, knowing the ambition of the nobility and their boldness,

considered that a bit to their mouths would be necessary to hold them in; and, on the other side, knowing the hatred of the people, founded in fear, against the nobles, he wished to protect them, yet he was not anxious for this to be the particular care of the king; therefore, to take away the reproach which he would

5 be liable to from the nobles for favouring the people, and from the people for favouring the nobles, he set up an arbiter, who should be one who could beat down the great and favour the lesser without reproach to the king. Neither could you have a better or a more prudent arrangement, or a greater source of security to the king and kingdom. From this one can draw another important conclusion,

10 that princes ought to leave affairs of reproach to the management of others, and keep those of grace in their own hands. And further, I consider that a prince ought to cherish the nobles, but not so as to make himself hated by the people.

It may appear, perhaps, to some who have examined the lives and deaths of the Roman emperors that many of them would be an example contrary to my

15 opinion, seeing that some of them lived nobly and showed great qualities of soul, nevertheless they have lost their empire or have been killed by subjects who have conspired against them. Wishing, therefore, to answer these objections, I will recall the characters of some of the emperors, and will show that the causes of their ruin were not different to those alleged by me; at the

20 same time I will only submit for consideration those things that are noteworthy to him who studies the affairs of those times.

It seems to me sufficient to take all those emperors who succeeded to the empire from Marcus the philosopher down to Maximinus; they were Marcus and his son Commodus, Pertinax, Julian, Severus and his son Antoninus Caracalla,

25 Macrinus, Heliogabalus, Alexander, and Maximinus.

There is first to note that, whereas in other principalities the ambition of the nobles and the insolence of the people only have to be contended with, the Roman emperors had a third difficulty in having to put up with the cruelty and avarice of their soldiers, a matter so beset with difficulties that it was the ruin of

30 many; for it was a hard thing to give satisfaction both to soldiers and people; because the people loved peace, and for this reason they loved the unaspiring prince, whilst the soldiers loved the warlike prince who was bold, cruel, and rapacious, which qualities they were quite willing he should exercise upon the people, so that they could get double pay and give vent to their own greed and

35 cruelty. Hence it arose that those emperors were always overthrown who, either by birth or training, had no great authority, and most of them, especially those who came new to the principality, recognizing the difficulty of these two opposing humours, were inclined to give satisfaction to the soldiers, caring little about injuring the people. Which course was necessary, because, as princes

40 cannot help being hated by someone, they ought, in the first place, to avoid

being hated by every one, and when they cannot compass this, they ought to endeavour with the utmost diligence to avoid the hatred of the most powerful. Therefore, those emperors who through inexperience had need of special favour adhered more readily to the soldiers than to the people; a course which turned
5   out advantageous to them or not, accordingly as the prince knew how to maintain authority over them.

From these causes it arose that Marcus, Pertinax, and Alexander, being all men of modest life, lovers of justice, enemies to cruelty, humane, and benignant, came to a sad end except Marcus; he alone lived and died honoured, because he
10 had succeeded to the throne by hereditary title, and owed nothing either to the soldiers or the people; and afterwards, being possessed of many virtues which made him respected, he always kept both orders in their places whilst he lived, and was neither hated nor despised.

But Pertinax was created emperor against the wishes of the soldiers, who,
15 being accustomed to live licentiously under Commodus, could not endure the honest life to which Pertinax wished to reduce them; thus, having given cause for hatred, to which hatred there was added contempt for his old age, he was overthrown at the very beginning of his administration. And here it should be noted that hatred is acquired as much by good works as by bad ones, therefore,
20 as I said before, a prince wishing to keep his state is very often forced to do evil; for when that body is corrupt whom you think you have need of to maintain yourself–it may be either the people or the soldiers or the nobles–you have to submit to its humours and to gratify them, and then good works will do you harm.
25 But let us come to Alexander, who was a man of such great goodness, that among the other praises which are accorded him is this, that in the fourteen years he held the empire no one was ever put to death by him unjudged; nevertheless, being considered effeminate and a man who allowed himself to be governed by his mother, he became despised, the army conspired against him,
30 and murdered him.

Turning now to the opposite characters of Commodus, Severus, Antoninus Caracalla, and Maximinus, you will find them all cruel and rapacious-men who, to satisfy their soldiers, did not hesitate to commit every kind of iniquity against the people; and all, except Severus, came to a bad end; but in Severus there was
35 so much valour that, keeping the soldiers friendly, although the people were oppressed by him, he reigned successfully; for his valour made him so much admired in the sight of the soldiers and people that the latter were kept in a way astonished and awed and the former respectful and satisfied. And because the actions of this man, as a new prince, were great, I wish to show briefly that he

knew well how to counterfeit the fox and the lion, which natures, as I said above, it is necessary for a prince to imitate.

Knowing the sloth of the Emperor Julian, he persuaded the army in Sclavonia, of which he was captain, that it would be right to go to Rome and avenge the death of Pertinax, who had been killed by the praetorian soldiers; and under this pretext, without appearing to aspire to the throne, he moved the army on Rome, and reached Italy before it was known that he had started. On his arrival at Rome, the Senate, through fear, elected him emperor and killed Julian. After this there remained for Severus, who wished to make himself master of the whole empire, two difficulties; one in Asia, where Niger, head of the Asiatic army, had caused himself to be proclaimed emperor; the other in the west where Albinus was, who also aspired to the throne. And as he considered it dangerous to declare himself hostile to both, he decided to attack Niger and to deceive Albinus. To the latter he wrote that, being elected emperor by the Senate, he was willing to share that dignity with him and sent him the title of Caesar; and, moreover, that the Senate had made Albinus his colleague; which things were accepted by Albinus as true. But after Severus had conquered and killed Niger, and settled oriental affairs, he returned to Rome and complained to the Senate that Albinus, little recognizing the benefits that he had received from him, had by treachery sought to murder him, and for this ingratitude he was compelled to punish him. Afterwards he sought him out in France, and took from him his government and life. He who will, therefore, carefully examine the actions of this man will find him a most valiant lion and a most cunning fox; he will find him feared and respected by every one, and not hated by the army; and it need not be wondered at that he, a new man, was able to hold the empire so well, because his supreme renown always protected him from that hatred which the people might have conceived against him for his violence.

But his son Antoninus was a most eminent man, and had very excellent qualities, which made him admirable in the sight of the people and acceptable to the soldiers, for he was a warlike man, most enduring of fatigue, a despiser of all delicate food and other luxuries, which caused him to be beloved by the armies. Nevertheless, his ferocity and cruelties were so great and so unheard of that, after endless single murders, he killed a large number of the people of Rome and all those of Alexandria. He became hated by the whole world, and also feared by those he had around him, to such an extent that he was murdered in the midst of his army by a centurion. And here it must be noted that such-like deaths, which are deliberately inflicted with a resolved and desperate courage, cannot be avoided by princes, because any one who does not fear to die can inflict them; but a prince may fear them the less because they are very rare; he has only to be careful not to do any grave injury to those whom he employs or has around him in the service of the state. Antoninus had not taken this care, but had contumeliously killed a brother of that centurion, whom also he daily threatened, yet retained in his bodyguard; which, as it turned out, was a rash thing to do, and proved the emperor's ruin.

5   But let us come to Commodus, to whom it should have been very easy to hold the empire, for, being the son of Marcus, he had inherited it, and he had only to follow in the footsteps of his father to please his people and soldiers; but, being by nature cruel and brutal, he gave himself up to amusing the soldiers and corrupting them, so that he might indulge his rapacity upon the people; on the other hand, not maintaining his dignity, often descending to the theatre to compete with gladiators, and doing other vile things, little worthy of the imperial majesty, he fell into contempt with the soldiers, and being hated by one party and despised by the other, he was conspired against and was killed.

      It remains to discuss the character of Maximinus. He was a very warlike man, and the armies, being disgusted with the effeminacy of Alexander, of whom I have already spoken, killed him and elected Maximinus to the throne. This he did not possess for long, for two things made him hated and despised; the one, his having kept sheep in Thrace, which brought him into contempt (it being well known to all, and considered a great indignity by every one), and the other, his having at the accession to his dominions deferred going to Rome and taking possession of the imperial seat; he had also gained a reputation for the utmost ferocity by having, through his prefects in Rome and elsewhere in the empire, practised many cruelties, so that the whole world was moved to anger at the meanness of his birth and to fear at his barbarity. First Africa rebelled, then the Senate with all the people of Rome, and all Italy conspired against him, to which may be added his own army; this latter, besieging Aquileia and meeting with difficulties in taking it, were disgusted with his cruelties, and fearing him less when they found so many against him, murdered him.

      I do not wish to discuss Heliogabalus, Macrinus, or Julian, who, being thoroughly contemptible, were quickly wiped out; but I will bring this discourse to a conclusion by saying that princes in our times have this difficulty of giving inordinate satisfaction to their soldiers in a far less degree, because, notwithstanding one has to give them some indulgence, that is soon done; none of these princes have armies that are veterans in the governance and administration of provinces, as were the armies of the Roman Empire; and whereas it was then more necessary to give satisfaction to the soldiers than to the people, it is now more necessary to all princes, except the Turk and the Soldan, to satisfy the people rather the soldiers, because the people are the more powerful.

From the above I have excepted the Turk, who always keeps round him twelve thousand infantry and fifteen thousand cavalry on which depend the security and strength of the kingdom, and it is necessary that, putting aside every consideration for the people, he should keep them his friends. The kingdom of

5 the Soldan is similar; being entirely in the hands of soldiers, it follows again that, without regard to the people, he must keep them his friends. But you must note that the state of the Soldan is unlike all other principalities, for the reason that it is like the Christian pontificate, which cannot be called either an hereditary or a newly formed principality; because the sons of the old prince are

10 not the heirs, but he who is elected to that position by those who have authority, and the sons remain only noblemen. And this being an ancient custom, it cannot be called a new principality, because there are none of those difficulties in it that are met with in new ones; for although the prince is new, the constitution of the state is old, and it is framed so as to receive him as if he were its hereditary lord.

15 But returning to the subject of our discourse, I say that whoever will consider it will acknowledge that either hatred or contempt has been fatal to the above-named emperors, and it will be recognized also how it happened that, a number of them acting in one way and a number in another, only one in each way came to a happy end and the rest to unhappy ones. Because it would have

20 been useless and dangerous for Pertinax and Alexander, being new princes, to imitate Marcus, who was heir to the principality; and likewise it would have been utterly destructive to Caracalla, Commodus, and Maximinus to have imitated Severus, they not having sufficient valour to enable them to tread in his footsteps. Therefore a prince, new to the principality, cannot imitate the actions

25 of Marcus, nor, again, is it necessary to follow those of Severus, but he ought to take from Severus those parts which are necessary to found his state, and from Marcus those which are proper and glorious to keep a state that may already be stable and firm.

CHAPTER XX:
Are fortresses, and many other things to which princes often resort, advantageous or hurtful?

1. Some princes, so as to hold securely the state, have disarmed their

30 subjects; others have kept their subject towns distracted by factions; others have fostered enmities against themselves; others have laid themselves out to gain over those whom they distrusted in the beginning of their governments; some have built fortresses; some have overthrown and destroyed them. And although one cannot give a final judgment on all of these things unless one possesses the

particulars of those states in which a decision has to be made, nevertheless I will speak as comprehensively as the matter of itself will admit.

2. There never was a new prince who has disarmed his subjects; rather when he has found them disarmed he has always armed them, because, by
5   arming them, those arms become yours, those men who were distrusted become faithful, and those who were faithful are kept so, and your subjects become your adherents. And whereas all subjects cannot be armed, yet when those whom you do arm are benefited, the others can be handled more freely, and this difference in their treatment, which they quite understand, makes the former your
10 dependents, and the latter, considering it to be necessary that those who have the most danger and service should have the most reward, excuse you. But when you disarm them, you at once offend them by showing that you distrust them, either for cowardice or for want of loyalty, and either of these opinions breeds hatred against you. And because you cannot remain unarmed, it follows that you
15 turn to mercenaries, which are of the character already shown; even if they should be good they would not be sufficient to defend you against powerful enemies and distrusted subjects. Therefore, as I have said, a new prince in a new principality has always distributed arms. Histories are full of examples. But when a prince acquires a new state, which he adds as a province to his old one,
20 then it is necessary to disarm the men of that state, except those who have been his adherents in acquiring it; and these again, with time and opportunity, should be rendered soft and effeminate; and matters should be managed in such a way that all the armed men in the state shall be your own soldiers who in your old state were living near you.
25   3. Our forefathers, and those who were reckoned wise, were accustomed to say that it was necessary to hold Pistoia by factions and Pisa by fortresses; and with this idea they fostered quarrels in some of their tributary towns so as to keep possession of them the more easily. This may have been well enough in those times when Italy was in a way balanced, but I do not believe that it can be
30 accepted as a precept for to-day, because I do not believe that factions can ever be of use; rather it is certain that when the enemy comes upon you in divided cities you are quickly lost, because the weakest party will always assist the outside forces and the other will not be able to resist. The Venetians, moved, as I believe, by the above reasons, fostered the Guelph and Ghibelline factions in
35 their tributary cities; and although they never allowed them to come to bloodshed, yet they nursed these disputes amongst them, so that the citizens, distracted by their differences, should not unite against them. Which, as we saw, did not afterwards turn out as expected, because, after the rout at Vaila, one party at once took courage and seized the state. Such methods argue, therefore,
40 weakness in the prince, because these factions will never be permitted in a

vigorous principality; such methods for enabling one the more easily to manage subjects are only useful in times of peace, but if war comes this policy proves fallacious.

4. Without doubt princes become great when they overcome the difficulties
5   and obstacles by which they are confronted, and therefore fortune, especially when she desires to make a new prince great, who has a greater necessity to earn renown than an hereditary one, causes enemies to arise and form designs against him, in order that he may have the opportunity of overcoming them, and by them to mount higher, as by a ladder which his enemies have raised. For this
10 reason many consider that a wise prince, when he has the opportunity, ought with craft to foster some animosity against himself, so that, having crushed it, his renown may rise higher.

5. Princes, especially new ones, have found more fidelity and assistance in those men who in the beginning of their rule were distrusted than among those
15 who in the beginning were trusted. Pandolfo Petrucci, Prince of Siena, ruled his state more by those who had been distrusted than by others. But on this question one cannot speak generally, for it varies so much with the individual; I will only say this, that those men who at the commencement of a princedom have been hostile, if they are of a description to need assistance to support themselves, can
20 always be gained over with the greatest ease, and they will be tightly held to serve the prince with fidelity, inasmuch as they know it to be very necessary for them to cancel by deeds the bad impression which he had formed of them; and thus the prince always extracts more profit from them than from those who, serving him in too much security, may neglect his affairs. And since the matter
25 demands it, I must not fail to warn a prince, who by means of secret favours has acquired a new state, that he must well consider the reasons which induced those to favour him who did so; and if it be not a natural affection towards him, but only discontent with their government, then he will only keep them friendly with great trouble and difficulty, for it will be impossible to satisfy them. And
30 weighing well the reasons for this in those examples which can be taken from ancient and modern affairs, we shall find that it is easier for the prince to make friends of those men who were contented under the former government, and are therefore his enemies, than of those who, being discontented with it, were favourable to him and encouraged him to seize it.

35 6. It has been a custom with princes, in order to hold their states more securely, to build fortresses that may serve as a bridle and bit to those who might design to work against them, and as a place of refuge from a first attack. I praise this system because it has been made use of formerly. Notwithstanding that, Messer Nicolo Vitelli in our times has been seen to demolish two fortresses in
40 Citta di Castello so that he might keep that state; Guido Ubaldo, Duke of

Urbino, on returning to his dominion, whence he had been driven by Cesare
Borgia, razed to the foundations all the fortresses in that province, and
considered that without them it would be more difficult to lose it; the Bentivogli
returning to Bologna came to a similar decision. Fortresses, therefore, are useful

5   or not according to circumstances; if they do you good in one way they injure
you in another. And this question can be reasoned thus: the prince who has more
to fear from the people than from foreigners ought to build fortresses, but he
who has more to fear from foreigners than from the people ought to leave them
alone. The castle of Milan, built by Francesco Sforza, has made, and will make,

10 more trouble for the house of Sforza than any other disorder in the state. For this
reason the best possible fortress is–not to be hated by the people, because,
although you may hold the fortresses, yet they will not save you if the people
hate you, for there will never be wanting foreigners to assist a people who have
taken arms against you. It has not been seen in our times that such fortresses

15 have been of use to any prince, unless to the Countess of Forli,[41] when the
Count Girolamo, her consort, was killed; for by that means she was able to
withstand the popular attack and wait for assistance from Milan, and thus
recover her state; and the posture of affairs was such at that time that the
foreigners could not assist the people. But fortresses were of little value to her

20 afterwards when Cesare Borgia attacked her, and when the people, her enemy,
were allied with foreigners. Therefore, it would have been safer for her, both
then and before, not to have been hated by the people than to have had the
fortresses. All these things considered then, I shall praise him who builds
fortresses as well as him who does not, and I shall blame whoever, trusting in

25 them, cares little about being hated by the people.

CHAPTER XXI:
How a prince should conduct himself so as to gain renown

Nothing makes a prince so much esteemed as great enterprises and setting a
fine example. We have in our time Ferdinand of Aragon, the present King of
Spain. He can almost be called a new prince, because he has risen, by fame and
glory, from being an insignificant king to be the foremost king in Christendom;

30 and if you will consider his deeds you will find them all great and some of them
extraordinary. In the beginning of his reign he attacked Granada, and this
enterprise was the foundation of his dominions. He did this quietly at first and
without any fear of hindrance, for he held the minds of the barons of Castile
occupied in thinking of the war and not anticipating any innovations; thus they

35 did not perceive that by these means he was acquiring power and authority over
them. He was able with the money of the Church and of the people to sustain his

armies, and by that long war to lay the foundation for the military skill which has since distinguished him. Further, always using religion as a plea, so as to undertake greater schemes, he devoted himself with pious cruelty to driving out and clearing his kingdom of the Moors; nor could there be a more admirable
5　example, nor one more rare. Under this same cloak he assailed Africa, he came down on Italy, he has finally attacked France; and thus his achievements and designs have always been great, and have kept the minds of his people in suspense and admiration and occupied with the issue of them. And his actions have arisen in such a way, one out of the other, that men have never been given
10　time to work steadily against him.

　　Again, it much assists a prince to set unusual examples in internal affairs, similar to those which are related of Messer Bernabo da Milano, who, when he had the opportunity, by any one in civil life doing some extraordinary thing, either good or bad, would take some method of rewarding or punishing him,
15　which would be much spoken about. And a prince ought, above all things, always endeavour in every action to gain for himself the reputation of being a great and remarkable man.

　　A prince is also respected when he is either a true friend or a downright enemy, that is to say, when, without any reservation, he declares himself in
20　favour of one party against the other; which course will always be more advantageous than standing neutral; because if two of your powerful neighbours come to blows, they are of such a character that, if one of them conquers, you have either to fear him or not. In either case it will always be more advantageous for you to declare yourself and to make war strenuously; because, in the first
25　case, if you do not declare yourself, you will invariably fall a prey to the conqueror, to the pleasure and satisfaction of him who has been conquered, and you will have no reasons to offer, nor anything to protect or to shelter you. Because he who conquers does not want doubtful friends who will not aid him in the time of trial; and he who loses will not harbour you because you did not
30　willingly, sword in hand, court his fate.

　　Antiochus went into Greece, being sent for by the Aetolians to drive out the Romans. He sent envoys to the Achaeans, who were friends of the Romans, exhorting them to remain neutral; and on the other hand the Romans urged them to take up arms. This question came to be discussed in the council of the
35　Achaeans, where the legate of Antiochus urged them to stand neutral. To this the Roman legate answered: "As for that which has been said, that it is better and more advantageous for your state not to interfere in our war, nothing can be more erroneous; because by not interfering you will be left, without favour or consideration, the guerdon of the conqueror." Thus it will always happen that he
40　who is not your friend will demand your neutrality, whilst he who is your friend

will entreat you to declare yourself with arms. And irresolute princes, to avoid present dangers, generally follow the neutral path, and are generally ruined. But when a prince declares himself gallantly in favour of one side, if the party with whom he allies himself conquers, although the victor may be powerful and may

5 have him at his mercy, yet he is indebted to him, and there is established a bond of amity; and men are never so shameless as to become a monument of ingratitude by oppressing you. Victories after all are never so complete that the victor must not show some regard, especially to justice. But if he with whom you ally yourself loses, you may be sheltered by him, and whilst he is able he

10 may aid you, and you become companions on a fortune that may rise again.

In the second case, when those who fight are of such a character that you have no anxiety as to who may conquer, so much the more is it greater prudence to be allied, because you assist at the destruction of one by the aid of another who, if he had been wise, would have saved him; and conquering, as it is

15 impossible that he should not do with your assistance, he remains at your discretion. And here it is to be noted that a prince ought to take care never to make an alliance with one more powerful than himself for the purposes of attacking others, unless necessity compels him, as is said above; because if he conquers you are at his discretion, and princes ought to avoid as much as

20 possible being at the discretion of any one. The Venetians joined with France against the Duke of Milan, and this alliance, which caused their ruin, could have been avoided. But when it cannot be avoided, as happened to the Florentines when the Pope and Spain sent armies to attack Lombardy, then in such a case, for the above reasons, the prince ought to favour one of the parties.

25 Never let any Government imagine that it can choose perfectly safe courses; rather let it expect to have to take very doubtful ones, because it is found in ordinary affairs that one never seeks to avoid one trouble without running into another; but prudence consists in knowing how to distinguish the character of troubles, and for choice to take the lesser evil.

30 A prince ought also to show himself a patron of ability, and to honour the proficient in every art. At the same time he should encourage his citizens to practise their callings peaceably, both in commerce and agriculture, and in every other following, so that the one should not be deterred from improving his possessions for fear lest they be taken away from him or another from opening

35 up trade for fear of taxes; but the prince ought to offer rewards to whoever wishes to do these things and designs in any way to honour his city or state.

Further, he ought to entertain the people with festivals and spectacles at convenient seasons of the year; and as every city is divided into guilds or into societies,[42] he ought to hold such bodies in esteem, and associate with them

40 sometimes, and show himself an example of courtesy and liberality;

nevertheless, always maintaining the majesty of his rank, for this he must never consent to abate in anything.

CHAPTER XXII:
Concerning the secretaries of princes

The choice of servants is of no little importance to a prince, and they are good or not according to the discrimination of the prince. And the first opinion

5   which one forms of a prince, and of his understanding, is by observing the men he has around him; and when they are capable and faithful he may always be considered wise, because he has known how to recognize the capable and to keep them faithful. But when they are otherwise one cannot form a good opinion of him, for the prime error which he made was in choosing them.

10   There were none who knew Messer Antonio da Venafro as the servant of Pandolfo Petrucci, Prince of Siena, who would not consider Pandolfo to be a very clever man in having Venafro for his servant. Because there are three classes of intellects: one which comprehends by itself; another which appreciates what others comprehended; and a third which neither comprehends

15   by itself nor by the showing of others; the first is the most excellent, the second is good, the third is useless. Therefore, it follows necessarily that, if Pandolfo was not in the first rank, he was in the second, for whenever one has judgment to know good and bad when it is said and done, although he himself may not have the initiative, yet he can recognize the good and the bad in his servant, and the

20   one he can praise and the other correct; thus the servant cannot hope to deceive him, and is kept honest.

But to enable a prince to form an opinion of his servant there is one test which never fails; when you see the servant thinking more of his own interests than of yours, and seeking inwardly his own profit in everything, such a man

25   will never make a good servant, nor will you ever be able to trust him; because he who has the state of another in his hands ought never to think of himself, but always of his prince, and never pay any attention to matters in which the prince is not concerned.

On the other hand, to keep his servant honest the prince ought to study him,

30   honouring him, enriching him, doing him kindnesses, sharing with him the honours and cares; and at the same time let him see that he cannot stand alone, so that many honours may not make him desire more, many riches make him wish for more, and that many cares may make him dread chances. When, therefore, servants, and princes towards servants, are thus disposed, they can

35   trust each other, but when it is otherwise, the end will always be disastrous for

either one or the other.

CHAPTER XXIII:
How flatterers should be avoided

I do not wish to leave out an important branch of this subject, for it is a danger from which princes are with difficulty preserved, unless they are very
5   careful and discriminating. It is that of flatterers, of whom courts are full, because men are so self-complacent in their own affairs, and in a way so deceived in them, that they are preserved with difficulty from this pest, and if they wish to defend themselves they run the danger of falling into contempt. Because there is no other way of guarding oneself from flatterers except letting
10   men understand that to tell you the truth does not offend you; but when every one may tell you the truth, respect for you abates.

Therefore a wise prince ought to hold a third course by choosing the wise men in his state, and giving to them only the liberty of speaking the truth to him, and then only of those things of which he inquires, and of none others; but he
15   ought to question them upon everything, and listen to their opinions, and afterwards form his own conclusions. With these councillors, separately and collectively, he ought to carry himself in such a way that each of them should know that, the more freely he shall speak, the more he shall be preferred; outside of these, he should listen to no one, pursue the thing resolved on, and be
20   steadfast in his resolutions. He who does otherwise is either overthrown by flatterers, or is so often changed by varying opinions that he falls into contempt.

I wish on this subject to adduce a modern example. Fra Luca, the man of affairs to Maximilian,[43] the present emperor, speaking of his majesty, said: He consulted with no one, yet never got his own way in anything. This arose
25   because of his following a practice the opposite to the above; for the emperor is a secretive man–he does not communicate his designs to any one, nor does he receive opinions on them. But as in carrying them into effect they become revealed and known, they are at once obstructed by those men whom he has around him, and he, being pliant, is diverted from them. Hence it follows that
30   those things he does one day he undoes the next, and no one ever understands what he wishes or intends to do, and no one can rely on his resolutions.

A prince, therefore, ought always to take counsel, but only when he wishes and not when others wish; he ought rather to discourage every one from offering advice unless he asks it; but, however, he ought to be a constant inquirer, and
35   afterwards a patient listener concerning the things of which he inquired; also, on learning that any one, on any consideration, has not told him the truth, he should let his anger be felt.

And if there are some who think that a prince who conveys an impression of his wisdom is not so through his own ability, but through the good advisers that he has around him, beyond doubt they are deceived, because this is an axiom which never fails: that a prince who is not wise himself will never take good
5   advice, unless by chance he has yielded his affairs entirely to one person who happens to be a very prudent man. In this case indeed he may be well governed, but it would not be for long, because such a governor would in a short time take away his state from him.

    But if a prince who is not inexperienced should take counsel from more
10   than one he will never get united counsels, nor will he know how to unite them. Each of the counsellors will think of his own interests, and the prince will not know how to control them or to see through them. And they are not to found otherwise, because men will always prove untrue to you unless they are kept honest by constraint. Therefore it must be inferred that good counsels,
15   whencesoever they come, are born of the wisdom of the prince, and not the wisdom of the prince from good counsels.

CHAPTER XXIV:
Why the princes of Italy have lost their states
    The previous suggestions, carefully observed, will enable a new prince to appear well established, and render him at once more secure and fixed in the state than if he had been long seated there. For the actions of a new prince are
20   more narrowly observed than those of an hereditary one, and when they are seen to be able they gain more men and bind far tighter than ancient blood; because men are attracted more by the present than by the past, and when they find the present good they enjoy it and seek no further; they will also make the utmost defence of a prince if he fails them not in other things. Thus it will be a double
25   glory for him to have established a new principality, and adorned and strengthened it with good laws, good arms, good allies, and with a good example; so will it be a double disgrace to him who, born a prince, shall lose his state by want of wisdom.

    And if those seigniors are considered who have lost their states in Italy in
30   our times, such as the King of Naples, the Duke of Milan, and others, there will be found in them, firstly, one common defect in regard to arms from the causes which have been discussed at length; in the next place, some one of them will be seen, either to have had the people hostile, or if he has had the people friendly, he has not known how to secure the nobles. In the absence of these defects states
35   that have power enough to keep an army in the field cannot be lost.

Philip of Macedon, not the father of Alexander the Great, but he who was conquered by Titus Quintius, had not much territory compared to the greatness of the Romans and of Greece who attacked him, yet being a warlike man who knew how to attract the people and secure the nobles, he sustained the war
5   against his enemies for many years, and if in the end he lost the dominion of some cities, nevertheless he retained the kingdom.

Therefore, do not let our princes accuse fortune for the loss of their principalities after so many years' possession, but rather their own sloth, because in quiet times they never thought there could be a change (it is a
10   common defect in man not to make any provision in the calm against the tempest), and when afterwards the bad times came they thought of flight and not of defending themselves, and they hoped that the people, disgusted with the insolence of the conquerors, would recall them. This course, when others fail, may be good, but it is very bad to have neglected all other expedients for that,
15   since you would never wish to fall because you trusted to be able to find someone later on to restore you. This again either does not happen, or, if it does, it will not be for your security, because that deliverance is of no avail which does not depend upon yourself; those only are reliable, certain, and durable that depend on yourself and your valour.

CHAPTER XXV:
What fortune can effect in human affairs and how to withstand her

20   It is not unknown to me how many men have had, and still have, the opinion that the affairs of the world are in such wise governed by fortune and by God that men with their wisdom cannot direct them and that no one can even help them; and because of this they would have us believe that it is not necessary to labour much in affairs, but to let chance govern them. This opinion
25   has been more credited in our times because of the great changes in affairs which have been seen, and may still be seen, every day, beyond all human conjecture. Sometimes pondering over this, I am in some degree inclined to their opinion. Nevertheless, not to extinguish our free will, I hold it to be true that Fortune is the arbiter of one-half of our actions,[44] but that she still leaves us to
30   direct the other half, or perhaps a little less.

I compare her to one of those raging rivers, which when in flood overflows the plains, sweeping away trees and buildings, bearing away the soil from place to place; everything flies before it, all yield to its violence, without being able in any way to withstand it; and yet, though its nature be such, it does not follow
35   therefore that men, when the weather becomes fair, shall not make provision, both with defences and barriers, in such a manner that, rising again, the waters

may pass away by canal, and their force be neither so unrestrained nor so dangerous. So it happens with fortune, who shows her power where valour has not prepared to resist her, and thither she turns her forces where she knows that barriers and defences have not been raised to constrain her.

5   And if you will consider Italy, which is the seat of these changes, and which has given to them their impulse, you will see it to be an open country without barriers and without any defence. For if it had been defended by proper valour, as are Germany, Spain, and France, either this invasion would not have made the great changes it has made or it would not have come at all. And this I consider

10   enough to say concerning resistance to fortune in general.

    But confining myself more to the particular, I say that a prince may be seen happy to-day and ruined to-morrow without having shown any change of disposition or character. This, I believe, arises firstly from causes that have already been discussed at length, namely, that the prince who relies entirely on

15   fortune is lost when it changes. I believe also that he will be successful who directs his actions according to the spirit of the times, and that he whose actions do not accord with the times will not be successful. Because men are seen, in affairs that lead to the end which every man has before him, namely, glory and riches, to get there by various methods; one with caution, another with haste;

20   one by force, another by skill; one by patience, another by its opposite; and each one succeeds in reaching the goal by a different method. One can also see of two cautious men the one attain his end, the other fail; and similarly, two men by different observances are equally successful, the one being cautious, the other impetuous; all this arises from nothing else than whether or not they conform in

25   their methods to the spirit of the times. This follows from what I have said, that two men working differently bring about the same effect, and of two working similarly, one attains his object and the other does not.

    Changes in estate also issue from this, for if, to one who governs himself with caution and patience, times and affairs converge in such a way that his

30   administration is successful, his fortune is made; but if times and affairs change, he is ruined if he does not change his course of action. But a man is not often found sufficiently circumspect to know how to accommodate himself to the change, both because he cannot deviate from what nature inclines him to do, and also because, having always prospered by acting in one way, he cannot be

35   persuaded that it is well to leave it; and, therefore, the cautious man, when it is time to turn adventurous, does not know how to do it, hence he is ruined; but had he changed his conduct with the times fortune would not have changed.

    Pope Julius the Second went to work impetuously in all his affairs, and found the times and circumstances conform so well to that line of action that he

40   always met with success. Consider his first enterprise against Bologna, Messer

Giovanni Bentivogli being still alive. The Venetians were not agreeable to it, nor was the King of Spain, and he had the enterprise still under discussion with the King of France; nevertheless he personally entered upon the expedition with his accustomed boldness and energy, a move which made Spain and the Venetians
5   stand irresolute and passive, the latter from fear, the former from desire to recover the kingdom of Naples; on the other hand, he drew after him the King of France, because that king, having observed the movement, and desiring to make the Pope his friend so as to humble the Venetians, found it impossible to refuse him. Therefore Julius with his impetuous action accomplished what no other
10   pontiff with simple human wisdom could have done; for if he had waited in Rome until he could get away, with his plans arranged and everything fixed, as any other pontiff would have done, he would never have succeeded. Because the King of France would have made a thousand excuses, and the others would have raised a thousand fears.
15   I will leave his other actions alone, as they were all alike, and they all succeeded, for the shortness of his life did not let him experience the contrary; but if circumstances had arisen which required him to go cautiously, his ruin would have followed, because he would never have deviated from those ways to which nature inclined him.
20   I conclude, therefore that, fortune being changeful and mankind steadfast in their ways, so long as the two are in agreement men are successful, but unsuccessful when they fall out. For my part I consider that it is better to be adventurous than cautious, because fortune is a woman, and if you wish to keep her under it is necessary to beat and ill-use her; and it is seen that she allows
25   herself to be mastered by the adventurous rather than by those who go to work more coldly. She is, therefore, always, woman-like, a lover of young men, because they are less cautious, more violent, and with more audacity command her.

CHAPTER XXVI:
An exhortation to liberate Italy from the barbarians

Having carefully considered the subject of the above discourses, and
30   wondering within myself whether the present times were propitious to a new prince, and whether there were elements that would give an opportunity to a wise and virtuous one to introduce a new order of things which would do honour to him and good to the people of this country, it appears to me that so many things concur to favour a new prince that I never knew a time more fit than the
35   present.

And if, as I said, it was necessary that the people of Israel should be captive so as to make manifest the ability of Moses; that the Persians should be oppressed by the Medes so as to discover the greatness of the soul of Cyrus; and that the Athenians should be dispersed to illustrate the capabilities of Theseus:

5 then at the present time, in order to discover the virtue of an Italian spirit, it was necessary that Italy should be reduced to the extremity that she is now in, that she should be more enslaved than the Hebrews, more oppressed than the Persians, more scattered than the Athenians; without head, without order, beaten, despoiled, torn, overrun; and to have endured every kind of desolation.

10 Although lately some spark may have been shown by one, which made us think he was ordained by God for our redemption, nevertheless it was afterwards seen, in the height of his career, that fortune rejected him; so that Italy, left as without life, waits for him who shall yet heal her wounds and put an end to the ravaging and plundering of Lombardy, to the swindling and taxing of the

15 kingdom and of Tuscany, and cleanse those sores that for long have festered. It is seen how she entreats God to send someone who shall deliver her from these wrongs and barbarous insolencies. It is seen also that she is ready and willing to follow a banner if only someone will raise it.

Nor is there to be seen at present one in whom she can place more hope
20 than in your illustrious house,[45] with its valour and fortune, favoured by God and by the Church of which it is now the chief, and which could be made the head of this redemption. This will not be difficult if you will recall to yourself the actions and lives of the men I have named. And although they were great and wonderful men, yet they were men, and each one of them had no more

25 opportunity than the present offers, for their enterprises were neither more just nor easier than this, nor was God more their friend than He is yours.

With us there is great justice, because that war is just which is necessary, and arms are hallowed when there is no other hope but in them. Here there is the greatest willingness, and where the willingness is great the difficulties cannot be

30 great if you will only follow those men to whom I have directed your attention. Further than this, how extraordinarily the ways of God have been manifested beyond example: the sea is divided, a cloud has led the way, the rock has poured forth water, it has rained manna, everything has contributed to your greatness; you ought to do the rest. God is not willing to do everything, and thus take away

35 our free will and that share of glory which belongs to us.

And it is not to be wondered at if none of the above-named Italians have been able to accomplish all that is expected from your illustrious house; and if in so many revolutions in Italy, and in so many campaigns, it has always appeared as if military virtue were exhausted, this has happened because the old order of

40 things was not good, and none of us have known how to find a new one. And

nothing honours a man more than to establish new laws and new ordinances when he himself was newly risen. Such things when they are well founded and dignified will make him revered and admired, and in Italy there are not wanting opportunities to bring such into use in every form.

5 Here there is great valour in the limbs whilst it fails in the head. Look attentively at the duels and the hand-to-hand combats, how superior the Italians are in strength, dexterity, and subtlety. But when it comes to armies they do not bear comparison, and this springs entirely from the insufficiency of the leaders, since those who are capable are not obedient, and each one seems to himself to

10 know, there having never been any one so distinguished above the rest, either by valour or fortune, that others would yield to him. Hence it is that for so long a time, and during so much fighting in the past twenty years, whenever there has been an army wholly Italian, it has always given a poor account of itself; the first witness to this is Il Taro, afterwards Allesandria, Capua, Genoa, Vaila,

15 Bologna, Mestri.[46]

If, therefore, your illustrious house wishes to follow these remarkable men who have redeemed their country, it is necessary before all things, as a true foundation for every enterprise, to be provided with your own forces, because there can be no more faithful, truer, or better soldiers. And although singly they

20 are good, altogether they will be much better when they find themselves commanded by their prince, honoured by him, and maintained at his expense. Therefore it is necessary to be prepared with such arms, so that you can be defended against foreigners by Italian valour.

And although Swiss and Spanish infantry may be considered very

25 formidable, nevertheless there is a defect in both, by reason of which a third order would not only be able to oppose them, but might be relied upon to overthrow them. For the Spaniards cannot resist cavalry, and the Switzers are afraid of infantry whenever they encounter them in close combat. Owing to this, as has been and may again be seen, the Spaniards are unable to resist French

30 cavalry, and the Switzers are overthrown by Spanish infantry. And although a complete proof of this latter cannot be shown, nevertheless there was some evidence of it at the battle of Ravenna, when the Spanish infantry were confronted by German battalions, who follow the same tactics as the Swiss; when the Spaniards, by agility of body and with the aid of their shields, got in

35 under the pikes of the Germans and stood out of danger, able to attack, while the Germans stood helpless, and, if the cavalry had not dashed up, all would have been over with them. It is possible, therefore, knowing the defects of both these infantries, to invent a new one, which will resist cavalry and not be afraid of infantry; this need not create a new order of arms, but a variation upon the old.

And these are the kind of improvements which confer reputation and power upon a new prince.

This opportunity, therefore, ought not to be allowed to pass for letting Italy at last see her liberator appear. Nor can one express the love with which he
5   would be received in all those provinces which have suffered so much from these foreign scourings, with what thirst for revenge, with what stubborn faith, with what devotion, with what tears. What door would be closed to him? Who would refuse obedience to him? What envy would hinder him? What Italian would refuse him homage? To all of us this barbarous dominion stinks. Let,
10   therefore, your illustrious house take up this charge with that courage and hope with which all just enterprises are undertaken, so that under its standard our native country may be ennobled, and under its auspices may be verified that saying of Petrarch:

Virtu contro al Furore Prendera l'arme, e fia il combatter corto: Che l'antico
15   valore Negli italici cuor non e ancor morto.

Virtue against fury shall advance the fight, And it i' th' combat soon shall put to flight: For the old Roman valour is not dead, Nor in th' Italians' brests extinguished.

Edward Dacre, 1640.

---

[1] Duke Lodovico was Lodovico Moro, a son of Francesco Sforza, who married Beatrice d'Este. He ruled over Milan from 1494 to 1500, and died in 1510.
[2] Louis XII, King of France, "The Father of the People," born 1462, died 1515.
[3] Charles VIII, King of France, born 1470, died 1498.
[4] Louis XII divorced his wife, Jeanne, daughter of Louis XI, and married in 1499 Anne of Brittany, widow of Charles VIII, in order to retain the Duchy of Brittany for the crown.
[5] The Archbishop of Rouen. He was Georges d'Amboise, created a cardinal by Alexander VI. Born 1460, died 1510.
[6] Hiero II, born about 307 B.C., died 216 B.C.
[7] "Le radici e corrispondenze," their roots (i.e. foundations) and correspondencies or relations with other states–a common meaning of "correspondence" and "correspondency" in the sixteenth and seventeenth centuries.
[8] Francesco Sforza, born 1401, died 1466. He married Bianca Maria Visconti, a natural daughter of Filippo Visconti, the Duke of Milan, on whose death he procured his own elevation to the duchy. Machiavelli was the accredited agent of the Florentine Republic to Cesare Borgia (1478- 1507) during the transactions which led up to the assassinations of the Orsini and Vitelli at Sinigalia, and along with his letters to his chiefs in Florence he has left an account, written ten years before "The Prince," of the proceedings of the duke in his "Descritione del modo tenuto dal duca Valentino nello ammazzare Vitellozzo Vitelli," etc., a translation of which is appended to the present work.
[9] Sinigalia, 31st December 1502.
[10] Ramiro d'Orco. Ramiro de Lorqua.
[11] Alexander VI died of fever, 18th August 1503.

[12] Julius II was Giuliano della Rovere, Cardinal of San Pietro ad Vincula, born 1443, died 1513.

[13] San Giorgio is Raffaello Riario. Ascanio is Ascanio Sforza.

[14] Agathocles the Sicilian, born 361 B.C., died 289 B.C.

[15] Mr. Burd suggests that this word probably comes near the modern equivalent of Machiavelli's thought when he speaks of "crudelta" than the more obvious "cruelties."

[16] Nabis, tyrant of Sparta, conquered by the Romans under Flamininus in 195 B.C.; killed 192 B.C.

[17] Messer Giorgio Scali. This event is to be found in Machiavelli's "Florentine History," Book III.

[18] Charles VIII invaded Italy in 1494.

[19] Pope Leo X was the Cardinal de' Medici.

[20] "With chalk in hand," "col gesso." This is one of the *bons mots* of Alexander VI, and refers to the ease with which Charles VIII seized Italy, implying that it was only necessary for him to send his quartermasters to chalk up the billets for his soldiers to conquer the country. Cf. "The History of Henry VII," by Lord Bacon: "King Charles had conquered the realm of Naples, and lost it again, in a kind of a felicity of a dream. He passed the whole length of Italy without resistance: so that it was true what Pope Alexander was wont to say: That the Frenchmen came into Italy with chalk in their hands, to mark up their lodgings, rather than with swords to fight."

[21] Battle of Caravaggio, 15th September 1448.

[22] Johanna II of Naples, the widow of Ladislao, King of Naples.

[23] Giovanni Acuto. An English knight whose name was Sir John Hawkwood. He fought in the English wars in France, and was knighted by Edward III; afterwards he collected a body of troops and went into Italy. These became the famous "White Company." He took part in many wars, and died in Florence in 1394. He was born about 1320 at Sible Hedingham, a village in Essex. He married Domnia, a daughter of Bernabo Visconti.

[24] Carmignuola. Francesco Bussone, born at Carmagnola about 1390, executed at Venice, 5th May 1432.

[25] Bartolomeo Colleoni of Bergamo; died 1457. Roberto of San Severino; died fighting for Venice against Sigismund, Duke of Austria, in 1487. "Primo capitano in Italia."– Machiavelli. Count of Pitigliano; Nicolo Orsini, born 1442, died 1510.

[26] Battle of Vaila in 1509.

[27] Alberigo da Conio. Alberico da Barbiano, Count of Cunio in Romagna. He was the leader of the famous "Company of St George," composed entirely of Italian soldiers. He died in 1409.

[28] Ferdinand V (F. II of Aragon and Sicily, F. III of Naples), surnamed "The Catholic," born 1542, died 1516.

[29] Joannes Cantacuzenus, born 1300, died 1383.

[30] Charles VII of France, surnamed "The Victorious," born 1403, died 1461.

[31] Louis XI, son of the above, born 1423, died 1483.

[32] "Many speakers to the House the other night in the debate on the reduction of armaments seemed to show a most lamentable ignorance of the conditions under which the British Empire maintains its existence. When Mr Balfour replied to the allegations that the Roman Empire sank under the weight of its military obligations, he said that this was 'wholly unhistorical.' He might well have added that the Roman power was at its zenith when every citizen acknowledged his liability to fight for the State, but that it

began to decline as soon as this obligation was no longer recognized."–Pall Mall Gazette, 15th May 1906.

[33] Philopoemen, "the last of the Greeks," born 252 B.C., died 183 B.C.

[34] During the rioting between the Cancellieri and Panciatichi factions in 1502 and 1503.

[35] . . . against my will, my fate A throne unsettled, and an infant state, Bid me defend my realms with all my pow'rs, And guard with these severities my shores.

[36] "Contesting," i.e. "striving for mastery." Mr Burd points out that this passage is imitated directly from Cicero's "De Officiis": "Nam cum sint duo genera decertandi, unum per disceptationem, alterum per vim; cumque illud proprium sit hominis, hoc beluarum; confugiendum est ad posterius, si uti non licet superiore."

[37] "Nondimanco sempre gli succederono gli inganni (ad votum)." The words "ad votum" are omitted in the Testina addition, 1550. Alexander never did what he said, Cesare never said what he did. (Italian Proverb)

[38] "Contrary to fidelity" or "faith," "contro alla fede," and "tutto fede," "altogether faithful," in the next paragraph. It is noteworthy that these two phrases, "contro alla fede" and "tutto fede," were omitted in the Testina edition, which was published with the sanction of the papal authorities. It may be that the meaning attached to the word "fede" was "the faith," i.e. the Catholic creed, and not as rendered here "fidelity" and "faithful." Observe that the word "religione" was suffered to stand in the text of the Testina, being used to signify indifferently every shade of belief, as witness "the religion," a phrase inevitably employed to designate the Huguenot heresy. South in his Sermon IX, p. 69, ed. 1843, comments on this passage as follows: "That great patron and Coryphaeus of this tribe, Nicolo Machiavel, laid down this for a master rule in his political scheme: 'That the show of religion was helpful to the politician, but the reality of it hurtful and pernicious.'"

[39] Ferdinand of Aragon. "When Machiavelli was writing 'The Prince' it would have been clearly impossible to mention Ferdinand's name here without giving offence." Burd's "Il Principe," p. 308.

[40] Giovanni Bentivogli, born in Bologna 1438, died at Milan 1508. He ruled Bologna from 1462 to 1506. Machiavelli's strong condemnation of conspiracies may get its edge from his own very recent experience (February 1513), when he had been arrested and tortured for his alleged complicity in the Boscoli conspiracy.

[41] Catherine Sforza, a daughter of Galeazzo Sforza and Lucrezia Landriani, born 1463, died 1509. It was to the Countess of Forli that Machiavelli was sent as envy on 1499. A letter from Fortunati to the countess announces the appointment: "I have been with the signori," wrote Fortunati, "to learn whom they would send and when. They tell me that Nicolo Machiavelli, a learned young Florentine noble, secretary to my Lords of the Ten, is to leave with me at once." Cf. "Catherine Sforza," by Count Pasolini, translated by P. Sylvester, 1898.

[42] "Guilds or societies," "in arti o in tribu." "Arti" were craft or trade guilds, cf. Florio: "Arte . . . a whole company of any trade in any city or corporation town." The guilds of Florence are most admirably described by Mr Edgcumbe Staley in his work on the subject (Methuen, 1906). Institutions of a somewhat similar character, called "artel," exist in Russia to-day, cf. Sir Mackenzie Wallace's "Russia," ed. 1905: "The sons . . . were always during the working season members of an artel. In some of the larger towns there are artels of a much more complex kind– permanent associations, possessing large capital, and pecuniarily responsible for the acts of the individual members." The word "artel," despite its apparent similarity, has, Mr Aylmer Maude assures me, no connection

with "ars" or "arte." Its root is that of the verb "rotisya," to bind oneself by an oath; and it is generally admitted to be only another form of "rota," which now signifies a "regimental company." In both words the underlying idea is that of a body of men united by an oath. "Tribu" were possibly gentile groups, united by common descent, and included individuals connected by marriage. Perhaps our words "sects" or "clans" would be most appropriate.

[43] Maximilian I, born in 1459, died 1519, Emperor of the Holy Roman Empire. He married, first, Mary, daughter of Charles the Bold; after her death, Bianca Sforza; and thus became involved in Italian politics.

[44] Frederick the Great was accustomed to say: "The older one gets the more convinced one becomes that his Majesty King Chance does three-quarters of the business of this miserable universe." Sorel's "Eastern Question."

[45] Giuliano de Medici. He had just been created a cardinal by Leo X. In 1523 Giuliano was elected Pope, and took the title of Clement VII.

[46] The battles of Il Taro, 1495; Alessandria, 1499; Capua, 1501; Genoa, 1507; Vaila, 1509; Bologna, 1511; Mestri, 1513.

Thomas Hobbes

Thomas Hobbes (b. 1588, Malmesbury, d. 1679, Derbyshire) was an English philosopher. Following his education at Oxford, he entered the household of William Cavendish (later Earl of Devonshire) and became a tutor and secretary to successive generations of Devonshire heirs, and later, through the Devonshire connections, a tutor to the future king Charles II. Hobbes spent the Civil War in exile in France, returning to England after quarrelling with other royalist exiles following the publication of *Leviathan* in 1651. Hobbes spent the rest of his life in and out of controversies concerning geometry, physics, the role (and lack thereof) of God in his philosophical works, determinism, and other topics.

Hobbes' principal political and philosophical works include *De Cive*, *De Corpore*, and *Leviathan*.

Along with Hugo Grotius and Samuel Pufendorf, Hobbes is considered to be one of the founders of the social contractarian tradition in political thought, and as such, has had a profound influence on the development of modern theories of state and legal authority.

Thomas Hobbes
LEVIATHAN
(1651)

*****

CHAPTER X.
Of power, worth, dignity, honour, and worthiness

THE POWER of a man, to take it universally, is his present means to obtain
some future apparent good, and is either original or instrumental.

Natural power is the eminence of the faculties of body, or mind; as
extraordinary strength, form, prudence, arts, eloquence, liberality, nobility.
5   Instrumental are those powers which, acquired by these, or by fortune, are
means and instruments to acquire more; as riches, reputation, friends, and the
secret working of God, which men call good luck. For the nature of power is, in
this point, like to fame, increasing as it proceeds; or like the motion of heavy
bodies, which, the further they go, make still the more haste.
10   The greatest of human powers is that which is compounded of the powers of
most men, united by consent, in one person, natural or civil, that has the use of
all their powers depending on his will; such as is the power of a Commonwealth:
or depending on the wills of each particular; such as is the power of a faction, or
of diverse. factions leagued. Therefore to have servants is power; to have friends
15   is power: for they are strengths united.

Also, riches joined with liberality is power; because it procureth friends and
servants: without liberality, not so; because in this case they defend not, but
expose men to envy, as a prey.

Reputation of power is power; because it draweth with it the adherence of
20   those that need protection.

So is reputation of love of a man's country, called popularity, for the same
reason.

Also, what quality soever maketh a man beloved or feared of many, or the
reputation of such quality, is power; because it is a means to have the assistance
25   and service of many.

Good success is power; because it maketh reputation of wisdom or good
fortune, which makes men either fear him or rely on him.

Affability of men already in power is increase of power; because it gaineth
love.

Reputation of prudence in the conduct of peace or war is power; because to prudent men we commit the government of ourselves more willingly than to others.

Nobility is power, not in all places, but only in those Commonwealths
5   where it has privileges; for in such privileges consisteth their power.

Eloquence is power; because it is seeming prudence.

Form is power; because being a promise of good, it recommendeth men to the favour of women and strangers.

The sciences are small powers; because not eminent, and therefore, not
10 acknowledged in any man; nor are at all, but in a few, and in them, but of a few things. For science is of that nature, as none can understand it to be, but such as in a good measure have attained it.

Arts of public use, as fortification, making of engines, and other instruments of war, because they confer to defence and victory, are power; and though the
15 true mother of them be science, namely, the mathematics yet, because they are brought into the light by the hand of the artificer, they be esteemed (the midwife passing with the vulgar for the mother) as his issue.

The value or worth of a man is, as of all other things, his price; that is to say, so much as would be given for the use of his power, and therefore is not
20 absolute, but a thing dependent on the need and judgement of another. An able conductor of soldiers is of great price in time of war present or imminent, but in peace not so. A learned and uncorrupt judge is much worth in time of peace, but not so much in war. And as in other things, so in men, not the seller, but the buyer determines the price. For let a man, as most men do, rate themselves at the
25 highest value they can, yet their true value is no more than it is esteemed by others.

The manifestation of the value we set on one another is that which is commonly called honouring and dishonouring. To value a man at a high rate is to honour him; at a low rate is to dishonour him. But high and low, in this case,
30 is to be understood by comparison to the rate that each man setteth on himself.

The public worth of a man, which is the value set on him by the Commonwealth, is that which men commonly call dignity. And this value of him by the Commonwealth is understood by offices of command, judicature, public employment; or by names and titles introduced for distinction of such
35 value.

To pray to another for aid of any kind is to honour; because a sign we have an opinion he has power to help; and the more difficult the aid is, the more is the honour.

To obey s to honour; because no man obeys them who they think have no
40 power to help or hurt them. And consequently to disobey is to dishonour.

To give great gifts to a man is to honour him; because it is buying of protection, and acknowledging of power. To give little gifts is to dishonour; because it is but alms, and signifies an opinion of the need of small helps.

To be sedulous in promoting another's good, also to flatter, is to honour; as a sign we seek his protection or aid. To neglect is to dishonour.

To give way or place to another, in any commodity, is to honour; being a confession of greater power. To arrogate is to dishonour.

To show any sign of love or fear of another is honour; for both to love and to fear is to value. To contemn, or less to love or fear than he expects, is to dishonour; for it is undervaluing.

To praise, magnify, or call happy is to honour; because nothing but goodness, power, and felicity is valued. To revile, mock, or pity is to dishonour.

To speak to another with consideration, to appear before him with decency and humility, is to honour him; as signs of fear to offend. To speak to him rashly, to do anything before him obscenely, slovenly, impudently is to dishonour.

To believe, to trust, to rely on another, is to honour him; sign of opinion of his virtue and power. To distrust, or not believe, is to dishonour.

To hearken to a man's counsel, or discourse of what kind soever, is to honour; as a sign we think him wise, or eloquent, or witty. To sleep, or go forth, or talk the while, is to dishonour.

To do those things to another which he takes for signs of honour, or which the law or custom makes so, is to honour; because in approving the honour done by others, he acknowledgeth the power which others acknowledge. To refuse to do them is to dishonour.

To agree with in opinion is to honour; as being a sign of approving his judgement and wisdom. To dissent is dishonour, and an upbraiding of error, and, if the dissent be in many things, of folly.

To imitate is to honour; for it is vehemently to approve. To imitate one's enemy is to dishonour.

To honour those another honours is to honour him; as a sign of approbation of his judgement. To honour his enemies is to dishonour him.

To employ in counsel, or in actions of difficulty, is to honour; as a sign of opinion of his wisdom or other power. To deny employment in the same cases to those that seek it is to dishonour.

All these ways of honouring are natural, and as well within, as without Commonwealths. But in Commonwealths where he or they that have the supreme authority can make whatsoever they please to stand for signs of honour, there be other honours.

A sovereign doth honour a subject with whatsoever title, or office, or employment, or action that he himself will have taken for a sign of his will to honour him.

The king of Persia honoured Mordecai when he appointed he should be
5 conducted through the streets in the king's garment, upon one of the king's horses, with a crown on his head, and a prince before him, proclaiming, "Thus shall it be done to him that the king will honour." And yet another king of Persia, or the same another time, to one that demanded for some great service to wear one of the king's robes, gave him leave so to do; but with this addition, that
10 he should wear it as the king's fool; and then it was dishonour. So that of civil honour, the fountain is in the person of the Commonwealth, and dependeth on the will of the sovereign, and is therefore temporary and called civil honour; such as are magistracy, offices, titles, and in some places coats and scutcheons painted: and men honour such as have them, as having so many signs of favour
15 in the Commonwealth, which favour is power.

Honourable is whatsoever possession, action, or quality is an argument and sign of power.

And therefore to be honoured, loved, or feared of many is honourable, as arguments of power. To be honoured of few or none, dishonourable.
20 Dominion and victory is honourable because acquired by power; and servitude, for need or fear, is dishonourable.

Good fortune, if lasting, honourable; as a sign of the favour of God. Ill and losses, dishonourable. Riches are honourable, for they are power. Poverty, dishonourable. Magnanimity, liberality, hope, courage, confidence, are
25 honourable; for they proceed from the conscience of power. Pusillanimity, parsimony, fear, diffidence, are dishonourable.

Timely resolution, or determination of what a man is to do, is honourable, as being the contempt of small difficulties and dangers. And irresolution, dishonourable, as a sign of too much valuing of little impediments and little
30 advantages: for when a man has weighed things as long as the time permits, and resolves not, the difference of weight is but little; and therefore if he resolve not, he overvalues little things, which is pusillanimity.

All actions and speeches that proceed, or seem to proceed, from much experience, science, discretion, or wit are honourable; for all these are powers.
35 Actions or words that proceed from error, ignorance, or folly, dishonourable.

Gravity, as far forth as it seems to proceed from a mind employed on something else, is honourable; because employment is a sign of power. But if it seem to proceed from a purpose to appear grave, it is dishonourable. For the gravity of the former is like the steadiness of a ship laden with merchandise; but
40 of the like the steadiness of a ship ballasted with sand and other trash.

To be conspicuous, that is to say, to be known, for wealth, office, great actions, or any eminent good is honourable; as a sign of the power for which he is conspicuous. On the contrary, obscurity is dishonourable.

To be descended from conspicuous parents is honourable; because they the more easily attain the aids and friends of their ancestors. On the contrary, to be descended from obscure parentage is dishonourable.

Actions proceeding from equity, joined with loss, are honourable; as signs of magnanimity: for magnanimity is a sign of power. On the contrary, craft, shifting, neglect of equity, is dishonourable.

Covetousness of great riches, and ambition of great honours, are honourable; as signs of power to obtain them. Covetousness, and ambition of little gains, or preferments, is dishonourable.

Nor does it alter the case of honour whether an action (so it be great and difficult, and consequently a sign of much power) be just or unjust: for honour consisteth only in the opinion of power. Therefore, the ancient heathen did not think they dishonoured, but greatly honoured the gods, when they introduced them in their poems committing rapes, thefts, and other great, but unjust or unclean acts; in so much as nothing is so much celebrated in Jupiter as his adulteries; nor in Mercury as his frauds and thefts; of whose praises, in a hymn of Homer, the greatest is this, that being born in the morning, he had invented music at noon, and before night stolen away the cattle of Apollo from his herdsmen.

Also amongst men, till there were constituted great Commonwealths, it was thought no dishonour to be a pirate, or a highway thief; but rather a lawful trade, not only amongst the Greeks, but also amongst all other nations; as is manifest by the of ancient time. And at this day, in this part of the world, private duels are, and always will be, honourable, though unlawful, till such time as there shall be honour ordained for them that refuse, and ignominy for them that make the challenge. For duels also are many times effects of courage, and the ground of courage is always strength or skill, which are power; though for the most part they be effects of rash speaking, and of the fear of dishonour, in one or both the combatants; who, engaged by rashness, are driven into the lists to avoid disgrace.

Scutcheons and coats of arms hereditary, where they have any their any eminent privileges, are honourable; otherwise not for their power consisteth either in such privileges, or in riches, or some such thing as is equally honoured in other men. This kind of honour, commonly called gentry, has been derived from the ancient Germans. For there never was any such thing known where the German customs were unknown. Nor is it now anywhere in use where the Germans have not inhabited. The ancient Greek commanders, when they went to

war, had their shields painted with such devices as they pleased; insomuch as an
unpainted buckler was a sign of poverty, and of a common soldier; but they
transmitted not the inheritance of them. The Romans transmitted the marks of
their families; but they were the images, not the devices of their ancestors.

5   Amongst the people of Asia, Africa, and America, there is not, nor was ever,
any such thing. Germans only had that custom; from whom it has been derived
into England, France, Spain and Italy, when in great numbers they either aided
the Romans or made their own conquests in these western parts of the world.

For Germany, being anciently, as all other countries in their beginnings,
10 divided amongst an infinite number of little lords, or masters of families, that
continually had wars one with another, those masters, or lords, principally to the
end they might, when they were covered with arms, be known by their
followers, and partly for ornament, both painted their armor, or their scutcheon,
or coat, with the picture of some beast, or other thing, and also put some eminent
15 and visible mark upon the crest of their helmets. And this ornament both of the
arms and crest descended by inheritance to their children; to the eldest pure, and
to the rest with some note of diversity, such as the old master, that is to say in
Dutch, the Here-alt, thought fit. But when many such families, joined together,
made a greater monarchy, this duty of the herald to distinguish scutcheons was
20 made a private office apart. And the issue of these lords is the great and ancient
gentry; which for the most part bear living creatures noted for courage and
rapine; or castles, battlements, belts, weapons, bars, palisades, and other notes of
war; nothing being then in honour, but virtue military. Afterwards, not only
kings, but popular Commonwealths, gave diverse manners of scutcheons to such
25 as went forth to the war, or returned from it, for encouragement or recompense
to their service. All which, by an observing reader, may be found in such ancient
histories, Greek and Latin, as make mention of the German nation and manners
in their times.

Titles of honour, such as are duke, count, marquis, and baron, are
30 honourable; as signifying the value set upon them by the sovereign power of the
Commonwealth: which titles were in old time titles of office and command
derived some from the Romans, some from the Germans and French. Dukes, in
Latin, duces, being generals in war; counts, comites, such as bore the general
company out of friendship, and were left to govern and defend places conquered
35 and pacified; marquises, marchioness, were counts that governed the marches,
or bounds of the Empire. Which titles of duke, count, and marquis came into the
Empire about the time of Constantine the Great, from the customs of the
German militia. But baron seems to have been a title of the Gauls, and signifies
a great man; such as were the kings' or princes' men whom they employed in
40 war about their persons; and seems to be derived from vir, to ber, and bar, that

signified the same in the language of the Gauls, that vir in Latin; and thence to bero and baro: so that such men were called berones, and after barones; and (in Spanish) varones. But he that would know more, particularly the original of titles of honour, may find it, as I have done this, in Mr. Selden's most excellent
5   treatise of that subject. In process of time these offices of honour, by occasion of trouble, and for reasons of good and peaceable government, were turned into mere titles, serving, for the most part, to distinguish the precedence, place, and order of subjects in the Commonwealth: and men were made dukes, counts, marquises, and barons of places, wherein they had neither possession nor
10   command, and other titles also were devised to the same end.

Worthiness is a thing different from the worth or value of a man, and also from his merit or desert, and consisteth in a particular power or ability for that whereof he is said to be worthy; which particular ability is usually named fitness, or aptitude.
15   For he is worthiest to be a commander, to be a judge, or to have any other charge, that is best fitted with the qualities required to the well discharging of it; and worthiest of riches, that has the qualities most requisite for the well using of them: any of which qualities being absent, one may nevertheless be a worthy man, and valuable for something else. Again, a man may be worthy of riches,
20   office, and employment that nevertheless can plead no right to have it before another, and therefore cannot be said to merit or deserve it. For merit presupposeth a right, and that the thing deserved is due by promise, of which I shall say more hereafter when I shall speak of contracts.

****

CHAPTER XIII.
Of the natural condition of mandkind as concerning their felicity and misery

NATURE hath made men so equal in the faculties of body and mind as that,
25   though there be found one man sometimes manifestly stronger in body or of quicker mind than another, yet when all is reckoned together the difference between man and man is not so considerable as that one man can thereupon claim to himself any benefit to which another may not pretend as well as he. For as to the strength of body, the weakest has strength enough to kill the strongest,
30   either by secret machination or by confederacy with others that are in the same danger with himself.

And as to the faculties of the mind, setting aside the arts grounded upon words, and especially that skill of proceeding upon general and infallible rules, called science, which very few have and but in few things, as being not a native

faculty born with us, nor attained, as prudence, while we look after somewhat else, I find yet a greater equality amongst men than that of strength. For prudence is but experience, which equal time equally bestows on all men in those things they equally apply themselves unto. That which may perhaps make
5   such equality incredible is but a vain conceit of one's own wisdom, which almost all men think they have in a greater degree than the vulgar; that is, than all men but themselves, and a few others, whom by fame, or for concurring with themselves, they approve. For such is the nature of men that howsoever they may acknowledge many others to be more witty, or more eloquent or more
10 learned, yet they will hardly believe there be many so wise as themselves; for they see their own wit at hand, and other men's at a distance. But this proveth rather that men are in that point equal, than unequal. For there is not ordinarily a greater sign of the equal distribution of anything than that every man is contented with his share.

15   From this equality of ability ariseth equality of hope in the attaining of our ends. And therefore if any two men desire the same thing, which nevertheless they cannot both enjoy, they become enemies; and in the way to their end (which is principally their own conservation, and sometimes their delectation only) endeavour to destroy or subdue one another. And from hence it comes to
20 pass that where an invader hath no more to fear than another man's single power, if one plant, sow, build, or possess a convenient seat, others may probably be expected to come prepared with forces united to dispossess and deprive him, not only of the fruit of his labour, but also of his life or liberty. And the invader again is in the like danger of another.

25   And from this diffidence of one another, there is no way for any man to secure himself so reasonable as anticipation; that is, by force, or wiles, to master the persons of all men he can so long till he see no other power great enough to endanger him: and this is no more than his own conservation requireth, and is generally allowed. Also, because there be some that, taking pleasure in
30 contemplating their own power in the acts of conquest, which they pursue farther than their security requires, if others, that otherwise would be glad to be at ease within modest bounds, should not by invasion increase their power, they would not be able, long time, by standing only on their defence, to subsist. And by consequence, such augmentation of dominion over men being necessary to a
35 man's conservation, it ought to be allowed him.

        Again, men have no pleasure (but on the contrary a great deal of grief) in keeping company where there is no power able to overawe them all. For every man looketh that his companion should value him at the same rate he sets upon himself, and upon all signs of contempt or undervaluing naturally endeavours, as
40 far as he dares (which amongst them that have no common power to keep them

in quiet is far enough to make them destroy each other), to extort a greater value from his contemners, by damage; and from others, by the example.

So that in the nature of man, we find three principal causes of quarrel. First, competition; secondly, diffidence; thirdly, glory.

5   The first maketh men invade for gain; the second, for safety; and the third, for reputation. The first use violence, to make themselves masters of other men's persons, wives, children, and cattle; the second, to defend them; the third, for trifles, as a word, a smile, a different opinion, and any other sign of undervalue, either direct in their persons or by reflection in their kindred, their friends, their
10 nation, their profession, or their name.

Hereby it is manifest that during the time men live without a common power to keep them all in awe, they are in that condition which is called war; and such a war as is of every man against every man. For war consisteth not in battle only, or the act of fighting, but in a tract of time, wherein the will to
15 contend by battle is sufficiently known: and therefore the notion of time is to be considered in the nature of war, as it is in the nature of weather. For as the nature of foul weather lieth not in a shower or two of rain, but in an inclination thereto of many days together: so the nature of war consisteth not in actual fighting, but in the known disposition thereto during all the time there is no
20 assurance to the contrary. All other time is peace.

Whatsoever therefore is consequent to a time of war, where every man is enemy to every man, the same consequent to the time wherein men live without other security than what their own strength and their own invention shall furnish them withal. In such condition there is no place for industry, because the fruit
25 thereof is uncertain: and consequently no culture of the earth; no navigation, nor use of the commodities that may be imported by sea; no commodious building; no instruments of moving and removing such things as require much force; no knowledge of the face of the earth; no account of time; no arts; no letters; no society; and which is worst of all, continual fear, and danger of violent death;
30 and the life of man, solitary, poor, nasty, brutish, and short.

It may seem strange to some man that has not well weighed these things that Nature should thus dissociate and render men apt to invade and destroy one another: and he may therefore, not trusting to this inference, made from the passions, desire perhaps to have the same confirmed by experience. Let him
35 therefore consider with himself: when taking a journey, he arms himself and seeks to go well accompanied; when going to sleep, he locks his doors; when even in his house he locks his chests; and this when he knows there be laws and public officers, armed, to revenge all injuries shall be done him; what opinion he has of his fellow subjects, when he rides armed; of his fellow citizens, when he
40 locks his doors; and of his children, and servants, when he locks his chests. Does

he not there as much accuse mankind by his actions as I do by my words? But neither of us accuse man's nature in it. The desires, and other passions of man, are in themselves no sin. No more are the actions that proceed from those passions till they know a law that forbids them; which till laws be made they
5 cannot know, nor can any law be made till they have agreed upon the person that shall make it.

It may peradventure be thought there was never such a time nor condition of war as this; and I believe it was never generally so, over all the world: but there are many places where they live so now. For the savage people in many places
10 of America, except the government of small families, the concord whereof dependeth on natural lust, have no government at all, and live at this day in that brutish manner, as I said before. Howsoever, it may be perceived what manner of life there would be, where there were no common power to fear, by the manner of life which men that have formerly lived under a peaceful government
15 use to degenerate into a civil war.

But though there had never been any time wherein particular men were in a condition of war one against another, yet in all times kings and persons of sovereign authority, because of their independency, are in continual jealousies, and in the state and posture of gladiators, having their weapons pointing, and
20 their eyes fixed on one another; that is, their forts, garrisons, and guns upon the frontiers of their kingdoms, and continual spies upon their neighbours, which is a posture of war. But because they uphold thereby the industry of their subjects, there does not follow from it that misery which accompanies the liberty of particular men.

25 To this war of every man against every man, this also is consequent; that nothing can be unjust. The notions of right and wrong, justice and injustice, have there no place. Where there is no common power, there is no law; where no law, no injustice. Force and fraud are in war the two cardinal virtues. Justice and injustice are none of the faculties neither of the body nor mind. If they were,
30 they might be in a man that were alone in the world, as well as his senses and passions. They are qualities that relate to men in society, not in solitude. It is consequent also to the same condition that there be no propriety, no dominion, no mine and thine distinct; but only that to be every man's that he can get, and for so long as he can keep it. And thus much for the ill condition which man by
35 mere nature is actually placed in; though with a possibility to come out of it, consisting partly in the passions, partly in his reason.

The passions that incline men to peace are: fear of death; desire of such things as are necessary to commodious living; and a hope by their industry to obtain them. And reason suggesteth convenient articles of peace upon which
40 men may be drawn to agreement. These articles are they which otherwise are

called the laws of nature, whereof I shall speak more particularly in the two
following chapters.

CHAPTER XIV.
Of the first and second natural laws, and of contracts

THE right of nature, which writers commonly call jus naturale, is the liberty
each man hath to use his own power as he will himself for the preservation of
5   his own nature; that is to say, of his own life; and consequently, of doing
anything which, in his own judgement and reason, he shall conceive to be the
aptest means thereunto.

By liberty is understood, according to the proper signification of the word,
the absence of external impediments; which impediments may oft take away
10   part of a man's power to do what he would, but cannot hinder him from using
the power left him according as his judgement and reason shall dictate to him.

A law of nature, lex naturalis, is a precept, or general rule, found out by
reason, by which a man is forbidden to do that which is destructive of his life, or
taketh away the means of preserving the same, and to omit that by which he
15   thinketh it may be best preserved. For though they that speak of this subject use
to confound jus and lex, right and law, yet they ought to be distinguished,
because right consisteth in liberty to do, or to forbear; whereas law determineth
and bindeth to one of them: so that law and right differ as much as obligation
and liberty, which in one and the same matter are inconsistent.

20   And because the condition of man (as hath been declared in the precedent
chapter) is a condition of war of every one against every one, in which case
every one is governed by his own reason, and there is nothing he can make use
of that may not be a help unto him in preserving his life against his enemies; it
followeth that in such a condition every man has a right to every thing, even to
25   one another's body. And therefore, as long as this natural right of every man to
every thing endureth, there can be no security to any man, how strong or wise
soever he be, of living out the time which nature ordinarily alloweth men to live.
And consequently it is a precept, or general rule of reason: that every man ought
to endeavour peace, as far as he has hope of obtaining it; and when he cannot
30   obtain it, that he may seek and use all helps and advantages of war. The first
branch of which rule containeth the first and fundamental law of nature, which
is: to seek peace and follow it. The second, the sum of the right of nature, which
is: by all means we can to defend ourselves.

From this fundamental law of nature, by which men are commanded to
35   endeavour peace, is derived this second law: that a man be willing, when others
are so too, as far forth as for peace and defence of himself he shall think it

necessary, to lay down this right to all things; and be contented with so much liberty against other men as he would allow other men against himself. For as long as every man holdeth this right, of doing anything he liketh; so long are all men in the condition of war. But if other men will not lay down their right, as

5 well as he, then there is no reason for anyone to divest himself of his: for that were to expose himself to prey, which no man is bound to, rather than to dispose himself to peace. This is that law of the gospel: Whatsoever you require that others should do to you, that do ye to them. And that law of all men, quod tibi fieri non vis, alteri ne feceris.

10 To lay down a man's right to anything is to divest himself of the liberty of hindering another of the benefit of his own right to the same. For he that renounceth or passeth away his right giveth not to any other man a right which he had not before, because there is nothing to which every man had not right by nature, but only standeth out of his way that he may enjoy his own original right

15 without hindrance from him, not without hindrance from another. So that the effect which redoundeth to one man by another man's defect of right is but so much diminution of impediments to the use of his own right original.

Right is laid aside, either by simply renouncing it, or by transferring it to another. By simply renouncing, when he cares not to whom the benefit thereof

20 redoundeth. By transferring, when he intendeth the benefit thereof to some certain person or persons. And when a man hath in either manner abandoned or granted away his right, then is he said to be obliged, or bound, not to hinder those to whom such right is granted, or abandoned, from the benefit of it: and that he ought, and it is duty, not to make void that voluntary act of his own: and

25 that such hindrance is injustice, and injury, as being sine jure; the right being before renounced or transferred. So that injury or injustice, in the controversies of the world, is somewhat like to that which in the disputations of scholars is called absurdity. For as it is there called an absurdity to contradict what one maintained in the beginning; so in the world it is called injustice, and injury

30 voluntarily to undo that which from the beginning he had voluntarily done. The way by which a man either simply renounceth or transferreth his right is a declaration, or signification, by some voluntary and sufficient sign, or signs, that he doth so renounce or transfer, or hath so renounced or transferred the same, to him that accepteth it. And these signs are either words only, or actions only; or,

35 as it happeneth most often, both words and actions. And the same are the bonds, by which men are bound and obliged: bonds that have their strength, not from their own nature (for nothing is more easily broken than a man's word), but from fear of some evil consequence upon the rupture.

Whensoever a man transferreth his right, or renounceth it, it is either in

40 consideration of some right reciprocally transferred to himself, or for some other

good he hopeth for thereby. For it is a voluntary act: and of the voluntary acts of every man, the object is some good to himself. And therefore there be some rights which no man can be understood by any words, or other signs, to have abandoned or transferred. As first a man cannot lay down the right of resisting
5 them that assault him by force to take away his life, because he cannot be understood to aim thereby at any good to himself. The same may be said of wounds, and chains, and imprisonment, both because there is no benefit consequent to such patience, as there is to the patience of suffering another to be wounded or imprisoned, as also because a man cannot tell when he seeth men
10 proceed against him by violence whether they intend his death or not. And lastly the motive and end for which this renouncing and transferring of right is introduced is nothing else but the security of a man's person, in his life, and in the means of so preserving life as not to be weary of it. And therefore if a man by words, or other signs, seem to despoil himself of the end for which those
15 signs were intended, he is not to be understood as if he meant it, or that it was his will, but that he was ignorant of how such words and actions were to be interpreted.

The mutual transferring of right is that which men call contract.

There is difference between transferring of right to the thing, the thing, and
20 transferring or tradition, that is, delivery of the thing itself. For the thing may be delivered together with the translation of the right, as in buying and selling with ready money, or exchange of goods or lands, and it may be delivered some time after.

Again, one of the contractors may deliver the thing contracted for on his
25 part, and leave the other to perform his part at some determinate time after, and in the meantime be trusted; and then the contract on his part is called pact, or covenant: or both parts may contract now to perform hereafter, in which cases he that is to perform in time to come, being trusted, his performance is called keeping of promise, or faith, and the failing of performance, if it be voluntary,
30 violation of faith.

When the transferring of right is not mutual, but one of the parties transferreth in hope to gain thereby friendship or service from another, or from his friends; or in hope to gain the reputation of charity, or magnanimity; or to deliver his mind from the pain of compassion; or in hope of reward in heaven;
35 this is not contract, but gift, free gift, grace: which words signify one and the same thing.

Signs of contract are either express or by inference. Express are words spoken with understanding of what they signify: and such words are either of the time present or past; as, I give, I grant, I have given, I have granted, I will that

178

this be yours: or of the future; as, I will give, I will grant, which words of the
future are called promise.

Signs by inference are sometimes the consequence of words; sometimes the
consequence of silence; sometimes the consequence of actions; sometimes the
5   consequence of forbearing an action: and generally a sign by inference, of any
contract, is whatsoever sufficiently argues the will of the contractor.

Words alone, if they be of the time to come, and contain a bare promise, are
an insufficient sign of a free gift and therefore not obligatory. For if they be of
the time to come, as, tomorrow I will give, they are a sign I have not given yet,
10   and consequently that my right is not transferred, but remaineth till I transfer it
by some other act. But if the words be of the time present, or past, as, I have
given, or do give to be delivered tomorrow, then is my tomorrow's right given
away today; and that by the virtue of the words, though there were no other
argument of my will. And there is a great difference in the signification of these
15   words, volo hoc tuum esse cras, and cras dabo; that is, between I will that this be
thine tomorrow, and, I will give it thee tomorrow: for the word I will, in the
former manner of speech, signifies an act of the will present; but in the latter, it
signifies a promise of an act of the will to come: and therefore the former words,
being of the present, transfer a future right; the latter, that be of the future,
20   transfer nothing. But if there be other signs of the will to transfer a right besides
words; then, though the gift be free, yet may the right be understood to pass by
words of the future: as if a man propound a prize to him that comes first to the
end of a race, the gift is free; and though the words be of the future, yet the right
passeth: for if he would not have his words so be understood, he should not have
25   let them run.

In contracts the right passeth, not only where the words are of the time
present or past, but also where they are of the future, because all contract is
mutual translation, or change of right; and therefore he that promiseth only,
because he hath already received the benefit for which he promiseth, is to be
30   understood as if he intended the right should pass: for unless he had been
content to have his words so understood, the other would not have performed his
part first. And for that cause, in buying, and selling, and other acts of contract, a
promise is equivalent to a covenant, and therefore obligatory.

He that performeth first in the case of a contract is said to merit that which
35   he is to receive by the performance of the other, and he hath it as due. Also
when a prize is propounded to many, which is to be given to him only that
winneth, or money is thrown amongst many to be enjoyed by them that catch it;
though this be a free gift, yet so to win, or so to catch, is to merit, and to have it
as due. For the right is transferred in the propounding of the prize, and in
40   throwing down the money, though it be not determined to whom, but by the

event of the contention. But there is between these two sorts of merit this difference, that in contract I merit by virtue of my own power and the contractor's need, but in this case of free gift I am enabled to merit only by the benignity of the giver: in contract I merit at the contractor's hand that he should depart with his right; in this case of gift, I merit not that the giver should part with his right, but that when he has parted with it, it should be mine rather than another's. And this I think to be the meaning of that distinction of the Schools between meritum congrui and meritum condigni. For God Almighty, having promised paradise to those men, hoodwinked with carnal desires, that can walk through this world according to the precepts and limits prescribed by him, they say he that shall so walk shall merit paradise ex congruo. But because no man can demand a right to it by his own righteousness, or any other power in himself, but by the free grace of God only, they say no man can merit paradise ex condigno. This, I say, I think is the meaning of that distinction; but because disputers do not agree upon the signification of their own terms of art longer than it serves their turn, I will not affirm anything of their meaning: only this I say; when a gift is given indefinitely, as a prize to be contended for, he that winneth meriteth, and may claim the prize as due.

If a covenant be made wherein neither of the parties perform presently, but trust one another, in the condition of mere nature (which is a condition of war of every man against every man) upon any reasonable suspicion, it is void: but if there be a common power set over them both, with right and force sufficient to compel performance, it is not void. For he that performeth first has no assurance the other will perform after, because the bonds of words are too weak to bridle men's ambition, avarice, anger, and other passions, without the fear of some coercive power; which in the condition of mere nature, where all men are equal, and judges of the justness of their own fears, cannot possibly be supposed. And therefore he which performeth first does but betray himself to his enemy, contrary to the right he can never abandon of defending his life and means of living.

But in a civil estate, where there a power set up to constrain those that would otherwise violate their faith, that fear is no more reasonable; and for that cause, he which by the covenant is to perform first is obliged so to do.

The cause of fear, which maketh such a covenant invalid, must be always something arising after the covenant made, as some new fact or other sign of the will not to perform, else it cannot make the covenant void. For that which could not hinder a man from promising ought not to be admitted as a hindrance of performing.

He that transferreth any right transferreth the means of enjoying it, as far as lieth in his power. As he that selleth land is understood to transfer the herbage and whatsoever grows upon it; nor can he that sells a mill turn away the stream that drives it. And they that give to a man the right of government in sovereignty are understood to give him the right of levying money to maintain soldiers, and of appointing magistrates for the administration of justice.

5   To make covenants with brute beasts is impossible, because not understanding our speech, they understand not, nor accept of any translation of right, nor can translate any right to another: and without mutual acceptation, there is no covenant.

    To make covenant with God is impossible but by mediation of such as God
10 speaketh to, either by revelation supernatural or by His lieutenants that govern under Him and in His name: for otherwise we know not whether our covenants be accepted or not. And therefore they that vow anything contrary to any law of nature, vow in vain, as being a thing unjust to pay such vow. And if it be a thing commanded by the law of nature, it is not the vow, but the law that binds them.

15   The matter or subject of a covenant is always something that falleth under deliberation, for to covenant is an act of the will; that is to say, an act, and the last act, of deliberation; and is therefore always understood to be something to come, and which judged possible for him that covenanteth to perform.

    And therefore, to promise that which is known to be impossible is no
20 covenant. But if that prove impossible afterwards, which before was thought possible, the covenant is valid and bindeth, though not to the thing itself, yet to the value; or, if that also be impossible, to the unfeigned endeavour of performing as much as is possible, for to more no man can be obliged.

    Men are freed of their covenants two ways; by performing, or by being
25 forgiven. For performance is the natural end of obligation, and forgiveness the restitution of liberty, as being a retransferring of that right in which the obligation consisted.

    Covenants entered into by fear, in the condition of mere nature, are obligatory. For example, if I covenant to pay a ransom, or service for my life, to
30 an enemy, I am bound by it. For it is a contract, wherein one receiveth the benefit of life; the other is to receive money, or service for it, and consequently, where no other law (as in the condition of mere nature) forbiddeth the performance, the covenant is valid. Therefore prisoners of war, if trusted with the payment of their ransom, are obliged to pay it: and if a weaker prince make a
35 disadvantageous peace with a stronger, for fear, he is bound to keep it; unless (as hath been said before) there ariseth some new and just cause of fear to renew the war. And even in Commonwealths, if I be forced to redeem myself from a thief by promising him money, I am bound to pay it, till the civil law discharge me. For whatsoever I may lawfully do without obligation, the same I may lawfully

covenant to do through fear: and what I lawfully covenant, I cannot lawfully break.

A former covenant makes void a later. For a man that hath passed away his right to one man today hath it not to pass tomorrow to another: and therefore the later promise passeth no right, but is null.

A covenant not to defend myself from force, by force, is always void. For (as I have shown before) no man can transfer or lay down his right to save himself from death, wounds, and imprisonment, the avoiding whereof is the only end of laying down any right; and therefore the promise of not resisting force, in no covenant transferreth any right, nor is obliging. For though a man may covenant thus, unless I do so, or so, kill me; he cannot covenant thus, unless I do so, or so, I will not resist you when you come to kill me. For man by nature chooseth the lesser evil, which is danger of death in resisting, rather than the greater, which is certain and present death in not resisting. And this is granted to be true by all men, in that they lead criminals to execution, and prison, with armed men, notwithstanding that such criminals have consented to the law by which they are condemned.

A covenant to accuse oneself, without assurance of pardon, is likewise invalid. For in the condition of nature where every man is judge, there is no place for accusation: and in the civil state the accusation is followed with punishment, which, being force, a man is not obliged not to resist. The same is also true of the accusation of those by whose condemnation a man falls into misery; as of a father, wife, or benefactor. For the testimony of such an accuser, if it be not willingly given, is presumed to be corrupted by nature, and therefore not to be received: and where a man's testimony is not to be credited, he is not bound to give it. Also accusations upon torture are not to be reputed as testimonies. For torture is to be used but as means of conjecture, and light, in the further examination and search of truth: and what is in that case confessed tendeth to the ease of him that is tortured, not to the informing of the torturers, and therefore ought not to have the credit of a sufficient testimony: for whether he deliver himself by true or false accusation, he does it by the right of preserving his own life.

The force of words being (as I have formerly noted) too weak to hold men to the performance of their covenants, there are in man's nature but two imaginable helps to strengthen it. And those are either a fear of the consequence of breaking their word, or a glory or pride in appearing not to need to break it. This latter is a generosity too rarely found to be presumed on, especially in the pursuers of wealth, command, or sensual pleasure, which are the greatest part of mankind. The passion to be reckoned upon is fear; whereof there be two very general objects: one, the power of spirits invisible; the other, the power of those

men they shall therein offend. Of these two, though the former be the greater power, yet the fear of the latter is commonly the greater fear. The fear of the former is in every man his own religion, which hath place in the nature of man before civil society. The latter hath not so; at least not place enough to keep men
5   to their promises, because in the condition of mere nature, the inequality of power is not discerned, but by the event of battle. So that before the time of civil society, or in the interruption thereof by war, there is nothing can strengthen a covenant of peace agreed on against the temptations of avarice, ambition, lust, or other strong desire, but the fear of that invisible power which they every one
10   worship as God, and fear as a revenger of their perfidy. All therefore that can be done between two men not subject to civil power is to put one another to swear by the God he feareth: which swearing, or oath, is a form of speech, added to a promise, by which he that promiseth signifieth that unless he perform he renounceth the mercy of his God, or calleth to him for vengeance on himself.
15   Such was the heathen form, Let Jupiter kill me else, as I kill this beast. So is our form, I shall do thus, and thus, so help me God. And this, with the rites and ceremonies which every one useth in his own religion, that the fear of breaking faith might be the greater.

By this it appears that an oath taken according to any other form, or rite,
20   than his that sweareth is in vain and no oath, and that there is no swearing by anything which the swearer thinks not God. For though men have sometimes used to swear by their kings, for fear, or flattery; yet they would have it thereby understood they attributed to them divine honour. And that swearing unnecessarily by God is but profaning of his name: and swearing by other
25   things, as men do in common discourse, is not swearing, but an impious custom, gotten by too much vehemence of talking.

It appears also that the oath adds nothing to the obligation. For a covenant, if lawful, binds in the sight of God, without the oath, as much as with it; if unlawful, bindeth not at all, though it be confirmed with an oath.

CHAPTER XV.
Of other laws of nature
30   FROM that law of nature by which we are obliged to transfer to another such rights as, being retained, hinder the peace of mankind, there followeth a third; which is this: that men perform their covenants made; without which covenants are in vain, and but empty words; and the right of all men to all things remaining, we are still in the condition of war.
35   And in this law of nature consisteth the fountain and original of justice. For where no covenant hath preceded, there hath no right been transferred, and every

man has right to everything and consequently, no action can be unjust. But when a covenant is made, then to break it is unjust and the definition of injustice is no other than the not performance of covenant. And whatsoever is not unjust is just.

But because covenants of mutual trust, where there is a fear of not performance on either part (as hath been said in the former chapter), are invalid, though the original of justice be the making of covenants, yet injustice actually there can be none till the cause of such fear be taken away; which, while men are in the natural condition of war, cannot be done. Therefore before the names of just and unjust can have place, there must be some coercive power to compel men equally to the performance of their covenants, by the terror of some punishment greater than the benefit they expect by the breach of their covenant, and to make good that propriety which by mutual contract men acquire in recompense of the universal right they abandon: and such power there is none before the erection of a Commonwealth. And this is also to be gathered out of the ordinary definition of justice in the Schools, for they say that justice is the constant will of giving to every man his own. And therefore where there is no own, that is, no propriety, there is no injustice; and where there is no coercive power erected, that is, where there is no Commonwealth, there is no propriety, all men having right to all things: therefore where there is no Commonwealth, there nothing is unjust. So that the nature of justice consisteth in keeping of valid covenants, but the validity of covenants begins not but with the constitution of a civil power sufficient to compel men to keep them: and then it is also that propriety begins.

The fool hath said in his heart, there is no such thing as justice, and sometimes also with his tongue, seriously alleging that every man's conservation and contentment being committed to his own care, there could be no reason why every man might not do what he thought conduced thereunto: and therefore also to make, or not make; keep, or not keep, covenants was not against reason when it conduced to one's benefit. He does not therein deny that there be covenants; and that they are sometimes broken, sometimes kept; and that such breach of them may be called injustice, and the observance of them justice: but he questioneth whether injustice, taking away the fear of God (for the same fool hath said in his heart there is no God), not sometimes stand with that reason which dictateth to every man his own good; and particularly then, when it conduceth to such a benefit as shall put a man in a condition to neglect not only the dispraise and revilings, but also the power of other men. The kingdom of God is gotten by violence: but what if it could be gotten by unjust violence? Were it against reason so to get it, when it is impossible to receive hurt by it? And if it be not against reason, it is not against justice: or else justice is not to be approved for good. From such reasoning as this, successful

wickedness hath obtained the name of virtue: and some that in all other things have disallowed the violation of faith, yet have allowed it when it is for the getting of a kingdom. And the heathen that believed that Saturn was deposed by his son Jupiter believed nevertheless the same Jupiter to be the avenger of
5   injustice, somewhat like to a piece of law in Coke's Commentaries on Littleton; where he says if the right heir of the crown be attainted of treason, yet the crown shall descend to him, and eo instante the attainder be void: from which instances a man will be very prone to infer that when the heir apparent of a kingdom shall kill him that is in possession, though his father, you may call it injustice, or by
10 what other name you will; yet it can never be against reason, seeing all the voluntary actions of men tend to the benefit of themselves; and those actions are most reasonable that conduce most to their ends. This specious reasoning is nevertheless false.
     For the question is not of promises mutual, where there is no security of
15 performance on either side, as when there is no civil power erected over the parties promising; for such promises are no covenants: but either where one of the parties has performed already, or where there is a power to make him perform, there is the question whether it be against reason; that is, against the benefit of the other to perform, or not. And I say it is not against reason. For the
20 manifestation whereof we are to consider; first, that when a man doth a thing, which notwithstanding anything can be foreseen and reckoned on tendeth to his own destruction, howsoever some accident, which he could not expect, arriving may turn it to his benefit; yet such events do not make it reasonably or wisely done. Secondly, that in a condition of war, wherein every man to every man, for
25 want of a common power to keep them all in awe, is an enemy, there is no man can hope by his own strength, or wit, to himself from destruction without the help of confederates; where every one expects the same defence by the confederation that any one else does: and therefore he which declares he thinks it reason to deceive those that help him can in reason expect no other means of
30 safety than what can be had from his own single power. He, therefore, that breaketh his covenant, and consequently declareth that he thinks he may with reason do so, cannot be received into any society that unite themselves for peace and defence but by the error of them that receive him; nor when he is received be retained in it without seeing the danger of their error; which errors a man
35 cannot reasonably reckon upon as the means of his security: and therefore if he be left, or cast out of society, he perisheth; and if he live in society, it is by the errors of other men, which he could not foresee nor reckon upon, and consequently against the reason of his preservation; and so, as all men that contribute not to his destruction forbear him only out of ignorance of what is
40 good for themselves.

As for the instance of gaining the secure and perpetual felicity of heaven by any way, it is frivolous; there being but one way imaginable, and that is not breaking, but keeping of covenant.

And for the other instance of attaining sovereignty by rebellion; it is
5   manifest that, though the event follow, yet because it cannot reasonably be expected, but rather the contrary, and because by gaining it so, others are taught to gain the same in like manner, the attempt thereof is against reason. Justice therefore, that is to say, keeping of covenant, is a rule of reason by which we are forbidden to do anything destructive to our life, and consequently a law of
10   nature.

There be some that proceed further and will not have the law of nature to be those rules which conduce to the preservation of man's life on earth, but to the attaining of an eternal felicity after death; to which they think the breach of covenant may conduce, and consequently be just and reasonable; such are they
15   that think it a work of merit to kill, or depose, or rebel against the sovereign power constituted over them by their own consent. But because there is no natural knowledge of man's estate after death, much less of the reward that is then to be given to breach of faith, but only a belief grounded upon other men's saying that they know it supernaturally or that they know those that knew them
20   that knew others that knew it supernaturally, breach of faith cannot be called a precept of reason or nature.

Others, that allow for a law of nature the keeping of faith, do nevertheless make exception of certain persons; as heretics, and such as use not to perform their covenant to others; and this also is against reason. For if any fault of a man
25   be sufficient to discharge our covenant made, the same ought in reason to have been sufficient to have hindered the making of it.

The names of just and unjust when they are attributed to men, signify one thing, and when they are attributed to actions, another. When they are attributed to men, they signify conformity, or inconformity of manners, to reason. But
30   when they are attributed to action they signify the conformity, or inconformity to reason, not of manners, or manner of life, but of particular actions. A just man therefore is he that taketh all the care he can that his actions may be all just; and an unjust man is he that neglecteth it. And such men are more often in our language styled by the names of righteous and unrighteous than just and unjust
35   though the meaning be the same. Therefore a righteous man does not lose that title by one or a few unjust actions that proceed from sudden passion, or mistake of things or persons, nor does an unrighteous man lose his character for such actions as he does, or forbears to do, for fear: because his will is not framed by the justice, but by the apparent benefit of what he is to do. That which gives to
40   human actions the relish of justice is a certain nobleness or gallantness of

courage, rarely found, by which a man scorns to be beholding for the contentment of his life to fraud, or breach of promise. This justice of the manners is that which is meant where justice is called a virtue; and injustice, a vice.

5   But the justice of actions denominates men, not just, but guiltless: and the injustice of the same (which is also called injury) gives them but the name of guilty.

Again, the injustice of manners is the disposition or aptitude to do injury, and is injustice before it proceed to act, and without supposing any individual
10   person injured. But the injustice of an action (that is to say, injury) supposeth an individual person injured; namely him to whom the covenant was made: and therefore many times the injury is received by one man when the damage redoundeth to another. As when the master commandeth his servant to give money to stranger; if it be not done, the injury is done to the master, whom he
15   had before covenanted to obey; but the damage redoundeth to the stranger, to whom he had no obligation, and therefore could not injure him. And so also in Commonwealths private men may remit to one another their debts, but not robberies or other violences, whereby they are endamaged; because the detaining of debt is an injury to themselves, but robbery and violence are
20   injuries to the person of the Commonwealth.

Whatsoever is done to a man, conformable to his own will signified to the doer, is not injury to him. For if he that doeth it hath not passed away his original right to do what he please by some antecedent covenant, there is no breach of covenant, and therefore no injury done him. And if he have, then his
25   will to have it done, being signified, is a release of that covenant, and so again there is no injury done him.

Justice of actions is by writers divided into commutative and distributive: and the former they say consisteth in proportion arithmetical; the latter in proportion geometrical. Commutative, therefore, they place in the equality of
30   value of the things contracted for; and distributive, in the distribution of equal benefit to men of equal merit. As if it were injustice to sell dearer than we buy, or to give more to a man than he merits. The value of all things contracted for is measured by the appetite of the contractors, and therefore the just value is that which they be contented to give. And merit (besides that which is by covenant,
35   where the performance on one part meriteth the performance of the other part, and falls under justice commutative, not distributive) is not due by justice, but is rewarded of grace only. And therefore this distinction, in the sense wherein it useth to be expounded, is not right. To speak properly, commutative justice is the justice of a contractor; that is, a performance of covenant in buying and

selling, hiring and letting to hire, lending and borrowing, exchanging, bartering, and other acts of contract.

And distributive justice, the justice of an arbitrator; that is to say, the act of defining what is just. Wherein, being trusted by them that make him arbitrator, if
5 he perform his trust, he is said to distribute to every man his own: and this is indeed just distribution, and may be called, though improperly, distributive justice, but more properly equity, which also is a law of nature, as shall be shown in due place.

As justice dependeth on antecedent covenant; so does gratitude depend on
10 antecedent grace; that is to say, antecedent free gift; and is the fourth law of nature, which may be conceived in this form: that a man which receiveth benefit from another of mere grace endeavour that he which giveth it have no reasonable cause to repent him of his good will. For no man giveth but with intention of good to himself, because gift is voluntary; and of all voluntary acts,
15 the object is to every man his own good; of which if men see they shall be frustrated, there will be no beginning of benevolence or trust, nor consequently of mutual help, nor of reconciliation of one man to another; and therefore they are to remain still in the condition of war, which is contrary to the first and fundamental law of nature which commandeth men to seek peace. The breach of
20 this law is called ingratitude, and hath the same relation to grace that injustice hath to obligation by covenant.

A fifth law of nature is complaisance; that is to say, that every man strive to accommodate himself to the rest. For the understanding whereof we may consider that there is in men's aptness to society a diversity of nature, rising
25 from their diversity of affections, not unlike to that we see in stones brought together for building of an edifice. For as that stone which by the asperity and irregularity of figure takes more room from others than itself fills, and for hardness cannot be easily made plain, and thereby hindereth the building, is by the builders cast away as unprofitable and troublesome: so also, a man that by
30 asperity of nature will strive to retain those things which to himself are superfluous, and to others necessary, and for the stubbornness of his passions cannot be corrected, is to be left or cast out of society as cumbersome thereunto. For seeing every man, not only by right, but also by necessity of nature, is supposed to endeavour all he can to obtain that which is necessary for his
35 conservation, he that shall oppose himself against it for things superfluous is guilty of the war that thereupon is to follow, and therefore doth that which is contrary to the fundamental law of nature, which commandeth to seek peace. The observers of this law may be called sociable, (the Latins call them commodi); the contrary, stubborn, insociable, forward, intractable.

A sixth law of nature is this: that upon caution of the future time, a man ought to pardon the offences past of them that, repenting, desire it. For pardon is nothing but granting of peace; which though granted to them that persevere in their hostility, be not peace, but fear; yet not granted to them that give caution of
5 the future time is sign of an aversion to peace, and therefore contrary to the law of nature.

A seventh is: that in revenges (that is, retribution of evil for evil), men look not at the greatness of the evil past, but the greatness of the good to follow. Whereby we are forbidden to inflict punishment with any other design than for
10 correction of the offender, or direction of others. For this law is consequent to the next before it, that commandeth pardon upon security of the future time. Besides, revenge without respect to the example and profit to come is a triumph, or glorying in the hurt of another, tending to no end (for the end is always somewhat to come); and glorying to no end is vain-glory, and contrary to
15 reason; and to hurt without reason tendeth to the introduction of war, which is against the law of nature, and is commonly styled by the name of cruelty.

And because all signs of hatred, or contempt, provoke to fight; insomuch as most men choose rather to hazard their life than not to be revenged, we may in the eighth place, for a law of nature, set down this precept: that no man by deed,
20 word, countenance, or gesture, declare hatred or contempt of another. The breach of which law is commonly called contumely.

The question who is the better man has no place in the condition of mere nature, where (as has been shown before) all men are equal. The inequality that now is has been introduced by the laws civil. I know that Aristotle in the first
25 book of his Politics, for a foundation of his doctrine, maketh men by nature, some more worthy to command, meaning the wiser sort, such as he thought himself to be for his philosophy; others to serve, meaning those that had strong bodies, but were not philosophers as he; as master and servant were not introduced by consent of men, but by difference of wit: which is not only against
30 reason, but also against experience. For there are very few so foolish that had not rather govern themselves than be governed by others: nor when the wise, in their own conceit, contend by force with them who distrust their own wisdom, do they always, or often, or almost at any time, get the victory. If nature therefore have made men equal, that equality is to be acknowledged: or if nature
35 have made men unequal, yet because men that think themselves equal will not enter into conditions of peace, but upon equal terms, such equality must be admitted. And therefore for the ninth law of nature, I put this: that every man acknowledge another for his equal by nature. The breach of this precept is pride.

On this law dependeth another: that at the entrance into conditions of peace,
40 no man require to reserve to himself any right which he is not content should he

189

reserved to every one of the rest. As it is necessary for all men that seek peace to lay down certain rights of nature; that is to say, not to have liberty to do all they list, so is it necessary for man's life to retain some: as right to govern their own bodies; enjoy air, water, motion, ways to go from place to place; and all things
5 else without which a man cannot live, or not live well. If in this case, at the making of peace, men require for themselves that which they would not have to be granted to others, they do contrary to the precedent law that commandeth the acknowledgement of natural equality, and therefore also against the law of nature. The observers of this law are those we call modest, and the breakers
10 arrogant men. The Greeks call the violation of this law pleonexia; that is, a desire of more than their share.

Also, if a man he trusted to judge between man and man, it is a precept of the law of nature that he deal equally between them. For without that, the controversies of men cannot be determined but by war. He therefore that is
15 partial in judgement, doth what in him lies to deter men from the use of judges and arbitrators, and consequently, against the fundamental law of nature, is the cause of war.

The observance of this law, from the equal distribution to each man of that which in reason belonged to him, is called equity, and (as I have said before)
20 distributive justice: the violation, acception of persons, prosopolepsia.

And from this followeth another law: that such things as cannot he divided be enjoyed in common, if it can be; and if the quantity of the thing permit, without stint; otherwise proportionably to the number of them that have right. For otherwise the distribution is unequal, and contrary to equity.
25 But some things there be that can neither be divided nor enjoyed in common. Then, the law of nature which prescribeth equity requireth: that the entire right, or else (making the use alternate) the first possession, be determined by lot. For equal distribution is of the law of nature; and other means of equal distribution cannot be imagined.
30 Of lots there be two sorts, arbitrary and natural. Arbitrary is that which is agreed on by the competitors; natural is either primogeniture (which the Greek calls kleronomia, which signifies, given by lot), or first seizure.

And therefore those things which cannot be enjoyed in common, nor divided, ought to be adjudged to the first possessor; and in some cases to the
35 first born, as acquired by lot.

It is also a law of nature: that all men that mediate peace he allowed safe conduct. For the law that commandeth peace, as the end, commandeth intercession, as the means; and to intercession the means is safe conduct.

And because, though men be never so willing to observe these laws, there
40 may nevertheless arise questions concerning a man's action; first, whether it

were done, or not done; secondly, if done, whether against the law, or not against the law; the former whereof is called a question of fact, the latter a question of right; therefore unless the parties to the question covenant mutually to stand to the sentence of another, they are as far from peace as ever. This
5 other, to whose sentence they submit, is called an arbitrator. And therefore it is of the law of nature that they that are at controversy submit their right to the judgement of an arbitrator.

And seeing every man is presumed to do all things in order to his own benefit, no man is a fit arbitrator in his own cause: and if he were never so fit,
10 yet equity allowing to each party equal benefit, if one be admitted to be judge, the other is to be admitted also; and so the controversy, that is, the cause of war, remains, against the law of nature.

For the same reason no man in any cause ought to be received for arbitrator to whom greater profit, or honour, or pleasure apparently ariseth out of the
15 victory of one party than of the other: for he hath taken, though an unavoidable bribe, yet a bribe; and no man can be obliged to trust him. And thus also the controversy and the condition of war remaineth, contrary to the law of nature.

And in a controversy of fact, the judge being to give no more credit to one than to the other, if there be no other arguments, must give credit to a third; or to
20 a third and fourth; or more: for else the question is undecided, and left to force, contrary to the law of nature.

These are the laws of nature, dictating peace, for a means of the conservation of men in multitudes; and which only concern the doctrine of civil society. There be other things tending to the destruction of particular men; as
25 drunkenness, and all other parts of intemperance, which may therefore also be reckoned amongst those things which the law of nature hath forbidden, but are not necessary to be mentioned, nor are pertinent enough to this place.

And though this may seem too subtle a deduction of the laws of nature to be taken notice of by all men, whereof the most part are too busy in getting food,
30 and the rest too negligent to understand; yet to leave all men inexcusable, they have been contracted into one easy sum, intelligible even to the meanest capacity; and that is: Do not that to another which thou wouldest not have done to thyself, which showeth him that he has no more to do in learning the laws of nature but, when weighing the actions of other men with his own they seem too
35 heavy, to put them into the other part of the balance, and his own into their place, that his own passions and self-love may add nothing to the weight; and then there is none of these laws of nature that will not appear unto him very reasonable.

The laws of nature oblige in foro interno; that is to say, they bind to a desire
40 they should take place: but in foro externo; that is, to the putting them in act, not

always. For he that should be modest and tractable, and perform all he promises in such time and place where no man else should do so, should but make himself a prey to others, and procure his own certain ruin, contrary to the ground of all laws of nature which tend to nature's preservation. And again, he that having

5   sufficient security that others shall observe the same laws towards him, observes them not himself, seeketh not peace, but war, and consequently the destruction of his nature by violence.

    And whatsoever laws bind in foro interno may be broken, not only by a fact contrary to the law, but also by a fact according to it, in case a man think it

10   contrary. For though his action in this case be according to the law, yet his purpose was against the law; which, where the obligation is in foro interno, is a breach.

    The laws of nature are immutable and eternal; for injustice, ingratitude, arrogance, pride, iniquity, acception of persons, and the rest can never be made

15   lawful. For it can never be that war shall preserve life, and peace destroy it.

    The same laws, because they oblige only to a desire and endeavour, mean an unfeigned and constant endeavour, are easy to be observed. For in that they require nothing but endeavour, he that endeavoureth their performance fulfilleth them; and he that fulfilleth the law is just.

20   And the science of them is the true and only moral philosophy. For moral philosophy is nothing else but the science of what is good and evil in the conversation and society of mankind. Good and evil are names that signify our appetites and aversions, which in different tempers, customs, and doctrines of men are different: and diverse men differ not only in their judgement on the

25   senses of what is pleasant and unpleasant to the taste, smell, hearing, touch, and sight; but also of what is conformable or disagreeable to reason in the actions of common life. Nay, the same man, in diverse times, differs from himself; and one time praiseth, that is, calleth good, what another time he dispraiseth, and calleth evil: from whence arise disputes, controversies, and at last war. And therefore so

30   long as a man is in the condition of mere nature, which is a condition of war, private appetite is the measure of good and evil: and consequently all men agree on this, that peace is good, and therefore also the way or means of peace, which (as I have shown before) are justice, gratitude, modesty, equity, mercy, and the rest of the laws of nature, are good; that is to say, moral virtues; and their

35   contrary vices, evil. Now the science of virtue and vice is moral philosophy; and therefore the true doctrine of the laws of nature is the true moral philosophy. But the writers of moral philosophy, though they acknowledge the same virtues and vices; yet, not seeing wherein consisted their goodness, nor that they come to be praised as the means of peaceable, sociable, and comfortable living, place them

in a mediocrity of passions: as if not the cause, but the degree of daring, made fortitude; or not the cause, but the quantity of a gift, made liberality.

These dictates of reason men used to call by the name of laws, but improperly: for they are but conclusions or theorems concerning what conduceth
5   to the conservation and defence of themselves; whereas law, properly, is the word of him that by right hath command over others. But yet if we consider the same theorems as delivered in the word of God that by right commandeth all things, then are they properly called laws.

CHAPTER XVI.
Of persons, authors, and things personated

A PERSON is he whose words or actions are considered, either as his own,
10   or as representing the words or actions of another man, or of any other thing to whom they are attributed, whether truly or by fiction.

When they are considered as his own, then is he called a natural person: and when they are considered as representing the words and actions of another, then is he a feigned or artificial person.

15   The word person is Latin, instead whereof the Greeks have prosopon, which signifies the face, as persona in Latin signifies the disguise, or outward appearance of a man, counterfeited on the stage; and sometimes more particularly that part of it which disguiseth the face, as a mask or vizard: and from the stage hath been translated to any representer of speech and action, as
20   well in tribunals as theatres. So that a person is the same that an actor is, both on the stage and in common conversation; and to personate is to act or represent himself or another; and he that acteth another is said to bear his person, or act in his name (in which sense Cicero useth it where he says, Unus sustineo tres personas; mei, adversarii, et judicis- I bear three persons; my own, my
25   adversary's, and the judge's), and is called in diverse occasions, diversely; as a representer, or representative, a lieutenant, a vicar, an attorney, a deputy, a procurator, an actor, and the like.

Of persons artificial, some have their words and actions owned by those whom they represent. And then the person is the actor, and he that owneth his
30   words and actions is the author, in which case the actor acteth by authority. For that which in speaking of goods and possessions is called an owner, and in Latin dominus in Greek kurios; speaking of actions, is called author. And as the right of possession is called dominion so the right of doing any action is called authority. So that by authority is always understood a right of doing any act; and
35   done by authority, done by commission or license from him whose right it is.

From hence it followeth that when the actor maketh a covenant by authority, he bindeth thereby the author no less than if he had made it himself; and no less subjecteth him to all the consequences of the same. And therefore all that hath been said formerly (Chapter XIV) of the nature of covenants between
5   man and man in their natural capacity is true also when they are made by their actors, representers, or procurators, that have authority from them, so far forth as is in their commission, but no further.

And therefore he that maketh a covenant with the actor, or representer, not knowing the authority he hath, doth it at his own peril. For no man is obliged by
10   a covenant whereof he is not author, nor consequently by a covenant made against or beside the authority he gave.

When the actor doth anything against the law of nature by command of the author, if he be obliged by former covenant to obey him, not he, but the author breaketh the law of nature: for though the action be against the law of nature, yet
15   it is not his; but, contrarily, to refuse to do it is against the law of nature that forbiddeth breach of covenant.

And he that maketh a covenant with the author, by mediation of the actor, not knowing what authority he hath, but only takes his word; in case such authority be not made manifest unto him upon demand, is no longer obliged: for
20   the covenant made with the author is not valid without his counter-assurance. But if he that so covenanteth knew beforehand he was to expect no other assurance than the actor's word, then is the covenant valid, because the actor in this case maketh himself the author. And therefore, as when the authority is evident, the covenant obligeth the author, not the actor; so when the authority is
25   feigned, it obligeth the actor only, there being no author but himself.

There are few things that are incapable of being represented by fiction. Inanimate things, as a church, a hospital, a bridge, may be personated by a rector, master, or overseer. But things inanimate cannot be authors, nor therefore give authority to their actors: yet the actors may have authority to procure their
30   maintenance, given them by those that are owners or governors of those things. And therefore such things cannot be personated before there be some state of civil government.

Likewise children, fools, and madmen that have no use of reason may be personated by guardians, or curators, but can be no authors during that time of
35   any action done by them, longer than (when they shall recover the use of reason) they shall judge the same reasonable. Yet during the folly he that hath right of governing them may give authority to the guardian. But this again has no place but in a state civil, because before such estate there is no dominion of persons.

An idol, or mere figment of the brain, may be personated, as were the gods
40   of the heathen, which, by such officers as the state appointed, were personated,

and held possessions, and other goods, and rights, which men from time to time dedicated and consecrated unto them. But idols cannot be authors: for an idol is nothing. The authority proceeded from the state, and therefore before introduction of civil government the gods of the heathen could not be
5   personated.

      The true God may be personated. As He was: first, Moses, who governed the Israelites, that were that were not his, but God's people; not in his own name, with hoc dicit Moses, but in God's name, with hoc dicit Dominus. Secondly, by the Son of Man, His own Son, our blessed Saviour Jesus Christ,
10   that came to reduce the Jews and induce all nations into the kingdom of his Father; not as of himself, but as sent from his Father. And thirdly, by the Holy Ghost, or Comforter, speaking and working in the Apostles; which Holy Ghost was a Comforter that came not of himself, but was sent and proceeded from them both.

15   A multitude of men are made one person when they are by one man, or one person, represented; so that it be done with the consent of every one of that multitude in particular. For it is the unity of the representer, not the unity of the represented, that maketh the person one. And it is the representer that beareth the person, and but one person: and unity cannot otherwise be understood in
20   multitude.

      And because the multitude naturally is not one, but many, they cannot be understood for one, but in any authors, of everything their representative saith or doth in their name; every man giving their common representer authority from himself in particular, and owning all the actions the representer doth, in case
25   they give him authority without stint: otherwise, when they limit him in what and how far he shall represent them, none of them owneth more than they gave him commission to act.

      And if the representative consist of many men, the voice of the greater number must be considered as the voice of them all. For if the lesser number
30   pronounce, for example, in the affirmative, and the greater in the negative, there will be negatives more than enough to destroy the affirmatives, and thereby the excess of negatives, standing uncontradicted, are the only voice the representative hath.

      And a representative of even number, especially when the number is not
35   great, whereby the contradictory voices are oftentimes equal, is therefore oftentimes mute and incapable of action. Yet in some cases contradictory voices equal in number may determine a question; as in condemning, or absolving, equality of votes, even in that they condemn not, do absolve; but not on the contrary condemn, in that they absolve not. For when a cause is heard, not to
40   condemn is to absolve; but on the contrary to say that not absolving is

condemning is not true. The like it is in deliberation of executing presently, or deferring till another time: for when the voices are equal, the not decreeing execution is a decree of dilation.

Or if the number be odd, as three, or more, men or assemblies, whereof
5   every one has, by a negative voice, authority to take away the effect of all the affirmative voices of the rest, this number is no representative; by the diversity of opinions and interests of men, it becomes oftentimes, and in cases of the greatest consequence, a mute person and unapt, as for many things else, so for the government of a multitude, especially in time of war.
10   Of authors there be two sorts. The first simply so called, which I have before defined to be him that owneth the action of another simply. The second is he that owneth an action or covenant of another conditionally; that is to say, he undertaketh to do it, if the other doth it not, at or before a certain time. And these authors conditional are generally called sureties, in Latin, fidejussores and
15   sponsores; and particularly for debt, praedes and for appearance before a judge or magistrate, vades.

CHAPTER XVII.
Of the causes, generation, and definition of a commonwealth
THE final cause, end, or design of men (who naturally love liberty, and dominion over others) in the introduction of that restraint upon themselves, in which we see them live in Commonwealths, is the foresight of their own
20   preservation, and of a more contented life thereby; that is to say, of getting themselves out from that miserable condition of war which is necessarily consequent, as hath been shown, to the natural passions of men when there is no visible power to keep them in awe, and tie them by fear of punishment to the performance of their covenants, and observation of those laws of nature set
25   down in the fourteenth and fifteenth chapters.

For the laws of nature, as justice, equity, modesty, mercy, and, in sum, doing to others as we would be done to, of themselves, without the terror of some power to cause them to be observed, are contrary to our natural passions, that carry us to partiality, pride, revenge, and the like. And covenants, without
30   the sword, are but words and of no strength to secure a man at all. Therefore, notwithstanding the laws of nature (which every one hath then kept, when he has the will to keep them, when he can do it safely), if there be no power erected, or not great enough for our security, every man will and may lawfully rely on his own strength and art for caution against all other men. And in all places, where
35   men have lived by small families, to rob and spoil one another has been a trade, and so far from being reputed against the law of nature that the greater spoils

they gained, the greater was their honour; and men observed no other laws
therein but the laws of honour; that is, to abstain from cruelty, leaving to men
their lives and instruments of husbandry. And as small families did then; so now
do cities and kingdoms, which are but greater families (for their own security),
5   enlarge their dominions upon all pretences of danger, and fear of invasion, or
assistance that may be given to invaders; endeavour as much as they can to
subdue or weaken their neighbours by open force, and secret arts, for want of
other caution, justly; and are remembered for it in after ages with honour.

Nor is it the joining together of a small number of men that gives them this
10 security; because in small numbers, small additions on the one side or the other
make the advantage of strength so great as is sufficient to carry the victory, and
therefore gives encouragement to an invasion. The multitude sufficient to
confide in for our security is not determined by any certain number, but by
comparison with the enemy we fear; and is then sufficient when the odds of the
15 enemy is not of so visible and conspicuous moment to determine the event of
war, as to move him to attempt.

And be there never so great a multitude; yet if their actions be directed
according to their particular judgements, and particular appetites, they can
expect thereby no defence, nor protection, neither against a common enemy, nor
20 against the injuries of one another. For being distracted in opinions concerning
the best use and application of their strength, they do not help, but hinder one
another, and reduce their strength by mutual opposition to nothing: whereby
they are easily, not only subdued by a very few that agree together, but also,
when there is no common enemy, they make war upon each other for their
25 particular interests. For if we could suppose a great multitude of men to consent
in the observation of justice, and other laws of nature, without a common power
to keep them all in awe, we might as well suppose all mankind to do the same;
and then there neither would be, nor need to be, any civil government or
Commonwealth at all, because there would be peace without subjection.
30 Nor is it enough for the security, which men desire should last all the time
of their life, that they be governed and directed by one judgement for a limited
time; as in one battle, or one war. For though they obtain a victory by their
unanimous endeavour against a foreign enemy, yet afterwards, when either they
have no common enemy, or he that by one part is held for an enemy is by
35 another part held for a friend, they must needs by the difference of their interests
dissolve, and fall again into a war amongst themselves.

It is true that certain living creatures, as bees and ants, live sociably one
with another (which are therefore by Aristotle numbered amongst political
creatures), and yet have no other direction than their particular judgements and
40 appetites; nor speech, whereby one of them can signify to another what he thinks

expedient for the common benefit: and therefore some man may perhaps desire to know why mankind cannot do the same. To which I answer,

First, that men are continually in competition for honour and dignity, which these creatures are not; and consequently amongst men there ariseth on that
5   ground, envy, and hatred, and finally war; but amongst these not so.

Secondly, that amongst these creatures the common good differeth not from the private; and being by nature inclined to their private, they procure thereby the common benefit. But man, whose joy consisteth in comparing himself with other men, can relish nothing but what is eminent.
10 Thirdly, that these creatures, having not, as man, the use of reason, do not see, nor think they see, any fault in the administration of their common business: whereas amongst men there are very many that think themselves wiser and abler to govern the public better than the rest, and these strive to reform and innovate, one this way, another that way; and thereby bring it into distraction and civil
15 war.

Fourthly, that these creatures, though they have some use of voice in making known to one another their desires and other affections, yet they want that art of words by which some men can represent to others that which is good in the likeness of evil; and evil, in the likeness of good; and augment or diminish
20 the apparent greatness of good and evil, discontenting men and troubling their peace at their pleasure.

Fifthly, irrational creatures cannot distinguish between injury and damage; and therefore as long as they be at ease, they are not offended with their fellows: whereas man is then most troublesome when he is most at ease; for then it is that
25 he loves to show his wisdom, and control the actions of them that govern the Commonwealth.

Lastly, the agreement of these creatures is natural; that of men is by covenant only, which is artificial: and therefore it is no wonder if there be somewhat else required, besides covenant, to make their agreement constant and
30 lasting; which is a common power to keep them in awe and to direct their actions to the common benefit.

The only way to erect such a common power, as may be able to defend them from the invasion of foreigners, and the injuries of one another, and thereby to secure them in such sort as that by their own industry and by the fruits
35 of the earth they may nourish themselves and live contentedly, is to confer all their power and strength upon one man, or upon one assembly of men, that may reduce all their wills, by plurality of voices, unto one will: which is as much as to say, to appoint one man, or assembly of men, to bear their person; and every one to own and acknowledge himself to be author of whatsoever he that so
40 beareth their person shall act, or cause to be acted, in those things which concern

the common peace and safety; and therein to submit their wills, every one to his will, and their judgements to his judgement. This is more than consent, or concord; it is a real unity of them all in one and the same person, made by covenant of every man with every man, in such manner as if every man should
5   say to every man: I authorise and give up my right of governing myself to this man, or to this assembly of men, on this condition; that thou give up, thy right to him, and authorise all his actions in like manner. This done, the multitude so united in one person is called a COMMONWEALTH; in Latin, CIVITAS. This is the generation of that great LEVIATHAN, or rather, to speak more reverently,
10   of that mortal god to which we owe, under the immortal God, our peace and defence. For by this authority, given him by every particular man in the Commonwealth, he hath the use of so much power and strength conferred on him that, by terror thereof, he is enabled to form the wills of them all, to peace at home, and mutual aid against their enemies abroad. And in him consisteth the
15   essence of the Commonwealth; which, to define it, is: one person, of whose acts a great multitude, by mutual covenants one with another, have made themselves every one the author, to the end he may use the strength and means of them all as he shall think expedient for their peace and common defence.

    And he that carryeth this person is called sovereign, and said to have
20   sovereign power; and every one besides, his subject.

    The attaining to this sovereign power is by two ways. One, by natural force: as when a man maketh his children to submit themselves, and their children, to his government, as being able to destroy them if they refuse; or by war subdueth his enemies to his will, giving them their lives on that condition. The other, is
25   when men agree amongst themselves to submit to some man, or assembly of men, voluntarily, on confidence to be protected by him against all others. This latter may be called a political Commonwealth, or Commonwealth by Institution; and the former, a Commonwealth by acquisition. And first, I shall speak of a Commonwealth by institution.

CHAPTER XVIII.
Of the rights of sovereigns by institution
30   A COMMONWEALTH is said to be instituted when a multitude of men do agree, and covenant, every one with every one, that to whatsoever man, or assembly of men, shall be given by the major part the right to present the person of them all, that is to say, to be their representative; every one, as well he that voted for it as he that voted against it, shall authorize all the actions and
35   judgements of that man, or assembly of men, in the same manner as if they were

his own, to the end to live peaceably amongst themselves, and be protected against other men.

From this institution of a Commonwealth are derived all the rights and faculties of him, or them, on whom the sovereign power is conferred by the
5   consent of the people assembled.

First, because they covenant, it is to be understood they are not obliged by former covenant to anything repugnant hereunto. And consequently they that have already instituted a Commonwealth, being thereby bound by covenant to own the actions and judgements of one, cannot lawfully make a new covenant
10 amongst themselves to be obedient to any other, in anything whatsoever, without his permission. And therefore, they that are subjects to a monarch cannot without his leave cast off monarchy and return to the confusion of a disunited multitude; nor transfer their person from him that beareth it to another man, other assembly of men: for they are bound, every man to every man, to
15 own and be reputed author of all that already is their sovereign shall do and judge fit to be done; so that any one man dissenting, all the rest should break their covenant made to that man, which is injustice: and they have also every man given the sovereignty to him that beareth their person; and therefore if they depose him, they take from him that which is his own, and so again it is
20 injustice. Besides, if he that attempteth to depose his sovereign be killed or punished by him for such attempt, he is author of his own punishment, as being, by the institution, author of all his sovereign shall do; and because it is injustice for a man to do anything for which he may be punished by his own authority, he is also upon that title unjust. And whereas some men have pretended for their
25 disobedience to their sovereign a new covenant, made, not with men but with God, this also is unjust: for there is no covenant with God but by mediation of somebody that representeth God's person, which none doth but God's lieutenant who hath the sovereignty under God. But this pretence of covenant with God is so evident a lie, even in the pretenders' own consciences, that it is not only an
30 act of an unjust, but also of a vile and unmanly disposition.

Secondly, because the right of bearing the person of them all is given to him they make sovereign, by covenant only of one to another, and not of him to any of them, there can happen no breach of covenant on the part of the sovereign; and consequently none of his subjects, by any pretence of forfeiture, can be
35 freed from his subjection. That he which is made sovereign maketh no covenant with his subjects before hand is manifest; because either he must make it with the whole multitude, as one party to the covenant, or he must make a several covenant with every man. With the whole, as one party, it is impossible, because as they are not one person: and if he make so many several covenants as there be
40 men, those covenants after he hath the sovereignty are void; because what act

soever can be pretended by any one of them for breach thereof is the act both of himself, and of all the rest, because done in the person, and by the right of every one of them in particular. Besides, if any one or more of them pretend a breach of the covenant made by the sovereign at his institution, and others or one other
5   of his subjects, or himself alone, pretend there was no such breach, there is in this case no judge to decide the controversy: it returns therefore to the sword again; and every man recovereth the right of protecting himself by his own strength, contrary to the design they had in the institution. It is therefore in vain to grant sovereignty by way of precedent covenant. The opinion that any
10   monarch receiveth his power by covenant, that is to say, on condition, proceedeth from want of understanding this easy truth: that covenants being but words, and breath, have no force to oblige, contain, constrain, or protect any man, but what it has from the public sword; that is, from the untied hands of that man, or assembly of men, that hath the sovereignty, and whose actions are
15   avouched by them all, and performed by the strength of them all, in him united. But when an assembly of men is made sovereign, then no man imagineth any such covenant to have passed in the institution: for no man is so dull as to say, for example, the people of Rome made a covenant with the Romans to hold the sovereignty on such or such conditions; which not performed, the Romans might
20   lawfully depose the Roman people. That men see not the reason to be alike in a monarchy and in a popular government proceedeth from the ambition of some that are kinder to the government of an assembly, whereof they may hope to participate, than of monarchy, which they despair to enjoy.

Thirdly, because the major part hath by consenting voices declared a
25   sovereign, he that dissented must now consent with the rest; that is, be contented to avow all the actions he shall do, or else justly be destroyed by the rest. For if he voluntarily entered into the congregation of them that were assembled, he sufficiently declared thereby his will, and therefore tacitly covenanted, to stand to what the major part should ordain: and therefore if he refuse to stand thereto,
30   or make protestation against any of their decrees, he does contrary to his covenant, and therefore unjustly. And whether he be of the congregation or not, and whether his consent be asked or not, he must either submit to their decrees or be left in the condition of war he was in before; wherein he might without injustice be destroyed by any man whatsoever.
35   Fourthly, because every subject is by this institution author of all the actions and judgements of the sovereign instituted, it follows that whatsoever he doth, can be no injury to any of his subjects; nor ought he to be by any of them accused of injustice. For he that doth anything by authority from another doth therein no injury to him by whose authority he acteth: but by this institution of a
40   Commonwealth every particular man is author of all the sovereign doth; and

consequently he that complaineth of injury from his sovereign complaineth of that whereof he himself is author, and therefore ought not to accuse any man but himself; no, nor himself of injury, because to do injury to oneself is impossible. It is true that they that have sovereign power may commit iniquity, but not
5   injustice or injury in the proper signification.

Fifthly, and consequently to that which was said last, no man that hath sovereign power can justly be put to death, or otherwise in any manner by his subjects punished. For seeing every subject is author of the actions of his sovereign, he punisheth another for the actions committed by himself.
10   And because the end of this institution is the peace and defence of them all, and whosoever has right to the end has right to the means, it belonged of right to whatsoever man or assembly that hath the sovereignty to be judge both of the means of peace and defence, and also of the hindrances and disturbances of the same; and to do whatsoever he shall think necessary to be done, both
15   beforehand, for the preserving of peace and security, by prevention of discord at home, and hostility from abroad; and when peace and security are lost, for the recovery of the same. And therefore,

Sixthly, it is annexed to the sovereignty to be judge of what opinions and doctrines are averse, and what conducing to peace; and consequently, on what
20   occasions, how far, and what men are to be trusted withal in speaking to multitudes of people; and who shall examine the doctrines of all books before they be published. For the actions of men proceed from their opinions, and in the well governing of opinions consisteth the well governing of men's actions in order to their peace and concord. And though in matter of doctrine nothing to be
25   regarded but the truth, yet this is not repugnant to regulating of the same by peace. For doctrine repugnant to peace can no more be true, than peace and concord can be against the law of nature. It is true that in a Commonwealth, where by the negligence or unskillfulness of governors and teachers false doctrines are by time generally received, the contrary truths may be generally
30   offensive: yet the most sudden and rough bustling in of a new truth that can be does never break the peace, but only sometimes awake the war. For those men that are so remissly governed that they dare take up arms to defend or introduce an opinion are still in war; and their condition, not peace, but only a cessation of arms for fear of one another; and they live, as it were, in the procincts of battle
35   continually. It belonged therefore to him that hath the sovereign power to be judge, or constitute all judges of opinions and doctrines, as a thing necessary to peace; thereby to prevent discord and civil war.

Seventhly, is annexed to the sovereignty the whole power of prescribing the rules whereby every man may know what goods he may enjoy, and what actions
40   he may do, without being molested by any of his fellow subjects: and this is it

men call propriety. For before constitution of sovereign power, as hath already
been shown, all men had right to all things, which necessarily causeth war: and
therefore this propriety, being necessary to peace, and depending on sovereign
power, is the act of that power, in order to the public peace. These rules of
5   propriety (or meum and tuum) and of good, evil, lawful, and unlawful in the
actions of subjects are the civil laws; that is to say, the laws of each
Commonwealth in particular; though the name of civil law be now restrained to
the ancient civil laws of the city of Rome; which being the head of a great part
of the world, her laws at that time were in these parts the civil law.
10   Eighthly, is annexed to the sovereignty the right of judicature; that is to say,
of hearing and deciding all controversies which may arise concerning law, either
civil or natural, or concerning fact. For without the decision of controversies,
there is no protection of one subject against the injuries of another; the laws
concerning meum and tuum are in vain, and to every man remaineth, from the
15   natural and necessary appetite of his own conservation, the right of protecting
himself by his private strength, which is the condition of war, and contrary to the
end for which every Commonwealth is instituted.
        Ninthly, is annexed to the sovereignty the right of making war and peace
with other nations and Commonwealths; that is to say, of judging when it is for
20   the public good, and how great forces are to be assembled, armed, and paid for
that end, and to levy money upon the subjects to defray the expenses thereof.
For the power by which the people are to be defended consisteth in their armies,
and the strength of an army in the union of their strength under one command;
which command the sovereign instituted, therefore hath, because the command
25   of the militia, without other institution, maketh him that hath it sovereign. And
therefore, whosoever is made general of an army, he that hath the sovereign
power is always generalissimo.
        Tenthly, is annexed to the sovereignty the choosing of all counsellors,
ministers, magistrates, and officers, both in peace and war. For seeing the
30   sovereign is charged with the end, which is the common peace and defence, he
is understood to have power to use such means as he shall think most fit for his
discharge.
        Eleventhly, to the sovereign is committed the power of rewarding with
riches or honour; and of punishing with corporal or pecuniary punishment, or
35   with ignominy, every subject according to the law he hath formerly made; or if
there be no law made, according as he shall judge most to conduce to the
encouraging of men to serve the Commonwealth, or deterring of them from
doing disservice to the same.
        Lastly, considering what values men are naturally apt to set upon
40   themselves, what respect they look for from others, and how little they value

other men; from whence continually arise amongst them, emulation, quarrels, factions, and at last war, to the destroying of one another, and diminution of their strength against a common enemy; it is necessary that there be laws of honour, and a public rate of the worth of such men as have deserved or are able
5 to deserve well of the Commonwealth, and that there be force in the hands of some or other to put those laws in execution. But it hath already been shown that not only the whole militia, or forces of the Commonwealth, but also the judicature of all controversies, is annexed to the sovereignty. To the sovereign therefore it belonged also to give titles of honour, and to appoint what order of
10 place and dignity each man shall hold, and what signs of respect in public or private meetings they shall give to one another.

These are the rights which make the essence of sovereignty, and which are the marks whereby a man may discern in what man, or assembly of men, the sovereign power is placed and resideth. For these are incommunicable and
15 inseparable. The power to coin money, to dispose of the estate and persons of infant heirs, to have pre-emption in markets, and all other statute prerogatives may be transferred by the sovereign, and yet the power to protect his subjects be retained. But if he transfer the militia, he retains the judicature in vain, for want of execution of the laws; or if he grant away the power of raising money, the
20 militia is in vain; or if he give away the government of doctrines, men will be frighted into rebellion with the fear of spirits. And so if we consider any one of the said rights, we shall presently see that the holding of all the rest will produce no effect in the conservation of peace and justice, the end for which all Commonwealths are instituted. And this division is it whereof it is said, a
25 kingdom divided in itself cannot stand: for unless this division precede, division into opposite armies can never happen. If there had not first been an opinion received of the greatest part of England that these powers were divided between the King and the Lords and the House of Commons, the people had never been divided and fallen into this Civil War; first between those that disagreed in
30 politics, and after between the dissenters about the liberty of religion, which have so instructed men in this point of sovereign right that there be few now in England that do not see that these rights are inseparable, and will be so generally acknowledged at the next return of peace; and so continue, till their miseries are forgotten, and no longer, except the vulgar be better taught than they have
35 hitherto been.

And because they are essential and inseparable rights, it follows necessarily that in whatsoever words any of them seem to be granted away, yet if the sovereign power itself be not in direct terms renounced and the name of sovereign no more given by the grantees to him that grants them, the grant is void: for when he has granted all he can, if we grant back the sovereignty, all is restored, as inseparably annexed thereunto.

This great authority being indivisible, and inseparably annexed to the sovereignty, there is little ground for the opinion of them that say of sovereign
5 kings, though they be singulis majores, of greater power than every one of their subjects, yet they be universis minores, of less power than them all together. For if by all together, they mean not the collective body as one person, then all together and every one signify the same; and the speech is absurd. But if by all together, they understand them as one person (which person the sovereign
10 bears), then the power of all together is the same with the sovereign's power; and so again the speech is absurd: which absurdity they see well enough when the sovereignty is in an assembly of the people; but in a monarch they see it not; and yet the power of sovereignty is the same in whomsoever it be placed.

And as the power, so also the honour of the sovereign, ought to be greater
15 than that of any or all the subjects. For in the sovereignty is the fountain of honour. The dignities of lord, earl, duke, and prince are his creatures. As in the presence of the master, the servants are equal, and without any honour at all; so are the subjects, in the presence of the sovereign. And though they shine some more, some less, when they are out of his sight; yet in his presence, they shine
20 no more than the stars in presence of the sun.

But a man may here object that the condition of subjects is very miserable, as being obnoxious to the lusts and other irregular passions of him or them that have so unlimited a power in their hands. And commonly they that live under a monarch think it the fault of monarchy; and they that live under the government
25 of democracy, or other sovereign assembly, attribute all the inconvenience to that form of Commonwealth; whereas the power in all forms, if they be perfect enough to protect them, is the same: not considering that the estate of man can never be without some incommodity or other; and that the greatest that in any form of government can possibly happen to the people in general is scarce
30 sensible, in respect of the miseries and horrible calamities that accompany a civil war, or that dissolute condition of masterless men without subjection to laws and a coercive power to tie their hands from rapine and revenge: nor considering that the greatest pressure of sovereign governors proceedeth, not from any delight or profit they can expect in the damage weakening of their
35 subjects, in whose vigour consisteth their own strength and glory, but in the restiveness of themselves that, unwillingly contributing to their own defence, make it necessary for their governors to draw from them what they can in time of peace that they may have means on any emergent occasion, or sudden need, to resist or take advantage on their enemies. For all men are by nature provided
40 of notable multiplying glasses (that is their passions and self-love) through

which every little payment appeareth a great grievance, but are destitute of those prospective glasses (namely moral and civil science) to see afar off the miseries that hang over them and cannot without such payments be avoided.

CHAPTER XIX.
Of the several kinds of commonwealth by institution, and of succession to the sovereign power

THE difference of Commonwealths consisteth in the difference of the
5   sovereign, or the person representative of all and every one of the multitude. And because the sovereignty is either in one man, or in an assembly of more than one; and into that assembly either every man hath right to enter, or not every one, but certain men distinguished from the rest; it is manifest there can be but three kinds of Commonwealth. For the representative must needs be one
10 man, or more; and if more, then it is the assembly of all, or but of a part. When the representative is one man, then is the Commonwealth a monarchy; when an assembly of all that will come together, then it is a democracy, or popular Commonwealth; when an assembly of a part only, then it is called an aristocracy. Other kind of Commonwealth there can be none: for either one, or
15 more, or all, must have the sovereign power (which I have shown to be indivisible) entire.

There be other names of government in the histories and books of policy; as tyranny and oligarchy; but they are not the names of other forms of government, but of the same forms misliked. For they that are discontented under monarchy
20 call it tyranny; and they that are displeased with aristocracy call it oligarchy: so also, they which find themselves grieved under a democracy call it anarchy, which signifies want of government; and yet I think no man believes that want of government is any new kind of government: nor by the same reason ought they to believe that the government is of one kind when they like it, and another
25 when they mislike it or are oppressed by the governors.

It is manifest that men who are in absolute liberty may, if they please, give authority to one man to represent them every one, as well as give such authority to any assembly of men whatsoever; and consequently may subject themselves, if they think good, to a monarch as absolutely as to other representative.
30 Therefore, where there is already erected a sovereign power, there can be no other representative of the same people, but only to certain particular ends, by the sovereign limited. For that were to erect two sovereigns; and every man to have his person represented by two actors that, by opposing one another, must needs divide that power, which (if men will live in peace) is indivisible; and
35 thereby reduce the multitude into the condition of war, contrary to the end for

which all sovereignty is instituted. And therefore as it is absurd to think that a sovereign assembly, inviting the people of their dominion to send up their deputies with power to make known their advice or desires should therefore hold such deputies, rather than themselves, for the absolute representative of the
5   people; so it is absurd also to think the same in a monarchy. And I know not how this so manifest a truth should of late be so little observed: that in a monarchy he that had the sovereignty from a descent of six hundred years was alone called sovereign, had the title of Majesty from every one of his subjects, and was unquestionably taken by them for their king, was notwithstanding never
10   considered as their representative; that name without contradiction passing for the title of those men which at his command were sent up by the people to carry their petitions and give him, if he permitted it, their advice. Which may serve as an admonition for those that are the true and absolute representative of a people, to instruct men in the nature of that office, and to take heed how they admit of
15   any other general representation upon any occasion whatsoever, if they mean to discharge the trust committed to them.

      The difference between these three kinds of Commonwealth consisteth, not in the difference of power, but in the difference of convenience or aptitude to produce the peace and security of the people; for which end they were instituted.
20   And to compare monarchy with the other two, we may observe: first, that whosoever beareth the person of the people, or is one of that assembly that bears it, beareth also his own natural person. And though he be careful in his politic person to procure the common interest, yet he is more, or no less, careful to procure the private good of himself, his family, kindred and friends; and for the
25   most part, if the public interest chance to cross the private, he prefers the private: for the passions of men are commonly more potent than their reason. From whence it follows that where the public and private interest are most closely united, there is the public most advanced. Now in monarchy the private interest is the same with the public. The riches, power, and honour of a monarch arise
30   only from the riches, strength, and reputation of his subjects. For no king can be rich, nor glorious, nor secure, whose subjects are either poor, or contemptible, or too weak through want, or dissension, to maintain a war against their enemies; whereas in a democracy, or aristocracy, the public prosperity confers not so much to the private fortune of one that is corrupt, or ambitious, as doth many
35   times a perfidious advice, a treacherous action, or a civil war.

      Secondly, that a monarch receiveth counsel of whom, when, and where he pleaseth; and consequently may hear the opinion of men versed in the matter about which he deliberates, of what rank or quality soever, and as long before the time of action and with as much secrecy as he will. But when a sovereign
40   assembly has need of counsel, none are admitted but such as have a right thereto

from the beginning; which for the most part are of those who have been versed more in the acquisition of wealth than of knowledge, and are to give their advice in long discourses which may, and do commonly, excite men to action, but not govern them in it. For the understanding is by the flame of the passions never

5 enlightened, but dazzled: nor is there any place or time wherein an assembly can receive counsel secrecy, because of their own multitude.

Thirdly, that the resolutions of a monarch are subject to no other inconstancy than that of human nature; but in assemblies, besides that of nature, there ariseth an inconstancy from the number. For the absence of a few that

10 would have the resolution, once taken, continue firm (which may happen by security, negligence, or private impediments), or the diligent appearance of a few of the contrary opinion, undoes today all that was concluded yesterday.

Fourthly, that a monarch cannot disagree with himself, out of envy or interest; but an assembly may; and that to such a height as may produce a civil

15 war.

Fifthly, that in monarchy there is this inconvenience; that any subject, by the power of one man, for the enriching of a favourite or flatterer, may be deprived of all he possesseth; which I confess is a great an inevitable inconvenience. But the same may as well happen where the sovereign power is

20 in an assembly: for their power is the same; and they are as subject to evil counsel, and to be seduced by orators, as a monarch by flatterers; and becoming one another's flatterers, serve one another's covetousness and ambition by turns. And whereas the favourites of monarchs are few, and they have none else to advance but their own kindred; the favourites of an assembly are many, and the

25 kindred much more numerous than of any monarch. Besides, there is no favourite of a monarch which cannot as well succour his friends as hurt his enemies: but orators, that is to say, favourites of sovereign assemblies, though they have great power to hurt, have little to save. For to accuse requires less eloquence (such is man's nature) than to excuse; and condemnation, than

30 absolution, more resembles justice.

Sixthly, that it is an inconvenience in monarchy that the sovereignty may descend upon an infant, or one that cannot discern between good and evil: and consisteth in this, that the use of his power must be in the hand of another man, or of some assembly of men, which are to govern by his right and in his name as

35 curators and protectors of his person and authority. But to say there is inconvenience in putting the use of the sovereign power into the hand of a man, or an assembly of men, is to say that all government is more inconvenient than confusion and civil war. And therefore all the danger that can be pretended must arise from the contention of those that, for an office of so great honour and

40 profit, may become competitors. To make it appear that this inconvenience

proceedeth not from that form of government we call monarchy, we are to
consider that the precedent monarch hath appointed who shall have the tuition of
his infant successor, either expressly by testament, or tacitly by not controlling
the custom in that case received: and then such inconvenience, if it happen, is to
5   be attributed, not to the monarchy, but to the ambition and injustice of the
subjects, which in all kinds of government, where the people are not well
instructed in their duty and the rights of sovereignty, is the same. Or else the
precedent monarch hath not at all taken order for such tuition; and then the law
of nature hath provided this sufficient rule, that the tuition shall be in him that
10 hath by nature most interest in the preservation of the authority of the infant, and
to whom least benefit can accrue by his death or diminution. For seeing every
man by nature seeketh his own benefit and promotion, to put an infant into the
power of those that can promote themselves by his destruction or damage is not
tuition, but treachery. So that sufficient provision being taken against all just
15 quarrel about the government under a child, if any contention arise to the
disturbance of the public peace, it is not to be attributed to the form of
monarchy, but to the ambition of subjects and ignorance of their duty. On the
other side, there is no great Commonwealth, the sovereignty whereof is in a
great assembly, which is not, as to consultations of peace, and war, and making
20 of laws, in the same condition as if the government were in a child. For as a
child wants the judgement to dissent from counsel given him, and is thereby
necessitated to take the advice of them, or him, to whom he is committed; so an
assembly wanteth the liberty to dissent from the counsel of the major part, be it
good or bad. And as a child has need of a tutor, or protector, to preserve his
25 person and authority; so also in great Commonwealths the sovereign assembly,
in all great dangers and troubles, have need of custodes libertatis; that is, of
dictators, or protectors of their authority; which are as much as temporary
monarchs to whom for a time they may commit the entire exercise of their
power; and have, at the end of that time, been oftener deprived thereof than
30 infant kings by their protectors, regents, or any other tutors.

Though the kinds of sovereignty be, as I have now shown, but three; that is
to say, monarchy, where one man has it; or democracy, where the general
assembly of subjects hath it; or aristocracy, where it is in an assembly of certain
persons nominated, or otherwise distinguished from the rest: yet he that shall
35 consider the particular Commonwealths that have been and are in the world will
not perhaps easily reduce them to three, and may thereby be inclined to think
there be other forms arising from these mingled together. As for example,
elective kingdoms; where kings have the sovereign power put into their hands
for a time; or kingdoms wherein the king hath a power limited: which
40 governments are nevertheless by most writers called monarchy. Likewise if a

popular or aristocratical Commonwealth subdue an enemy's country, and govern the same by a president, procurator, or other magistrate, this may seem perhaps, at first sight, to be a democratical or aristocratical government. But it is not so. For elective kings are not sovereigns, but ministers of the sovereign; nor limited
5   kings sovereigns, but ministers of them that have the sovereign power; nor are those provinces which are in subjection to a democracy or aristocracy of another Commonwealth democratically or aristocratically governed, but monarchically.

And first, concerning an elective king, whose power is limited to his life, as it is in many places of Christendom at this day; or to certain years or months, as
10   the dictator's power amongst the Romans; if he have right to appoint his successor, he is no more elective but hereditary. But if he have no power to elect his successor, then there is some other man, or assembly known, which after his decease may elect a new; or else the Commonwealth dieth, and dissolveth with him, and returneth to the condition of war. If it be known who have the power to
15   give the sovereignty after his death, it is known also that the sovereignty was in them before: for none have right to give that which they have not right to possess, and keep to themselves, if they think good. But if there be none that can give the sovereignty after the decease of him that was first elected, then has he power, nay he is obliged by the law of nature, to provide, by establishing his
20   successor, to keep to those that had trusted him with the government from relapsing into the miserable condition of civil war. And consequently he was, when elected, a sovereign absolute.

Secondly, that king whose power is limited is not superior to him, or them, that have the power to limit it; and he that is not superior is not supreme; that is
25   to say, not sovereign. The sovereignty therefore was always in that assembly which had the right to limit him, and by consequence the government not monarchy, but either democracy or aristocracy; as of old time in Sparta, where the kings had a privilege to lead their armies, but the sovereignty was in the Ephori.
30   Thirdly, whereas heretofore the Roman people governed the land of Judea, for example, by a president; yet was not Judea therefore a democracy, because they were not governed by any assembly into which any of them had right to enter; nor by an aristocracy, because they were not governed by any assembly into which any man could enter by their election: but they were governed by one
35   person, which though as to the people of Rome was an assembly of the people, or democracy; yet as to the people of Judea, which had no right at all of participating in the government, was a monarch. For though where the people are governed by an assembly, chosen by themselves out of their own number, the government is called a democracy, or aristocracy; yet when they are

governed by an assembly not of their own choosing, it is a monarchy; not of one man over another man, but of one people over another people.

Of all these forms of government, the matter being mortal, so that not only monarchs, but also whole assemblies die, it is necessary for the conservation of
5   the peace of men that as there was order taken for an artificial man, so there be order also taken for an artificial eternity of life; without which men that are governed by an assembly should return into the condition of war in every age; and they that are governed by one man, as soon as their governor dieth. This artificial eternity is that which men call the right of succession.
10   There is no perfect form of government, where the disposing of the succession is not in the present sovereign. For if it be in any other particular man, or private assembly, it is in a person subject, and may be assumed by the sovereign at his pleasure; and consequently the right is in himself. And if it be in no particular man, but left to a new choice; then is the Commonwealth
15   dissolved, and the right is in him that can get it, contrary to the intention of them that did institute the Commonwealth for their perpetual, and not temporary, security.

In a democracy, the whole assembly cannot fail unless the multitude that are to be governed fail. And therefore questions of the right of succession have in
20   that form of government no place at all.

In an aristocracy, when any of the assembly dieth, the election of another into his room belonged to the assembly, as the sovereign, to whom belonged the choosing of all counsellors and officers. For that which the representative doth, as actor, every one of the subjects doth, as author. And though the sovereign
25   assembly may give power to others to elect new men, for supply of their court, yet it is still by their authority that the election is made; and by the same it may, when the public shall require it, be recalled.

The greatest difficulty about the right of succession is in monarchy: and the difficulty ariseth from this, that at first sight, it is not manifest who is to appoint
30   the successor; nor many times who it is whom he hath appointed. For in both these cases, there is required a more exact ratiocination than every man is accustomed to use. As to the question who shall appoint the successor of a monarch that hath the sovereign authority; that is to say, who shall determine of the right of inheritance (for elective kings and princes have not the sovereign
35   power in propriety, but in use only), we are to consider that either he that is in possession has right to dispose of the succession, or else that right is again in the dissolved multitude. For the death of him that hath the sovereign power in property leaves the multitude without any sovereign at all; that is, without any representative in whom they should be united, and be capable of doing any one
40   action at all: and therefore they are incapable of election of any new monarch,

every man having equal right to submit himself to such as he thinks best able to protect him; or, if he can, protect himself by his own sword; which is a return to confusion and to the condition of a war of every man against every man, contrary to the end for which monarchy had its first institution. Therefore it is
5   manifest that by the institution of monarchy, the disposing of the successor is always left to the judgement and will of the present possessor.

And for the question which may arise sometimes, who it is that the monarch in possession hath designed to the succession and inheritance of his power, it is determined by his express words and testament; or by other tacit signs sufficient.
10   By express words, or testament, when it is declared by him in his lifetime, viva voce, or by writing; as the first emperors of Rome declared who should be their heirs. For the word heir does not of itself imply the children or nearest kindred of a man; but whomsoever a man shall any way declare he would have to succeed him in his estate. If therefore a monarch declare expressly that such a
15   man shall be his heir, either by word or writing, then is that man immediately after the decease of his predecessor invested in the right of being monarch.

But where testament and express words are wanting, other natural signs of the will are to be followed: whereof the one is custom. And therefore where the custom is that the next of kindred absolutely succeedeth, there also the next of
20   kindred hath right to the succession; for that, if the will of him that was in possession had been otherwise, he might easily have declared the same in his lifetime. And likewise where the custom is that the next of the male kindred succeedeth, there also the right of succession is in the next of the kindred male, for the same reason. And so it is if the custom were to advance the female. For
25   whatsoever custom a man may by a word control, and does not, it is a natural sign he would have that custom stand.

But where neither custom nor testament hath preceded, there it is to he understood; first, that a monarch's will is that the government remain monarchical, because he hath approved that government in himself. Secondly,
30   that a child of his own, male or female, be preferred before any other, because men are presumed to be more inclined by nature to advance their own children than the children of other men; and of their own, rather a male than a female, because men are naturally fitter than women for actions of labour and danger. Thirdly, where his own issue faileth, rather a brother than a stranger, and so still
35   the nearer in blood rather than the more remote, because it is always presumed that the nearer of kin is the nearer in affection; and it is evident that a man receives always, by reflection, the most honour from the greatness of his nearest kindred.

But if it be lawful for a monarch to dispose of the succession by words of
40   contract, or testament, men may perhaps object a great inconvenience: for he

212

may sell or give his right of governing to a stranger; which, because strangers (that is, men not used to live under the same government, nor speaking the same language) do commonly undervalue one another, may turn to the oppression of his subjects, which is indeed a great inconvenience: but it proceedeth not
5   necessarily from the subjection to a stranger's government, but from the unskillfulness of the governors, ignorant of the true rules of politics. And therefore the Romans, when they had subdued many nations, to make their government digestible were wont to take away that grievance as much as they thought necessary by giving sometimes to whole nations, and sometimes to
10   principal men of every nation they conquered, not only the privileges, but also the name of Romans; and took many of them into the Senate, and offices of charge, even in the Roman city. And this was it our most wise king, King James, aimed at in endeavouring the union of his two realms of England and Scotland. Which, if he could have obtained, had in all likelihood prevented the civil wars
15   which both those kingdoms, at this present, miserable. It is not therefore any injury to the people for a monarch to dispose of the succession by will; though by the fault of many princes, it hath been sometimes found inconvenient. Of the lawfulness of it, this also is an argument; that whatsoever inconvenience can arrive by giving a kingdom to a stranger, may arrive also by so marrying with
20   strangers, as the right of succession may descend upon them: yet this by all men is accounted lawful.

CHAPTER XX.
Of dominion paternal and despotical

A COMMONWEALTH by acquisition is that where the sovereign power is acquired by force; and it is acquired by force when men singly, or many together by plurality of voices, for fear of death, or bonds, do authorise all the actions of
25   that man, or assembly, that hath their lives and liberty in his power.

And this kind of dominion, or sovereignty, differeth from sovereignty by institution only in this, that men who choose their sovereign do it for fear of one another, and not of him whom they institute: but in this case, they subject themselves to him they are afraid of. In both cases they do it for fear: which is to
30   be noted by them that hold all such covenants, as proceed from fear of death or violence, void: which, if it were true, no man in any kind of Commonwealth could be obliged to obedience. It is true that in a Commonwealth once instituted, or acquired, promises proceeding from fear of death or violence are no covenants, nor obliging, when the thing promised is contrary to the laws; but the
35   reason is not because it was made upon fear, but because he that promiseth hath no right in the thing promised. Also, when he may lawfully perform, and doth

not, it is not the invalidity of the covenant that absolveth him, but the sentence of the sovereign. Otherwise, whensoever a man lawfully promiseth, he unlawfully breaketh: but when the sovereign, who is the actor, acquitteth him, then he is acquitted by him that extorted the promise, as by the author of such
5   absolution.

But the rights and consequences of sovereignty are the same in both. His power cannot, without his consent, be transferred to another: he cannot forfeit it: he cannot be accused by any of his subjects of injury: he cannot be punished by them: he is judge of what is necessary for peace, and judge of doctrines: he is
10   sole legislator, and supreme judge of controversies, and of the times and occasions of war and peace: to him it belonged to choose magistrates, counsellors, commanders, and all other officers and ministers; and to determine of rewards and punishments, honour and order. The reasons whereof are the same which are alleged in the precedent chapter for the same rights and
15   consequences of sovereignty by institution.

Dominion is acquired two ways: by generation and by conquest. The right of dominion by generation is that which the parent hath over his children, and is called paternal. And is not so derived from the generation, as if therefore the parent had dominion over his child because he begat him, but from the child's
20   consent, either express or by other sufficient arguments declared. For as to the generation, God hath ordained to man a helper, and there be always two that are equally parents: the dominion therefore over the child should belong equally to both, and he be equally subject to both, which is impossible; for no man can obey two masters. And whereas some have attributed the dominion to the man
25   only, as being of the more excellent sex, they misreckon in it. For there is not always that difference of strength or prudence between the man and the woman as that the right can be determined without war. In Commonwealths this controversy is decided by the civil law: and for the most part, but not always, the sentence is in favour of the father, because for the most part Commonwealths
30   have been erected by the fathers, not by the mothers of families. But the question lieth now in the state of mere nature where there are supposed no laws of matrimony, no laws for the education of children, but the law of nature and the natural inclination of the sexes, one to another, and to their children. In this condition of mere nature, either the parents between themselves dispose of the
35   dominion over the child by contract, or do not dispose thereof at all. If they dispose thereof, the right passeth according to the contract. We find in history that the Amazons contracted with the men of the neighbouring countries, to whom they had recourse for issue, that the issue male should be sent back, but the female remain with themselves: so that the dominion of the females was in
40   the mother.

If there be no contract, the dominion is in the mother. For in the condition of mere nature, where there are no matrimonial laws, it cannot be known who is the father unless it be declared by the mother; and therefore the right of dominion over the child dependeth on her will, and is consequently hers. Again,

5 seeing the infant is first in the power of the mother, so as she may either nourish or expose it; if she nourish it, it oweth its life to the mother, and is therefore obliged to obey her rather than any other; and by consequence the dominion over it is hers. But if she expose it, and another find and nourish it, dominion is in him that nourisheth it. For it ought to obey him by whom it is preserved,

10 because preservation of life being the end for which one man becomes subject to another, every man is supposed to promise obedience to him in whose power it is to save or destroy him.

If the mother be the father's subject, the child is in the father's power; and if the father be the mother's subject (as when a sovereign queen marrieth one of

15 her subjects), the child is subject to the mother, because the father also is her subject.

If a man and a woman, monarchs of two several kingdoms, have a child, and contract concerning who shall have the dominion of him, the right of the dominion passeth by the contract. If they contract not, the dominion followeth

20 the dominion of the place of his residence. For the sovereign of each country hath dominion over all that reside therein.

He that hath the dominion over the child hath dominion also over the children of the child, and over their children's children. For he that hath dominion over the person of a man hath dominion over all that is his, without

25 which dominion were but a title without the effect.

The right of succession to paternal dominion proceedeth in the same manner as doth the right of succession to monarchy, of which I have already sufficiently spoken in the precedent chapter.

Dominion acquired by conquest, or victory in war, is that which some

30 writers call despotical from Despotes, which signifieth a lord or master, and is the dominion of the master over his servant. And this dominion is then acquired to the victor when the vanquished, to avoid the present stroke of death, covenanteth, either in express words or by other sufficient signs of the will, that so long as his life and the liberty of his body is allowed him, the victor shall

35 have the use thereof at his pleasure. And after such covenant made, the vanquished is a servant, and not before: for by the word servant (whether it be derived from servire, to serve, or from servare, to save, which I leave to grammarians to dispute) is not meant a captive, which is kept in prison, or bonds, till the owner of him that took him, or bought him of one that did, shall

40 consider what to do with him: for such men, commonly called slaves, have no

215

obligation at all; but may break their bonds, or the prison; and kill, or carry away captive their master, justly: but one that, being taken, hath corporal liberty allowed him; and upon promise not to run away, nor to do violence to his master, is trusted by him.

5   It is not therefore the victory that giveth the right of dominion over the vanquished, but his own covenant. Nor is he obliged because he is conquered; that is to say, beaten, and taken, or put to flight; but because he cometh in and submitteth to the victor; nor is the victor obliged by an enemy's rendering himself, without promise of life, to spare him for this his yielding to discretion;
10 which obliges not the victor longer than in his own discretion he shall think fit.

And that which men do when they demand, as it is now called, quarter (which the Greeks called Zogria, taking alive) is to evade the present fury of the victor by submission, and to compound for their life with ransom or service: and therefore he that hath quarter hath not his life given, but deferred till further
15 deliberation; for it is not a yielding on condition of life, but to discretion. And then only is his life in security, and his service due, when the victor hath trusted him with his corporal liberty. For slaves that work in prisons, or fetters, do it not of duty, but to avoid the cruelty of their task-masters.

The master of the servant is master also of all he hath, and may exact the
20 use thereof; that is to say, of his goods, of his labour, of his servants, and of his children, as often as he shall think fit. For he holdeth his life of his master by the covenant of obedience; that is, of owning and authorising whatsoever the master shall do. And in case the master, if he refuse, kill him, or cast him into bonds, or otherwise punish him for his disobedience, he is himself the author of the same,
25 and cannot accuse him of injury.

In sum, the rights and consequences of both paternal and despotical dominion are the very same with those of a sovereign by institution; and for the same reasons: which reasons are set down in the precedent chapter. So that for a man that is monarch of diverse nations, he hath in one the sovereignty by
30 institution of the people assembled, and in another by conquest; that is by the submission of each particular, to avoid death or bonds; to demand of one nation more than of the other, from the title of conquest, as being a conquered nation, is an act of ignorance of the rights of sovereignty. For the sovereign is absolute over both alike; or else there is no sovereignty at all, and so every man may
35 lawfully protect himself, if he can, with his own sword, which is the condition of war.

By eat family, if it be not part of some Commonwealth, is of itself, as to the rights of sovereignty, a little monarchy; whether that family consist of a man and his children, or of a man and his servants, or of a man and his children and
40 servants together; wherein the father or master is the sovereign. But yet a family

is not properly a Commonwealth, unless it be of that power by its own number, or by other opportunities, as not to be subdued without the hazard of war. For where a number of men are manifestly too weak to defend themselves united, every one may use his own reason in time of danger to save his own life, either
5   by flight, or by submission to the enemy, as he shall think best; in the same manner as a very small company of soldiers, surprised by an army, may cast down their arms and demand quarter, or run away rather than be put to the sword. And thus much shall suffice concerning what I find by speculation, and deduction, of sovereign rights, from the nature, need, and designs of men in
10   erecting of Commonwealths, and putting themselves under monarchs or assemblies entrusted with power enough for their protection.

    Let us now consider what the Scripture teacheth in the same point. To Moses the children of Israel say thus: "Speak thou to us, and we will hear thee; but let not God speak to us, lest we die."[1] This is absolute obedience to Moses.
15   Concerning the right of kings, God Himself, by the mouth of Samuel, saith, "This shall be the right of the king you will have to reign over you. He shall take your sons, and set them to drive his chariots, and to be his horsemen, and to run before his chariots, and gather in his harvest; and to make his engines of war, and instruments of his chariots; and shall take your daughters to make perfumes,
20   to be his cooks, and bakers. He shall take your fields, your vineyards, and your olive-yards, and give them to his servants. He shall take the tithe of your corn and wine, and give it to the men of his chamber, and to his other servants. He shall take your man-servants, and your maidservants, and the choice of your youth, and employ them in his business. He shall take the tithe of your flocks;
25   and you shall be his servants."[2] This is absolute power, and summed up in the last words, you shall be his servants. Again, when the people heard what power their king was to have, yet they consented thereto, and say thus, "We will be as all other nations, and our king shall judge our causes, and go before us, to conduct our wars."[3] Here is confirmed the right that sovereigns have, both to the
30   militia and to all judicature; in which is contained as absolute power as one man can possibly transfer to another. Again, the prayer of King Solomon to God was this: "Give to thy servant understanding, to judge thy people, and to discern between good and evil."[4] It belonged therefore to the sovereign to be judge, and to prescribe the rules of discerning good and evil: which rules are laws; and
35   therefore in him is the legislative power. Saul sought the life of David; yet when it was in his power to slay Saul, and his servants would have done it, David forbade them, saying, "God forbid I should do such an act against my Lord, the anointed of God."[5] For obedience of servants St. Paul saith, "Servants obey your masters in all things";[6] and, "Children obey your parents in all things."[7] There is
40   simple obedience in those that are subject to paternal or despotical dominion.

Again, "The scribes and Pharisees sit in Moses' chair, and therefore all that they shall bid you observe, that observe and do."[8] There again is simple obedience. And St. Paul, "Warn them that they subject themselves to princes, and to those that are in authority, and obey them."[9] This obedience is also simple. Lastly, our
5   Saviour Himself acknowledges that men ought to pay such taxes as are by kings imposed, where He says, "Give to Caesar that which is Caesar's"; and paid such taxes Himself. And that the king's word is sufficient to take anything from any subject, when there is need; and that the king is judge of that need: for He Himself, as king of the Jews, commanded his Disciples to take the ass and ass's
10   colt to carry him into Jerusalem, saying, "Go into the village over against you, and you shall find a she ass tied, and her colt with her; untie them, and bring them to me. And if any man ask you, what you mean by it, say the Lord hath need of them: and they will let them go."[10] They will not ask whether his necessity be a sufficient title; nor whether he be judge of that necessity; but
15   acquiesce in the will of the Lord.
    To these places may be added also that of Genesis, "You shall be as gods, knowing good and evil."[11] And, "Who told thee that thou wast naked? Hast thou eaten of the tree, of which I commanded thee thou shouldest not eat?"[12] For the cognizance or judicature of good and evil, being forbidden by the name of the
20   fruit of the tree of knowledge, as a trial of Adam's obedience, the devil to inflame the ambition of the woman, to whom that fruit already seemed beautiful, told her that by tasting it they should be as gods, knowing good and evil. Whereupon having both eaten, they did indeed take upon them God's office, which is judicature of good and evil, but acquired no new ability to distinguish
25   between them aright. And whereas it is said that, having eaten, they saw they were naked; no man hath so interpreted that place as if they had been formerly blind, and saw not their own skins: the meaning is plain that it was then they first judged their nakedness (wherein it was God's will to create them) to be uncomely; and by being ashamed did tacitly censure God Himself. And
30   thereupon God saith, "Hast thou eaten," etc., as if He should say, doest thou that owest me obedience take upon thee to judge of my commandments? Whereby it is clearly, though allegorically, signified that the commands of them that have the right to command are not by their subjects to be censured nor disputed.
    So that it appeareth plainly, to my understanding, both from reason and
35   Scripture, that the sovereign power, whether placed in one man, as in monarchy, or in one assembly of men, as in popular and aristocratical Commonwealths, is as great as possibly men can be imagined to make it. And though of so unlimited a power, men may fancy many evil consequences, yet the consequences of the want of it, which is perpetual war of every man against his neighbour, are much
40   worse. The condition of man in this life shall never be without inconveniences;

but there happeneth in no Commonwealth any great inconvenience but what proceeds from the subjects' disobedience and breach of those covenants from which the Commonwealth hath its being. And whosoever, thinking sovereign power too great, will seek to make it less, must subject himself to the power that
5 can limit it; that is to say, to a greater.

The greatest objection is that of the practice; when men ask where and when such power has by subjects been acknowledged. But one may ask them again, when or where has there been a kingdom long free from sedition and civil war? In those nations whose Commonwealths have been long-lived, and not been
10 destroyed but by foreign war, the subjects never did dispute of the sovereign power. But howsoever, an argument from the practice of men that have not sifted to the bottom, and with exact reason weighed the causes and nature of Commonwealths, and suffer daily those miseries that proceed from the ignorance thereof, is invalid. For though in all places of the world men should
15 lay the foundation of their houses on the sand, it could not thence be inferred that so it ought to be. The skill of making and maintaining Commonwealths consisteth in certain rules, as doth arithmetic and geometry; not, as tennis play, on practice only: which rules neither poor men have the leisure, nor men that have had the leisure have hitherto had the curiosity or the method, to find out.

CHAPTER XXI.
Of liberty of subjects

20 LIBERTY, or freedom, signifieth properly the absence of opposition (by opposition, I mean external impediments of motion); and may be applied no less to irrational and inanimate creatures than to rational. For whatsoever is so tied, or environed, as it cannot move but within a certain space, which space is determined by the opposition of some external body, we say it hath not liberty to
25 go further. And so of all living creatures, whilst they are imprisoned, or restrained with walls or chains; and of the water whilst it is kept in by banks or vessels that otherwise would spread itself into a larger space; we use to say they are not at liberty to move in such manner as without those external impediments they would. But when the impediment of motion is in the constitution of the
30 thing itself, we use not to say it wants the liberty, but the power, to move; as when a stone lieth still, or a man is fastened to his bed by sickness.

And according to this proper and generally received meaning of the word, a freeman is he that, in those things which by his strength and wit he is able to do, is not hindered to do what he has a will to. But when the words free and liberty
35 are applied to anything but bodies, they are abused; for that which is not subject to motion is not to subject to impediment: and therefore, when it is said, for

example, the way is free, no liberty of the way is signified, but of those that walk in it without stop. And when we say a gift is free, there is not meant any liberty of the gift, but of the giver, that was not bound by any law or covenant to give it. So when we speak freely, it is not the liberty of voice, or pronunciation, but of the man, whom no law hath obliged to speak otherwise than he did. Lastly, from the use of the words free will, no liberty can be inferred of the will, desire, or inclination, but the liberty of the man; which consisteth in this, that he finds no stop in doing what he has the will, desire, or inclination to do.

Fear and liberty are consistent: as when a man throweth his goods into the sea for fear the ship should sink, he doth it nevertheless very willingly, and may refuse to do it if he will; it is therefore the action of one that was free: so a man sometimes pays his debt, only for fear of imprisonment, which, because no body hindered him from detaining, was the action of a man at liberty. And generally all actions which men do in Commonwealths, for fear of the law, are actions which the doers had liberty to omit.

Liberty and necessity are consistent: as in the water that hath not only liberty, but a necessity of descending by the channel; so, likewise in the actions which men voluntarily do, which, because they proceed their will, proceed from liberty, and yet because every act of man's will and every desire and inclination proceedeth from some cause, and that from another cause, in a continual chain (whose first link is in the hand of God, the first of all causes), proceed from necessity. So that to him that could see the connexion of those causes, the necessity of all men's voluntary actions would appear manifest. And therefore God, that seeth and disposeth all things, seeth also that the liberty of man in doing what he will is accompanied with the necessity of doing that which God will and no more, nor less. For though men may do many things which God does not command, nor is therefore author of them; yet they can have no passion, nor appetite to anything, of which appetite God's will is not the cause. And did not His will assure the necessity of man's will, and consequently of all that on man's will dependeth, the liberty of men would be a contradiction and impediment to the omnipotence and liberty of God. And this shall suffice, as to the matter in hand, of that natural liberty, which only is properly called liberty.

But as men, for the attaining of peace and conservation of themselves thereby, have made an artificial man, which we call a Commonwealth; so also have they made artificial chains, called civil laws, which they themselves, by mutual covenants, have fastened at one end to the lips of that man, or assembly, to whom they have given the sovereign power, and at the other to their own ears. These bonds, in their own nature but weak, may nevertheless be made to hold, by the danger, though not by the difficulty of breaking them.

In relation to these bonds only it is that I am to speak now of the liberty of subjects. For seeing there is no Commonwealth in the world wherein there be rules enough set down for the regulating of all the actions and words of men (as being a thing impossible): it followeth necessarily that in all kinds of actions, by
5   the laws pretermitted, men have the liberty of doing what their own reasons shall suggest for the most profitable to themselves. For if we take liberty in the proper sense, for corporal liberty; that is to say, freedom from chains and prison, it were very absurd for men to clamour as they do for the liberty they so manifestly enjoy. Again, if we take liberty for an exemption from laws, it is no less absurd
10 for men to demand as they do that liberty by which all other men may be masters of their lives. And yet as absurd as it is, this is it they demand, not knowing that the laws are of no power to protect them without a sword in the hands of a man, or men, to cause those laws to be put in execution. The liberty of a subject lieth therefore only in those things which, in regulating their actions,
15 the sovereign hath pretermitted: such as is the liberty to buy, and sell, and otherwise contract with one another; to choose their own abode, their own diet, their own trade of life, and institute their children as they themselves think fit; and the like.
      Nevertheless we are not to understand that by such liberty the sovereign
20 power of life and death is either abolished or limited. For it has been already shown that nothing the sovereign representative can do to a subject, on what pretence soever, can properly be called injustice or injury; because every subject is author of every act the sovereign doth, so that he never wanteth right to any thing, otherwise than as he himself is the subject of God, and bound thereby to
25 observe the laws of nature. And therefore it may and doth often happen in Commonwealths that a subject may be put to death by the command of the sovereign power, and yet neither do the other wrong; as when Jephthah caused his daughter to be sacrificed: in which, and the like cases, he that so dieth had liberty to do the action, for which he is nevertheless, without injury, put to death.
30 And the same holdeth also in a sovereign prince that putteth to death an innocent subject. For though the action be against the law of nature, as being contrary to equity (as was the killing of Uriah by David); yet it was not an injury to Uriah, but to God. Not to Uriah, because the right to do what he pleased was given him by Uriah himself; and yet to God, because David was God's subject and
35 prohibited all iniquity by the law of nature. Which distinction, David himself, when he repented the fact, evidently confirmed, saying, "To thee only have I sinned." In the same manner, the people of Athens, when they banished the most potent of their Commonwealth for ten years, thought they committed no injustice; and yet they never questioned what crime he had done, but what hurt
40 he would do: nay, they commanded the banishment of they knew not whom; and

every citizen bringing his oyster shell into the market place, written with the name of him he desired should be banished, without actually accusing him sometimes banished an Aristides, for his reputation of justice; and sometimes a scurrilous jester, as Hyperbolus, to make a jest of it. And yet a man cannot say the sovereign people of Athens wanted right to banish them; or an Athenian the liberty to jest, or to be just.

The liberty whereof there is so frequent and honourable mention in the histories and philosophy of the ancient Greeks and Romans, and in the writings and discourse of those that from them have received all their learning in the politics, is not the liberty of particular men, but the liberty of the Commonwealth: which is the same with that which every man then should have, if there were no civil laws nor Commonwealth at all. And the effects of it also be the same. For as amongst masterless men, there is perpetual war of every man against his neighbour; no inheritance to transmit to the son, nor to expect from the father; no propriety of goods or lands; no security; but a full and absolute liberty in every particular man: so in states and Commonwealths not dependent on one another, every Commonwealth, not every man, has an absolute liberty to do what it shall judge, that is to say, what that man or assembly that representeth it shall judge, most conducing to their benefit. But withal, they live in the condition of a perpetual war, and upon the confines of battle, with their frontiers armed, and cannons planted against their neighbours round about. The Athenians and Romans were free; that is, free Commonwealths: not that any particular men had the liberty to resist their own representative, but that their representative had the liberty to resist, or invade, other people. There is written on the turrets of the city of Luca in great characters at this day, the word LIBERTAS; yet no man can thence infer that a particular man has more liberty or immunity from the service of the Commonwealth there than in Constantinople. Whether a Commonwealth be monarchical or popular, the freedom is still the same.

But it is an easy thing for men to be deceived by the specious name of liberty; and, for want of judgement to distinguish, mistake that for their private inheritance and birthright which is the right of the public only. And when the same error is confirmed by the authority of men in reputation for their writings on this subject, it is no wonder if it produce sedition and change of government. In these western parts of the world we are made to receive our opinions concerning the institution and rights of Commonwealths from Aristotle, Cicero, and other men, Greeks and Romans, that, living under popular states, derived those rights, not from the principles of nature, but transcribed them into their books out of the practice of their own Commonwealths, which were popular; as the grammarians describe the rules of language out of the practice of the time; or

the rules of poetry out of the poems of Homer and Virgil. And because the Athenians were taught (to keep them from desire of changing their government) that they were freemen, and all that lived under monarchy were slaves; therefore Aristotle puts it down in his Politics "In democracy, liberty is to be supposed:
5   for it is commonly held that no man is free in any other government."[13] And as Aristotle, so Cicero and other writers have grounded their civil doctrine on the opinions of the Romans, who were taught to hate monarchy: at first, by them that, having deposed their sovereign, shared amongst them the sovereignty of Rome; and afterwards by their successors. And by reading of these Greek and
10   Latin authors, men from their childhood have gotten a habit, under a false show of liberty, of favouring tumults, and of licentious controlling the actions of their sovereigns; and again of controlling those controllers; with the effusion of so much blood, as I think I may truly say there was never anything so dearly bought as these western parts have bought the learning of the Greek and Latin
15   tongues.

To come now to the particulars of the true liberty of a subject; that is to say, what are the things which, though commanded by the sovereign, he may nevertheless without injustice refuse to do; we are to consider what rights we pass away when we make a Commonwealth; or, which is all one, what liberty
20   we deny ourselves by owning all the actions, without exception, of the man or assembly we make our sovereign. For in the act of our submission consisteth both our obligation and our liberty; which must therefore be inferred by arguments taken from thence; there being no obligation on any man which ariseth not from some act of his own; for all men equally are by nature free. And
25   because such arguments must either be drawn from the express words, "I authorise all his actions," or from the intention of him that submitteth himself to his power (which intention is to be understood by the end for which he so submitteth), the obligation and liberty of the subject is to be derived either from those words, or others equivalent, or else from the end of the institution of
30   sovereignty; namely, the peace of the subjects within themselves, and their defence against a common enemy.

First therefore, seeing sovereignty by institution is by covenant of every one to every one; and sovereignty by acquisition, by covenants of the vanquished to the victor, or child to the parent; it is manifest that every subject has liberty in all
35   those things the right whereof cannot by covenant be transferred. I have shown before, in the fourteenth Chapter, that covenants not to defend a man's own body are void. Therefore,

If the sovereign command a man, though justly condemned, to kill, wound, or maim himself; or not to resist those that assault him; or to abstain from the use of food, air, medicine, or any other thing without which he cannot live; yet hath that man the liberty to disobey.

If a man be interrogated by the sovereign, or his authority, concerning a crime done by himself, he is not bound (without assurance of pardon) to confess it; because no man, as I have shown in the same chapter, can be obliged by covenant to accuse himself.

Again, the consent of a subject to sovereign power is contained in these words, "I authorise, or take upon me, all his actions"; in which there is no restriction at all of his own former natural liberty: for by allowing him to kill me, I am not bound to kill myself when he commands me. It is one thing to say, "Kill me, or my fellow, if you please"; another thing to say, "I will kill myself, or my fellow." It followeth, therefore, that

No man is bound by the words themselves, either to kill himself or any other man; and consequently, that the obligation a man may sometimes have, upon the command of the sovereign, to execute any dangerous or dishonourable office, dependeth not on the words of our submission, but on the intention; which is to be understood by the end thereof. When therefore our refusal to obey frustrates the end for which the sovereignty was ordained, then there is no liberty to refuse; otherwise, there is.

Upon this ground a man that is commanded as a soldier to fight against the enemy, though his sovereign have right enough to punish his refusal with death, may nevertheless in many cases refuse, without injustice; as when he substituteth a sufficient soldier in his place: for in this case he deserteth not the service of the Commonwealth. And there is allowance to be made for natural timorousness, not only to women (of whom no such dangerous duty is expected), but also to men of feminine courage. When armies fight, there is on one side, or both, a running away; yet when they do it not out of treachery, but fear, they are not esteemed to do it unjustly, but dishonourably. For the same reason, to avoid battle is not injustice, but cowardice. But he that enrolleth himself a soldier, or taketh impressed money, taketh away the excuse of a timorous nature, and is obliged, not only to go to the battle, but also not to run from it without his captain's leave. And when the defence of the Commonwealth requireth at once the help of all that are able to bear arms, every one is obliged; because otherwise the institution of the Commonwealth, which they have not the purpose or courage to preserve, was in vain.

To resist the sword of the Commonwealth in defence of another man, guilty or innocent, no man hath liberty; because such liberty takes away from the sovereign the means of protecting us, and is therefore destructive of the very essence of government. But in case a great many men together have already resisted the sovereign power unjustly, or committed some capital crime for

which every one of them expecteth death, whether have they not the liberty then
to join together, and assist, and defend one another? Certainly they have: for
they but defend their lives, which the guilty man may as well do as the innocent.
There was indeed injustice in the first breach of their duty: their bearing of arms
5   subsequent to it, though it be to maintain what they have done, is no new unjust
act. And if it be only to defend their persons, it is not unjust at all. But the offer
of pardon taketh from them to whom it is offered the plea of self-defence, and
maketh their perseverance in assisting or defending the rest unlawful.

As for other liberties, they depend on the silence of the law. In cases where
10 the sovereign has prescribed no rule, there the subject hath the liberty to do, or
forbear, according to his own discretion. And therefore such liberty is in some
places more, and in some less; and in some times more, in other times less,
according as they that have the sovereignty shall think most convenient. As for
example, there was a time when in England a man might enter into his own land,
15 and dispossess such as wrongfully possessed it, by force. But in after times that
liberty of forcible entry was taken away by a statute made by the king in
Parliament. And in some places of the world men have the liberty of many
wives: in other places, such liberty is not allowed.

If a subject have a controversy with his sovereign of debt, or of right of
20 possession of lands or goods, or concerning any service required at his hands, or
concerning any penalty, corporal or pecuniary, grounded on a precedent law, he
hath the same liberty to sue for his right as if it were against a subject, and
before such judges as are appointed by the sovereign. For seeing the sovereign
demandeth by force of a former law, and not by virtue of his power, he declareth
25 thereby that he requireth no more than shall appear to be due by that law. The
suit therefore is not contrary to the will of the sovereign, and consequently the
subject hath the liberty to demand the hearing of his cause, and sentence
according to that law. But if he demand or take anything by pretence of his
power, there lieth, in that case, no action of law: for all that is done by him in
30 virtue of his power is done by the authority of every subject, and consequently,
he that brings an action against the sovereign brings it against himself.

If a monarch, or sovereign assembly, grant a liberty to all or any of his
subjects, which grant standing, he is disabled to provide for their safety; the
grant is void, unless he directly renounce or transfer the sovereignty to another.
35 For in that he might openly (if it had been his will), and in plain terms, have
renounced or transferred it and did not, it is to be understood it was not his will,
but that the grant proceeded from ignorance of the repugnancy between such a
liberty and the sovereign power: and therefore the sovereignty is still retained,
and consequently all those powers which are necessary to the exercising thereof;

such as are the power of war and peace, of judicature, of appointing officers and counsellors, of levying money, and the rest named in the eighteenth Chapter.

The obligation of subjects to the sovereign is understood to last as long, and no longer, than the power lasteth by which he is able to protect them. For the right men have by nature to protect themselves, when none else can protect them, can by no covenant be relinquished. The sovereignty is the soul of the Commonwealth; which, once departed from the body, the members do no more receive their motion from it. The end of obedience is protection; which, wheresoever a man seeth it, either in his own or in another's sword, nature applieth his obedience to it, and his endeavour to maintain it. And though sovereignty, in the intention of them that make it, be immortal; yet is it in its own nature, not only subject to violent death by foreign war, but also through the ignorance and passions of men it hath in it, from the very institution, many seeds of a natural mortality, by intestine discord.

If a subject be taken prisoner in war, or his person or his means of life be within the guards of the enemy, and hath his life and corporal liberty given him on condition to be subject to the victor, he hath liberty to accept the condition; and, having accepted it, is the subject of him that took him; because he had no other way to preserve himself. The case is the same if he be detained on the same terms in a foreign country. But if a man be held in prison, or bonds, or is not trusted with the liberty of his body, he cannot be understood to be bound by covenant to subjection, and therefore may, if he can, make his escape by any means whatsoever.

If a monarch shall relinquish the sovereignty, both for himself and his heirs, his subjects return to the absolute liberty of nature; because, though nature may declare who are his sons, and who are the nearest of his kin, yet it dependeth on his own will, as hath been said in the precedent chapter, who shall be his heir. If therefore he will have no heir, there is no sovereignty, nor subjection. The case is the same if he die without known kindred, and without declaration of his heir. For then there can no heir be known, and consequently no subjection be due.

If the sovereign banish his subject, during the banishment he is not subject. But he that is sent on a message, or hath leave to travel, is still subject; but it is by contract between sovereigns, not by virtue of the covenant of subjection. For whosoever entereth into another's dominion is subject to all the laws thereof, unless he have a privilege by the amity of the sovereigns, or by special license.

If a monarch subdued by war render himself subject to the victor, his subjects are delivered from their former obligation, and become obliged to the victor. But if he be held prisoner, or have not the liberty of his own body, he is not understood to have given away the right of sovereignty; and therefore his subjects are obliged to yield obedience to the magistrates formerly placed, governing not in their own name, but in his. For, his right remaining, the question is only of the administration; that is to say, of the magistrates and officers; which if he have not means to name, he is supposed to approve those which he himself had formerly appointed.

****

CHAPTER XXVI.
Of civil laws

5   BY civil laws, I understand the laws that men are therefore bound to observe, because they are members, not of this or that Commonwealth in particular, but of a Commonwealth. For the knowledge of particular laws belongeth to them that profess the study of the laws of their several countries; but the knowledge of civil law in general, to any man. The ancient law of Rome

10   was called their civil law, from the word civitas, which signifies a Commonwealth: and those countries which, having been under the Roman Empire and governed by that law, retain still such part thereof as they think fit, call that part the civil law to distinguish it from the rest of their own civil laws. But that is not it I intend to speak of here; my design being not to show what is

15   law here and there, but what is law; as Plato, Aristotle, Cicero, and diverse others have done, without taking upon them the profession of the study of the law.

      And first it is manifest that law in general is not counsel, but command; nor a command of any man to any man, but only of him whose command is

20   addressed to one formerly obliged to obey him. And as for civil law, it addeth only the name of the person commanding, which is persona civitatis, the person of the Commonwealth.

      Which considered, I define civil law in this manner. Civil law is to every subject those rules which the Commonwealth hath commanded him, by word,

25   writing, or other sufficient sign of the will, to make use of for the distinction of right and wrong; that is to say, of that is contrary and what is not contrary to the rule.

      In which definition there is nothing that is that is not at first sight evident. For every man seeth that some laws are addressed to all the subjects in general;

30   some to particular provinces; some to particular vocations; and some to particular men; and are therefore laws to every of those to whom the command is directed, and to none else. As also, that laws are the rules of just and unjust, nothing being reputed unjust that is not contrary to some law. Likewise, that none can make laws but the Commonwealth, because our subjection is to the

Commonwealth only; and that commands are to be signified by sufficient signs, because a man knows not otherwise how to obey them. And therefore, whatsoever can from this definition by necessary consequence be deduced, ought to be acknowledged for truth. Now I deduce from it this that followeth.

5   1. The legislator in all Commonwealths is only the sovereign, be he one man, as in a monarchy, or one assembly of men, as in a democracy or aristocracy. For the legislator is he that maketh the law. And the Commonwealth only prescribes and commandeth the observation of those rules which we call law: therefore the Commonwealth is the legislator. But the Commonwealth is no
10   person, nor has capacity to do anything but by the representative, that is, the sovereign; and therefore the sovereign is the sole legislator. For the same reason, none can abrogate a law made, but the sovereign, because a law is not abrogated but by another law that forbiddeth it to be put in execution.

       2. The sovereign of a Commonwealth, be it an assembly or one man, is not
15   subject to the civil laws. For having power to make and repeal laws, he may, when he pleaseth, free himself from that subjection by repealing those laws that trouble him, and making of new; and consequently he was free before. For he is free that can be free when he will: nor is it possible for any person to be bound to himself, because he that can bind can release; and therefore he that is bound
20   to himself only is not bound.

       3. When long use obtaineth the authority of a law, it is not the length of time that maketh the authority, but the will of the sovereign signified by his silence (for silence is sometimes an signified by his silence (for silence is sometimes an argument of consent); and it is no longer law, than the sovereign
25   shall be silent therein. And therefore if the sovereign shall have a question of right grounded, not upon his present will, but upon the laws formerly made, the length of time shall bring no prejudice to his right: but the question shall be judged by equity. For many unjust actions and unjust sentences go uncontrolled a longer time than any man can remember. And our lawyers account no customs
30   law but such as reasonable, and that evil customs are to be abolished: but the judgement of what is reasonable, and of what is to be abolished, belonged to him that maketh the law, which is the sovereign assembly or monarch.

       4. The law of nature and the civil law contain each other and are of equal extent. For the laws of nature, which consist in equity, justice, gratitude, and
35   other moral virtues on these depending, in the condition of mere nature (as I have said before in the end of the fifteenth Chapter), are not properly laws, but qualities that dispose men to peace and to obedience. When a Commonwealth is once settled, then are they actually laws, and not before; as being then the commands of the Commonwealth; and therefore also civil laws: for it is the
40   sovereign power that obliges men to obey them. For the differences of private

men, to declare what is equity, what is justice, and is moral virtue, and to make them binding, there is need of the ordinances of sovereign power, and punishments to be ordained for such as shall break them; which ordinances are therefore part of the civil law. The law of nature therefore is a part of the civil

5 law in all Commonwealths of the world. Reciprocally also, the civil law is a part of the dictates of nature. For justice, that is to say, performance of covenant, and giving to every man his own, is a dictate of the law of nature. But every subject in a Commonwealth hath covenanted to obey the civil law; either one with another, as when they assemble to make a common representative, or with the

10 representative itself one by one when, subdued by the sword, they promise obedience that they may receive life; and therefore obedience to the civil law is part also of the law of nature. Civil and natural law are not different kinds, but different parts of law; whereof one part, being written, is called civil the other unwritten, natural. But the right of nature, that is, the natural liberty of man, may

15 by the civil law be abridged and restrained: nay, the end of making laws is no other but such restraint, without which there cannot possibly be any peace. And law was brought into the world for nothing else but to limit the natural liberty of particular men in such manner as they might not hurt, but assist one another, and join together against a common enemy.

20   5. If the sovereign of one Commonwealth subdue a people that have lived under other written laws, and afterwards govern them by the same laws by which they were governed before, yet those laws are the civil laws of the victor, and not of the vanquished Commonwealth. For the legislator is he, not by whose authority the laws were first made, but by whose authority they now continue to

25 be laws. And therefore where there be diverse provinces within the dominion of a Commonwealth, and in those provinces diversity of laws, which commonly are called the customs of each several province, we are not to understand that such customs have their force only from length of time; but that they were anciently laws written, or otherwise made known, for the constitutions and

30 statutes of their sovereigns; and are now laws, not by virtue of the prescription of time, but by the constitutions of their present sovereigns. But if an unwritten law, in all the provinces of a dominion, shall be generally observed, and no iniquity appear in the use thereof, that law can be no other but a law of nature, equally obliging all mankind.

35   6. Seeing then all laws, written and unwritten, have their authority and force from the will of the Commonwealth; that is to say, from the will of the representative, which in a monarchy is the monarch, and in other Commonwealths the sovereign assembly; a man may wonder from whence proceed such opinions as are found in the books of lawyers of eminence in

40 several Commonwealths, directly or by consequence making the legislative

power depend on private men or subordinate judges. As for example, that the common law hath no controller but the Parliament; which is true only where a parliament has the sovereign power, and cannot be assembled nor dissolved, but by their own discretion. For if there be a right in any else to dissolve them, there

5   is a right also to control them, and consequently to control their controllings. And if there be no such right, then the controller of laws is not parlamentum, but rex in parlamento. And where a parliament is sovereign, if it should assemble never so many or so wise men from the countries subject to them, for whatsoever cause, yet there is no man will believe that such an assembly hath

10   thereby acquired to themselves a legislative power. Item, that the two arms of a Commonwealth are force and justice; the first whereof is in the king, the other deposited in the hands of the Parliament. As if a Commonwealth could consist where the force were in any hand which justice had not the authority to command and govern.

15   7. That law can never be against reason, our lawyers are agreed: and that not the letter (that is, every construction of it), but that which is according to the intention of the legislator, is the law. And it is true: but the doubt is of whose reason it is that shall be received for law. It is not meant of any private reason; for then there would be as much contradiction in the laws as there is in the

20   Schools; nor yet, as Sir Edward Coke makes it, an "Artificial perfection of reason, gotten by long study, observation, and experience," as his was. For it is possible long study may increase and confirm erroneous sentences: and where men build on false grounds, the more they build, the greater is the ruin: and of those that study and observe with equal time and diligence, the reasons and

25   resolutions are, and must remain, discordant: and therefore it is not that juris prudentia, or wisdom of subordinate judges, but the reason of this our artificial man the Commonwealth, and his command, that maketh law: and the Commonwealth being in their representative but one person, there cannot easily arise any contradiction in the laws; and when there doth, the same reason is able,

30   by interpretation or alteration, to take it away. In all courts of justice, the sovereign (which is the person of the Commonwealth) is he that judgeth: the subordinate judge ought to have regard to the reason which moved his sovereign to make such law, that his sentence may be according thereunto, which then is his sovereigns sentence; otherwise it is his own, and an unjust one.

35   8. From this, that the law is a command, and a command consisteth in declaration or manifestation of the will of him that commandeth, by voice, writing, or some other sufficient argument of the same, we may understand that the command of the Commonwealth is law only to those that have means to take notice of it. Over natural fools, children, or madmen there is no law, no more

40   than over brute beasts; nor are they capable of the title of just or unjust, because

they had never power to make any covenant or to understand the consequences thereof, and consequently never took upon them to authorize the actions of any sovereign, as they must do that make to themselves a Commonwealth. And as those from whom nature or accident hath taken away the notice of all laws in
5   general; so also every man, from whom any accident not proceeding from his own default, hath taken away the means to take notice of any particular law, is excused if he observe it not; and to speak properly, that law is no law to him. It is therefore necessary to consider in this place what arguments and signs be sufficient for the knowledge of what is the law; that is to say, what is the will of
10   the sovereign, as well in monarchies as in other forms of government.

And first, if it be a law that obliges all the subjects without exception, and is not written, nor otherwise published in such places as they may take notice thereof, it is a law of nature. For whatever men are to take knowledge of for law, not upon other men's words, but every one from his own reason, must be such
15   as is agreeable to the reason of all men; which no law can be, but the law of nature. The laws of nature therefore need not any publishing nor proclamation; as being contained in this one sentence, approved by all the world, Do not that to another which thou thinkest unreasonable to be done by another to thyself.

Secondly, if it be a law that obliges only some condition of men, or one
20   particular man, and be not written, nor published by word, then also it is a law of nature, and known by the same arguments and signs that distinguish those in such a condition from other subjects. For whatsoever law is not written, or some way published by him that makes it law, can be known no way but by the reason of him that is to obey it; and is therefore also a law not only civil, but natural.
25   For example, if the sovereign employ a public minister, without written instructions what to do, he is obliged to take for instructions the dictates of reason: as if he make a judge, the judge is to take notice that his sentence ought to be according to the reason of his sovereign, which being always understood to be equity, he is bound to it by the law of nature: or if an ambassador, he is, in all
30   things not contained in his written instructions, to take for instruction that which reason dictates to be most conducing to his sovereign's interest; and so of all other ministers of the sovereignty, public and private. All which instructions of natural reason may be comprehended under one name of fidelity, which is a branch of natural justice.
35   The law of nature excepted, it belonged to the essence of all other laws to be made known to every man that shall be obliged to obey them, either by word, or writing, or some other act known to proceed from the sovereign authority. For the will of another cannot be understood but by his own word, or act, or by conjecture taken from his scope and purpose; which in the person of the
40   Commonwealth is to be supposed always consonant to equity and reason. And

in ancient time, before letters were in common use, the laws were many times put into verse; that the rude people, taking pleasure in singing or reciting them, might the more easily retain them in memory. And for the same reason Solomon adviseth a man to bind the Ten Commandments upon his ten fingers.[14] And for
5 the Law which Moses gave to the people of Israel at the renewing of the Covenant, he biddeth them to teach it their children, by discoursing of it both at home and upon the way, at going to bed and at rising from bed; and to write it upon the posts and doors of their houses;[15] and to assemble the people, man, woman, and child, to hear it read.[16]
10 Nor is it enough the law be written and published, but also that there be manifest signs that it proceedeth from the will of the sovereign. For private men, when they have, or think they have, force enough to secure their unjust designs, and convoy them safely to their ambitious ends, may publish for laws what they please, without or against the legislative authority. There is therefore requisite,
15 not only a declaration of the law, but also sufficient signs of the author and authority. The author or legislator is supposed in every Commonwealth to be evident, because he is the sovereign, who, having been constituted by the consent of every one, is supposed by every one to be sufficiently known. And though the ignorance and security of men be such, for the most part, as that
20 when the memory of the first constitution of their Commonwealth is worn out, they do not consider by whose power they use to be defended against their enemies, and to have their industry protected, and to be righted when injury is done them; yet because no man that considers can make question of it, no excuse can be derived from the ignorance of where the sovereignty is placed.
25 And it is a dictate of natural reason, and consequently an evident law of nature, that no man ought to weaken that power the protection whereof he hath himself demanded or wittingly received against others. Therefore of who is sovereign, no man, but by his own fault (whatsoever evil men suggest), can make any doubt. The difficulty cocsisteth in the evidence of the authority derived from
30 him; the removing whereof dependeth on the knowledge of the public registers, public counsels, public ministers, and public seals; by which all laws are sufficiently verified; verified, I say, not authorized: for the verification is but the testimony and record; not the authority of the law, which consisteth in the command of the sovereign only.
35 If therefore a man have a question of injury, depending on the law of nature; that is to say, on common equity; the sentence of the judge, that by commission hath authority to take cognizance of such causes, is a sufficient verification of the law of nature in that individual case. For though the advice of one that professeth the study of the law be useful for the avoiding of contention, yet it is

but advice: it is the judge must tell men what is law, upon the hearing of the controversy.

But when the question is of injury, or crime, upon a written law, every man by recourse to the registers by himself or others may, if he will, be sufficiently
5 informed, before he do such injury, or commit the crime, whether it be an injury or not; nay, he ought to do so: for when a man doubts whether the act he goeth about be just or unjust, and may inform himself if he will, the doing is unlawful. In like manner, he that supposeth himself injured, in a case determined by the written law, which he may by himself or others see and consider; if he complain
10 before he consults with the law, he does unjustly, and bewrayeth a disposition rather to vex other men than to demand his own right.

If the question be of obedience to a public officer, to have seen his commission with the public seal, and heard it read, or to have had the means to be informed of it, if a man would, is a sufficient verification of his authority. For
15 every man is obliged to do his best endeavour to inform himself of all written laws that may concern his own future actions.

The legislator known, and the laws either by writing or by the light of nature sufficiently published, there wanteth yet another very material circumstance to make them obligatory. For it is not the letter, but the
20 intendment, or meaning; that is to say, the authentic interpretation of the law (which is the sense of the legislator), in which the nature of the law consisteth; and therefore the interpretation of all laws dependeth on the authority sovereign; and the interpreters can be none but those which the sovereign, to whom only the subject oweth obedience, shall appoint. For else, by the craft of an
25 interpreter, the law may be made to bear a sense contrary to that of the sovereign, by which means the interpreter becomes the legislator.

All laws, written and unwritten, have need of interpretation. The unwritten law of nature, though it be easy to such as without partiality and passion make use of their natural reason, and therefore leaves the violators thereof without
30 excuse; yet considering there be very few, perhaps none, that in some cases are not blinded by self-love, or some other passion, it is now become of all laws the most obscure, and has consequently the greatest need of able interpreters. The written laws, if laws, if they be short, are easily misinterpreted, for the diverse significations of a word or two; if long, they be more obscure by the diverse
35 significations of many words: in so much as no written law, delivered in few or many words, can be well understood without a perfect understanding of the final causes for which the law was made; the knowledge of which final causes is in the legislator. To him therefore there cannot be any knot in the law insoluble, either by finding out the ends to undo it by, or else by making what ends he will

(as Alexander did with his sword in the Gordian knot) by the legislative power; which no other interpreter can do.

The interpretation of the laws of nature in a Commonwealth dependeth not on the books of moral philosophy. The authority of writers, without the authority of the Commonwealth, maketh not their opinions law, be they never so true. That which I have written in this treatise concerning the moral virtues, and of their necessity for the procuring and maintaining peace, though it be evident truth, is not therefore presently law, but because in all Commonwealths in the world it is part of the civil law. For though it be naturally reasonable, yet it is by the sovereign power that it is law: otherwise, it were a great error to call the laws of nature unwritten law; whereof we see so many volumes published, and in them so many contradictions of one another and of themselves.

The interpretation of the law of nature is the sentence of the judge constituted by the sovereign authority to hear and determine such controversies as depend thereon, and consisteth in the application of the law to the present case. For in the act of judicature the judge doth no more but consider whether the demand of the party be consonant to natural reason and equity; and the sentence he giveth is therefore the interpretation of the law of nature; which interpretation is authentic, not because it is his private sentence, but because he giveth it by authority of the sovereign, whereby it becomes the sovereign's sentence; which is law for that time to the parties pleading.

But because there is no judge subordinate, nor sovereign, but may err in a judgement equity; if afterward in another like case he find it more consonant to equity to give a contrary sentence, he is obliged to do it. No man's error becomes his own law, nor obliges him to persist in it. Neither, for the same reason, becomes it a law to other judges, though sworn to follow it. For though a wrong sentence given by authority of the sovereign, if he know and allow it, in such laws as are mutable, be a constitution of a new law in cases in which every little circumstance is the same; yet in laws immutable, such as are the laws of nature, they are no laws to the same or other judges in the like cases for ever after. Princes succeed one another; and one judge passeth, another cometh; nay, heaven and earth shall pass; but not one tittle of the law of nature shall pass; for it is the eternal law of God. Therefore all the sentences of precedent judges that have ever been cannot all together make a law contrary to natural equity. Nor any examples of former judges can warrant an unreasonable sentence, or discharge the present judge of the trouble of studying what is equity (in the case he is to judge) from the principles of his own natural reason. For example sake, it is against the law of nature to punish the innocent; and innocent is he that acquitteth himself judicially and is acknowledged for innocent by the judge. Put the case now that a man is accused of a capital crime, and seeing the power and

malice of some enemy, and the frequent corruption and partiality of judges, runneth away for fear of the event, and afterwards is taken and brought to a legal trial, and maketh it sufficiently appear he was not guilty of the crime, and being thereof acquitted is nevertheless condemned to lose his goods; this is a manifest
5 condemnation of the innocent. I say therefore that there is no place in the world where this can be an interpretation of a law of nature, or be made a law by the sentences of precedent judges that had done the same. For he that judged it first judged unjustly; and no injustice can be a pattern of judgement to succeeding judges. A written law may forbid innocent men to fly, and they may be punished
10 for flying: but that flying for fear of injury should be taken for presumption of guilt, after a man is already absolved of the crime judicially, is contrary to the nature of a presumption, which hath no place after judgement given. Yet this is set down by a great lawyer for the common law of England: "If a man," saith he, "that is innocent be accused of felony, and for fear flyeth for the same; albeit he
15 judicially acquitteth himself of the felony; yet if it be found that he fled for the felony, he shall, notwithstanding his innocency, forfeit all his goods, chattels, debts, and duties. For as to the forfeiture of them, the law will admit no proof against the presumption in law, grounded upon his flight." Here you see an innocent man, judicially acquitted, notwithstanding his innocency (when no
20 written law forbade him to fly) after his acquittal, upon a presumption in law, condemned to lose all the goods he hath. If the law ground upon his flight a presumption of the fact, which was capital, the sentence ought to have been capital: the presumption were not of the fact, for what then ought he to lose his goods? This therefore is no law of England; nor is the condemnation grounded
25 upon a presumption of law, but upon the presumption of the judges. It is also against law to say that no proof shall be admitted against a presumption of law. For all judges, sovereign and subordinate, if they refuse to hear proof, refuse to do justice: for though the sentence be just, yet the judges that condemn, without hearing the proofs offered, are unjust judges; and their presumption is but
30 prejudice; which no man ought to bring with him to the seat of justice whatsoever precedent judgements or examples he shall pretend to follow. There be other things of this nature, wherein men's judgements have been perverted by trusting to precedents: but this is enough to show that though the sentence of the judge be a law to the party pleading, yet it is no law any judge that shall succeed
35 him in that office.

In like manner, when question is of the meaning of written laws, he is not the interpreter of them that writeth a commentary upon them. For commentaries are commonly more subject to cavil than the text, and therefore need other commentaries; and so there will be no end of such interpretation. And therefore
40 unless there be an interpreter authorized by the sovereign, from which the

subordinate judges are not to recede, the interpreter can be no other than the ordinary judges, in the same manner as they are in cases of the unwritten law; and their sentences are to be taken by them that plead for laws in that particular case, but not to bind other judges in like cases to give like judgements. For a
5 judge may err in the interpretation even of written laws; but no error of a subordinate judge can change the law, which is the general sentence of the sovereign.

In written laws men use to make a difference between the letter and the sentence of the law: and when by the letter is meant whatsoever can be gathered
10 from the bare words, it is well distinguished. For the significations of almost all are either in themselves, or in the metaphorical use of them, ambiguous; and may be drawn in argument to make many senses; but there is only one sense of the law. But if by the letter be meant the literal sense, then the letter and the sentence or intention of the law is all one. For the literal sense is that which the
15 legislator intended should by the letter of the law be signified. Now the intention of the legislator is always supposed to be equity: for it were a great contumely for a judge to think otherwise of the sovereign. He ought therefore, if the word of the law do not fully authorize a reasonable sentence, to supply it with the law of nature; or if the case be difficult, to respite judgement till he have received
20 more ample authority. For example, a written law ordaineth that he which is thrust out of his house by force shall be restored by force. It happens that a man by negligence leaves his house empty, and returning is kept out by force, in which case there is no special law ordained. It is evident that this case is contained in the same law; for else there is no remedy for him at all, which is to
25 be supposed against the intention of the legislator. Again, the word of the law commandeth to judge according to the evidence. A man is accused falsely of a fact which the judge himself saw done by another, and not by him that is accused. In this case neither shall the letter of the law be followed to the condemnation of the innocent, nor shall the judge give sentence against the
30 evidence of the witnesses, because the letter of the law is to the contrary; but procure of the sovereign that another be made judge, and himself witness. So that the incommodity that follows the bare words of a written law may lead him to the intention of the law, whereby to interpret the same the better; though no incommodity can warrant a sentence against the law. For every judge of right
35 and wrong is not judge of what is commodious or incommodious to the Commonwealth.

The abilities required in a good interpreter of the law, that is to say, in a good judge, are not the same with those of an advocate; namely, the study of the laws. For a judge, as he ought to take notice of the fact from none but the
40 witnesses, so also he ought to take notice of the law from nothing but the

236

statutes and constitutions of the sovereign, alleged in the pleading, or declared to
him by some that have authority from the sovereign power to declare them; and
need not take care beforehand what he shall judge; for it shall be given him what
he shall say concerning the fact, by witnesses; and what he shall say in point of
5   law, from those that shall in their pleadings show it, and by authority interpret it
upon the place. The Lords of Parliament in England were judges, and most
difficult causes have been heard and determined by them; yet few of them were
much versed in the study of the laws, and fewer had made profession of them;
and though they consulted with lawyers that were appointed to be present there
10 for that purpose, yet they alone had the authority of giving sentence. In like
manner, in the ordinary trials of right, twelve men of the common people are the
judges and give sentence, not only of the fact, but of the right; and pronounce
simply for the complainant or for the defendant; that is to say, are judges not
only of the fact, but also of the right; and in a question of crime, not only
15 determine whether done or not done, but also whether it be murder, homicide,
felony, assault, and the like, which are determinations of law: but because they
are not supposed to know the law of themselves, there is one that hath authority
to inform them of it in the particular case they are to judge of. But yet if they
judge not according to that he tells them, they are not subject thereby to any
20 penalty; unless it be made appear they did it against their consciences, or had
been corrupted by reward.

The things that make a good judge or good interpreter of the laws are, first,
a right understanding of that principal law of nature called equity; which,
depending not on the reading of other men's writings, but on the goodness of a
25 man's own natural reason and meditation, is presumed to be in those most that
had most leisure, and had the most inclination to meditate thereon. Secondly,
contempt of unnecessary riches and preferments. Thirdly, to be able in
judgement to divest himself of all fear, anger, hatred, love, and compassion.
Fourthly, and lastly, patience to hear, diligent attention in hearing, and memory
30 to retain, digest, and apply what he hath heard.

The difference and division of the laws has been made in diverse manners,
according to the different methods of those men that have written of them. For it
is a thing that dependeth on nature, but on the scope of the writer, and is
subservient to every man's proper method. In the Institutions of Justinian, we
35 find seven sorts of civil laws:

1. The edicts, constitutions, and epistles of prince; that is, of the emperor,
because the whole power of the people was in him. Like these are the
proclamations of the kings of England.

2. The decrees of the whole people of Rome, comprehending the Senate,
40 when they were put to the question by the Senate. These were laws, at first, by

the virtue of the sovereign power residing in the people; and such of them as by the emperors were not abrogated remained laws by the authority imperial. For all laws that bind are understood to be laws by his authority that has power to repeal them. Somewhat like to these laws are the Acts of Parliament in England.

5   3. The decrees of the common people, excluding the Senate, when they were put to the question by the tribune of the people. For such of them as were not abrogated by the emperors, remained laws by the authority imperial. Like to these were the orders of the House of Commons in England.

    4. Senatus consulta, the orders of the Senate: because when the people of
10 Rome grew so numerous as it was inconvenient to assemble them, it was thought fit by the emperor that men should consult the Senate instead of the people: and these have some resemblance with the Acts of Council.

    5. The edicts of praetors, and in some cases of the aediles: such as are the chief justices in the courts of England.

15   6. Responsa prudentum, which were the sentences and opinions of those lawyers to whom the emperor gave authority to interpret the law, the law, and to give answer to such as in matter of law demanded their advice; which answers the judges in giving judgement were obliged by the constitutions of the emperor to observe: and should be like the reports of cases judged, if other judges be by
20 the law of England bound to observe them. For the judges of the common law of England are not properly judges, but juris consulti; of whom the judges, who are either the lords, or twelve men of the country, are in point of law to ask advice.

    7. Also, unwritten customs, which in their own nature are an imitation of law, by the tacit consent of the emperor, in case they be not contrary to the law
25 of nature, are very laws.

    Another division of laws is into natural and positive. Natural are those which have been laws from all eternity, and are called not only natural, but also moral laws, consisting in the moral virtues; as justice, equity, and all habits of the mind that conduce to peace and charity, of which I have already spoken in
30 the fourteenth and fifteenth Chapters.

    Positive are those which have not been from eternity, but have been made laws by the will of those that have had the sovereign power over others, and are either written or made known to men by some other argument of the will of their legislator.

35   Again, of positive laws some are human, some divine: and of human positive laws, some are distributive, some penal. Distributive are those that determine the rights of the subjects, declaring to every man what it is by which he acquireth and holdeth a propriety in lands or goods, and a right or liberty of action: and these speak to all the subjects. Penal are those which declare what
40 penalty shall be inflicted on those that violate the law; and speak to the ministers

and officers ordained for execution. For though every one ought to be informed of the punishments ordained beforehand for their transgression; nevertheless the command is not addressed to the delinquent (who cannot be supposed will faithfully punish himself), but to public ministers appointed to see the penalty
5 executed. And these penal laws are for the most part written together with the laws distributive, and are sometimes called judgements. For all laws are general judgements, or sentences of the legislator; as also every particular judgement is a law to him whose case is judged.

Divine positive laws (for natural laws, being eternal and universal, are all
10 divine) are those which, being the commandments of God, not from all eternity, nor universally addressed to all men, but only to a certain people or to certain persons, are declared for such by those whom God hath authorized to declare them. But this authority of man to declare what be these positive of God, how can it be known? God may command a man, by a supernatural way, to deliver
15 laws to other men. But because it is of the essence of law that he who is to be obliged be assured of the authority of him that declareth it, which we cannot naturally take notice to be from God, how can a man without supernatural revelations be assured of the revelation received by the declarer? And how can he be bound to obey bound to obey them? For the first question, how a man can
20 be assured of the revelation of another without a revelation particularly to himself, it is evidently impossible: for though a man may be induced to believe such revelation, from the miracles they see him do, or from seeing the extraordinary sanctity of his life, or from seeing the extraordinary wisdom, or extraordinary felicity of his actions, all which are marks of God's extraordinary
25 favour; yet they are not assured evidences of special revelation. Miracles are marvellous works; but that which is marvellous to one may not be so to another. Sanctity may be feigned; and the visible felicities of this world are most often the work of God by natural and ordinary causes. And therefore no man can infallibly know by natural reason that another has had a supernatural revelation
30 of God's will but only a belief; every one, as the signs thereof shall appear greater or lesser, a firmer or a weaker belief.

But for the second, how he can be bound to obey them, it is not so hard. For if the law declared be not against the law of nature, which is undoubtedly God's law, and he undertake to obey it, he is bound by his own act; bound I say to obey
35 it, but not bound to believe it: for men's belief, and interior cogitations, are not subject to the commands, but only to the operation of God, ordinary or extraordinary. Faith of supernatural law is not a fulfilling, but only an assenting to the same; and not a duty that we exhibit to God, but a gift which God freely giveth to whom He pleaseth; as also unbelief is not a breach of any of His laws,
40 but a rejection of them all, except the laws natural. But this that I say will be

made yet clearer by, the examples and testimonies concerning this point in Holy Scripture. The covenant God made with Abraham in a supernatural manner was thus, "This is the covenant which thou shalt observe between me and thee and thy seed after thee."[17] Abraham's seed had not this revelation, nor were yet in

5 being; yet they are a party to the covenant, and bound to obey what Abraham should declare to them for God's law; which they could not be but in virtue of the obedience they owed to their parents, who (if they be subject to no other earthly power, as here in the case of Abraham) have sovereign power over their children and servants. Again, where God saith to Abraham, "In thee shall all

10 nations of the earth be blessed: for I know thou wilt command thy children and thy house after thee to keep the way of the Lord, and to observe righteousness and judgement," it is manifest the obedience of his family, who had no revelation, depended on their former obligation to obey their sovereign. At Mount Sinai Moses only went up to God; the people were forbidden to approach

15 on pain of death; yet were they bound to obey all that Moses declared to them for God's law. Upon what ground, but on this submission of their own, "Speak thou to us, and we will hear thee; but let not God speak to us, lest we die"? By which two places it sufficiently appeareth that in a Commonwealth a subject that has no certain and assured revelation particularly to himself concerning the will

20 of God is to obey for such the command of the Commonwealth: for if men were at liberty to take for God's commandments their own dreams and fancies, or the dreams and fancies of private men, scarce two men would agree upon what is God's commandment; and yet in respect of them every man would despise the commandments of the Commonwealth. I conclude, therefore, that in all things

25 not contrary to the moral law (that is to say, to the law of nature), all subjects are bound to obey that for divine law which is declared to be so by the laws of the Commonwealth. Which also is evident to any man's reason; for whatsoever is not against the law of nature may be made law in the name of them that have the sovereign power; there is no reason men should be the less obliged by it when it

30 is propounded in the name of God. Besides, there is no place in the world where men are permitted to pretend other commandments of God than are declared for such by the Commonwealth. Christian states punish those that revolt from Christian religion; and all other states, those that set up any religion by them forbidden. For in whatsoever is not regulated by the Commonwealth, it is equity

35 (which is the law of nature, and therefore an eternal law of God) that every man equally enjoy his liberty.

There is also another distinction of laws into fundamental and not fundamental: but I could never see in any author what a fundamental law signifieth. Nevertheless one may very reasonably distinguish laws in that

40 manner.

For a fundamental law in every Commonwealth is that which, being taken away, the Commonwealth faileth and is utterly dissolved, as a building whose foundation is destroyed. And therefore a fundamental law is that by which subjects are bound to uphold whatsoever power is given to the sovereign,
5   whether a monarch or a sovereign assembly, without which the Commonwealth cannot stand; such as is the power of war and peace, of judicature, of election of officers, and of doing whatsoever he shall think necessary for the public good. Not fundamental is that, the abrogating whereof draweth not with it the dissolution of the Commonwealth; such as are the laws concerning controversies
10   between subject and subject. Thus much of the division of laws.

I find the words lex civilis and jus civile, that is to say, and law and right civil, promiscuously used for the same thing, even in the most learned authors; which nevertheless ought not to be so. For right is liberty, namely that liberty which the civil law leaves us: but civil law is an obligation, and takes from us
15   the liberty which the law of nature gave us. Nature gave a right to every man to secure himself by his own strength, and to invade a suspected neighbour by way of prevention: but the civil law takes away that liberty, in all cases where the protection of the law may be safely stayed for. Insomuch as lex and jus are as different as obligation and liberty.

20   Likewise laws and charters are taken promiscuously for the same thing. Yet charters are donations of the sovereign; and not laws, but exemptions from law. The phrase of a law is jubeo, injungo; I command and enjoin: the phrase of a charter is dedi, concessi; I have given, I have granted: but what is given or granted to a man is not forced upon him by a law. A law may be made to bind
25   all the subjects of a Commonwealth: a liberty or charter is only to one man or some one part of the people. For to say all the people of a Commonwealth have liberty in any case whatsoever is to say that, in such case, there hath been no law made; or else, having been made, is now abrogated.

****

CHAPTER XXIX.
Of those things that weaken or tend to the dissolution of a commonwealth

THOUGH nothing can be immortal which mortals make; yet, if men had
30   the use of reason they pretend to, their Commonwealths might be secured, at least, from perishing by internal diseases. For by the nature of their institution, they are designed to live as long as mankind, or as the laws of nature, or as justice itself, which gives them life. Therefore when they come to be dissolved, not by external violence, but intestine disorder, the fault is not in men as they are
35   the matter, but as they are the makers and orderers of them. For men, as they

become at last weary of irregular jostling and hewing one another, and desire with all their hearts to conform themselves into one firm and lasting edifice; so for want both of the art of making fit laws to square their actions by, and also of humility and patience to suffer the rude and cumbersome points of their present greatness to be taken off, they cannot without the help of a very able architect be compiled into any other than a crazy building, such as, hardly lasting out their own time, must assuredly fall upon the heads of their posterity.

Amongst the infirmities therefore of a Commonwealth, I will reckon in the first place those that arise from an imperfect institution, and resemble the diseases of a natural body, which proceed from a defectuous procreation.

Of which this is one: that a man to obtain a kingdom is sometimes content with less power than to the peace and defence of the Commonwealth is necessarily required. From whence it cometh to pass that when the exercise of the power laid by is for the public safety to be resumed, it hath the resemblance of an unjust act, which disposeth great numbers of men, when occasion is presented, to rebel; in the same manner as the bodies of children gotten by diseased parents are subject either to untimely death, or to purge the ill quality derived from their vicious conception, by breaking out into biles and scabs. And when kings deny themselves some such necessary power, it is not always (though sometimes) out of ignorance of what is necessary to the office they undertake, but many times out of a hope to recover the same again at their pleasure: wherein they reason not well; because such as will hold them to their promises shall be maintained against them by foreign Commonwealths; who in order to the good of their own subjects let slip few occasions to weaken the estate of their neighbours. So was Thomas Becket, Archbishop of Canterbury, supported against Henry the Second by the Pope; the subjection of ecclesiastics to the Commonwealth having been dispensed with by William the Conqueror at his reception, when he took an oath not to infringe the liberty of the Church. And so were the barons, whose power was by William Rufus, to have their help in transferring the succession from his elder brother to himself, increased to a degree inconsistent with the sovereign power, maintained in their rebellion against King John by the French.

Nor does this happen in monarchy only. For whereas the style of the ancient Roman Commonwealth was, "The Senate and People of Rome"; neither senate nor people pretended to the whole power; which first caused the seditions of Tiberius Gracchus, Caius Gracchus, Lucius Saturninus, and others; and afterwards the wars between the senate and the people under Marius and Sylla; and again under Pompey and Caesar to the extinction of their democracy and the setting up of monarchy.

The people of Athens bound themselves but from one only action, which was that no man on pain of death should propound the renewing of the war for the island of Salamis; and yet thereby, if Solon had not caused to be given out he was mad, and afterwards in gesture and habit of a madman, and in verse,
5   propounded it to the people that flocked about him, they had had an enemy perpetually in readiness, even at the gates of their city: such damage, or shifts, are all Commonwealths forced to that have their power never so little limited.

In the second place, I observe the diseases of a Commonwealth that proceed from the poison of seditious doctrines, whereof one is that every private man is
10   judge of good and evil actions. This is true in the condition of mere nature, where there are no civil laws; and also under civil government in such cases as are not determined by the law. But otherwise, it is manifest that the measure of good and evil actions is the civil law; and the judge the legislator, who is always representative of the Commonwealth. From this false doctrine, men are disposed
15   to debate with themselves and dispute the commands of the Commonwealth, and afterwards to obey or disobey them as in their private judgments they shall think fit; whereby the Commonwealth is distracted and weakened.

Another doctrine repugnant to civil society is that whatsoever a man does against his conscience is sin; and it dependeth on the presumption of making
20   himself judge of good and evil. For a man's conscience and his judgement is the same thing; and as the judgement, so also the conscience may be erroneous. Therefore, though he that is subject to no civil law sinneth in all he does against his conscience, because he has no other rule to follow but his own reason, yet it is not so with him that lives in a Commonwealth, because the law is the public
25   conscience by which he hath already undertaken to be guided. Otherwise in such diversity as there is of private consciences, which are but private opinions, the Commonwealth must needs be distracted, and no man dare to obey the sovereign power farther than it shall seem good in his own eyes.

It hath been also commonly taught that faith and sanctity are not to be
30   attained by study and reason, but by supernatural inspiration or infusion. Which granted, I see not why any man should render a reason of his faith; or why every Christian should not be also a prophet; or why any man should take the law of his country rather than his own inspiration for the rule of his action. And thus we fall again into the fault of taking upon us to judge of good and evil; or to make
35   judges of it such private men as pretend to be supernaturally inspired, to the dissolution of all civil government. Faith comes by hearing, and hearing by those accidents which guide us into the presence of them that speak to us; which accidents are all contrived by God Almighty, and yet are not supernatural, but only, for the great number of them that concur to every effect, unobservable.
40   Faith and sanctity are indeed not very frequent; but yet they are not miracles, but

243

brought to pass by education, discipline, correction, and other natural ways by which God worketh them in His elect, at such time as He thinketh fit. And these three opinions, pernicious to peace and government, have in this part of the world proceeded chiefly from tongues and pens of unlearned divines; who,
5 joining the words of Holy Scripture together otherwise is agreeable to reason, do what they can to make men think that sanctity and natural reason cannot stand together.

A fourth opinion repugnant to the nature of a Commonwealth is this: that he that hath the sovereign power is subject to the civil laws. It is true that
10 sovereigns are all subject to the laws of nature, because such laws be divine and divine and cannot by any man or Commonwealth be abrogated. But to those laws which the sovereign himself, that is, which the Commonwealth, maketh, he is not subject. For to be subject to laws is to be to be subject to the Commonwealth, that is, to the sovereign representative, that is, to himself which
15 is not subjection, but freedom from the laws. Which error, because it setteth the laws above the sovereign, setteth also a judge above him, and a power to punish him; which is to make a new sovereign; and again for the same reason a third to punish the second; and so continually without end, to the confusion and dissolution of the Commonwealth.
20 A fifth doctrine that tendeth to the dissolution of a Commonwealth is that every private man has an absolute propriety in his goods, such as excludeth the right of the sovereign. Every man has indeed a propriety that excludes the right of every other subject: and he has it only from the sovereign power, without the protection whereof every other man should have right to the same. But the right
25 of the sovereign also be excluded, he cannot perform the office they have put him into, which is to defend them both from foreign enemies and from the injuries of one another; and consequently there is no longer a Commonwealth.

And if the propriety of subjects exclude not the right of the sovereign representative to their goods; much less, to their offices of judicature or
30 execution in which they represent the sovereign himself.

There is a sixth doctrine, plainly and directly against the essence of a Commonwealth, and it is this: that the sovereign power may be divided. For what is it to divide the power of a Commonwealth, but to dissolve it; for powers divided mutually destroy each other. And for these doctrines men are chiefly
35 beholding to some of those that, making profession of the laws, endeavour to make them depend upon their own learning, and not upon the legislative power.

And as false doctrine, so also oftentimes the example of different government in a neighbouring nation disposeth men to alteration of the form already settled. So the people of the Jews were stirred up to reject God, and to
40 call upon the prophet Samuel for a king after the manner of the nations: so also

244

the lesser cities of Greece were continually disturbed with seditions of the aristocratical and democratical factions; one part of almost every Commonwealth desiring to imitate the Lacedaemonians; the other, the Athenians. And I doubt not but many men have been contented to see the late
5   troubles in England out of an imitation of the Low Countries, supposing there needed no more to grow rich than to change, as they had done, the form of their government. For the constitution of man's nature is of itself subject to desire novelty: when therefore they are provoked to the same by the neighbourhood also of those that have been enriched by it, it is almost impossible to be content
10   with those that solicit them to change; and love the first beginnings, though they be grieved with the continuance of disorder; like hot bloods that, having gotten the itch, tear themselves with their own nails till they can endure the smart no longer.

     And as to rebellion in particular against monarchy, one of the most frequent
15   causes of it is the reading of the books of policy and histories of the ancient Greeks and Romans; from which young men, and all others that are unprovided of the antidote of solid reason, receiving a strong and delightful impression of the great exploits of war achieved by the conductors of their armies, receive withal a pleasing idea of all they have done besides; and imagine their great
20   prosperity not to have proceeded from the emulation of particular men, but from the virtue of their popular form of government not considering the frequent seditions and civil wars produced by the imperfection of their policy. From the reading, I say, of such books, men have undertaken to kill their kings, because the Greek and Latin writers in their books and discourses of policy make it
25   lawful and laudable for any man so to do, provided before he do it he call him tyrant. For they say not regicide, that is, killing of a king, but tyrannicide, that is, killing of a tyrant, is lawful. From the same books they that live under a monarch conceive an the opinion that the subjects in a popular Commonwealth enjoy liberty, but that in a monarchy they are all slaves. I say, they that live
30   under a monarchy conceive such an opinion; not that they live under a popular government: for they find no such matter. In sum, I cannot imagine how anything can be more prejudicial to a monarchy than the allowing of such books to be publicly read, without present applying such correctives of discreet masters as are fit to take away their venom: which venom I will not doubt to compare to
35   the biting of a mad dog, which is a disease that physicians call hydrophobia, or fear of water. For as he that is so bitten has a continual torment of thirst, and yet abhorreth water; and is in such an estate as if the poison endeavoured to convert him into a dog; so when a monarchy is once bitten to the quick by those democratical writers that continually snarl at that estate, it wanteth nothing more

than a strong monarch, which nevertheless out of a certain tyrannophobia, or fear of being strongly governed, when they have him, they abhor.

As there have been doctors that hold there be three souls in a man; so there be also that think there may be more souls, that is, more sovereigns, than one in a Commonwealth; and set up a supremacy against the sovereignty; canons against laws; and a ghostly authority against the civil; working on men's minds with words and distinctions that of themselves signify nothing, but bewray, by their obscurity, that there walketh (as some think invisibly) another kingdom, as it were a kingdom of fairies, in the dark. Now seeing it is manifest that the civil power and the power of the Commonwealth is the same thing; and that supremacy, and the power of making canons, and granting faculties, implieth a Commonwealth; it followeth that where one is sovereign, another supreme; where one can make laws, and another make canons; there must needs be two Commonwealths, of one and the same subjects; which is a kingdom divided in itself, and cannot stand. For notwithstanding the insignificant distinction of temporal and ghostly, they are still two kingdoms, and every subject is subject to two masters. For seeing the ghostly power challengeth the right to declare what is sin, it challengeth by consequence to declare what is law, sin being nothing but the transgression of the law; and again, the civil power challenging to declare what is law, every subject must obey two masters, who both will have their commands be observed as law, which is impossible. Or, if it be but one kingdom, either the civil, which is the power of the Commonwealth, must be subordinate to the ghostly, and then there is no sovereignty but the ghostly; or the ghostly must be subordinate to the temporal, and then there is no supremacy but the temporal. When therefore these two powers oppose one another, the Commonwealth cannot but be in great danger of civil war and dissolution. For the civil authority being more visible, and standing in the clearer light of natural reason, cannot choose but draw to it in all times a very considerable part of the people: and the spiritual, though it stand in the darkness of School distinctions and hard words; yet, because the fear of darkness and ghosts is greater than other fears, cannot want a party sufficient to trouble, and sometimes to destroy, a Commonwealth. And this is a disease which not unfitly may be compared to the epilepsy, or falling sickness (which the Jews took to be one kind of possession by spirits), in the body natural. For as in this disease there is an unnatural spirit or wind in the head that obstructeth the roots of the nerves and, moving them violently, taketh the motion which naturally they should have from the power of the soul in the brain; thereby causeth violent and irregular motions, which men call convulsions, in the parts; insomuch as he that is seized therewith falleth down sometimes into the water, and sometimes into the fire, as a man deprived of his senses: so also in the body politic, when the spiritual power moveth the

members of a Commonwealth by the terror of punishments and hope of rewards, which are the nerves of it, otherwise than by the civil power, which is the soul of the Commonwealth, they ought to be moved; and by strange and hard words suffocates their understanding; it must needs thereby distract the people, and
5 either overwhelm the Commonwealth with oppression, or cast it into the fire of a civil war.

Sometimes also in the merely civil government there be more than one soul: as when the power of levying money, which is the nutritive faculty, has depended on a general assembly; the power of conduct and command, which is
10 the motive faculty, on one man; and the power of making laws, which is the rational faculty, on the accidental consent, not only of those two, but also of a third: this endangereth the Commonwealth, sometimes for want of consent to good laws, but most often for want of such nourishment as is necessary to life and motion. For although few perceive that such government is not government,
15 but division of the Commonwealth into three factions, and call it mixed monarchy; yet the truth is that it is not one independent Commonwealth, but three independent factions; nor one representative person, but three. In the kingdom of God there may be three persons independent, without breach of unity in God that reigneth; but where men reign, that be subject to diversity of
20 opinions, it cannot be so. And therefore if the king bear the person of the people, and the general assembly bear also the person of the people, and another assembly bear the person of a part of the people, they are not one person, nor one sovereign; but three persons, and three sovereigns.

To what disease in the natural body of man I may exactly compare this
25 irregularity of a Commonwealth, I know not. But I have seen a man that had another man growing out of his side, with a head, arms, breast, and stomach of his own: if he had had another man growing out of his other side, the comparison might then have been exact.

Hitherto I have named such diseases of a Commonwealth as are of the
30 greatest and most present danger. There be other, not so great, which nevertheless are not unfit to be observed. As first, the difficulty of raising money for the necessary uses of the Commonwealth, especially in the approach of war. This difficulty ariseth from the opinion that every subject hath of a propriety in his lands and goods exclusive of the sovereign's right to the use of the same.
35 From whence it cometh to pass that the sovereign power, which foreseeth the necessities and dangers of the Commonwealth, finding the passage of money to the public treasury obstructed by the tenacity of the people, whereas it ought to extend itself, to encounter and prevent such dangers in their beginnings, contracteth itself as long as it can, and when it cannot longer, struggles with the
40 people by stratagems of law to obtain little sums, which, not sufficing, he is fain

at last violently to open the way for present supply or perish; and, being put often to these extremities, at last reduceth the people to their due temper, or else the Commonwealth must perish. Insomuch as we may compare this distemper very aptly to an ague; wherein, the fleshy parts being congealed, or by

5   venomous matter obstructed, the veins which by their natural course empty themselves into the heart, are not (as they ought to be) supplied from the arteries, whereby there succeedeth at first a cold contraction and trembling of the limbs; and afterwards a hot and strong endeavour of the heart to force a passage for the blood; and before it can do that, contenteth itself with the small

10   refreshments of such things as cool for a time, till, if nature be strong enough, it break at last the contumacy of the parts obstructed, and dissipateth the venom into sweat; or, if nature be too weak, the patient dieth.

     Again, there is sometimes in a Commonwealth a disease which resembleth the pleurisy; and that is when the treasury of the Commonwealth, flowing out of

15   its due course, is gathered together in too much abundance in one or a few private men, by monopolies or by farms of the public revenues; in the same manner as the blood in a pleurisy, getting into the membrane of the breast, breedeth there an inflammation, accompanied with a fever and painful stitches.

     Also, the popularity of a potent subject, unless the Commonwealth have

20   very good caution of his fidelity, is a dangerous disease; because the people, which should receive their motion from the authority of the sovereign, by the flattery and by the reputation of an ambitious man, are drawn away from their obedience to the laws to follow a man of whose virtues and designs they have no knowledge. And this is commonly of more danger in a popular government than

25   in a monarchy, because an army is of so great force and multitude as it may easily be made believe they are the people. By this means it was that Julius Caesar, who was set up by the people against the senate, having won to himself the affections of his army, made himself master both of senate and people. And this proceeding of popular and ambitious men is plain rebellion, and may be

30   resembled to the effects of witchcraft.

     Another infirmity of a Commonwealth is the immoderate greatness of a town, when it is able to furnish out of its own circuit the number and expense of a great army; as also the great number of corporations, which are as it were many lesser Commonwealths in the bowels of a greater, like worms in the

35   entrails of a natural man. To may be added, liberty of disputing against absolute power by pretenders to political prudence; which though bred for the most part in the lees of the people, yet animated by false doctrines are perpetually meddling with the fundamental laws, to the molestation of the Commonwealth, like the little worms which physicians call ascarides.

We may further add the insatiable appetite, or bulimia, of enlarging dominion, with the incurable wounds thereby many times received from the enemy; and the wens, of ununited conquests, which are many times a burden, and with less danger lost than kept; as also the lethargy of ease, and

5 consumption of riot and vain expense.

Lastly, when in a war, foreign or intestine, the enemies get a final victory, so as, the forces of the Commonwealth keeping the field no longer, there is no further protection of subjects in their loyalty, then is the Commonwealth dissolved, and every man at liberty to protect himself by such courses as his own

10 discretion shall suggest unto him. For the sovereign is the public soul, giving life and motion to the Commonwealth, which expiring, the members are governed by it no more than the carcass of a man by his departed, though immortal, soul. For though the right of a sovereign monarch cannot be extinguished by the act of another, yet the obligation of the members may. For he that wants protection

15 may seek it anywhere; and, when he hath it, is obliged (without fraudulent pretence of having submitted himself out of fear) to protect his protection as long as he is able. But when the power of an assembly is once suppressed, the right of the same perisheth utterly, because the assembly itself is extinct; and consequently, there is no possibility for sovereignty to re-enter.

CHAPTER XXX.
Of the office of the sovereign representative

20 THE office of the sovereign, be it a monarch or an assembly, consisteth in the end for which he was trusted with the sovereign power, namely the procuration of the safety of the people, to which he is obliged by the law of nature, and to render an account thereof to God, the Author of that law, and to none but Him. But by safety here is not meant a bare preservation, but also all

25 other contentments of life, which every man by lawful industry, without danger or hurt to the Commonwealth, shall acquire to himself.

And this is intended should be done, not by care applied to individuals, further than their protection from injuries when they shall complain; but by a general providence, contained in public instruction, both of doctrine and

30 example; and in the making and executing of good laws to which individual persons may apply their own cases.

And because, if the essential rights of sovereignty (specified before in the eighteenth Chapter) be taken away, the Commonwealth is thereby dissolved, and every man returneth into the condition and calamity of a war with every other

35 man, which is the greatest evil that can happen in this life; it is the office of the sovereign to maintain those rights entire, and consequently against his duty,

first, to transfer to another or to lay from himself any of them. For he that deserteth the means deserteth the ends; and he deserteth the means that, being the sovereign, acknowledgeth himself subject to the civil laws, and renounceth the power of supreme judicature; or of making war or peace by his own
5   authority; or of judging of the necessities of the Commonwealth; or of levying money and soldiers when and as much as in his own conscience he shall judge necessary; or of making officers and ministers both of war and peace; or of appointing teachers, and examining what doctrines are conformable or contrary to the defence, peace, and good of the people. Secondly, it is against his duty to
10   let the people be ignorant or misinformed of the grounds and reasons of those his essential rights, because thereby men are easy to be seduced and drawn to resist him when the Commonwealth shall require their use and exercise.

And the grounds of these rights have the rather need drafter need to be diligently and truly taught, because they cannot be maintained by any civil law
15   or terror of legal punishment. For a civil law that shall forbid rebellion (and such is all resistance to the essential rights of sovereignty) is not, as a civil law, any obligation but by virtue only of the law of nature that forbiddeth the violation of faith; which natural obligation, if men know not, they cannot know the right of any law the sovereign maketh. And for the punishment, they take it but for an
20   act of hostility; which when they think they have strength enough, they will endeavour, by acts of hostility, to avoid.

As I have heard some say that justice is but a word, without substance; and that whatsoever a man can by force or art acquire to himself, not only in the condition of war, but also in a Commonwealth, is his own, which I have already
25   shown to be false: so there be also that maintain that there are no grounds, nor principles of reason, to sustain those essential rights which make sovereignty absolute. For if there were, they would have been found out in some place or other; whereas we see there has not hitherto been any Commonwealth where those rights have been acknowledged, or challenged. Wherein they argue as ill,
30   as if the savage people of America should deny there were any grounds or principles of reason so to build a house as to last as long as the materials, because they never yet saw any so well built. Time and industry produce every day new knowledge. And as the art of well building is derived from principles of reason, observed by industrious men that had long studied the nature of
35   materials, and the diverse effects of figure and proportion, long after mankind began, though poorly, to build: so, long time after men have begun to constitute Commonwealths, imperfect and apt to relapse into disorder, there may principles of reason be found out, by industrious meditation, to make their constitution, excepting by external violence, everlasting. And such are those which I have in
40   this discourse set forth: which, whether they come not into the sight of those that

have power to make use of them, or be neglected by them or not, concerneth my particular interest, at this day, very little. But supposing that these of mine are not such principles of reason; yet I am sure they are principles from authority of Scripture, as I shall make it appear when I shall come to speak of the kingdom
5   of God, administered by Moses, over the Jews, His peculiar people by covenant.
But they say again that though the principles be right, yet common people are not of capacity enough to be made to understand them. I should be glad that the rich and potent subjects of a kingdom, or those that are accounted the most learned, were no less incapable than they. But all men know that the
10   obstructions to this kind of doctrine proceed not so much from the difficulty of the matter, as from the interest of them that are to learn. Potent men digest hardly anything that setteth up a power to bridle their affections; and learned men, anything that discovereth their errors, and thereby their authority: whereas the common people's minds, unless they be tainted with dependence on the
15   potent, or scribbled over with the opinions of their doctors, are like clean paper, fit to receive whatsoever by public authority shall be imprinted in them. Shall whole nations be brought to acquiesce in the great mysteries of Christian religion, which are above reason; and millions of men be made believe that the same body may be in innumerable places at one and the same time, which is
20   against reason; and shall not men be able, by their teaching and preaching, protected by the law, to make that received which is so consonant to reason that any unprejudicated man needs no more to learn it than to hear it? I conclude therefore that in the instruction of the people in the essential rights which are the natural and fundamental laws of sovereignty, there is no difficulty, whilst a
25   sovereign has his power entire, but what proceeds from his own fault, or the fault of those whom he trusteth in the administration of the Commonwealth; and consequently, it is his duty to cause them so to be instructed; and not only his duty, but his benefit also, and security against the danger that may arrive to himself in his natural person from rebellion.
30   And, to descend to particulars, the people are to be taught, first, that they ought not to be in love with any form of government they see in their neighbour nations, more than with their own, nor, whatsoever present prosperity they behold in nations that are otherwise governed than they, to desire change. For the prosperity of a people ruled by an aristocratical or democratical assembly
35   cometh not from aristocracy, nor from democracy, but from the obedience and concord of the subjects: nor do the people flourish in a monarchy because one man has the right to rule them, but because they obey him. Take away in any kind of state the obedience, and consequently the concord of the people, and they shall not only not flourish, but in short time be dissolved. And they that go
40   about by disobedience to do no more than reform the Commonwealth shall find

they do thereby destroy it; like the foolish daughters of Peleus, in the fable, which desiring to renew the youth of their decrepit father, did by the counsel of Medea cut him in pieces and boil him, together with strange herbs, but made not of him a new man. This desire of change is like the breach of the first of God's
5 Commandments: for there God says, Non habebis Deos alienos: "Thou shalt not have the Gods of other nations"; and in another place concerning kings, that they are gods.

Secondly, they are to be taught that they ought not to be led with admiration of the virtue of any of their fellow subjects, how high soever he stand, nor how
10 conspicuously soever he shine in the Commonwealth; nor of any assembly, except the sovereign assembly, so as to defer to them any obedience or honour appropriate to the sovereign only, whom, in their particular stations, they represent; nor to receive any influence from them, but such as is conveyed by them from the sovereign authority. For that sovereign cannot be imagined to
15 love his people as he ought that is not jealous of them, but suffers them by the flattery of popular men to be seduced from their loyalty, as they have often been, not only secretly, but openly, so as to proclaim marriage with them in facie ecclesiae by preachers, and by publishing the same in the open streets: which may fitly be compared to the violation of the second of the Ten Commandments.
20 Thirdly, in consequence to this, they ought to be informed how great a fault it is to speak evil of the sovereign representative, whether one man or an assembly of men; or to argue and dispute his power, or any way to use his name irreverently, whereby he may be brought into contempt with his people, and their obedience, in which the safety of the Commonwealth consisteth, slackened.
25 Which doctrine the third Commandment by resemblance pointeth to.

Fourthly, seeing people cannot be taught this, nor, when it is taught, remember it, nor after one generation past so much as know in whom the sovereign power is placed, without setting apart from their ordinary labour some certain times in which they may attend those that are appointed to instruct them;
30 it is necessary that some such times be determined wherein they may assemble together, and, after prayers and praises given to God, the Sovereign of sovereigns, hear those their duties told them, and the positive laws, such as generally concern them all, read and expounded, and be put in mind of the authority that maketh them laws. To this end had the Jews every seventh day a
35 Sabbath, in which the law was read and expounded; and in the solemnity whereof they were put in mind that their king was God; that having created the world in six days, He rested on the seventh day; and by their resting on it from their labour, that that God was their king, which redeemed them from their servile and painful labour in Egypt, and gave them a time, after they had
40 rejoiced in God, to take joy also in themselves, by lawful recreation. So that the

first table of the Commandments is spent all in setting down the sum of God's absolute power; not only as God, but as King by pact, in peculiar, of the Jews; and may therefore give light to those that have sovereign power conferred on them by the consent of men, to see what doctrine they ought to teach their
5   subjects.

And because the first instruction of children dependeth on the care of their parents, it is necessary that they should be obedient to them whilst they are under their tuition; and not only so, but that also afterwards, as gratitude requireth, they acknowledge the benefit of their education by external signs of
10   honour. To which end they are to be taught that originally the father of every man was also his sovereign lord, with power over him of life and death; and that the fathers of families, when by instituting a Commonwealth they resigned that absolute power, yet it was never intended they should lose the honour due unto them for their education. For to relinquish such right was not necessary to the
15   institution of sovereign power; nor would there be any reason why any man should desire to have children, or take the care to nourish and instruct them, if they were afterwards to have no other benefit from them than from other men. And this accordeth with the fifth Commandment.

Again, every sovereign ought to cause justice to be taught, which,
20   consisting in taking from no man what is his, is as much as to say, to cause men to be taught not to deprive their neighbours, by violence or fraud, of anything which by the sovereign authority is theirs. Of things held in propriety, those that are dearest to a man are his own life and limbs; and in the next degree, in most men, those that concern conjugal affection; and after them riches and means of
25   living. Therefore the people are to be taught to abstain from violence to one another's person by private revenges, from violation of conjugal honour, and from forcible rapine and fraudulent surreption of one another's goods. For which purpose also it is necessary they be shown the evil consequences of false judgment, by corruption either of judges or witnesses, whereby the distinction of
30   propriety is taken away, and justice becomes of no effect: all which things are intimated in the sixth, seventh, eighth, and ninth Commandments.

Lastly, they are to be taught that not only the unjust facts, but the designs and intentions to do them, though by accident hindered, are injustice; which consisteth in the pravity of the will, as well as in the irregularity of the act. And
35   this is the intention of the tenth Commandment, and the sum of the second table; which is reduced all to this one commandment of mutual charity, "Thou shalt love thy neighbour as thy self"; as the sum of the first table is reduced to "the love of God"; whom they had then newly received as their king.

As for the means and conduits by which the people may receive this
40   instruction, we are to search by what means so many opinions contrary to the

peace of mankind, upon weak and false principles, have nevertheless been so deeply rooted in them. I mean those which I have in the precedent the precedent chapter specified: as that men shall judge of what is lawful and unlawful, not by the law itself, but by their own consciences; that is to say, by their own private
5   judgements: that subjects sin in obeying the commands of the Commonwealth, unless they themselves have first judged them to be lawful: that their propriety in their riches is such as to exclude the dominion which the Commonwealth hath the same: that it is lawful for subjects to kill such as they call tyrants: that the sovereign power may be divided, and the like; which come to be instilled into
10   the people by this means. They whom necessity or covetousness keepeth attent on their trades and labour; and they, on the other side, whom superfluity or sloth carrieth after their sensual pleasures (which two sorts of men take up the greatest part of mankind), being diverted from the deep meditation which the of truth, not only in the matter of natural justice, but also of all other sciences necessarily
15   requireth, receive the notions of their duty chiefly from divines in the pulpit, and partly from such of their neighbours or familiar acquaintance as having the faculty of discoursing readily and plausibly seem wiser and better learned in cases of law and conscience than themselves. And the divines, and such others as make show of learning, derive their knowledge from the universities, and
20   from the schools of law, or from the books which by men eminent in those schools and universities have been published. It is therefore manifest that the instruction of the people dependeth wholly on the right teaching of youth in the universities. But are not, may some man say, the universities of England learned enough already to do that? Or is it, you will undertake to teach the universities?
25   Hard questions. Yet to the first, I doubt not to answer: that till towards the latter end of Henry the Eighth, the power of the Pope was always upheld against the power of the Commonwealth, principally by the universities; and that the doctrines by so many preachers against the sovereign power of the king, and by so many lawyers and others that had their education there, is a sufficient
30   argument that, though the universities were not authors of those false doctrines, yet they knew not how to plant the true. For in such a contradiction of opinions, it is most certain that they have not been sufficiently instructed; and it is no wonder, if they yet retain a relish of that subtle liquor wherewith they were first seasoned against the civil authority. But to the latter question, it is not fit nor
35   needful for me to say either aye or no: for any man that sees what I am doing may easily perceive what I think.

The safety of the people requireth further, from him or them that have the sovereign power, that justice be equally administered to all degrees of people; that is, that as well the rich and mighty, as poor and obscure persons, may be
40   righted of the injuries done them; so as the great may have no greater hope of

254

impunity, when they do violence, dishonour, or any injury to the meaner sort, than when one of these does the like to one of them: for in this consisteth equity; to which, as being a precept of the law of nature, a sovereign is as much subject as any of the meanest of his people. All breaches of the law are offences against
5   the Commonwealth: but there be some that are also against private persons. Those that concern the Commonwealth only may without breach of equity be pardoned; for every man may pardon what is done against himself, according to his own discretion. But an offence against a private man cannot in equity be pardoned without the consent of him that is injured; or reasonable satisfaction.
10   The inequality of subjects proceedeth from the acts of sovereign power, and therefore has no more place in the presence of the sovereign; that is to say, in a court of justice, than the inequality between kings and their subjects in the presence of the King of kings. The honour of great persons is to be valued for their beneficence, and the aids they give to men of inferior rank, or not at all.
15   And the violences, oppressions, and injuries they do are not extenuated, but aggravated, by the greatness of their persons, because they have least need to commit them. The consequences of this partiality towards the great proceed in this manner. Impunity maketh insolence; insolence, hatred; and hatred, an endeavour to pull down all oppressing and contumelious greatness, though with
20   the ruin of the Commonwealth.

To equal justice appertaineth also the equal imposition of taxes; the equality whereof dependeth not on the equality of riches, but on the equality of the debt that every man oweth to the Commonwealth for his defence. It is not enough for a man to labour for the maintenance of his life; but also to fight, if need be, for
25   the securing of his labour. They must either do as the Jews did after their return from captivity, in re-edifying the Temple, build with one hand and hold the sword in the other, or else they must hire others to fight for them. For the impositions that are laid on the people by the sovereign power are nothing else but the wages due to them that hold the public sword to defend private men in
30   the exercise of several trades and callings. Seeing then the benefit that every one receiveth thereby is the enjoyment of life, which is equally dear to poor and rich, the debt which a poor man oweth them that defend his life is the same which a rich man oweth for the defence of his; saving that the rich, who have the service of the poor, may be debtors not only for their own persons, but for many more.
35   Which considered, the equality of imposition consisteth rather in the equality of that which is consumed, than of the riches of the persons that consume the same. For what reason is there that he which laboureth much and, sparing the fruits of his labour, consumeth little should be more charged than he that, living idly, getteth little and spendeth all he gets; seeing the one hath no more protection
40   from the Commonwealth than the other? But when the impositions are laid upon

those things which men consume, every man payeth equally for what he useth; nor is the Commonwealth defrauded by the luxurious waste of private men.

And whereas many men, by accident inevitable, become unable to maintain themselves by their labour, they ought not to be left to the charity of private
5   persons, but to be provided for, as far forth as the necessities of nature require, by the laws of the Commonwealth. For as it is uncharitableness in any man to neglect the impotent; so it is in the sovereign of a Commonwealth, to expose them to the hazard of such uncertain charity.

But for such as have strong bodies the case is otherwise; they are to be
10   forced to work; and to avoid the excuse of not finding employment, there ought to be such laws as may encourage all manner of arts; as navigation, agriculture, fishing, and all manner of manufacture that requires labour. The multitude of poor and yet strong people still increasing, they are to be transplanted into countries not sufficiently inhabited; where nevertheless they are not to
15   exterminate those they find there; but constrain them to inhabit closer together, and not range a great deal of ground to snatch what they find, but to court each little plot with art and labour, to give them their sustenance in due season. And when all the world is overcharged with inhabitants, then the last remedy of all is war, which provideth for every man, by victory or death.
20   To the care of the sovereign belongeth the making of good laws. But what is a good law? By a good law, I mean not a just law: for no law can be unjust. The law is made by the sovereign power, and all that is done by such power is warranted and owned by every one of the people; and that which every man will have so, no man can say is unjust. It is in the laws of a Commonwealth, as in the
25   laws of gaming: whatsoever the gamesters all agree on is injustice to none of them. A good law is that which is needful, for the good of the people, and withal perspicuous.

For the use of laws (which are but rules authorized) is not to bind the people from all voluntary actions, but to direct and keep them in such a motion as not to
30   hurt themselves by their own impetuous desires, rashness, or indiscretion; as hedges are set, not to stop travellers, but to keep them in the way. And therefore a law that is not needful, having not the true end of a law, is not good. A law may be conceived to be good when it is for the benefit of the sovereign, though it be not necessary for the people, but it is not so. For the good of the sovereign
35   and people cannot be separated. It is a weak sovereign that has weak subjects; and a weak people whose sovereign wanteth power to rule them at his will. Unnecessary laws are not good laws, but traps for money which, where the right of sovereign power is acknowledged, are superfluous; and where it is not acknowledged, insufficient to defend the people.

The perspicuity consisteth not so much in the words of the law itself, as in a declaration of the causes and motives for which it was made. That is it that shows us the meaning of the legislator; and the meaning of the legislator known, the law is more easily understood by few than many words. For all words are
5 subject to ambiguity; and therefore multiplication of words in the body of the law is multiplication of ambiguity: besides it seems to imply, by too much diligence, that whosoever can evade the words is without the compass of the law. And this is a cause of many unnecessary processes. For when I consider how short were the laws of ancient times, and how they grew by degrees still
10 longer, methinks I see a contention between the penners and pleaders of the law; the former seeking to circumscribe the latter, and the latter to evade their circumscriptions; and that the pleaders have got the victory. It belongeth therefore to the office of a legislator (such as is in all Commonwealths the supreme representative, be it one man or an assembly) to make the reason
15 perspicuous why the law was made, and the body of the law itself as short, but in as proper and significant terms, as may be.

It belongeth also to the office of the sovereign to make a right application of punishments and rewards. And seeing the end of punishing is not revenge and discharge of choler, but correction either of the offender or of others by his
20 example, the severest punishments are to be inflicted for those crimes that are of most danger to the public; such as are those which proceed from malice to the government established; those that spring from contempt of justice; those that provoke indignation in the multitude; and those which, unpunished, seem authorized, as when they are committed by sons, servants, or favourites of men
25 in authority: for indignation carrieth men, not only against the actors and authors of injustice, but against all power that is likely to protect them; as in the case of Tarquin, when for the insolent act of one of his sons he was driven out of Rome, and the monarchy itself dissolved. But crimes of infirmity; such as are those which proceed from great provocation, from great fear, great need, or from
30 ignorance whether the fact be a great crime or not, there is place many times for lenity, without prejudice to the Commonwealth; and lenity, when there is such place for it, is required by the law of nature. The punishment of the leaders and teachers in a commotion; not the poor seduced people, when they are punished, can profit the Commonwealth by their example. To be severe to people is to
35 punish ignorance which may in great part be imputed to the sovereign, whose fault it was they were no better instructed.

In like manner it belongeth to the office and duty of the sovereign to apply his rewards always so as there may arise from them benefit to the Commonwealth: wherein consisteth their use and end; and is then done when
40 they that have well served the Commonwealth are, with as little expense of the

common treasury as is possible, so well recompensed as others thereby may be encouraged, both to serve the same as faithfully as they can, and to study the arts by which they may be enabled to do it better. To buy with money or preferment, from a popular ambitious subject to be quiet and desist from making ill

5 impressions in the minds of the people, has nothing of the nature of reward (which is ordained not for disservice, but for service past); nor a sign of gratitude, but of fear; nor does it tend to the benefit, but to the damage of the public. It is a contention with ambition, that of Hercules with the monster Hydra, which, having many heads, for every one that was vanquished there grew up

10 three. For in like manner, when the stubbornness of one popular man is overcome with reward, there arise many more by the example, that do the same mischief in hope of like benefit: and as all sorts of manufacture, so also malice increaseth by being vendible. And though sometimes a civil war may be deferred by such ways as that, yet the danger grows still the greater, and the

15 public ruin more assured. It is therefore against the duty of the sovereign, to whom the public safety is committed, to reward those that aspire to greatness by disturbing the peace of their country, and not rather to oppose the beginnings of such men with a little danger, than after a longer time with greater.

Another business of the sovereign is to choose good counsellors; I mean

20 such whose advice he is to take in the government of the Commonwealth. For this word counsel (consilium, corrupted from considium) is of a large signification, and comprehendeth all assemblies of men that sit together, not only to deliberate what is to be done hereafter, but also to judge of facts past, and of law for the present. I take it here in the first sense only: and in this sense,

25 there is no choice of counsel, neither in a democracy nor aristocracy; because the persons counselling are members of the person counselled. The choice of counsellors therefore is proper to monarchy, in which the sovereign that endeavoureth not to make choice of those that in every kind are the most able, dischargeth not his office as he ought to do. The most able counsellors are they

30 that have least hope of benefit by giving evil counsel, and most knowledge of those things that conduce to the peace and defence of the Commonwealth. It is a hard matter to know who expecteth benefit from public troubles; but the signs that guide to a just suspicion is the soothing of the people in their unreasonable or irremediable grievances by men whose estates are not sufficient to discharge

35 their accustomed expenses, and may easily be observed by any one whom it concerns to know it. But to know who has most knowledge of the public affairs is yet harder; and they that know them need them a great deal the less. For to know who knows the rules almost of any art is a great degree of the knowledge of the same art, because no man can be assured of the truth of another's rules but

40 he that is first taught to understand them. But the best signs of knowledge of any

art are much conversing in it and constant good effects of it. Good counsel comes not by lot, nor by inheritance; and therefore there is no more reason to expect good advice from the rich or noble in matter of state, than in delineating the dimensions of a fortress; unless we shall think there needs no method in the

5 study of the politics, as there does in the study of geometry, but only to be lookers on; which is not so. For the politics is the harder study of the two. Whereas in these parts of Europe it hath been taken for a right of certain persons to have place in the highest council of state by inheritance, it derived from the conquests of the ancient Germans; wherein many absolute lords, joining

10 together to conquer other nations, would not enter into the confederacy without such privileges as might be marks of difference, in time following, between their posterity and the posterity of their subjects; which privileges being inconsistent with the sovereign power, by the favour of the sovereign they may seem to keep; but contending for them as their right, they must needs by degrees let them go,

15 and have at last no further honour than adhereth naturally to their abilities.

And how able soever be the counsellors in any affair, the benefit of their counsel is greater when they give every one his advice, and the reasons of it apart, than when they do it in an assembly by way of orations; and when they have premeditated, than when they speak on the sudden; both because they have

20 more time to survey the consequences of action, and are less subject to be carried away to contradiction through envy, emulation, or other passions arising from the difference of opinion.

The best counsel, in those things that concern not other nations, but only the ease and benefit the subjects may enjoy, by laws that look only inward, is to be

25 taken from the general informations and complaints of the people of each province, who are best acquainted with their own wants, and ought therefore, when they demand nothing in derogation of the essential rights of sovereignty, to be diligently taken notice of. For without those essential rights, as I have often before said, the Commonwealth cannot at all subsist.

30 A commander of an army in chief, if he be not popular, shall not be beloved, nor feared as he ought to be by his army, and consequently cannot perform that office with good success. He must therefore be industrious, valiant, affable, liberal and fortunate, that he may gain an opinion both of sufficiency and of loving his soldiers. This is popularity, and breeds in the soldiers both

35 desire and courage to recommend themselves to his favour; and protects the severity of the general, in punishing, when need is, the mutinous or negligent soldiers. But this love of soldiers, if caution be not given of the commander's fidelity, is a dangerous thing to sovereign power; especially when it is in the hands of an assembly not popular. It belongeth therefore to the safety of the

people, both that they be good conductors and faithful subjects, to whom the sovereign commits his armies.

But when the sovereign himself is popular; that is, reverenced and beloved of his people, there is no danger at all from the popularity of a subject. For
5   soldiers are never so generally unjust as to side with their captain, though they love him, against their sovereign, when they love not only his person, but also his cause. And therefore those who by violence have at any time suppressed the power of their lawful sovereign, before they could settle themselves in his place, have been always put to the trouble of contriving their titles to save the people
10   from the shame of receiving them. To have a known right to sovereign power is so popular a quality as he that has it needs no more, for his own part, to turn the hearts of his subjects to him, but that they see him able absolutely to govern his own family: nor, on the part of his enemies, but a disbanding of their armies. For the greatest and most active part of mankind has never hitherto been well
15   contented with the present.

Concerning the offices of one sovereign to another, which are comprehended in that law which is commonly called the law of nations, I need not say anything in this place, because the law of nations and the law of nature is the same thing. And every sovereign hath the same right in procuring the safety
20   of his people, that any particular man can have in procuring the safety of his own body. And the same law that dictateth to men that have no civil government what they ought to do, and what to avoid in regard of one another, dictateth the same to Commonwealths; that is, to the consciences of sovereign princes and sovereign assemblies; there being no court of natural justice, but in the
25   conscience only, where not man, but God reigneth; whose laws, such of them as oblige all mankind, in respect of God, as he is the Author of nature, are natural; and in respect of the same God, as he is King of kings, are laws. But of the kingdom of God, as King of kings, and as King also of a peculiar people, I shall speak in the rest of this discourse.

****

A REVIEW AND CONCLUSION

30   FROM the contrariety of some of the natural faculties of the mind, one to another, as also of one passion to another, and from their reference to conversation, there has been an argument taken to infer an impossibility that any one man should be sufficiently disposed to all sorts of civil duty. The severity of judgement, they say, makes men censorious and unapt to pardon the errors and
35   infirmities of other men: and on the other side, celerity of fancy makes the thoughts less steady than is necessary to discern exactly between right and

wrong. Again, in all deliberations, and in all pleadings, the faculty of solid reasoning is necessary: for without it, the resolutions of men are rash, and their sentences unjust: and yet if there be not powerful eloquence, which procureth attention and consent, the effect of reason will be little. But these are contrary
5   faculties; the former being grounded upon principles of truth; the other upon opinions already received, true or false; and upon the passions and interests of men, which are different and mutable.

And amongst the passions, courage (by which I mean the contempt of wounds and violent death) inclineth men to private revenges, and sometimes to
10   endeavour the unsettling of the public peace: and timorousness many times disposeth to the desertion of the public defence. Both these, they say, cannot stand together in the same person.

And to consider the contrariety of men's opinions and manners in general, it is, they say, impossible to entertain a constant civil amity with all those with
15   whom the business of the world constrains us to converse: which business consisteth almost in nothing else but a perpetual contention for honour, riches, and authority.

To which I answer that these are indeed great difficulties, but not impossibilities: for by education and discipline, they may be, and are sometimes,
20   reconciled. Judgement and fancy may have place in the same man; but by turns; as the end which he aimeth at requireth. As the Israelites in Egypt were sometimes fastened to their labour of making bricks, and other times were ranging abroad to gather straw: so also may the judgement sometimes be fixed upon one certain consideration, and the fancy at another time wandering about
25   the world. So also reason and eloquence (though not perhaps in the natural sciences, yet in the moral) may stand very well together. For wheresoever there is place for adorning and preferring of error, there is much more place for adorning and preferring of truth, if they have it to adorn. Nor is there any repugnancy between fearing the laws, and not fearing a public enemy; nor
30   between abstaining from injury, and pardoning it in others. There is therefore no such inconsistence of human nature with civil duties, as some think. I have known clearness of judgement, and largeness of fancy; strength of reason, and graceful elocution; a courage for the war, and a fear for the laws, and all eminently in one man; and that was my most noble and honoured friend, Mr.
35   Sidney Godolphin; who, hating no man, nor hated of any, was unfortunately slain in the beginning of the late civil war, in the public quarrel, by an undiscerned and an undiscerning hand.

To the Laws of Nature declared in the fifteenth Chapter, I would have this added: that every man is bound by nature, as much as in him lieth, to protect in
40   war the authority by which he is himself protected in time of peace. For he that

pretendeth a right of nature to preserve his own body, cannot pretend a right of nature to destroy him by whose strength he is preserved: it is a manifest contradiction of himself. And though this law may be drawn by consequence from some of those that are there already mentioned, yet the times require to
5   have it inculcated and remembered.

And because I find by diverse English books lately printed that the civil wars have not yet sufficiently taught men in what point of time it is that a subject becomes obliged to the conqueror; nor what is conquest; nor how it comes about that it obliges men to obey his laws: therefore for further
10 satisfaction of men therein, I say, the point of time wherein a man becomes subject to a conqueror is that point wherein, having liberty to submit to him, he consenteth, either by express words or by other sufficient sign, to be his subject. When it is that a man hath the liberty to submit, I have shown before in the end of the twenty-first Chapter; namely, that for him that hath no obligation to his
15 former sovereign but that of an ordinary subject, it is then when the means of his life is within the guards and garrisons of the enemy; for it is then that he hath no longer protection from him, but is protected by the adverse party for his contribution. Seeing therefore such contribution is everywhere, as a thing inevitable, notwithstanding it be an assistance to the enemy, esteemed lawful; a
20 total submission, which is but an assistance to the enemy, cannot be esteemed unlawful. Besides, if a man consider that they submit, assist the enemy but with part of their estates, whereas they that refuse, assist him with the whole, there is no reason to call their submission or composition an assistance, but rather a detriment, to the enemy. But if a man, besides the obligation of a subject, hath
25 taken upon him a new obligation of a soldier, then he hath not the liberty to submit to a new power, as long as the old one keeps the field and giveth him means of subsistence, either in his armies or garrisons: for in this case, he cannot complain of want of protection and means to live as a soldier. But when that also fails, a soldier also may seek his protection wheresoever he has most hope to
30 have it, and may lawfully submit himself to his new master. And so much for the time when he may do it lawfully, if he will. It therefore he do it, he is undoubtedly bound to be a true subject: for a contract lawfully made cannot lawfully be broken.

By this also a man may understand when it is that men may be said to be
35 conquered; and in what the nature of conquest, and the right of a conqueror consisteth: for this submission is it implieth them all. Conquest is not the victory itself; but the acquisition, by victory, of a right over the persons of men. He therefore that is slain is overcome, but not conquered: he that is taken and put into prison or chains is not conquered, though overcome; for he is still an
40 enemy, and may save himself if he can: but he that upon promise of obedience

hath his life and liberty allowed him, is then conquered and a subject; and not
before. The Romans used to say that their general had pacified such a province,
that is to say, in English, conquered it; and that the country was pacified by
victory when the people of it had promised imperata facere, that is, to do what
5 the Roman people commanded them: this was to be conquered. But this promise
may be either express or tacit: express, by promise; tacit, by other signs. As, for
example, a man that hath not been called to make such an express promise,
because he is one whose power perhaps is not considerable; yet if he live under
their protection openly, he is understood to submit himself to the government:
10 but if he live there secretly, he is liable to anything that may be done to a spy
and enemy of the state. I say not, he does any injustice (for acts of open hostility
bear not that name); but that he may be justly put to death. Likewise, if a man,
when his country is conquered, be out of it, he is not conquered, nor subject: but
if at his return he submit to the government, he is bound to obey it. So that
15 conquest, to define it, is the acquiring of the right of sovereignty by victory.
Which right is acquired in the people's submission, by which they contract with
the victor, promising obedience, for life and liberty.

In the twenty-ninth Chapter I have set down for one of the causes of the
dissolutions of Commonwealths their imperfect generation, consisting in the
20 want of an absolute and arbitrary legislative power; for want whereof, the civil
sovereign is fain to handle the sword of justice unconstantly, and as if it were
too hot for him to hold: one reason whereof (which I have not there mentioned)
is this, that they will all of them justify the war by which their power was at first
gotten, and whereon, as they think, their right dependeth, and not on the
25 possession. As if, for example, the right of the kings of England did depend on
the goodness of the cause of William the Conqueror, and upon their lineal and
directest descent from him; by which means, there would perhaps be no tie of
the subjects' obedience to their sovereign at this day in all the world: wherein
whilst they needlessly think to justify themselves, they justify all the successful
30 rebellions that ambition shall at any time raise against them and their successors.
Therefore I put down for one of the most effectual seeds of the death of any
state, that the conquerors require not only a submission of men's actions to them
for the future, but also an approbation of all their actions past; when there is
scarce a Commonwealth in the world whose beginnings can in conscience be
35 justified.

And because the name of tyranny signifieth nothing more nor less than the
name of sovereignty, be it in one or many men, saving that they that use the
former word are understood to be angry with them they call tyrants; I think the
toleration of a professed hatred of tyranny is a toleration of hatred to
40 Commonwealth in general, and another evil seed, not differing much from the

former. For to the justification of the cause of a conqueror, the reproach of the cause of the conquered is for the most part necessary: but neither of them necessary for the obligation of the conquered. And thus much I have thought fit to say upon the review of the first and second part of this discourse.

5   In the thirty-fifth Chapter, I have sufficiently declared out of the Scripture that in the Commonwealth of the Jews, God Himself was made the Sovereign, by pact with the people; who were therefore called His "peculiar people," to distinguish them from the rest of the world, over whom God reigned, not by their consent, but by His own power: and that in this kingdom Moses was God's

10   lieutenant on earth; and that it was he that told them what laws God appointed them to be ruled by. But I have omitted to set down who were the officers appointed to do execution; especially in capital punishments; not then thinking it a matter of so necessary consideration as I find it since. We know that generally in all Commonwealths, the execution of corporeal punishments was either put

15   upon the guards, or other soldiers of the sovereign power, or given to those in whom want of means, contempt of honour, and hardness of heart concurred to make them sue for such an office. But amongst the Israelites it was a positive law of God their Sovereign that he that was convicted of a capital crime should be stoned to death by the people; and that the witnesses should cast the first

20   stone, and after the witnesses, then the rest of the people. This was a law that designed who were to be the executioners; but not that any one should throw a stone at him before conviction and sentence, where the congregation was judge. The witnesses were nevertheless to be heard before they proceeded to execution, unless the fact were committed in the presence of the congregation itself, or in

25   sight of the lawful judges; for then there needed no other witnesses but the judges themselves. Nevertheless, this manner of proceeding, being not thoroughly understood, hath given occasion to a dangerous opinion, that any man may kill another, in some cases, by a right of zeal; as if the executions done upon offenders in the kingdom of God in old time proceeded not from the

30   sovereign command, but from the authority of private zeal: which, if we consider the texts that seem to favour it, is quite contrary.

     First, where the Levites fell upon the people that had made and worshipped the golden calf, and slew three thousand of them, it was by the commandment of Moses from the mouth of God; as is manifest, Exodus, 32. 27. And when the son

35   of a woman of Israel had blasphemed God, they that heard it did not kill him, but brought him before Moses, who put him under custody, till God should give sentence against him; as appears, Leviticus, 24. 11, 12. Again, when Phinehas killed Zimri and Cozbi,[18] it was not by right of private zeal: their crime was committed in the sight of the assembly; there needed no witness; the law was

40   known, and he the heir apparent to the sovereignty; and, which is the principal

point, the lawfulness of his act depended wholly upon a subsequent ratification by Moses, whereof he had no cause to doubt. And this presumption of a future ratification is sometimes necessary to the safety of a Commonwealth; as in a sudden rebellion any man that can suppress it by his own power in the country
5   where it begins, without express law or commission, may lawfully do it, and provide to have it ratified, or pardoned, whilst it is in doing, or after it is done. Also, it is expressly said, "Whosoever shall kill the murderer shall kill him upon the word of witnesses":[19] but witnesses suppose a formal judicature, and consequently condemn that pretence of jus zelotarum. The Law of Moses
10 concerning him that enticeth to idolatry, that is to say, in the kingdom of God to a renouncing of his allegiance, forbids to conceal him, and commands the accuser to cause him to be put to death, and to cast the first stone at him;[20] but not to kill him before he be condemned. And the process against idolatry is exactly set down: for God there speaketh to the people as Judge, and
15 commandeth them, when a man is accused of idolatry, to enquire diligently of the fact, and finding it true, then to stone him; but still the hand of the witness throweth the first stone.[21] This is not private zeal, but public condemnation. In like manner when a father hath a rebellious son, the law is that he shall bring him before the judges of the town, and all the people of the town shall stone
20 him.[22] Lastly, by pretence of these laws it was that St. Stephen was stoned, and not by pretence of private zeal: for before he was carried away to execution, he had pleaded his cause before the high priest. There is nothing in all this, nor in any other part of the Bible, to countenance executions by private zeal; which, being oftentimes but a conjunction of ignorance and passion, is against both the
25 justice and peace of a Commonwealth.

    In the thirty-sixth Chapter I have said that it is not declared in what manner God spoke supernaturally to Moses: not that He spoke not to him sometimes by dreams and visions, and by a supernatural voice, as to other prophets; for the manner how He spoke unto him from the mercy seat is expressly set down in
30 these words, "From that time forward, when Moses entered into Tabernacle of the congregation to speak with God, he heard a voice which spake unto him from over the mercy seat, which is over the Ark of the testimony; from between the cherubims he spake unto him."[23] But it is not declared in what consisted the pre-eminence of the manner of God's speaking to Moses, above that of His
35 speaking to other prophets, as to Samuel and to Abraham, to whom He also spoke by a voice (that is, by vision), unless the difference consist in the clearness of the vision. For "face to face," and "mouth to mouth," cannot be literally understood of the infiniteness and incomprehensibility of the Divine Nature.

And as to the whole doctrine, I see not yet, but the principles of it are true and proper, and the ratiocination solid. For I ground the civil right of sovereigns, and both the duty and liberty of subjects, upon the known natural inclinations of mankind, and upon the articles of the law of nature; of which no man, that

5   pretends but reason enough to govern his private family, ought to be ignorant. And for the power ecclesiastical of the same sovereigns, I ground it on such texts as are both evident in themselves and consonant to the scope of the whole Scripture, and therefore am persuaded that he that shall read it with a purpose only to be informed, shall be informed by it. But for those that by writing or

10   public discourse, or by their eminent actions, have already engaged themselves to the maintaining of contrary opinions, they will not be so easily satisfied. For in such cases, it is natural for men, at one and the same time, both to proceed in reading and to lose their attention in the search of objections to that they had read before: of which, in a time wherein the interests of men are changed (seeing

15   much of that doctrine which serveth to the establishing of a new government must needs be contrary to that which conduced to the dissolution of the old), there cannot choose but be very many.

In that part which treateth of a Christian Commonwealth, there are some new doctrines which, it may be, in a state where the contrary were already fully

20   determined, were a fault for a subject without leave to divulge, as being a usurpation of the place of a teacher. But in this time that men call not only for peace, but also for truth, to offer such doctrines as I think true, and that manifestly tend to peace and loyalty, to the consideration of those that are yet in deliberation, is no more but to offer new wine, to be put into new casks, that

25   both may be preserved together. And I suppose that then, when novelty can breed no trouble nor disorder in a state, men are not generally so much inclined to the reverence of antiquity as to prefer ancient errors before new and well-proved truth.

There is nothing I distrust more than my elocution, which nevertheless I am

30   confident (excepting the mischances of the press) is not obscure. That I have neglected the ornament of quoting ancient poets, orators, and philosophers, contrary to the custom of late time, whether I have done well or ill in it, proceedeth from my judgement, grounded on many reasons. For first, all truth of doctrine dependeth either upon reason or upon Scripture; both which give credit

35   to many, but never receive it from any writer. Secondly, the matters in question are not of fact, but of right, wherein there is no place for witnesses. There is scarce any of those old writers that contradicteth not sometimes both himself and others; which makes their testimonies insufficient. Fourthly, such opinions as are taken only upon credit of antiquity are not intrinsically the judgement of

40   those that cite them, but words that pass, like gaping, from mouth to mouth.

Fifthly, it is many times with a fraudulent design that men stick their corrupt doctrine with the cloves of other men's wit. Sixthly, I find not that the ancients they cite took it for an ornament to do the like with those that wrote before them. Seventhly, it is an argument of indigestion, when Greek and Latin sentences
5 unchewed come up again, as they use to do, unchanged. Lastly, though I reverence those men of ancient time that either have written truth perspicuously, or set us in a better way to find it out ourselves; yet to the antiquity itself I think nothing due. For if we will reverence the age, the present is the oldest: if the antiquity of the writer, I am not sure that generally they to whom such honour is
10 given, were more ancient when they wrote than I am that am writing: but if it be well considered, the praise of ancient authors proceeds not from the reverence of the dead, but from the competition and mutual envy of the living.

To conclude, there is nothing in this whole discourse, nor in that I wrote before of the same subject in Latin, as far as I can perceive, contrary either to the
15 word of God or to good manners; or to the disturbance of the public tranquillity. Therefore I think it may be profitably printed, and more profitably taught in the Universities, in case they also think so, whom the judgement of the same belongeth. For seeing the Universities are the fountains of civil and moral doctrine, from whence the preachers and the gentry, drawing such water as they
20 find, use to sprinkle the same (both from the pulpit and in their conversation) upon the people, there ought certainly to be great care taken, to have it pure, both from the venom of heathen politicians, and from the incantation of deceiving spirits. And by that means the most men, knowing their duties, will be the less subject to serve the ambition of a few discontented persons in their
25 purposes against the state, and be the less grieved with the contributions necessary for their peace and defence; and the governors themselves have the less cause to maintain at the common charge any greater army than is necessary to make good the public liberty against the invasions and encroachments of foreign enemies.
30 And thus I have brought to an end my discourse of civil and ecclesiastical government, occasioned by the disorders of the present time, without partiality, without application, and without other design than to set before men's eyes the mutual relation between protection and obedience; of which the condition of human nature, and the laws divine, both natural and positive, require an
35 inviolable observation. And though in the revolution of states there can be no very good constellation for truths of this nature to be born under (as having an angry aspect from the dissolvers of an old government, and seeing but the backs of them that erect a new); yet I cannot think it will be condemned at this time, either by the public judge of doctrine, or by any that desires the continuance of
40 public peace. And in this hope I return to my interrupted speculation of bodies

natural; wherein, if God give me health to finish it, I hope the novelty will as much please as in the doctrine of this artificial body it useth to offend. For such truth as opposeth no man's profit nor pleasure is to all men welcome.

---

[1] Exodus, 20. 19
[2] I Samuel, 8. 11-17
[3] Ibid., 8. 19, 20
[4] I Kings, 3. 9
[5] I Samuel, 24. 6
[6] Colossians, 3. 22
[7] Ibid., 3. 20
[8] Matthew, 23. 2, 3
[9] Titus, 3. 1
[10] Matthew, 21. 2, 3
[11] Genesis, 3. 5
[12] Ibid., 3. 11
[13] Aristotle, Politics, Bk VI
[14] Proverbs, 7. 3
[15] Deuteronomy, 11. 19
[16] Ibid., 31. 12
[17] Genesis, 17. 10
[18] Numbers, 25. 6, 7
[19] Ibid., 35. 30
[20] Deuteronomy, 13. 8
[21] Ibid., 17. 4, 5, 6
[22] Ibid., 21. 18-21
[23] Numbers, 7. 89

John Locke

John Locke (b. 1632, Sommerset, d. 1704, Essex) was an English philosopher. He studied philosophy and medicine at Oxford, and largely because of his medical training, he came to the attention of Anthony Ashley Cooper, 1ˢᵗ Earl of Shaftesbury, later the Lord Chancellor of the King's Government. Through his associations with Shaftesbury, Locke came to play a prominent role in Whig circles and to perform sensitive political tasks on behalf of the Whig government of Shaftesbury and of the Whig party more generally. Among these tasks was the drafting of the Fundamental Constitution of the Carolinas and the writing of the Whig response, in the form of the *First Treatise of Government*, to the defense of absolutism in Sir Robert Filmer's *Patriarcha*.

Locke's important philosophical works include the clearly political *First* and *Second Treatises of Government*, and *A Letter Concerning Toleration*, as well as *An Essay Concerning Human Understanding*, which provided an influential defense of epistemological empiricism.

Locke is, perhaps, the central figure in the development of modern ideas of liberty, religious toleration, and governmental restraint. His theories has had a profound impact on the American founding fathers, especially James Madison and Thomas Jefferson, as well as on the development of contemporary libertarian political theory, especially in the work of Robert Nozick.

John Locke
A LETTER CONCERNING TOLERATION
(1689)

Honoured Sir,

Since you are pleased to inquire what are my thoughts about the mutual toleration of Christians in their different professions of religion, I must needs
5   answer you freely that I esteem that toleration to be the chief characteristic mark of the true Church. For whatsoever some people boast of the antiquity of places and names, or of the pomp of their outward worship; others, of the reformation of their discipline; all, of the orthodoxy of their faith — for everyone is orthodox to himself — these things, and all others of this nature, are much rather marks of
10 men striving for power and empire over one another than of the Church of Christ. Let anyone have never so true a claim to all these things, yet if he be destitute of charity, meekness, and good-will in general towards all mankind, even to those that are not Christians, he is certainly yet short of being a true Christian himself. "The kings of the Gentiles exercise leadership over them,"
15 said our Saviour to his disciples, "but ye shall not be so."[1] The business of true religion is quite another thing. It is not instituted in order to the erecting of an external pomp, nor to the obtaining of ecclesiastical dominion, nor to the exercising of compulsive force, but to the regulating of men's lives, according to the rules of virtue and piety. Whosoever will list himself under the banner of
20 Christ, must, in the first place and above all things, make war upon his own lusts and vices. It is in vain for any man to unsurp the name of Christian, without holiness of life, purity of manners, benignity and meekness of spirit. "Let everyone that nameth the name of Christ, depart from iniquity."[2] "Thou, when thou art converted, strengthen thy brethren," said our Lord to Peter.[3] It would,
25 indeed, be very hard for one that appears careless about his own salvation to persuade me that he were extremely concerned for mine. For it is impossible that those should sincerely and heartily apply themselves to make other people Christians, who have not really embraced the Christian religion in their own hearts. If the Gospel and the apostles may be credited, no man can be a Christian
30 without charity and without that faith which works, not by force, but by love. Now, I appeal to the consciences of those that persecute, torment, destroy, and kill other men upon pretence of religion, whether they do it out of friendship and kindness towards them or no? And I shall then indeed, and not until then, believe they do so, when I shall see those fiery zealots correcting, in the same
35 manner, their friends and familiar acquaintance for the manifest sins they commit against the precepts of the Gospel; when I shall see them persecute with

fire and sword the members of their own communion that are tainted with
enormous vices and without amendment are in danger of eternal perdition; and
when I shall see them thus express their love and desire of the salvation of their
souls by the infliction of torments and exercise of all manner of cruelties. For if
5   it be out of a principle of charity, as they pretend, and love to men's souls that
they deprive them of their estates, maim them with corporal punishments, starve
and torment them in noisome prisons, and in the end even take away their lives
— I say, if all this be done merely to make men Christians and procure their
salvation, why then do they suffer whoredom, fraud, malice, and such-like
10   enormities, which (according to the apostle)[4] manifestly relish of heathenish
corruption, to predominate so much and abound amongst their flocks and
people? These, and such-like things, are certainly more contrary to the glory of
God, to the purity of the Church, and to the salvation of souls, than any
conscientious dissent from ecclesiastical decisions, or separation from public
15   worship, whilst accompanied with innocence of life. Why, then, does this
burning zeal for God, for the Church, and for the salvation of souls — burning I
say, literally, with fire and faggot — pass by those moral vices and
wickednesses, without any chastisement, which are acknowledged by all men to
be diametrically opposite to the profession of Christianity, and bend all its
20   nerves either to the introducing of ceremonies, or to the establishment of
opinions, which for the most part are about nice and intricate matters, that
exceed the capacity of ordinary understandings? Which of the parties contending
about these things is in the right, which of them is guilty of schism or heresy,
whether those that domineer or those that suffer, will then at last be manifest
25   when the causes of their separation comes to be judged of He, certainly, that
follows Christ, embraces His doctrine, and bears His yoke, though he forsake
both father and mother, separate from the public assemblies and ceremonies of
his country, or whomsoever or whatsoever else he relinquishes, will not then be
judged a heretic.
30   Now, though the divisions that are amongst sects should be allowed to be
never so obstructive of the salvation of souls; yet, nevertheless, adultery,
fornication, uncleanliness, lasciviousness, idolatry, and such-like things, cannot
be denied to be works of the flesh, concerning which the apostle has expressly
declared that "they who do them shall not inherit the kingdom of God."[5]
35   Whosoever, therefore, is sincerely solicitous about the kingdom of God and
thinks it his duty to endeavour the enlargement of it amongst men, ought to
apply himself with no less care and industry to the rooting out of these
immoralities than to the extirpation of sects. But if anyone do otherwise, and
whilst he is cruel and implacable towards those that differ from him in opinion,
40   he be indulgent to such iniquities and immoralities as are unbecoming the name

of a Christian, let such a one talk never so much of the Church, he plainly demonstrates by his actions that it is another kingdom he aims at and not the advancement of the kingdom of God.

That any man should think fit to cause another man — whose salvation he heartily desires — to expire in torments, and that even in an unconverted state, would, I confess, seem very strange to me, and I think, to any other also. But nobody, surely, will ever believe that such a carriage can proceed from charity, love, or goodwill. If anyone maintain that men ought to be compelled by fire and sword to profess certain doctrines, and conform to this or that exterior worship, without any regard had unto their morals; if anyone endeavour to convert those that are erroneous unto the faith, by forcing them to profess things that they do not believe and allowing them to practise things that the Gospel does not permit, it cannot be doubted indeed but such a one is desirous to have a numerous assembly joined in the same profession with himself; but that he principally intends by those means to compose a truly Christian Church is altogether incredible. It is not, therefore, to be wondered at if those who do not really contend for the advancement of the true religion, and of the Church of Christ, make use of arms that do not belong to the Christian warfare. If, like the Captain of our salvation, they sincerely desired the good of souls, they would tread in the steps and follow the perfect example of that Prince of Peace, who sent out His soldiers to the subduing of nations, and gathering them into His Church, not armed with the sword, or other instruments of force, but prepared with the Gospel of peace and with the exemplary holiness of their conversation. This was His method. Though if infidels were to be converted by force, if those that are either blind or obstinate were to be drawn off from their errors by armed soldiers, we know very well that it was much more easy for Him to do it with armies of heavenly legions than for any son of the Church, how potent soever, with all his dragoons.

The toleration of those that differ from others in matters of religion is so agreeable to the Gospel of Jesus Christ, and to the genuine reason of mankind, that it seems monstrous for men to be so blind as not to perceive the necessity and advantage of it in so clear a light. I will not here tax the pride and ambition of some, the passion and uncharitable zeal of others. These are faults from which human affairs can perhaps scarce ever be perfectly freed; but yet such as nobody will bear the plain imputation of, without covering them with some specious colour; and so pretend to commendation, whilst they are carried away by their own irregular passions. But, however, that some may not colour their spirit of persecution and unchristian cruelty with a pretence of care of the public weal and observation of the laws; and that others, under pretence of religion, may not seek impunity for their libertinism and licentiousness; in a word, that

none may impose either upon himself or others, by the pretences of loyalty and obedience to the prince, or of tenderness and sincerity in the worship of God; I esteem it above all things necessary to distinguish exactly the business of civil government from that of religion and to settle the just bounds that lie between
5 the one and the other. If this be not done, there can be no end put to the controversies that will be always arising between those that have, or at least pretend to have, on the one side, a concernment for the interest of men's souls, and, on the other side, a care of the commonwealth.

The commonwealth seems to me to be a society of men constituted only for
10 the procuring, preserving, and advancing their own civil interests.

Civil interests I call life, liberty, health, and indolency of body; and the possession of outward things, such as money, lands, houses, furniture, and the like.

It is the duty of the civil magistrate, by the impartial execution of equal
15 laws, to secure unto all the people in general and to every one of his subjects in particular the just possession of these things belonging to this life. If anyone presume to violate the laws of public justice and equity, established for the preservation of those things, his presumption is to be checked by the fear of punishment, consisting of the deprivation or diminution of those civil interests,
20 or goods, which otherwise he might and ought to enjoy. But seeing no man does willingly suffer himself to be punished by the deprivation of any part of his goods, and much less of his liberty or life, therefore, is the magistrate armed with the force and strength of all his subjects, in order to the punishment of those that violate any other man's rights.
25 Now that the whole jurisdiction of the magistrate reaches only to these civil concernments, and that all civil power, right and dominion, is bounded and confined to the only care of promoting these things; and that it neither can nor ought in any manner to be extended to the salvation of souls, these following considerations seem unto me abundantly to demonstrate.
30 First, because the care of souls is not committed to the civil magistrate, any more than to other men. It is not committed unto him, I say, by God; because it appears not that God has ever given any such authority to one man over another as to compel anyone to his religion. Nor can any such power be vested in the magistrate by the consent of the people, because no man can so far abandon the
35 care of his own salvation as blindly to leave to the choice of any other, whether prince or subject, to prescribe to him what faith or worship he shall embrace. For no man can, if he would, conform his faith to the dictates of another. All the life and power of true religion consist in the inward and full persuasion of the mind; and faith is not faith without believing. Whatever profession we make, to
40 whatever outward worship we conform, if we are not fully satisfied in our own

mind that the one is true and the other well pleasing unto God, such profession and such practice, far from being any furtherance, are indeed great obstacles to our salvation. For in this manner, instead of expiating other sins by the exercise of religion, I say, in offering thus unto God Almighty such a worship as we
5   esteem to be displeasing unto Him, we add unto the number of our other sins those also of hypocrisy and contempt of His Divine Majesty.

In the second place, the care of souls cannot belong to the civil magistrate, because his power consists only in outward force; but true and saving religion consists in the inward persuasion of the mind, without which nothing can be
10   acceptable to God. And such is the nature of the understanding, that it cannot be compelled to the belief of anything by outward force. Confiscation of estate, imprisonment, torments, nothing of that nature can have any such efficacy as to make men change the inward judgement that they have framed of things.

It may indeed be alleged that the magistrate may make use of arguments,
15   and, thereby; draw the heterodox into the way of truth, and procure their salvation. I grant it; but this is common to him with other men. In teaching, instructing, and redressing the erroneous by reason, he may certainly do what becomes any good man to do. Magistracy does not oblige him to put off either humanity or Christianity; but it is one thing to persuade, another to command;
20   one thing to press with arguments, another with penalties. This civil power alone has a right to do; to the other, goodwill is authority enough. Every man has commission to admonish, exhort, convince another of error, and, by reasoning, to draw him into truth; but to give laws, receive obedience, and compel with the sword, belongs to none but the magistrate. And, upon this ground, I affirm that
25   the magistrate's power extends not to the establishing of any articles of faith, or forms of worship, by the force of his laws. For laws are of no force at all without penalties, and penalties in this case are absolutely impertinent, because they are not proper to convince the mind. Neither the profession of any articles of faith, nor the conformity to any outward form of worship (as has been already said),
30   can be available to the salvation of souls, unless the truth of the one and the acceptableness of the other unto God be thoroughly believed by those that so profess and practise. But penalties are no way capable to produce such belief. It is only light and evidence that can work a change in men's opinions; which light can in no manner proceed from corporal sufferings, or any other outward
35   penalties.

In the third place, the care of the salvation of men's souls cannot belong to the magistrate; because, though the rigour of laws and the force of penalties were capable to convince and change men's minds, yet would not that help at all to the salvation of their souls. For there being but one truth, one way to heaven,
40   what hope is there that more men would be led into it if they had no rule but the

276

religion of the court and were put under the necessity to quit the light of their own reason, and oppose the dictates of their own consciences, and blindly to resign themselves up to the will of their governors and to the religion which either ignorance, ambition, or superstition had chanced to establish in the
5   countries where they were born? In the variety and contradiction of opinions in religion, wherein the princes of the world are as much divided as in their secular interests, the narrow way would be much straitened; one country alone would be in the right, and all the rest of the world put under an obligation of following their princes in the ways that lead to destruction; and that which heightens the
10 absurdity, and very ill suits the notion of a Deity, men would owe their eternal happiness or misery to the places of their nativity.

     These considerations, to omit many others that might have been urged to the same purpose, seem unto me sufficient to conclude that all the power of civil government relates only to men's civil interests, is confined to the care of the
15 things of this world, and hath nothing to do with the world to come.

     Let us now consider what a church is. A church, then, I take to be a voluntary society of men, joining themselves together of their own accord in order to the public worshipping of God in such manner as they judge acceptable to Him, and effectual to the salvation of their souls.
20   I say it is a free and voluntary society. Nobody is born a member of any church; otherwise the religion of parents would descend unto children by the same right of inheritance as their temporal estates, and everyone would hold his faith by the same tenure he does his lands, than which nothing can be imagined more absurd. Thus, therefore, that matter stands. No man by nature is bound
25 unto any particular church or sect, but everyone joins himself voluntarily to that society in which he believes he has found that profession and worship which is truly acceptable to God. The hope of salvation, as it was the only cause of his entrance into that communion, so it can be the only reason of his stay there. For if afterwards he discover anything either erroneous in the doctrine or
30 incongruous in the worship of that society to which he has joined himself, why should it not be as free for him to go out as it was to enter? No member of a religious society can be tied with any other bonds but what proceed from the certain expectation of eternal life. A church, then, is a society of members voluntarily uniting to that end.
35   It follows now that we consider what is the power of this church and unto what laws it is subject.

     Forasmuch as no society, how free soever, or upon whatsoever slight occasion instituted, whether of philosophers for learning, of merchants for commerce, or of men of leisure for mutual conversation and discourse, no
40 church or company, I say, can in the least subsist and hold together, but will

presently dissolve and break in pieces, unless it be regulated by some laws, and the members all consent to observe some order. Place and time of meeting must be agreed on; rules for admitting and excluding members must be established; distinction of officers, and putting things into a regular course, and suchlike,

5   cannot be omitted. But since the joining together of several members into this church-society, as has already been demonstrated, is absolutely free and spontaneous, it necessarily follows that the right of making its laws can belong to none but the society itself; or, at least (which is the same thing), to those whom the society by common consent has authorised thereunto.

10   Some, perhaps, may object that no such society can be said to be a true church unless it have in it a bishop or presbyter, with ruling authority derived from the very apostles, and continued down to the present times by an uninterrupted succession.

To these I answer: In the first place, let them show me the edict by which

15   Christ has imposed that law upon His Church. And let not any man think me impertinent, if in a thing of this consequence I require that the terms of that edict be very express and positive; for the promise He has made us,[6] that "wheresoever two or three are gathered together" in His name, He will be in the midst of them, seems to imply the contrary. Whether such an assembly want

20   anything necessary to a true church, pray do you consider. Certain I am that nothing can be there wanting unto the salvation of souls, which is sufficient to our purpose.

Next, pray observe how great have always been the divisions amongst even those who lay so much stress upon the Divine institution and continued

25   succession of a certain order of rulers in the Church. Now, their very dissension unavoidably puts us upon a necessity of deliberating and, consequently, allows a liberty of choosing that which upon consideration we prefer.

And, in the last place, I consent that these men have a ruler in their church, established by such a long series of succession as they judge necessary, provided

30   I may have liberty at the same time to join myself to that society in which I am persuaded those things are to be found which are necessary to the salvation of my soul. In this manner ecclesiastical liberty will be preserved on all sides, and no man will have a legislator imposed upon him but whom himself has chosen.

But since men are so solicitous about the true church, I would only ask them

35   here, by the way, if it be not more agreeable to the Church of Christ to make the conditions of her communion consist in such things, and such things only, as the Holy Spirit has in the Holy Scriptures declared, in express words, to be necessary to salvation; I ask, I say, whether this be not more agreeable to the Church of Christ than for men to impose their own inventions and

40   interpretations upon others as if they were of Divine authority, and to establish

by ecclesiastical laws, as absolutely necessary to the profession of Christianity, such things as the Holy Scriptures do either not mention, or at least not expressly command? Whosoever requires those things in order to ecclesiastical communion, which Christ does not require in order to life eternal, he may,
5   perhaps, indeed constitute a society accommodated to his own opinion and his own advantage; but how that can be called the Church of Christ which is established upon laws that are not His, and which excludes such persons from its communion as He will one day receive into the Kingdom of Heaven, I understand not. But this being not a proper place to inquire into the marks of the
10   true church, I will only mind those that contend so earnestly for the decrees of their own society, and that cry out continually, "The Church! the Church!" with as much noise, and perhaps upon the same principle, as the Ephesian silversmiths did for their Diana; this, I say, I desire to mind them of, that the Gospel frequently declares that the true disciples of Christ must suffer
15   persecution; but that the Church of Christ should persecute others, and force others by fire and sword to embrace her faith and doctrine, I could never yet find in any of the books of the New Testament.

    The end of a religious society (as has already been said) is the public worship of God and, by means thereof, the acquisition of eternal life. All
20   discipline ought, therefore, to tend to that end, and all ecclesiastical laws to be thereunto confined. Nothing ought nor can be transacted in this society relating to the possession of civil and worldly goods. No force is here to be made use of upon any occasion whatsoever. For force belongs wholly to the civil magistrate, and the possession of all outward goods is subject to his jurisdiction.

25   But, it may be asked, by what means then shall ecclesiastical laws be established, if they must be thus destitute of all compulsive power? I answer: They must be established by means suitable to the nature of such things, whereof the external profession and observation — if not proceeding from a thorough conviction and approbation of the mind — is altogether useless and
30   unprofitable. The arms by which the members of this society are to be kept within their duty are exhortations, admonitions, and advices. If by these means the offenders will not be reclaimed, and the erroneous convinced, there remains nothing further to be done but that such stubborn and obstinate persons, who give no ground to hope for their reformation, should be cast out and separated
35   from the society. This is the last and utmost force of ecclesiastical authority. No other punishment can thereby be inflicted than that, the relation ceasing between the body and the member which is cut off. The person so condemned ceases to be a part of that church.

    These things being thus determined, let us inquire, in the next place: How
40   far the duty of toleration extends, and what is required from everyone by it?

And, first, I hold that no church is bound, by the duty of toleration, to retain any such person in her bosom as, after admonition, continues obstinately to offend against the laws of the society. For, these being the condition of communion and the bond of the society, if the breach of them were permitted
5   without any animadversion the society would immediately be thereby dissolved. But, nevertheless, in all such cases care is to be taken that the sentence of excommunication, and the execution thereof, carry with it no rough usage of word or action whereby the ejected person may any wise be damnified in body or estate. For all force (as has often been said) belongs only to the magistrate,
10   nor ought any private persons at any time to use force, unless it be in self-defence against unjust violence. Excommunication neither does, nor can, deprive the excommunicated person of any of those civil goods that he formerly possessed. All those things belong to the civil government and are under the magistrate's protection. The whole force of excommunication consists only in
15   this: that, the resolution of the society in that respect being declared, the union that was between the body and some member comes thereby to be dissolved; and, that relation ceasing, the participation of some certain things which the society communicated to its members, and unto which no man has any civil right, comes also to cease. For there is no civil injury done unto the
20   excommunicated person by the church minister's refusing him that bread and wine, in the celebration of the Lord's Supper, which was not bought with his but other men's money.

What I say concerning the mutual toleration of private persons differing another person in his civil enjoyments because he is of another church or
25   religion. All the rights and franchises that belong to him as a man, or as a denizen, are inviolably to be preserved to him. These are not the business of religion. No violence nor injury is to be offered him, whether he be Christian or Pagan. Nay, we must not content ourselves with the narrow measures of bare justice; charity, bounty, and liberality must be added to it. This the Gospel
30   enjoins, this reason directs, and this that natural fellowship we are born into requires of us. If any man err from the right way, it is his own misfortune, no injury to thee; nor therefore art thou to punish him in the things of this life because thou supposest he will be miserable in that which is to come.

What I say concerning the mutual toleration of private persons differing
35   from one another in religion, I understand also of particular churches which stand, as it were, in the same relation to each other as private persons among themselves: nor has any one of them any manner of jurisdiction over any other; no, not even when the civil magistrate (as it sometimes happens) comes to be of this or the other communion. For the civil government can give no new right to
40   the church, nor the church to the civil government. So that, whether the

magistrate join himself to any church, or separate from it, the church remains always as it was before — a free and voluntary society. It neither requires the power of the sword by the magistrate's coming to it, nor does it lose the right of instruction and excommunication by his going from it. This is the fundamental
5   and immutable right of a spontaneous society — that it has power to remove any of its members who transgress the rules of its institution; but it cannot, by the accession of any new members, acquire any right of jurisdiction over those that are not joined with it. And therefore peace, equity, and friendship are always mutually to be observed by particular churches, in the same manner as by
10 private persons, without any pretence of superiority or jurisdiction over one another.

     That the thing may be made clearer by an example, let us suppose two churches — the one of Arminians, the other of Calvinists — residing in the city of Constantinople. Will anyone say that either of these churches has right to
15 deprive the members of the other of their estates and liberty (as we see practised elsewhere) because of their differing from it in some doctrines and ceremonies, whilst the Turks, in the meanwhile, silently stand by and laugh to see with what inhuman cruelty Christians thus rage against Christians? But if one of these churches hath this power of treating the other ill, I ask which of them it is to
20 whom that power belongs, and by what right? It will be answered, undoubtedly, that it is the orthodox church which has the right of authority over the erroneous or heretical. This is, in great and specious words, to say just nothing at all. For every church is orthodox to itself; to others, erroneous or heretical. For whatsoever any church believes, it believes to be true and the contrary unto
25 those things it pronounce; to be error. So that the controversy between these churches about the truth of their doctrines and the purity of their worship is on both sides equal; nor is there any judge, either at Constantinople or elsewhere upon earth, by whose sentence it can be determined. The decision of that question belongs only to the Supreme judge of all men, to whom also alone
30 belongs the punishment of the erroneous. In the meanwhile, let those men consider how heinously they sin, who, adding injustice, if not to their error, yet certainly to their pride, do rashly and arrogantly take upon them to misuse the servants of another master, who are not at all accountable to them.

     Nay, further: if it could be manifest which of these two dissenting churches
35 were in the right, there would not accrue thereby unto the orthodox any right of destroying the other. For churches have neither any jurisdiction in worldly matters, nor are fire and sword any proper instruments wherewith to convince men's minds of error, and inform them of the truth. Let us suppose, nevertheless, that the civil magistrate inclined to favour one of them and to put
40 his sword into their hands that (by his consent) they might chastise the dissenters

as they pleased. Will any man say that any right can be derived unto a Christian church over its brethren from a Turkish emperor? An infidel, who has himself no authority to punish Christians for the articles of their faith, cannot confer such an authority upon any society of Christians, nor give unto them a right
5   which he has not himself. This would be the case at Constantinople; and the reason of the thing is the same in any Christian kingdom. The civil power is the same in every place. Nor can that power, in the hands of a Christian prince, confer any greater authority upon the Church than in the hands of a heathen; which is to say, just none at all.
10   Nevertheless, it is worthy to be observed and lamented that the most violent of these defenders of the truth, the opposers of errors, the exclaimers against schism do hardly ever let loose this their zeal for God, with which they are so warmed and inflamed, unless where they have the civil magistrate on their side. But so soon as ever court favour has given them the better end of the staff, and
15   they begin to feel themselves the stronger, then presently peace and charity are to be laid aside. Otherwise they are religiously to be observed. Where they have not the power to carry on persecution and to become masters, there they desire to live upon fair terms and preach up toleration. When they are not strengthened with the civil power, then they can bear most patiently and unmovedly the
20   contagion of idolatry, superstition, and heresy in their neighbourhood; of which on other occasions the interest of religion makes them to be extremely apprehensive. They do not forwardly attack those errors which are in fashion at court or are countenanced by the government. Here they can be content to spare their arguments; which yet (with their leave) is the only right method of
25   propagating truth, which has no such way of prevailing as when strong arguments and good reason are joined with the softness of civility and good usage.
        Nobody, therefore, in fine, neither single persons nor churches, nay, nor even commonwealths, have any just title to invade the civil rights and worldly
30   goods of each other upon pretence of religion. Those that are of another opinion would do well to consider with themselves how pernicious a seed of discord and war, how powerful a provocation to endless hatreds, rapines, and slaughters they thereby furnish unto mankind. No peace and security, no, not so much as common friendship, can ever be established or preserved amongst men so long
35   as this opinion prevails, that dominion is founded in grace and that religion is to be propagated by force of arms.
        In the third place, let us see what the duty of toleration requires from those who are distinguished from the rest of mankind (from the laity, as they please to call us) by some ecclesiastical character and office; whether they be bishops,
40   priests, presbyters, ministers, or however else dignified or distinguished. It is not

282

my business to inquire here into the original of the power or dignity of the clergy. This only I say, that, whencesoever their authority be sprung, since it is ecclesiastical, it ought to be confined within the bounds of the Church, nor can it in any manner be extended to civil affairs, because the Church itself is a thing
5 absolutely separate and distinct from the commonwealth. The boundaries on both sides are fixed and immovable. He jumbles heaven and earth together, the things most remote and opposite, who mixes these two societies, which are in their original, end, business, and in everything perfectly distinct and infinitely different from each other. No man, therefore, with whatsoever ecclesiastical
10 office he be dignified, can deprive another man that is not of his church and faith either of liberty or of any part of his worldly goods upon the account of that difference between them in religion. For whatsoever is not lawful to the whole Church cannot by any ecclesiastical right become lawful to any of its members.

But this is not all. It is not enough that ecclesiastical men abstain from
15 violence and rapine and all manner of persecution. He that pretends to be a successor of the apostles, and takes upon him the office of teaching, is obliged also to admonish his hearers of the duties of peace and goodwill towards all men, as well towards the erroneous as the orthodox; towards those that differ from them in faith and worship as well as towards those that agree with them
20 therein. And he ought industriously to exhort all men, whether private persons or magistrates (if any such there be in his church), to charity, meekness, and toleration, and diligently endeavour to ally and temper all that heat and unreasonable averseness of mind which either any man's fiery zeal for his own sect or the craft of others has kindled against dissenters. I will not undertake to
25 represent how happy and how great would be the fruit, both in Church and State, if the pulpits everywhere sounded with this doctrine of peace and toleration, lest I should seem to reflect too severely upon those men whose dignity I desire not to detract from, nor would have it diminished either by others or themselves. But this I say, that thus it ought to be. And if anyone that professes himself to be a
30 minister of the Word of God, a preacher of the gospel of peace, teach otherwise, he either understands not or neglects the business of his calling and shall one day give account thereof unto the Prince of Peace. If Christians are to be admonished that they abstain from all manner of revenge, even after repeated provocations and multiplied injuries, how much more ought they who suffer
35 nothing, who have had no harm done them, forbear violence and abstain from all manner of ill-usage towards those from whom they have received none! This caution and temper they ought certainly to use towards those. who mind only their own business and are solicitous for nothing but that (whatever men think of them) they may worship God in that manner which they are persuaded is
40 acceptable to Him and in which they have the strongest hopes of eternal

salvation. In private domestic affairs, in the management of estates, in the conservation of bodily health, every man may consider what suits his own convenience and follow what course he likes best. No man complains of the ill-management of his neighbour's affairs. No man is angry with another for an error committed in sowing his land or in marrying his daughter. Nobody corrects a spendthrift for consuming his substance in taverns. Let any man pull down, or build, or make whatsoever expenses he pleases, nobody murmurs, nobody controls him; he has his liberty. But if any man do not frequent the church, if he do not there conform his behaviour exactly to the accustomed ceremonies, or if he brings not his children to be initiated in the sacred mysteries of this or the other congregation, this immediately causes an uproar. The neighbourhood is filled with noise and clamour. Everyone is ready to be the avenger of so great a crime, and the zealots hardly have the patience to refrain from violence and rapine so long till the cause be heard and the poor man be, according to form, condemned to the loss of liberty, goods, or life. Oh, that our ecclesiastical orators of every sect would apply themselves with all the strength of arguments that they are able to the confounding of men's errors! But let them spare their persons. Let them not supply their want of reasons with the instruments of force, which belong to another jurisdiction and do ill become a Churchman's hands. Let them not call in the magistrate's authority to the aid of their eloquence or learning, lest perhaps, whilst they pretend only love for the truth, this their intemperate zeal, breathing nothing but fire and sword, betray their ambition and show that what they desire is temporal dominion. For it will be very difficult to persuade men of sense that he who with dry eyes and satisfaction of mind can deliver his brother to the executioner to be burnt alive, does sincerely and heartily concern himself to save that brother from the flames of hell in the world to come.

In the last place, let us now consider what is the magistrate's duty in the business of toleration, which certainly is very considerable.

We have already proved that the care of souls does not belong to the magistrate. Not a magisterial care, I mean (if I may so call it), which consists in prescribing by laws and compelling by punishments. But a charitable care, which consists in teaching, admonishing, and persuading, cannot be denied unto any man. The care, therefore, of every man's soul belongs unto himself and is to be left unto himself. But what if he neglect the care of his soul? I answer: What if he neglect the care of his health or of his estate, which things are nearlier related to the government of the magistrate than the other? Will the magistrate provide by an express law that such a one shall not become poor or sick? Laws provide, as much as is possible, that the goods and health of subjects be not injured by the fraud and violence of others; they do not guard them from the

negligence or ill-husbandry of the possessors themselves. No man can be forced to be rich or healthful whether he will or no. Nay, God Himself will not save men against their wills. Let us suppose, however, that some prince were desirous to force his subjects to accumulate riches, or to preserve the health and strength
5   of their bodies. Shall it be provided by law that they must consult none but Roman physicians, and shall everyone be bound to live according to their prescriptions? What, shall no potion, no broth, be taken, but what is prepared either in the Vatican, suppose, or in a Geneva shop? Or, to make these subjects rich, shall they all be obliged by law to become merchants or musicians? Or,
10   shall everyone turn victualler, or smith, because there are some that maintain their families plentifully and grow rich in those professions? But, it may be said, there are a thousand ways to wealth, but one only way to heaven. It is well said, indeed, especially by those that plead for compelling men into this or the other way. For if there were several ways that led thither, there would not be so much
15   as a pretence left for compulsion. But now, if I be marching on with my utmost vigour in that way which, according to the sacred geography, leads straight to Jerusalem, why am I beaten and ill-used by others because, perhaps, I wear not buskins; because my hair is not of the right cut; because, perhaps, I have not been dipped in the right fashion; because I eat flesh upon the road, or some other
20   food which agrees with my stomach; because I avoid certain by-ways, which seem unto me to lead into briars or precipices; because, amongst the several paths that are in the same road, I choose that to walk in which seems to be the straightest and cleanest; because I avoid to keep company with some travellers that are less grave and others that are more sour than they ought to be; or, in
25   fine, because I follow a guide that either is, or is not, clothed in white, or crowned with a mitre? Certainly, if we consider right, we shall find that, for the most part, they are such frivolous things as these that (without any prejudice to religion or the salvation of souls, if not accompanied with superstition or hypocrisy) might either be observed or omitted. I say they are such-like things as
30   these which breed implacable enmities amongst Christian brethren, who are all agreed in the substantial and truly fundamental part of religion.

     But let us grant unto these zealots, who condemn all things that are not of their mode, that from these circumstances are different ends. What shall we conclude from thence? There is only one of these which is the true way to
35   eternal happiness: but in this great variety of ways that men follow, it is still doubted which is the right one. Now, neither the care of the commonwealth, nor the right enacting of laws, does discover this way that leads to heaven more certainly to the magistrate than every private man's search and study discovers it unto himself. I have a weak body, sunk under a languishing disease, for which (I
40   suppose) there is one only remedy, but that unknown. Does it therefore belong

unto the magistrate to prescribe me a remedy, because there is but one, and because it is unknown? Because there is but one way for me to escape death, will it therefore be safe for me to do whatsoever the magistrate ordains? Those things that every man ought sincerely to inquire into himself, and by meditation, study, search, and his own endeavours, attain the knowledge of, cannot be looked upon as the peculiar possession of any sort of men. Princes, indeed, are born superior unto other men in power, but in nature equal. Neither the right nor the art of ruling does necessarily carry along with it the certain knowledge of other things, and least of all of true religion. For if it were so, how could it come to pass that the lords of the earth should differ so vastly as they do in religious matters? But let us grant that it is probable the way to eternal life may be better known by a prince than by his subjects, or at least that in this incertitude of things the safest and most commodious way for private persons is to follow his dictates. You will say: "What then?" If he should bid you follow merchandise for your livelihood, would you decline that course for fear it should not succeed? I answer: I would turn merchant upon the prince's command, because, in case I should have ill-success in trade, he is abundantly able to make up my loss some other way. If it be true, as he pretends, that he desires I should thrive and grow rich, he can set me up again when unsuccessful voyages have broken me. But this is not the case in the things that regard the life to come; if there I take a wrong course, if in that respect I am once undone, it is not in the magistrate's power to repair my loss, to ease my suffering, nor to restore me in any measure, much less entirely, to a good estate. What security can be given for the Kingdom of Heaven?

Perhaps some will say that they do not suppose this infallible judgement, that all men are bound to follow in the affairs of religion, to be in the civil magistrate, but in the Church. What the Church has determined, that the civil magistrate orders to be observed; and he provides by his authority that nobody shall either act or believe in the business of religion otherwise than the Church teaches. So that the judgement of those things is in the Church; the magistrate himself yields obedience thereunto and requires the like obedience from others. I answer: Who sees not how frequently the name of the Church, which was venerable in time of the apostles, has been made use of to throw dust in the people's eyes in the following ages? But, however, in the present case it helps us not. The one only narrow way which leads to heaven is not better known to the magistrate than to private persons, and therefore I cannot safely take him for my guide, who may probably be as ignorant of the way as myself, and who certainly is less concerned for my salvation than I myself am. Amongst so many kings of the Jews, how many of them were there whom any Israelite, thus blindly following, had not fallen into idolatry and thereby into destruction? Yet,

nevertheless, you bid me be of good courage and tell me that all is now safe and secure, because the magistrate does not now enjoin the observance of his own decrees in matters of religion, but only the decrees of the Church. Of what Church, I beseech you? of that, certainly, which likes him best. As if he that
5 compels me by laws and penalties to enter into this or the other Church, did not interpose his own judgement in the matter. What difference is there whether he lead me himself, or deliver me over to be led by others? I depend both ways upon his will, and it is he that determines both ways of my eternal state. Would an Israelite that had worshipped Baal upon the command of his king have been
10 in any better condition because somebody had told him that the king ordered nothing in religion upon his own head, nor commanded anything to be done by his subjects in divine worship but what was approved by the counsel of priests, and declared to be of divine right by the doctors of their Church? If the religion of any Church become, therefore, true and saving, because the head of that sect,
15 the prelates and priests, and those of that tribe, do all of them, with all their might, extol and praise it, what religion can ever be accounted erroneous, false, and destructive? I am doubtful concerning the doctrine of the Socinians, I am suspicious of the way of worship practised by the Papists, or Lutherans; will it be ever a jot safer for me to join either unto the one or the other of those
20 Churches, upon the magistrate's command, because he commands nothing in religion but by the authority and counsel of the doctors of that Church?

But, to speak the truth, we must acknowledge that the Church (if a convention of clergymen, making canons, must be called by that name) is for the most part more apt to be influenced by the Court than the Court by the Church.
25 How the Church was under the vicissitude of orthodox and Arian emperors is very well known. Or if those things be too remote, our modern English history affords us fresh examples in the reigns of Henry VIII, Edward VI, Mary, and Elizabeth, how easily and smoothly the clergy changed their decrees, their articles of faith, their form of worship, everything according to the inclination of
30 those kings and queens. Yet were those kings and queens of such different minds in point of religion, and enjoined thereupon such different things, that no man in his wits (I had almost said none but an atheist) will presume to say that any sincere and upright worshipper of God could, with a safe conscience, obey their several decrees. To conclude, it is the same thing whether a king that
35 prescribes laws to another man's religion pretend to do it by his own judgement, or by the ecclesiastical authority and advice of others. The decisions of churchmen, whose differences and disputes are sufficiently known, cannot be any sounder or safer than his; nor can all their suffrages joined together add a new strength to the civil power. Though this also must be taken notice of — that

princes seldom have any regard to the suffrages of ecclesiastics that are not favourers of their own faith and way of worship.

But, after all, the principal consideration, and which absolutely determines this controversy, is this: Although the magistrate's opinion in religion be sound, and the way that he appoints be truly Evangelical, yet, if I be not thoroughly persuaded thereof in my own mind, there will be no safety for me in following it. No way whatsoever that I shall walk in against the dictates of my conscience will ever bring me to the mansions of the blessed. I may grow rich by an art that I take not delight in; I may be cured of some disease by remedies that I have not faith in; but I cannot be saved by a religion that I distrust and by a worship that I abhor. It is in vain for an unbeliever to take up the outward show of another man's profession. Faith only and inward sincerity are the things that procure acceptance with God. The most likely and most approved remedy can have no effect upon the patient, if his stomach reject it as soon as taken; and you will in vain cram a medicine down a sick man's throat, which his particular constitution will be sure to turn into poison. In a word, whatsoever may be doubtful in religion, yet this at least is certain, that no religion which I believe not to be true can be either true or profitable unto me. In vain, therefore, do princes compel their subjects to come into their Church communion, under pretence of saving their souls. If they believe, they will come of their own accord, if they believe not, their coming will nothing avail them. How great soever, in fine, may be the pretence of good-will and charity, and concern for the salvation of men's souls, men cannot be forced to be saved whether they will or no. And therefore, when all is done, they must be left to their own consciences.

Having thus at length freed men from all dominion over one another in matters of religion, let us now consider what they are to do. All men know and acknowledge that God ought to be publicly worshipped; why otherwise do they compel one another unto the public assemblies? Men, therefore, constituted in this liberty are to enter into some religious society, that they meet together, not only for mutual edification, but to own to the world that they worship God and offer unto His Divine Majesty such service as they themselves are not ashamed of and such as they think not unworthy of Him, nor unacceptable to Him; and, finally, that by the purity of doctrine, holiness of life, and decent form of worship, they may draw others unto the love of the true religion, and perform such other things in religion as cannot be done by each private man apart.

These religious societies I call Churches; and these, I say, the magistrate ought to tolerate, for the business of these assemblies of the people is nothing but what is lawful for every man in particular to take care of — I mean the salvation of their souls; nor in this case is there any difference between the National Church and other separated congregations.

288

But as in every Church there are two things especially to be considered — the outward form and rites of worship, and the doctrines and articles of things must be handled each distinctly that so the whole matter of toleration may the more clearly be understood.

5   Concerning outward worship, I say, in the first place, that the magistrate has no power to enforce by law, either in his own Church, or much less in another, the use of any rites or ceremonies whatsoever in the worship of God. And this, not only because these Churches are free societies, but because whatsoever is practised in the worship of God is only so far justifiable as it is believed by those
10 that practise it to be acceptable unto Him. Whatsoever is not done with that assurance of faith is neither well in itself, nor can it be acceptable to God. To impose such things, therefore, upon any people, contrary to their own judgment, is in effect to command them to offend God, which, considering that the end of all religion is to please Him, and that liberty is essentially necessary to that end,
15 appears to be absurd beyond expression.

But perhaps it may be concluded from hence that I deny unto the magistrate all manner of power about indifferent things, which, if it be not granted, the whole subject-matter of law-making is taken away. No, I readily grant that indifferent things, and perhaps none but such, are subjected to the legislative
20 power. But it does not therefore follow that the magistrate may ordain whatsoever he pleases concerning anything that is indifferent. The public good is the rule and measure of all law-making. If a thing be not useful to the commonwealth, though it be never so indifferent, it may not presently be established by law.

25 And further, things never so indifferent in their own nature, when they are brought into the Church and worship of God, are removed out of the reach of the magistrate's jurisdiction, because in that use they have no connection at all with civil affairs. The only business of the Church is the salvation of souls, and it no way concerns the commonwealth, or any member of it, that this or the other
30 ceremony be there made use of. Neither the use nor the omission of any ceremonies in those religious assemblies does either advantage or prejudice the life, liberty, or estate of any man. For example, let it be granted that the washing of an infant with water is in itself an indifferent thing, let it be granted also that the magistrate understand such washing to be profitable to the curing or
35 preventing of any disease the children are subject unto, and esteem the matter weighty enough to be taken care of by a law. In that case he may order it to be done. But will any one therefore say that a magistrate has the same right to ordain by law that all children shall be baptised by priests in the sacred font in order to the purification of their souls? The extreme difference of these two
40 cases is visible to every one at first sight. Or let us apply the last case to the

child of a Jew, and the thing speaks itself. For what hinders but a Christian magistrate may have subjects that are Jews? Now, if we acknowledge that such an injury may not be done unto a Jew as to compel him, against his own opinion, to practise in his religion a thing that is in its nature indifferent, how can we
5   maintain that anything of this kind may be done to a Christian?

      Again, things in their own nature indifferent cannot, by any human authority, be made any part of the worship of God — for this very reason: because they are indifferent. For, since indifferent things are not capable, by any virtue of their own, to propitiate the Deity, no human power or authority can
10   confer on them so much dignity and excellency as to enable them to do it. In the common affairs of life that use of indifferent things which God has not forbidden is free and lawful, and therefore in those things human authority has place. But it is not so in matters of religion. Things indifferent are not otherwise lawful in the worship of God than as they are instituted by God Himself and as
15   He, by some positive command, has ordained them to be made a part of that worship which He will vouchsafe to accept at the hands of poor sinful men. Nor, when an incensed Deity shall ask us, "Who has required these, or such-like things at your hands?" will it be enough to answer Him that the magistrate commanded them. If civil jurisdiction extend thus far, what might not lawfully
20   be introduced into religion? What hodgepodge of ceremonies, what superstitious inventions, built upon the magistrate's authority, might not (against conscience) be imposed upon the worshippers of God? For the greatest part of these ceremonies and superstitions consists in the religious use of such things as are in their own nature indifferent; nor are they sinful upon any other account than
25   because God is not the author of them. The sprinkling of water and the use of bread and wine are both in their own nature and in the ordinary occasions of life altogether indifferent. Will any man, therefore, say that these things could have been introduced into religion and made a part of divine worship if not by divine institution? If any human authority or civil power could have done this, why
30   might it not also enjoin the eating of fish and drinking of ale in the holy banquet as a part of divine worship? Why not the sprinkling of the blood of beasts in churches, and expiations by water or fire, and abundance more of this kind? But these things, how indifferent soever they be in common uses, when they come to be annexed unto divine worship, without divine authority, they are as
35   abominable to God as the sacrifice of a dog. And why is a dog so abominable? What difference is there between a dog and a goat, in respect of the divine nature, equally and infinitely distant from all affinity with matter, unless it be that God required the use of one in His worship and not of the other? We see, therefore, that indifferent things, how much soever they be under the power of
40   the civil magistrate, yet cannot, upon that pretence, be introduced into religion

and imposed upon religious assemblies, because, in the worship of God, they wholly cease to be indifferent. He that worships God does it with design to please Him and procure His favour. But that cannot be done by him who, upon the command of another, offers unto God that which he knows will be
5   displeasing to Him, because not commanded by Himself. This is not to please God, or appease his wrath, but willingly and knowingly to provoke Him by a manifest contempt, which is a thing absolutely repugnant to the nature and end of worship.

     But it will be here asked: "If nothing belonging to divine worship be left to
10   human discretion, how is it then that Churches themselves have the power of ordering anything about the time and place of worship and the like?" To this I answer that in religious worship we must distinguish between what is part of the worship itself and what is but a circumstance. That is a part of the worship which is believed to be appointed by God and to be well-pleasing to Him, and
15   therefore that is necessary. Circumstances are such things which, though in general they cannot be separated from worship, yet the particular instances or modifications of them are not determined, and therefore they are indifferent. Of this sort are the time and place of worship, habit and posture of him that worships. These are circumstances, and perfectly indifferent, where God has not
20   given any express command about them. For example: amongst the Jews the time and place of their worship and the habits of those that officiated in it were not mere circumstances, but a part of the worship itself, in which, if anything were defective, or different from the institution, they could not hope that it would be accepted by God. But these, to Christians under the liberty of the
25   Gospel, are mere circumstances of worship, which the prudence of every Church may bring into such use as shall be judged most subservient to the end of order, decency, and edification. But, even under the Gospel, those who believe the first or the seventh day to be set apart by God, and consecrated still to His worship, to them that portion of time is not a simple circumstance, but a real part of
30   Divine worship, which can neither be changed nor neglected.

     In the next place: As the magistrate has no power to impose by his laws the use of any rites and ceremonies in any Church, so neither has he any power to forbid the use of such rites and ceremonies as are already received, approved, and practised by any Church; because, if he did so, he would destroy the Church
35   itself: the end of whose institution is only to worship God with freedom after its own manner.

     You will say, by this rule, if some congregations should have a mind to sacrifice infants, or (as the primitive Christians were falsely accused) lustfully pollute themselves in promiscuous uncleanness, or practise any other such
40   heinous enormities, is the magistrate obliged to tolerate them, because they are

committed in a religious assembly? I answer: No. These things are not lawful in the ordinary course of life, nor in any private house; and therefore neither are they so in the worship of God, or in any religious meeting. But, indeed, if any people congregated upon account of religion should be desirous to sacrifice a

5 calf, I deny that that ought to be prohibited by a law. Meliboeus, whose calf it is, may lawfully kill his calf at home, and burn any part of it that he thinks fit. For no injury is thereby done to any one, no prejudice to another man's goods. And for the same reason he may kill his calf also in a religious meeting. Whether the doing so be well-pleasing to God or no, it is their part to consider that do it. The

10 part of the magistrate is only to take care that the commonwealth receive no prejudice, and that there be no injury done to any man, either in life or estate. And thus what may be spent on a feast may be spent on a sacrifice. But if peradventure such were the state of things that the interest of the commonwealth required all slaughter of beasts should be forborne for some while, in order to

15 the increasing of the stock of cattle that had been destroyed by some extraordinary murrain, who sees not that the magistrate, in such a case, may forbid all his subjects to kill any calves for any use whatsoever? Only it is to be observed that, in this case, the law is not made about a religious, but a political matter; nor is the sacrifice, but the slaughter of calves, thereby prohibited.

20   By this we see what difference there is between the Church and the Commonwealth. Whatsoever is lawful in the Commonwealth cannot be prohibited by the magistrate in the Church. Whatsoever is permitted unto any of his subjects for their ordinary use, neither can nor ought to be forbidden by him to any sect of people for their religious uses. If any man may lawfully take bread

25 or wine, either sitting or kneeling in his own house, the law ought not to abridge him of the same liberty in his religious worship; though in the Church the use of bread and wine be very different and be there applied to the mysteries of faith and rites of Divine worship. But those things that are prejudicial to the commonweal of a people in their ordinary use and are, therefore, forbidden by

30 laws, those things ought not to be permitted to Churches in their sacred rites. Only the magistrate ought always to be very careful that he do not misuse his authority to the oppression of any Church, under pretence of public good.

It may be said: "What if a Church be idolatrous, is that also to be tolerated by the magistrate?" I answer: What power can be given to the magistrate for the

35 suppression of an idolatrous Church, which may not in time and place be made use of to the ruin of an orthodox one? For it must be remembered that the civil power is the same everywhere, and the religion of every prince is orthodox to himself. If, therefore, such a power be granted unto the civil magistrate in spirituals as that at Geneva, for example, he may extirpate, by violence and

40 blood, the religion which is there reputed idolatrous, by the same rule another

magistrate, in some neighbouring country, may oppress the reformed religion and, in India, the Christian. The civil power can either change everything in religion, according to the prince's pleasure, or it can change nothing. If it be once permitted to introduce anything into religion by the means of laws and
5   penalties, there can be no bounds put to it; but it will in the same manner be lawful to alter everything, according to that rule of truth which the magistrate has framed unto himself. No man whatsoever ought, therefore, to be deprived of his terrestrial enjoyments upon account of his religion. Not even Americans, subjected unto a Christian prince, are to be punished either in body or goods for
10 not embracing our faith and worship. If they are persuaded that they please God in observing the rites of their own country and that they shall obtain happiness by that means, they are to be left unto God and themselves. Let us trace this matter to the bottom. Thus it is: An inconsiderable and weak number of Christians, destitute of everything, arrive in a Pagan country; these foreigners
15 beseech the inhabitants, by the bowels of humanity, that they would succour them with the necessaries of life; those necessaries are given them, habitations are granted, and they all join together, and grow up into one body of people. The Christian religion by this means takes root in that country and spreads itself, but does not suddenly grow the strongest. While things are in this condition peace,
20 friendship, faith, and equal justice are preserved amongst them. At length the magistrate becomes a Christian, and by that means their party becomes the most powerful. Then immediately all compacts are to be broken, all civil rights to be violated, that idolatry may be extirpated; and unless these innocent Pagans, strict observers of the rules of equity and the law of Nature and no ways offending
25 against the laws of the society, I say, unless they will forsake their ancient religion and embrace a new and strange one, they are to be turned out of the lands and possessions of their forefathers and perhaps deprived of life itself. Then, at last, it appears what zeal for the Church, joined with the desire of dominion, is capable to produce, and how easily the pretence of religion, and of
30 the care of souls, serves for a cloak to covetousness, rapine, and ambition.

Now whosoever maintains that idolatry is to be rooted out of any place by laws, punishments, fire, and sword, may apply this story to himself. For the reason of the thing is equal, both in America and Europe. And neither Pagans there, nor any dissenting Christians here, can, with any right, be deprived of
35 their worldly goods by the predominating faction of a court-church; nor are any civil rights to be either changed or violated upon account of religion in one place more than another.

But idolatry, say some, is a sin and therefore not to be tolerated. If they said it were therefore to be avoided, the inference were good. But it does not follow
40 that because it is a sin it ought therefore to be punished by the magistrate. For it

does not belong unto the magistrate to make use of his sword in punishing everything, indifferently, that he takes to be a sin against God. Covetousness, uncharitableness, idleness, and many other things are sins by the consent of men, which yet no man ever said were to be punished by the magistrate. The reason is because they are not prejudicial to other men's rights, nor do they break the public peace of societies. Nay, even the sins of lying and perjury are nowhere punishable by laws; unless, in certain cases, in which the real turpitude of the thing and the offence against God are not considered, but only the injury done unto men's neighbours and to the commonwealth. And what if in another country, to a Mahometan or a Pagan prince, the Christian religion seem false and offensive to God; may not the Christians for the same reason, and after the same manner, be extirpated there?

But it may be urged farther that, by the law of Moses, idolaters were to be rooted out. True, indeed, by the law of Moses; but that is not obligatory to us Christians. Nobody pretends that everything generally enjoined by the law of Moses ought to be practised by Christians; but there is nothing more frivolous than that common distinction of moral, judicial, and ceremonial law, which men ordinarily make use of. For no positive law whatsoever can oblige any people but those to whom it is given. "Hear, O Israel," sufficiently restrains the obligations of the law of Moses only to that people. And this consideration alone is answer enough unto those that urge the authority of the law of Moses for the inflicting of capital punishment upon idolaters. But, however, I will examine this argument a little more particularly.

The case of idolaters, in respect of the Jewish commonwealth, falls under a double consideration. The first is of those who, being initiated in the Mosaical rites, and made citizens of that commonwealth, did afterwards apostatise from the worship of the God of Israel. These were proceeded against as traitors and rebels, guilty of no less than high treason. For the commonwealth of the Jews, different in that from all others, was an absolute theocracy; nor was there, or could there be, any difference between that commonwealth and the Church. The laws established there concerning the worship of One Invisible Deity were the civil laws of that people and a part of their political government, in which God Himself was the legislator. Now, if any one can shew me where there is a commonwealth at this time, constituted upon that foundation, I will acknowledge that the ecclesiastical laws do there unavoidably become a part of the civil, and that the subjects of that government both may and ought to be kept in strict conformity with that Church by the civil power. But there is absolutely no such thing under the Gospel as a Christian commonwealth. There are, indeed, many cities and kingdoms that have embraced the faith of Christ, but they have retained their ancient form of government, with which the law of Christ hath not

at all meddled. He, indeed, hath taught men how, by faith and good works, they may obtain eternal life; but He instituted no commonwealth. He prescribed unto His followers no new and peculiar form of government, nor put He the sword into any magistrate's hand, with commission to make use of it in forcing men to
5   forsake their former religion and receive His.

Secondly, foreigners and such as were strangers to the commonwealth of Israel were not compelled by force to observe the rites of the Mosaical law; but, on the contrary, in the very same place where it is ordered that an Israelite that was an idolater should be put to death,[7] there it is provided that strangers should
10   not be vexed nor oppressed. I confess that the seven nations that possessed the land which was promised to the Israelites were utterly to be cut off; but this was not singly because they were idolaters. For if that had been the reason, why were the Moabites and other nations to be spared? No: the reason is this. God being in a peculiar manner the King of the Jews, He could not suffer the adoration of any
15   other deity (which was properly an act of high treason against Himself) in the land of Canaan, which was His kingdom. For such a manifest revolt could no ways consist with His dominion, which was perfectly political in that country. All idolatry was, therefore, to be rooted out of the bounds of His kingdom because it was an acknowledgment of another god, that is say, another king,
20   against the laws of Empire. The inhabitants were also to be driven out, that the entire possession of the land might be given to the Israelites. And for the like reason the Emims and the Horims were driven out of their countries by the children of Esau and Lot; and their lands, upon the same grounds, given by God to the invaders.[8] But, though all idolatry was thus rooted out of the land of
25   Canaan, yet every idolater was not brought to execution. The whole family of Rahab, the whole nation of the Gibeonites, articled with Joshua, and were allowed by treaty; and there were many captives amongst the Jews who were idolaters. David and Solomon subdued many countries without the confines of the Land of Promise and carried their conquests as far as Euphrates. Amongst so
30   many captives taken, so many nations reduced under their obedience, we find not one man forced into the Jewish religion and the worship of the true God and punished for idolatry, though all of them were certainly guilty of it. If any one, indeed, becoming a proselyte, desired to be made a denizen of their commonwealth, he was obliged to submit to their laws; that is, to embrace their
35   religion. But this he did willingly, on his own accord, not by constraint. He did not unwillingly submit, to show his obedience, but he sought and solicited for it as a privilege. And, as soon as he was admitted, he became subject to the laws of the commonwealth, by which all idolatry was forbidden within the borders of the land of Canaan. But that law (as I have said) did not reach to any of those

regions, however subjected unto the Jews, that were situated without those bounds.

Thus far concerning outward worship. Let us now consider articles of faith. The articles of religion are some of them practical and some speculative.

5 Now, though both sorts consist in the knowledge of truth, yet these terminate simply in the understanding, those influence the will and manners. Speculative opinions, therefore, and articles of faith (as they are called) which are required only to be believed, cannot be imposed on any Church by the law of the land. For it is absurd that things should be enjoined by laws which are not in men's

10 power to perform. And to believe this or that to be true does not depend upon our will. But of this enough has been said already. "But." will some say; "let men at least profess that they believe." A sweet religion, indeed, that obliges men to dissemble and tell lies, both to God and man, for the salvation of their souls! If the magistrate thinks to save men thus, he seems to understand little of

15 the way of salvation. And if he does it not in order to save them, why is he so solicitous about the articles of faith as to enact them by a law?

Further, the magistrate ought not to forbid the preaching or professing of any speculative opinions in any Church because they have no manner of relation to the civil rights of the subjects. If a Roman Catholic believe that to be really

20 the body of Christ which another man calls bread, he does no injury thereby to his neighbour. If a Jew do not believe the New Testament to be the Word of God, he does not thereby alter anything in men's civil rights. If a heathen doubt of both Testaments, he is not therefore to be punished as a pernicious citizen. The power of the magistrate and the estates of the people may be equally secure

25 whether any man believe these things or no. I readily grant that these opinions are false and absurd. But the business of laws is not to provide for the truth of opinions, but for the safety and security of the commonwealth and of every particular man's goods and person. And so it ought to be. For the truth certainly would do well enough if she were once left to shift for herself. She seldom has

30 received and, I fear, never will receive much assistance from the power of great men, to whom she is but rarely known and more rarely welcome. She is not taught by laws, nor has she any need of force to procure her entrance into the minds of men. Errors, indeed, prevail by the assistance of foreign and borrowed succours. But if Truth makes not her way into the understanding by her own

35 light, she will be but the weaker for any borrowed force violence can add to her. Thus much for speculative opinions. Let us now proceed to practical ones.

A good life, in which consist not the least part of religion and true piety, concerns also the civil government; and in it lies the safety both of men's souls and of the commonwealth. Moral actions belong, therefore, to the jurisdiction

40 both of the outward and inward court; both of the civil and domestic governor; I

mean both of the magistrate and conscience. Here, therefore, is great danger, lest one of these jurisdictions intrench upon the other, and discord arise between the keeper of the public peace and the overseers of souls. But if what has been already said concerning the limits of both these governments be rightly considered, it will easily remove all difficulty in this matter.

Every man has an immortal soul, capable of eternal happiness or misery; whose happiness depending upon his believing and doing those things in this life which are necessary to the obtaining of God's favour, and are prescribed by God to that end. It follows from thence, first, that the observance of these things is the highest obligation that lies upon mankind and that our utmost care, application, and diligence ought to be exercised in the search and performance of them; because there is nothing in this world that is of any consideration in comparison with eternity. Secondly, that seeing one man does not violate the right of another by his erroneous opinions and undue manner of worship, nor is his perdition any prejudice to another man's affairs, therefore, the care of each man's salvation belongs only to himself. But I would not have this understood as if I meant hereby to condemn all charitable admonitions and affectionate endeavours to reduce men from errors, which are indeed the greatest duty of a Christian. Any one may employ as many exhortations and arguments as he pleases, towards the promoting of another man's salvation. But all force and compulsion are to be forborne. Nothing is to be done imperiously. Nobody is obliged in that matter to yield obedience unto the admonitions or injunctions of another, further than he himself is persuaded. Every man in that has the supreme and absolute authority of judging for himself. And the reason is because nobody else is concerned in it, nor can receive any prejudice from his conduct therein.

But besides their souls, which are immortal, men have also their temporal lives here upon earth; the state whereof being frail and fleeting, and the duration uncertain, they have need of several outward conveniences to the support thereof, which are to be procured or preserved by pains and industry. For those things that are necessary to the comfortable support of our lives are not the spontaneous products of nature, nor do offer themselves fit and prepared for our use. This part, therefore, draws on another care and necessarily gives another employment. But the pravity of mankind being such that they had rather injuriously prey upon the fruits of other men's labours than take pains to provide for themselves, the necessity of preserving men in the possession of what honest industry has already acquired and also of preserving their liberty and strength, whereby they may acquire what they farther want, obliges men to enter into society with one another, that by mutual assistance and joint force they may secure unto each other their properties, in the things that contribute to the comfort and happiness of this life, leaving in the meanwhile to every man the care of his own eternal happiness, the attainment whereof can neither be facilitated by another man's industry, nor can the loss of it turn to another man's prejudice, nor the hope of it be forced from him by any external violence. But, forasmuch as men thus entering into societies, grounded upon their mutual

5 compacts of assistance for the defence of their temporal goods, may, nevertheless, be deprived of them, either by the rapine and fraud of their fellow citizens, or by the hostile violence of foreigners, the remedy of this evil consists in arms, riches, and multitude of citizens; the remedy of the other in laws; and the care of all things relating both to one and the other is committed by the

10 society to the civil magistrate. This is the original, this is the use, and these are the bounds of the legislative (which is the supreme) power in every commonwealth. I mean that provision may be made for the security of each man's private possessions; for the peace, riches, and public commodities of the whole people; and, as much as possible, for the increase of their inward strength

15 against foreign invasions.

These things being thus explained, it is easy to understand to what end the legislative power ought to be directed and by what measures regulated; and that is the temporal good and outward prosperity of the society; which is the sole reason of men's entering into society, and the only thing they seek and aim at in

20 it. And it is also evident what liberty remains to men in reference to their eternal salvation, and that is that every one should do what he in his conscience is persuaded to be acceptable to the Almighty, on whose good pleasure and acceptance depends their eternal happiness. For obedience is due, in the first place, to God and, afterwards to the laws.

25 But some may ask: "What if the magistrate should enjoin anything by his authority that appears unlawful to the conscience of a private person?" I answer that, if government be faithfully administered and the counsels of the magistrates be indeed directed to the public good, this will seldom happen. But if, perhaps, it do so fall out, I say, that such a private person is to abstain from

30 the action that he judges unlawful, and he is to undergo the punishment which it is not unlawful for him to bear. For the private judgement of any person concerning a law enacted in political matters, for the public good, does not take away the obligation of that law, nor deserve a dispensation. But if the law, indeed, be concerning things that lie not within the verge of the magistrate's

35 authority (as, for example, that the people, or any party amongst them, should be compelled to embrace a strange religion, and join in the worship and ceremonies of another Church), men are not in these cases obliged by that law, against their consciences. For the political society is instituted for no other end, but only to secure every man's possession of the things of this life. The care of each man's

40 soul and of the things of heaven, which neither does belong to the

commonwealth nor can be subjected to it, is left entirely to every man's self. Thus the safeguard of men's lives and of the things that belong unto this life is the business of the commonwealth; and the preserving of those things unto their owners is the duty of the magistrate. And therefore the magistrate cannot take
5   away these worldly things from this man or party and give them to that; nor change propriety amongst fellow subjects (no not even by a law), for a cause that has no relation to the end of civil government, I mean for their religion, which whether it be true or false does no prejudice to the worldly concerns of their fellow subjects, which are the things that only belong unto the care of the
10   commonwealth.

But what if the magistrate believe such a law as this to be for the public good? I answer: As the private judgement of any particular person, if erroneous, does not exempt him from the obligation of law, so the private judgement (as I may call it) of the magistrate does not give him any new right of imposing laws
15   upon his subjects, which neither was in the constitution of the government granted him, nor ever was in the power of the people to grant, much less if he make it his business to enrich and advance his followers and fellow-sectaries with the spoils of others. But what if the magistrate believe that he has a right to make such laws and that they are for the public good, and his subjects believe
20   the contrary? Who shall be judge between them? I answer: God alone. For there is no judge upon earth between the supreme magistrate and the people. God, I say, is the only judge in this case, who will retribute unto every one at the last day according to his deserts; that is, according to his sincerity and uprightness in endeavouring to promote piety, and the public weal, and peace of mankind. But
25   What shall be done in the meanwhile? I answer: The principal and chief care of every one ought to be of his own soul first, and, in the next place, of the public peace; though yet there are very few will think it is peace there, where they see all laid waste.

There are two sorts of contests amongst men, the one managed by law, the
30   other by force; and these are of that nature that where the one ends, the other always begins. But it is not my business to inquire into the power of the magistrate in the different constitutions of nations. I only know what usually happens where controversies arise without a judge to determine them. You will say, then, the magistrate being the stronger will have his will and carry his point.
35   Without doubt; but the question is not here concerning the doubtfulness of the event, but the rule of right.

But to come to particulars. I say, first, no opinions contrary to human society, or to those moral rules which are necessary to the preservation of civil society, are to be tolerated by the magistrate. But of these, indeed, examples in
40   any Church are rare. For no sect can easily arrive to such a degree of madness as

that it should think fit to teach, for doctrines of religion, such things as manifestly undermine the foundations of society and are, therefore, condemned by the judgement of all mankind; because their own interest, peace, reputation, everything would be thereby endangered.

5   Another more secret evil, but more dangerous to the commonwealth, is when men arrogate to themselves, and to those of their own sect, some peculiar prerogative covered over with a specious show of deceitful words, but in effect opposite to the civil right of the community. For example: we cannot find any sect that teaches, expressly and openly, that men are not obliged to keep their
10   promise; that princes may be dethroned by those that differ from them in religion; or that the dominion of all things belongs only to themselves. For these things, proposed thus nakedly and plainly, would soon draw on them the eye and hand of the magistrate and awaken all the care of the commonwealth to a watchfulness against the spreading of so dangerous an evil. But, nevertheless,
15   we find those that say the same things in other words. What else do they mean who teach that faith is not to be kept with heretics? Their meaning, forsooth, is that the privilege of breaking faith belongs unto themselves; for they declare all that are not of their communion to be heretics, or at least may declare them so whensoever they think fit. What can be the meaning of their asserting that kings
20   excommunicated forfeit their crowns and kingdoms? It is evident that they thereby arrogate unto themselves the power of deposing kings, because they challenge the power of excommunication, as the peculiar right of their hierarchy. That dominion is founded in grace is also an assertion by which those that maintain it do plainly lay claim to the possession of all things. For they are
25   not so wanting to themselves as not to believe, or at least as not to profess themselves to be the truly pious and faithful. These, therefore, and the like, who attribute unto the faithful, religious, and orthodox, that is, in plain terms, unto themselves, any peculiar privilege or power above other mortals, in civil concernments; or who upon pretence of religion do challenge any manner of
30   authority over such as are not associated with them in their ecclesiastical communion, I say these have no right to be tolerated by the magistrate; as neither those that will not own and teach the duty of tolerating all men in matters of mere religion. For what do all these and the like doctrines signify, but that they may and are ready upon any occasion to seize the Government and possess
35   themselves of the estates and fortunes of their fellow subjects; and that they only ask leave to be tolerated by the magistrate so long until they find themselves strong enough to effect it?

Again: That Church can have no right to be tolerated by the magistrate which is constituted upon such a bottom that all those who enter into it do
40   thereby ipso facto deliver themselves up to the protection and service of another

prince. For by this means the magistrate would give way to the settling of a foreign jurisdiction in his own country and suffer his own people to be listed, as it were, for soldiers against his own Government. Nor does the frivolous and fallacious distinction between the Court and the Church afford any remedy to
5   this inconvenience; especially when both the one and the other are equally subject to the absolute authority of the same person, who has not only power to persuade the members of his Church to whatsoever he lists, either as purely religious, or in order thereunto, but can also enjoin it them on pain of eternal fire. It is ridiculous for any one to profess himself to be a Mahometan only in his
10   religion, but in everything else a faithful subject to a Christian magistrate, whilst at the same time he acknowledges himself bound to yield blind obedience to the Mufti of Constantinople, who himself is entirely obedient to the Ottoman Emperor and frames the feigned oracles of that religion according to his pleasure. But this Mahometan living amongst Christians would yet more
15   apparently renounce their government if he acknowledged the same person to be head of his Church who is the supreme magistrate in the state.

Lastly, those are not at all to be tolerated who deny the being of a God. Promises, covenants, and oaths, which are the bonds of human society, can have no hold upon an atheist. The taking away of God, though but even in thought,
20   dissolves all; besides also, those that by their atheism undermine and destroy all religion, can have no pretence of religion whereupon to challenge the privilege of a toleration. As for other practical opinions, though not absolutely free from all error, if they do not tend to establish domination over others, or civil impunity to the Church in which they are taught, there can be no reason why
25   they should not be tolerated.

It remains that I say something concerning those assemblies which, being vulgarly called and perhaps having sometimes been conventicles and nurseries of factions and seditions, are thought to afford against this doctrine of toleration. But this has not happened by anything peculiar unto the genius of such
30   assemblies, but by the unhappy circumstances of an oppressed or ill-settled liberty. These accusations would soon cease if the law of toleration were once so settled that all Churches were obliged to lay down toleration as the foundation of their own liberty, and teach that liberty of conscience is every man's natural right, equally belonging to dissenters as to themselves; and that nobody ought to
35   be compelled in matters of religion either by law or force. The establishment of this one thing would take away all ground of complaints and tumults upon account of conscience; and these causes of discontents and animosities being once removed, there would remain nothing in these assemblies that were not more peaceable and less apt to produce disturbance of state than in any other

meetings whatsoever. But let us examine particularly the heads of these accusations.

You will say that assemblies and meetings endanger the public peace and threaten the commonwealth. I answer: If this be so, why are there daily such numerous meetings in markets and Courts of Judicature? Why are crowds upon the Exchange and a concourse of people in cities suffered? You will reply: "Those are civil assemblies, but these we object against are ecclesiastical." I answer: It is a likely thing, indeed, that such assemblies as are altogether remote from civil affairs should be most apt to embroil them. Oh, but civil assemblies are composed of men that differ from one another in matters of religion, but these ecclesiastical meetings are of persons that are all of one opinion. As if an agreement in matters of religion were in effect a conspiracy against the commonwealth; or as if men would not be so much the more warmly unanimous in religion the less liberty they had of assembling. But it will be urged still that civil assemblies are open and free for any one to enter into, whereas religious conventicles are more private and thereby give opportunity to clandestine machinations. I answer that this is not strictly true, for many civil assemblies are not open to everyone. And if some religious meetings be private, who are they (I beseech you) that are to be blamed for it, those that desire, or those that forbid their being public! Again, you will say that religious communion does exceedingly unite men's minds and affections to one another and is therefore the more dangerous. But if this be so, why is not the magistrate afraid of his own Church; and why does he not forbid their assemblies as things dangerous to his Government? You will say because he himself is a part and even the head of them. As if he were not also a part of the commonwealth, and the head of the whole people!

Let us therefore deal plainly. The magistrate is afraid of other Churches, but not of his own, because he is kind and favourable to the one, but severe and cruel to the other. These he treats like children, and indulges them even to wantonness. Those he uses as slaves and, how blamelessly soever they demean themselves, recompenses them no otherwise than by galleys, prisons, confiscations, and death. These he cherishes and defends; those he continually scourges and oppresses. Let him turn the tables. Or let those dissenters enjoy but the same privileges in civils as his other subjects, and he will quickly find that these religious meetings will be no longer dangerous. For if men enter into seditious conspiracies, it is not religion inspires them to it in their meetings, but their sufferings and oppressions that make them willing to ease themselves. Just and moderate governments are everywhere quiet, everywhere safe; but oppression raises ferments and makes men struggle to cast off an uneasy and tyrannical yoke. I know that seditions are very frequently raised upon pretence

of religion, but it is as true that for religion subjects are frequently ill treated and live miserably. Believe me, the stirs that are made proceed not from any peculiar temper of this or that Church or religious society, but from the common disposition of all mankind, who when they groan under any heavy burthen
5 endeavour naturally to shake off the yoke that galls their necks. Suppose this business of religion were let alone, and that there were some other distinction made between men and men upon account of their different complexions, shapes, and features, so that those who have black hair (for example) or grey eyes should not enjoy the same privileges as other citizens; that they should not
10 be permitted either to buy or sell, or live by their callings; that parents should not have the government and education of their own children; that all should either be excluded from the benefit of the laws, or meet with partial judges; can it be doubted but these persons, thus distinguished from others by the colour of their hair and eyes, and united together by one common persecution, would be
15 as dangerous to the magistrate as any others that had associated themselves merely upon the account of religion? Some enter into company for trade and profit, others for want of business have their clubs for claret. Neighbourhood joins some and religion others. But there is only one thing which gathers people into seditious commotions, and that is oppression.
20 You will say "What, will you have people to meet at divine service against the magistrate's will?" I answer: Why, I pray, against his will? Is it not both lawful and necessary that they should meet? Against his will, do you say? That is what I complain of; that is the very root of all the mischief. Why are assemblies less sufferable in a church than in a theatre or market? Those that
25 meet there are not either more vicious or more turbulent than those that meet elsewhere. The business in that is that they are ill used, and therefore they are not to be suffered. Take away the partiality that is used towards them in matters of common right; change the laws, take away the penalties unto which they are subjected, and all things will immediately become safe and peaceable; nay,
30 those that are averse to the religion of the magistrate will think themselves so much the more bound to maintain the peace of the commonwealth as their condition is better in that place than elsewhere; and all the several separate congregations, like so many guardians of the public peace, will watch one another, that nothing may be innovated or changed in the form of the
35 government, because they can hope for nothing better than what they already enjoy — that is, an equal condition with their fellow-subjects under a just and moderate government. Now if that Church which agrees in religion with the prince be esteemed the chief support of any civil government, and that for no other reason (as has already been shown) than because the prince is kind and the
40 laws are favourable to it, how much greater will be the security of government

where all good subjects, of whatsoever Church they be, without any distinction upon account of religion, enjoying the same favour of the prince and the same benefit of the laws, shall become the common support and guard of it, and where none will have any occasion to fear the severity of the laws but those that do
5   injuries to their neighbours and offend against the civil peace?

That we may draw towards a conclusion. The sum of all we drive at is that every man may enjoy the same rights that are granted to others. Is it permitted to worship God in the Roman manner? Let it be permitted to do it in the Geneva form also. Is it permitted to speak Latin in the market-place? Let those that have
10   a mind to it be permitted to do it also in the Church. Is it lawful for any man in his own house to kneel, stand, sit, or use any other posture; and to clothe himself in white or black, in short or in long garments? Let it not be made unlawful to eat bread, drink wine, or wash with water in the church. In a word, whatsoever things are left free by law in the common occasions of life, let them remain free
15   unto every Church in divine worship. Let no man's life, or body, or house, or estate, suffer any manner of prejudice upon these accounts. Can you allow of the Presbyterian discipline? Why should not the Episcopal also have what they like? Ecclesiastical authority, whether it be administered by the hands of a single person or many, is everywhere the same; and neither has any jurisdiction in
20   things civil, nor any manner of power of compulsion, nor anything at all to do with riches and revenues.

Ecclesiastical assemblies and sermons are justified by daily experience and public allowance. These are allowed to people of some one persuasion; why not to all? If anything pass in a religious meeting seditiously and contrary to the
25   public peace, it is to be punished in the same manner and no otherwise than as if it had happened in a fair or market. These meetings ought not to be sanctuaries for factious and flagitious fellows. Nor ought it to be less lawful for men to meet in churches than in halls; nor are one part of the subjects to be esteemed more blamable for their meeting together than others. Every one is to be accountable
30   for his own actions, and no man is to be laid under a suspicion or odium for the fault of another. Those that are seditious, murderers, thieves, robbers, adulterers, slanderers, etc., of whatsoever Church, whether national or not, ought to be punished and suppressed. But those whose doctrine is peaceable and whose manners are pure and blameless ought to be upon equal terms with their fellow-
35   subjects. Thus if solemn assemblies, observations of festivals, public worship be permitted to any one sort of professors, all these things ought to be permitted to the Presbyterians, Independents, Anabaptists, Arminians, Quakers, and others, with the same liberty. Nay, if we may openly speak the truth, and as becomes one man to another, neither Pagan nor Mahometan, nor Jew, ought to be
40   excluded from the civil rights of the commonwealth because of his religion. The

Gospel commands no such thing. The Church which "judgeth not those that are without"[9] wants it not. And the commonwealth, which embraces indifferently all men that are honest, peaceable, and industrious, requires it not. Shall we suffer a Pagan to deal and trade with us, and shall we not suffer him to pray unto
5 and worship God? If we allow the Jews to have private houses and dwellings amongst us, why should we not allow them to have synagogues? Is their doctrine more false, their worship more abominable, or is the civil peace more endangered by their meeting in public than in their private houses? But if these things may be granted to Jews and Pagans, surely the condition of any Christians
10 ought not to be worse than theirs in a Christian commonwealth.

You will say, perhaps: "Yes, it ought to be; because they are more inclinable to factions, tumults, and civil wars." I answer: Is this the fault of the Christian religion? If it be so, truly the Christian religion is the worst of all religions and ought neither to be embraced by any particular person, nor
15 tolerated by any commonwealth. For if this be the genius, this the nature of the Christian religion, to be turbulent and destructive to the civil peace, that Church itself which the magistrate indulges will not always be innocent. But far be it from us to say any such thing of that religion which carries the greatest opposition to covetousness, ambition, discord, contention, and all manner of
20 inordinate desires, and is the most modest and peaceable religion that ever was. We must, therefore, seek another cause of those evils that are charged upon religion. And, if we consider right, we shall find it to consist wholly in the subject that I am treating of. It is not the diversity of opinions (which cannot be avoided), but the refusal of toleration to those that are of different opinions
25 (which might have been granted), that has produced all the bustles and wars that have been in the Christian world upon account of religion. The heads and leaders of the Church, moved by avarice and insatiable desire of dominion, making use of the immoderate ambition of magistrates and the credulous superstition of the giddy multitude, have incensed and animated them against
30 those that dissent from themselves, by preaching unto them, contrary to the laws of the Gospel and to the precepts of charity, that schismatics and heretics are to be outed of their possessions and destroyed. And thus have they mixed together and confounded two things that are in themselves most different, the Church and the commonwealth. Now as it is very difficult for men patiently to suffer
35 themselves to be stripped of the goods which they have got by their honest industry, and, contrary to all the laws of equity, both human and divine, to be delivered up for a prey to other men's violence and rapine; especially when they are otherwise altogether blameless; and that the occasion for which they are thus treated does not at all belong to the jurisdiction of the magistrate, but entirely to
40 the conscience of every particular man for the conduct of which he is

accountable to God only; what else can be expected but that these men, growing weary of the evils under which they labour, should in the end think it lawful for them to resist force with force, and to defend their natural rights (which are not forfeitable upon account of religion) with arms as well as they can? That this has been hitherto the ordinary course of things is abundantly evident in history, and that it will continue to be so hereafter is but too apparent in reason. It cannot indeed, be otherwise so long as the principle of persecution for religion shall prevail, as it has done hitherto, with magistrate and people, and so long as those that ought to be the preachers of peace and concord shall continue with all their art and strength to excite men to arms and sound the trumpet of war. But that magistrates should thus suffer these incendiaries and disturbers of the public peace might justly be wondered at if it did not appear that they have been invited by them unto a participation of the spoil, and have therefore thought fit to make use of their covetousness and pride as means whereby to increase their own power. For who does not see that these good men are, indeed, more ministers of the government than ministers of the Gospel and that, by flattering the ambition and favouring the dominion of princes and men in authority, they endeavour with all their might to promote that tyranny in the commonwealth which otherwise they should not be able to establish in the Church? This is the unhappy agreement that we see between the Church and State. Whereas if each of them would contain itself within its own bounds — the one attending to the worldly welfare of the commonwealth, the other to the salvation of souls — it is impossible that any discord should ever have happened between them. Sed pudet hoec opprobria. etc. God Almighty grant, I beseech Him, that the gospel of peace may at length be preached, and that civil magistrates, growing more careful to conform their own consciences to the law of God and less solicitous about the binding of other men's consciences by human laws, may, like fathers of their country, direct all their counsels and endeavours to promote universally the civil welfare of all their children, except only of such as are arrogant, ungovernable, and injurious to their brethren; and that all ecclesiastical men, who boast themselves to be the successors of the Apostles, walking peaceably and modestly in the Apostles' steps, without intermeddling with State Affairs, may apply themselves wholly to promote the salvation of souls.

FAREWELL.

PERHAPS it may not be amiss to add a few things concerning heresy and schism. A Turk is not, nor can be, either heretic or schismatic to a Christian; and if any man fall off from the Christian faith to Mahometism, he does not thereby become a heretic or schismatic, but an apostate and an infidel. This nobody doubts of; and by this it appears that men of different religions cannot be heretics or schismatics to one another.

We are to inquire, therefore, what men are of the same religion. Concerning which it is manifest that those who have one and the same rule of faith and worship are of the same religion; and those who have not the same rule of faith and worship are of different religions. For since all things that belong unto that
5   religion are contained in that rule, it follows necessarily that those who agree in one rule are of one and the same religion, and vice versa. Thus Turks and Christians are of different religions, because these take the Holy Scriptures to be the rule of their religion, and those the Alcoran. And for the same reason there may be different religions also even amongst Christians. The Papists and
10   Lutherans, though both of them profess faith in Christ and are therefore called Christians, yet are not both of the same religion, because these acknowledge nothing but the Holy Scriptures to be the rule and foundation of their religion, those take in also traditions and the decrees of Popes and of these together make the rule of their religion; and thus the Christians of St. John (as they are called)
15   and the Christians of Geneva are of different religions, because these also take only the Scriptures, and those I know not what traditions, for the rule of their religion.

This being settled, it follows, first, that heresy is a separation made in ecclesiastical communion between men of the same religion for some opinions
20   no way contained in the rule itself; and, secondly, that amongst those who acknowledge nothing but the Holy Scriptures to be their rule of faith, heresy is a separation made in their Christian communion for opinions not contained in the express words of Scripture. Now this separation may be made in a twofold manner:
25   1. When the greater part, or by the magistrate's patronage the stronger part, of the Church separates itself from others by excluding them out of her communion because they will not profess their belief of certain opinions which are not the express words of the Scripture. For it is not the paucity of those that are separated, nor the authority of the magistrate, that can make any man guilty
30   of heresy, but he only is a heretic who divides the Church into parts, introduces names and marks of distinction, and voluntarily makes a separation because of such opinions.

2. When any one separates himself from the communion of a Church because that Church does not publicly profess some certain opinions which the
35   Holy Scriptures do not expressly teach.

Both these are heretics because they err in fundamentals, and they err obstinately against knowledge; for when they have determined the Holy Scriptures to be the only foundation of faith, they nevertheless lay down certain propositions as fundamental which are not in the Scripture, and because others
40   will not acknowledge these additional opinions of theirs, nor build upon them as

if they were necessary and fundamental, they therefore make a separation in the Church, either by withdrawing themselves from others, or expelling the others from them. Nor does it signify anything for them to say that their confessions and symbols are agreeable to Scripture and to the analogy of faith; for if they be
5 conceived in the express words of Scripture, there can be no question about them, because those things are acknowledged by all Christians to be of divine inspiration and therefore fundamental. But if they say that the articles which they require to be professed are consequences deduced from the Scripture, it is undoubtedly well done of them who believe and profess such things as seem
10 unto them so agreeable to the rule of faith. But it would be very ill done to obtrude those things upon others unto whom they do not seem to be the indubitable doctrines of the Scripture; and to make a separation for such things as these, which neither are nor can be fundamental, is to become heretics; for I do not think there is any man arrived to that degree of madness as that he dare
15 give out his consequences and interpretations of Scripture as divine inspirations and compare the articles of faith that he has framed according to his own fancy with the authority of Scripture. I know there are some propositions so evidently agreeable to Scripture that nobody can deny them to be drawn from thence, but about those, therefore, there can be no difference. This only I say — that
20 however clearly we may think this or the other doctrine to be deduced from Scripture, we ought not therefore to impose it upon others as a necessary article of faith because we believe it to be agreeable to the rule of faith, unless we would be content also that other doctrines should be imposed upon us in the same manner, and that we should be compelled to receive and profess all the
25 different and contradictory opinions of Lutherans, Calvinists, Remonstrants, Anabaptists, and other sects which the contrivers of symbols, systems, and confessions are accustomed to deliver to their followers as genuine and necessary deductions from the Holy Scripture. I cannot but wonder at the extravagant arrogance of those men who think that they themselves can explain
30 things necessary to salvation more clearly than the Holy Ghost, the eternal and infinite wisdom of God.

Thus much concerning heresy, which word in common use is applied only to the doctrinal part of religion. Let us now consider schism, which is a crime near akin to it; for both these words seem unto me to signify an ill-grounded
35 separation in ecclesiastical communion made about things not necessary. But since use, which is the supreme law in matter of language, has determined that heresy relates to errors in faith, and schism to those in worship or discipline, we must consider them under that distinction.

Schism, then, for the same reasons that have already been alleged, is
40 nothing else but a separation made in the communion of the Church upon

account of something in divine worship or ecclesiastical discipline that is not any necessary part of it. Now, nothing in worship or discipline can be necessary to Christian communion but what Christ our legislator, or the Apostles by inspiration of the Holy Spirit, have commanded in express words.

5   In a word, he that denies not anything that the Holy Scriptures teach in express words, nor makes a separation upon occasion of anything that is not manifestly contained in the sacred text — however he may be nicknamed by any sect of Christians and declared by some or all of them to be utterly void of true Christianity — yet in deed and in truth this man cannot be either a heretic or

10   schismatic.

These things might have been explained more largely and more advantageously, but it is enough to have hinted at them thus briefly to a person of your parts.

---

[1] Luke 22. 25.
[2] II Tim. 2. 19.
[3] Luke 22. 32.
[4] Rom. I.
[5] Gal. 5.
[6] Matt. 18. 20.
[7] Exod. 22, 20, 21.
[8] Deut. 2.
[9] I Cor. 5. 12, 13.

John Locke
AN ESSAY CONCERNING THE TRUE ORIGINAL, EXTENT, AND END OF CIVIL GOVERNMENT
(1690)

CHAPTER I

§. 1. It having been shewn in the foregoing discourse,

1. That *Adam* had not, either by natural right of fatherhood, or by positive donation from God, any such authority over his children, or dominion over the world, as is pretended:

5   2. That if he had, his heirs, yet, had no right to it:

3. That if his heirs had, there being no law of nature nor positive law of God that determines which is the right heir in all cases that may arise, the right of succession, and consequently of bearing rule, could not have been certainly determined:

10   4. That if even that had been determined, yet the knowledge of which is the eldest line of *Adam*'s posterity, being so long since utterly lost, that in the races of mankind and families of the world, there remains not to one above another, the least pretence to be the eldest house, and to have the right of inheritance:

All these premises having, as I think, been clearly made out, it is impossible
15   that the rulers now on earth should make any benefit, or derive any the least shadow of authority from that, which is held to be the fountain of all power, *Adam's private dominion and paternal jurisdiction;* so that he that will not give just occasion to think that all government in the world is the product only of force and violence, and that men live together by no other rules but that of
20   beasts, where the strongest carries it, and so lay a foundation for perpetual disorder and mischief, tumult, sedition and rebellion, (things that the followers of that hypothesis so loudly cry out against) must of necessity find out another rise of government, another original of political power, and another way of designing and knowing the persons that have it, than what Sir *Robert Filmer*
25   hath taught us.

§. 2. To this purpose, I think it may not be amiss, to set down what I take to be political power; that the power of a *magistrate* over a subject may be distinguished from that of a *father* over his children, a *master* over his servant, a *husband* over his wife, and a *lord* over his slave. All which distinct powers
30   happening sometimes together in the same man, if he be considered under these different relations, it may help us to distinguish these powers one from another, and shew the difference betwixt a ruler of a common-wealth, a father of a family, and a captain of a galley.

§. 3. Political power, then, I take to be a *right* of making laws with penalties of death, and consequently all less penalties, for the regulating and preserving of property, and of employing the force of the community, in the execution of such laws, and in the defence of the common-wealth from foreign injury; and all this only for the public good

---

CHAPTER II.
Of the State of Nature.

§. 4. TO understand political power right, and derive it from its original, we must consider, what state all men are naturally in, and that is, a *state of perfect freedom* to order their actions, and dispose of their possessions and persons, as they think fit, within the bounds of the law of nature, without asking leave, or
5   depending upon the will of any other man.

A *state* also *of equality,* wherein all the power and jurisdiction is reciprocal, no one having more than another; there being nothing more evident, than that creatures of the same species and rank, promiscuously born to all the same advantages of nature, and the use of the same faculties, should also be equal one
10   amongst another without subordination or subjection, unless the lord and master of them all should, by any manifest declaration of his will, set one above another, and confer on him, by an evident and clear appointment, an undoubted right to dominion and sovereignty.

§. 5. This *equality* of men by nature, the judicious *Hooker* looks upon as so
15   evident in itself, and beyond all question, that he makes it the foundation of that obligation to mutual love amongst men, on which he builds the duties they owe one another, and from whence he derives the great maxims *of justice* and *charity.* His words are,

The like natural inducement hath brought men to know that it is no less
20   *their duty, to love others than themselves; for seeing those things which are*
equal, must needs all have one measure; if I cannot but wish to receive good,
even as much at every man's hands, as any man can wish unto his own soul,
how should I look to have any part of my desire herein satisfied, unless myself
be careful to satisfy the like desire, which is undoubtedly in other men, being of
25   *one and the same nature? To have any thing offered them repugnant to this*
desire, must needs in all respects grieve them as much as me; so that if I do
harm, I must look to suffer, there being no reason that others should shew
greater measure of love to me, than they have by me shewed unto them: my
desire therefore to be loved of my equals in nature, as much as possible may be,
30   *imposeth upon me a natural duty of bearing to them-ward fully the like*
affection; from which relation of equality between ourselves and them that are

312

as ourselves, what several rules and canons natural reason hath drawn, for
direction of life, no man is ignorant. Eccl. Pol. Lib. 1.

    §. 6. But though this be *a state of liberty,* yet *it is not a state of licence:*
though man in that state have an uncontroulable liberty to dispose of his person
5 or possessions, yet he has not liberty to destroy himself, or so much as any
creature in his possession, but where some nobler use than its bare preservation
calls for it. The *state of nature* has a law of nature to govern it, which obliges
every one: and reason, which is that law, teaches all mankind, who will but
consult it, that being all *equal and independent,* no one ought to harm another in
10 his life, health, liberty, or possessions: for men being all the workmanship of one
omnipotent, and infinitely wise maker; all the servants of one sovereign master,
sent into the world by his order, and about his business; they are his property,
whose workmanship they are, made to last during his, not one another's
pleasure: and being furnished with like faculties, sharing all in one community
15 of nature, there cannot be supposed any such *subordination* among us, that may
authorize us to destroy one another, as if we were made for one another's uses,
as the inferior ranks of creatures are for our's. Every one, as he is *bound to*
preserve himself, and not to quit his station wilfully, so by the like reason, when
his own preservation comes not in competition, ought he, as much as he can, *to*
20 *preserve the rest of mankind,* and may not, unless it be to do justice on an
offender, take away, or impair the life, or what tends to the preservation of the
life, the liberty, health, limb, or goods of another.

    §. 7. And that all men may be restrained from invading others rights, and
from doing hurt to one another, and the law of nature be observed, which willeth
25 the peace and *preservation of all mankind,* the *execution* of the law of nature is,
in that state, put into every man's hands, whereby every one has a right to
punish the transgressors of that law to such a degree, as may hinder its violation:
for the *law of nature* would, as all other laws that concern men in this world, be
in vain, if there were no body that in the state of nature had a *power to execute*
30 that law, and thereby preserve the innocent and restrain offenders. And if any
one in the state of nature may punish another for any evil he has done, every one
may do so: for in that *state of perfect equality,* where naturally there is no
superiority or jurisdiction of one over another, what any may do in prosecution
of that law, every one must needs have a right to do.

35   *§. 8.* And thus, in the state of nature, *one man comes by a power over*
another; but yet no absolute or arbitrary power, to use a criminal, when he has
got him in his hands, according to the passionate heats, or boundless
extravagancy of his own will; but only to retribute to him, so far as calm reason
and conscience dictate, what is proportionate to his transgression, which is so
40 much as may serve for *reparation* and *restraint:* for these two are the only

reasons, why one man may lawfully do harm to another, which is that we call *punishment.* In transgressing the law of nature, the offender declares himself to live by another rule than that of reason and common equity, which is that measure God has set to the actions of men, for their mutual security; and so he
5   becomes dangerous to mankind, the tye, which is to secure them from injury and violence, being slighted and broken by him. Which being a trespass against the whole species, and the peace and safety of it, provided for by the law of nature, every man upon this score, by the right he hath to preserve mankind in general, may restrain, or where it is necessary, destroy things noxious to them, and so
10   may bring such evil on any one, who hath transgressed that law, as may make him repent the doing of it, and thereby deter him, and by his example others, from doing the like mischief. And in this case, and upon this ground, *every man hath a right to punish the offender, and be executioner of the law of nature.*
         §. 9. I doubt not but this will seem a very strange doctrine to some men: but
15   before they condemn it, I desire them to resolve me, by what right any prince or state can put to death, or *punish an alien,* for any crime he commits in their country. It is certain their laws, by virtue of any sanction they receive from the promulgated will of the legislative, reach not a stranger: they speak not to him, nor, if they did, is he bound to hearken to them. The legislative authority, by
20   which they are in force over the subjects of that common-wealth, hath no power over him. Those who have the supreme power of making laws in *England, France* or *Holland,* are to an *Indian,* but like the rest of the world, men without authority: and therefore, if by the law of nature every man hath not a power to punish offences against it, as he soberly judges the case to require, I see not how
25   the magistrates of any community can *punish an alien* of another country; since, in reference to him, they can have no more power than what every man naturally may have over another.
         §. 10. Besides the crime which consists in violating the law, and varying from the right rule of reason, whereby a man so far becomes degenerate, and
30   declares himself to quit the principles of human nature, and to be a noxious creature, there is commonly *injury* done to some person or other, and some other man receives damage by his transgression: in which case he who hath received any damage, has, besides the right of punishment common to him with other men, a particular right to seek *reparation* from him that has done it: and any
35   other person, who finds it just, may also join with him that is injured, and assist him in recovering from the offender so much as may make satisfaction for the harm he has suffered.
         §. 11. From these *two distinct rights,* the one of *punishing* the crime *for restraint,* and preventing the like offence, which right of punishing is in every
40   body; the other of taking *reparation,* which belongs only to the injured party,

comes it to pass that the magistrate, who by being magistrate hath the common right of punishing put into his hands, can often, where the public good demands not the execution of the law, *remit* the punishment of criminal offences by his own authority, but yet cannot *remit* the satisfaction due to any private man for
5   the damage he has received. That, he who has suffered the damage has a right to demand in his own name, and he alone can remit: the damnified person has this power of appropriating to himself the goods or service of the offender, *by right of self-preservation,* as every man has a power to punish the crime, to prevent its being committed again, *by the right he has of preserving all mankind,* and doing
10   all reasonable things he can in order to that end: and thus it is, that every man, in the state of nature, has a power to kill a murderer, both *to deter* others from doing the like injury, which no reparation can compensate, by the example of the punishment that attends it from every body, and also to secure men from the attempts of a criminal, who having renounced reason, the common rule and
15   measure God hath given to mankind, hath, by the unjust violence and slaughter he hath committed upon one, declared war against all mankind, and therefore may be destroyed as a *lion* or a *tyger,* one of those wild savage beasts, with whom men can have no society nor security: and upon this is grounded that great law of nature, *Whoso sheddeth man's blood, by man shall his blood be*
20   *shed.* And *Cain* was so fully convinced, that every one had a right to destroy such a criminal, that after the murder of his brother, he cries out, *Every one that findeth me, shall slay me;* so plain was it writ in the hearts of all mankind.

    §. 12. By the same reason may a man in the state of nature *punish the lesser breaches* of that law. It will perhaps be demanded, with death? I answer, each
25   transgression may be *punished* to that *degree,* and with so much *severity,* as will suffice to make it an ill bargain to the offender, give him cause to repent, and terrify others from doing the like. Every offence, that can be committed in the state of nature, may in the state of nature be also punished equally, and as far forth as it may, in a common-wealth: for though it would be besides my present
30   purpose, to enter here into the particulars of the law of nature, or its *measures of punishment;* yet, it is certain there is such a law, and that too, as intelligible and plain to a rational creature, and a studier of that law, as the positive laws of common-wealths; nay, possibly plainer; as much as reason is easier to be understood, than the fancies and intricate contrivances of men, following
35   contrary and hidden interests put into words; for so truly are a great part of the *municipal laws* of countries, which are only so far right, as they are founded on the law of nature, by which they are to be regulated and interpreted.

    §. 13. To this strange doctrine, *viz.* That *in the state of nature every one has the executive power* of the law of nature, I doubt not but it will be objected, that
40   it is unreasonable for men to be judges in their own cases, that self-love will

make men partial to themselves and their friends: and on the other side, that ill nature, passion and revenge will carry them too far in punishing others; and hence nothing but confusion and disorder will follow, and that therefore God hath certainly appointed government to restrain the partiality and violence of
5   men. I easily grant, that *civil government* is the proper remedy for the inconveniencies of the state of nature, which must certainly be great, where men may be judges in their own case, since it is easy to be imagined, that he who was so unjust as to do his brother an injury, will scarce be so just as to condemn himself for it: but I shall desire those who make this objection, to remember, that
10 *absolute monarchs* are but men; and if government is to be the remedy of those evils, which necessarily follow from men's being judges in their own cases, and the state of nature is therefore not to be endured, I desire to know what kind of government that is, and how much better it is than the state of nature, where one man, commanding a multitude, has the liberty to be judge in his own case, and
15 may do to all his subjects whatever he pleases, without the least liberty to any one to question or controul those who execute his pleasure? and in whatsoever he doth, whether led by reason, mistake or passion, must be submitted to? much better it is in the state of nature, wherein men are not bound to submit to the unjust will of another: and if he that judges, judges amiss in his own, or any
20 other case, he is answerable for it to the rest of mankind.

     §. 14. It is often asked as a mighty objection, *where are,* or ever were there any *men in such a state of nature?* To which it may suffice as an answer at present, that since all princes and rulers of *independent* governments all through the world, are in a state of nature, it is plain the world never was, nor ever will
25 be, without numbers of men in that state. I have named all governors of *independent communities,* whether they are, or are not, in league with others: for it is not every compact that puts an end to the state of nature between men, but only this one of agreeing together mutually to enter into one community, and make one body politic; other promises, and compacts, men may make one with
30 another, and yet still be in the state of nature. The promises and bargains for truck, *&c.* between the two men in the desert island, mentioned by *Garcilasso de la Vega,* in his history of *Peru;* or between a *Swiss* and an *Indian,* in the woods of *America,* are binding to them, though they are perfectly in a state of nature, in reference to one another: for truth and keeping of faith belongs to men, as men,
35 and not as members of society.

     §. 15. To those that say, there were never any men in the state of nature, I will not only oppose the authority of the judicious *Hooker, Eccl. Pol. lib.* i. *sect.* 10. where he says, *The laws which have been hitherto mentioned,* i. e. the laws of nature, *do bind men absolutely, even as they are men, although they have*
40 *never any settled fellowship, never any solemn agreement amongst themselves*

what to do, or not to do: but forasmuch as we are not by ourselves sufficient to
furnish ourselves with competent store of things, needful for such a life as our
nature doth desire, a life fit for the dignity of man; therefore to supply those
defects and imperfections which are in us, as living single and solely by
5   *ourselves, we are naturally induced to seek communion and fellowship with*
others: this was the cause of men's uniting themselves at first in politic societies.
But I moreover affirm, that all men are naturally in that state, and remain so, till
by their own consents they make themselves members of some politic society;
and I doubt not in the sequel of this discourse, to make it very clear
10 ⸻⸻⸻⸻⸻

CHAPTER III.
Of the State of War.

§. 16. THE *state of war* is a state of *enmity* and *destruction:* and therefore
15 declaring by word or action, not a passionate and hasty, but a sedate settled
design upon another man's life, *puts him in a state of war* with him against
whom he has declared such an intention, and so has exposed his life to the
other's power to be taken away by him, or any one that joins with him in his
defence, and espouses his quarrel; it being reasonable and just, I should have a
20 right to destroy that which threatens me with destruction: for, *by the*
fundamental law of nature, man being to be preserved as much as possible,
when all cannot be preserved, the safety of the innocent is to be preferred: and
one may destroy a man who makes war upon him, or has discovered an enmity
to his being, for the same reason that he may kill a *wolf* or a *lion;* because such
25 men are not under the ties of the common-law of reason, have no other rule, but
that of force and violence, and so may be treated as beasts of prey, those
dangerous and noxious creatures, that will be sure to destroy him whenever he
falls into their power.

§. 17. And hence it is, that he who attempts to get another man into his
30 absolute power, does thereby *put himself into a state of war* with him; it being to
be understood as a declaration of a design upon his life: for I have reason to
conclude, that he who would get me into his power without my consent, would
use me as he pleased when he had got me there, and destroy me too when he had
a fancy to it; for no body can desire to *have me in his absolute power,* unless it
35 be to compel me by force to that which is against the right of my freedom, *i. e.*
make me a slave. To be free from such force is the only security of my
preservation; and reason bids me look on him, as an enemy to my preservation,
who would take away that *freedom* which is the fence to it; so that he who
makes an *attempt to enslave* me, thereby puts himself into a state of war with
40 me. He that, in the state of nature, *would take away the freedom* that belongs to

any one in that state, must necessarily be supposed to have a design to take away every thing else, that *freedom* being the foundation of all the rest; as he that, in the state of society, would take away the *freedom* belonging to those of that society or common-wealth, must be supposed to design to take away from them
5 every thing else, and so be looked on as *in a state of war.*

§. 18. This makes it lawful for a man to *kill a thief,* who has not in the least hurt him, nor declared any design upon his life, any farther than, by the use of force, so to get him in his power, as to take away his money, or what he pleases, from him; because using force, where he has no right, to get me into his power,
10 let his pretence be what it will, I have no reason to suppose, that he, who would *take away my liberty,* would not, when he had me in his power, take away every thing else. And therefore it is lawful for me to treat him as one who has *put himself into a state of war* with me, *i. e.* kill him if I can; for to that hazard does he justly expose himself, whoever introduces a state of war, and is aggressor in
15 it.

§. 19. And here we have the plain *difference between the state of nature and the state of war,* which however some men have confounded, are as far distant, as a state of peace, good will, mutual assistance and preservation, and a state of enmity, malice, violence and mutual destruction, are one from another.
20 Men living together according to reason, without a common superior on earth, with authority to judge between them, is *properly the state of nature.* But force, or a declared design of force, upon the person of another, where there is no common superior on earth to appeal to for relief, *is the state of war:* and it is the want of such an appeal gives a man the right of war even against an *aggressor,*
25 tho' he be in society and a fellow subject. Thus a *thief,* whom I cannot harm, but by appeal to the law, for having stolen all that I am worth, I may kill, when he sets on me to rob me but of my horse or coat; because the law, which was made for my preservation, where it cannot interpose to secure my life from present force, which, if lost, is capablce and injury, however coloured with the name,
30 pretences, or forms of law, the end whereof being to protect and redress the innocent, by an unbiassed application of it, to all who are under it; where-ever that is not *bona fide* done, *war is made* upon the sufferers, who having no appeal on earth to right them, they are left to the only remedy in such cases, an appeal to heaven.
35 §. 21. To avoid this *state of war* (wherein there is no appeal but to heaven, and wherein every the least difference is apt to end, where there is no authority to decide between the contenders) is one great reason of men's putting themselves into society, and quitting the state of nature: for where there is an authority, a power on earth, from which relief can be had by *appeal,* there the
40 continuance of the *state of war* is excluded, and the controversy is decided by

that power. Had there been any such court, any superior jurisdiction on earth, to determine the right between *Jephtha* and the *Ammonites,* they had never come to a *state of war:* but we see he was forced to appeal to heaven. *The Lord the Judge* (says he) *be judge this day between the children of* Israel *and the children of*

5 Ammon, *Judg.* xi. 27. and then prosecuting, and relying on his *appeal,* he leads out his army to battle: and therefore in such controversies, where the question is put, *who shall be judge?* It cannot be meant, who shall decide the controversy; every one knows what *Jephtha* here tells us, that *the Lord the Judge* shall judge. Where there is no judge on earth, the appeal lies to God in heaven. That question

10 then cannot mean, who shall judge, whether another hath put himself in a *state of war* with me, and whether I may, as *Jephtha* did, *appeal to heaven* in it? of that I myself can only be judge in my own conscience, as I will answer it, at the great day, to the supreme judge of all men.

CHAPTER IV.
Of slavery.

15 *§. 22.* THE *natural liberty* of man is to be free from any superior power on earth, and not to be under the will or legislative authority of man, but to have only the law of nature for his rule. The *liberty of man,* in society, is to be under no other legislative power, but that established, by consent, in the common-wealth; nor under the dominion of any will, or restraint of any law, but what that

20 legislative shall enact, according to the trust put in it. Freedom then is not what Sir *Robert Filmer* tells us, *Observations, A.* 55. *a liberty for every one to do what he lists, to live as he pleases, and not to be tied by any laws:* but *freedom of men under government* is, to have a standing rule to live by, common to every one of that society, and made by the legislative power erected in it; a liberty to

25 follow my own will in all things, where the rule prescribes not; and not to be subject to the inconstant, uncertain, unknown, arbitrary will of another man: as *freedom of nature* is, to be under no other restraint but the law of nature.

§. 23. This *freedom* from absolute, arbitrary power, is so necessary to, and closely joined with a man's preservation, that he cannot part with it, but by what

30 forfeits his preservation and life together: for a man, not having the power of his own life, *cannot,* by compact, or his own consent, *enslave himself* to any one, nor put himself under the absolute, arbitrary power of another, to take away his life, when he pleases. No body can give more power than he has himself; and he that cannot take away his own life, cannot give another power over it. Indeed,

35 having by his fault forfeited his own life, by some act that deserves death; he, to whom he has forfeited it, may (when he has him in his power) delay to take it, and make use of him to his own service, and he does him no injury by it: for,

whenever he finds the hardship of his slavery outweigh the value of his life, it is in his power, by resisting the will of his master, to draw on himself the death he desires.

§. 24. This is the perfect condition of *slavery,* which is nothing else, but *the*
5   *state of war continued, between a lawful conqueror and a captive:* for, if once *compact* enter between them, and make an agreement for a limited power on the one side, and obedience on the other, the *state of war and slavery* ceases, as long as the compact endures: for, as has been said, no man can, by agreement, pass over to another that which he hath not in himself, a power over his own life.
10   I confess, we find among the *Jews,* as well as other nations, that men did sell themselves; but, it is plain, this was only to *drudgery, not to slavery:* for, it is evident, the person sold was not under an absolute, arbitrary, despotical power: for the master could not have power to kill him, at any time, whom, at a certain time, he was obliged to let go free out of his service; and the master of
15   such a servant was so far from having an arbitrary power over his life, that he could not, at pleasure, so much as maim him, but the loss of an eye, or tooth, set him free, *Exod.* xxi

---

CHAPTER V.
Of property.

§. 25. WHether we consider natural *reason,* which tells us, that men, being
20   once born, have a right to their preservation, and consequently to meat and drink, and such other things as nature affords for their subsistence: or *revelation,* which gives us an account of those grants God made of the world to *Adam,* and to *Noah,* and his sons, it is very clear, that God, as king *David* says, *Psal.* CXV. 16. *has given the earth to the children of men;* given it to mankind in common.
25   But this being supposed, it seems to some a very great difficulty, how any one should ever come to have a *property* in any thing: I will not content myself to answer, that if it be difficult to make out *property,* upon a supposition that God gave the world to *Adam,* and his posterity in common, it is impossible that any man, but one universal monarch, should have any *property* upon a supposition,
30   that God gave the world to *Adam,* and his heirs in succession, exclusive of all the rest of his posterity. But I shall endeavour to shew, how men might come to have a *property* in several parts of that which God gave to mankind in common, and that without any express compact of all the commoners.

§. 26. God, who hath given the world to men in common, hath also given
35   them reason to make use of it to the best advantage of life, and convenience. The earth, and all that is therein, is given to men for the support and comfort of their being. And tho' all the fruits it naturally produces, and beasts it feeds, belong to

320

mankind in common, as they are produced by the spontaneous hand of nature; and no body has originally a private dominion, exclusive of the rest of mankind, in any of them, as they are thus in their natural state: yet being given for the use of men, there must of necessity be *a means to appropriate* them some way or

5   other, before they can be of any use, or at all beneficial to any particular man. The fruit, or venison, which nourishes the wild *Indian,* who knows no inclosure, and is still a tenant in common, must be his, and so his, *i. e.* a part of him, that another can no longer have any right to it, before it can do him any good for the support of his life.

10   *§. 27.* Though the earth, and all inferior creatures, be common to all men, yet every man has a *property* in his own *person:* this no body has any right to but himself. The *labour* of his body, and the *work* of his hands, we may say, are properly his. Whatsoever then he removes out of the state that nature hath provided, and left it in, he hath mixed his *labour* with, and joined to it something

15   that is his own, and thereby makes it his *property.* It being by him removed from the common state nature hath placed it in, it hath by this *labour* something annexed to it, that excludes the common right of other men: for this *labour* being the unquestionable property of the labourer, no man but he can have a right to what that is once joined to, at least where there is enough, and as good,

20   left in common for others.

  §. 28. He that is nourished by the acorns he picked up under an oak, or the apples he gathered from the trees in the wood, has certainly appropriated them to himself. No body can deny but the nourishment is his. I ask then, when did they begin to be his? when he digested? or when he eat? or when he boiled? or when

25   he brought them home? or when he picked them up? and it is plain, if the first gathering made them not his, nothing else could. That *labour* put a distinction between them and common: that added something to them more than nature, the common mother of all, had done; and so they became his private right. And will any one say, he had no right to those acorns or apples, he thus appropriated,

30   because he had not the consent of all mankind to make them his? Was it a robbery thus to assume to himself what belonged to all in common? If such a consent as that was necessary, man had starved, notwithstanding the plenty God had given him. We see in *commons,* which remain so by compact, that it is the taking any part of what is common, and removing it out of the state nature

35   leaves it in, which *begins the property;* without which the common is of no use. And the taking of this or that part, does not depend on the express consent of all the commoners. Thus the grass my horse has bit; the turfs my servant has cut; and the ore I have digged in any place, where I have a right to them in common with others, become my *property,* without the assignation or consent of any

body. The *labour* that was mine, removing them out of that common state they were in, hath *fixed* my *property* in them.

§. *29.* By making an explicit consent of every commoner, necessary to any one's appropriating to himself any part of what is given in common, children or
5 servants could not cut the meat, which their father or master had provided for them in common, without assigning to every one his peculiar part. Though the water running in the fountain be every one's, yet who can doubt, but that in the pitcher is his only who drew it out? His *labour* hath taken it out of the hands of nature, where it was common, and belonged equally to all her children, and *hath*
10 thereby *appropriated* it to himself.

§. *30.* Thus this law of reason makes the deer that *Indian*'s who hath killed it; it is allowed to be his goods, who hath bestowed his labour upon it, though before it was the common right of every one. And amongst those who are counted the civilized part of mankind, who have made and multiplied positive
15 laws to determine *property,* this original law of nature, for the *beginning of property,* in what was before common, still takes place; and by virtue thereof, what fish any one catches in the ocean, that great and still remaining common of mankind; or what ambergrise any one takes up here, is by the *labour* that removes it out of that common state nature left it in, *made* his *property,* who
20 takes that pains about it. And even amongst us, the hare that any one is hunting, is thought his who pursues her during the chase: for being a beast that is still looked upon as common, and no man's private possession; whoever has employed so much *labour* about any of that kind, as to find and pursue her, has thereby removed her from the state of nature, wherein she was common, and
25 hath *begun a property.*

§. *31.* It will perhaps be objected to this, that if gathering the acorns, or other fruits of the earth, *&c.* makes a right to them, then any one may *ingross* as much as he will. To which I answer, Not so. The same law of nature, that does by this means give us property, does also *bound* that *property* too. *God has*
30 *given us all things richly,* 1 Tim. vi. 12. is the voice of reason confirmed by inspiration. But how far has he given it us? *To enjoy.* As much as any one can make use of to any advantage of life before it spoils, so much he may by his labour fix a property in: whatever is beyond this, is more than his share, and belongs to others. Nothing was made by God for man to spoil or destroy. And
35 thus, considering the plenty of natural provisions there was a long time in the world, and the few spenders; and to how small a part of that provision the industry of one man could extend itself, and ingross it to the prejudice of others; especially keeping within the *bounds,* set by reason, of what might serve for his *use;* there could be then little room for quarrels or contentions about property so
40 established.

§. 32. But the *chief matter of property* being now not the fruits of the earth, and the beasts that subsist on it, but *the earth itself;* as that which takes in and carries with it all the rest; I think it is plain, that *property* in that too is acquired as the former. *As much land* as a man tills, plants, improves, cultivates, and can
5   use the product of, so much is his *property.* He by his labour does, as it were, inclose it from the common. Nor will it invalidate his right, to say every body else has an equal title to it; and therefore he cannot appropriate, he cannot inclose, without the consent of all his fellow-commoners, all mankind. God, when he gave the world in common to all mankind, commanded man also to
10 labour, and the penury of his condition required it of him. God and his reason commanded him to subdue the earth, *i. e.* improve it for the benefit of life, and therein lay out something upon it that was his own, his labour. He that in obedience to this command of God, subdued, tilled and sowed any part of it, thereby annexed to it something that was his *property,* which another had no
15 title to, nor could without injury take from him.

§. 33. Nor was this *appropriation* of any parcel of *land,* by improving it, any prejudice to any other man, since there was still enough, and as good left; and more than the yet unprovided could use. So that, in effect, there was never the less left for others because of his inclosure for himself: for he that leaves as
20 much as another can make use of, does as good as take nothing at all. No body could think himself injured by the drinking of another man, though he took a good draught, who had a whole river of the same water left him to quench his thirst: and the case of land and water, where there is enough of both, is perfectly the same.

25 *§. 34.* God gave the world to men in common; but since he gave it them for their benefit, and the greatest conveniencies of life they were capable to draw from it, it cannot be supposed he meant it should always remain common and uncultivated. He gave it to the use of the industrious and rational, (and *labour* was to be *his title* to it;) not to the fancy or covetousness of the quarrelsome and
30 contentious. He that had as good left for his improvement, as was already taken up, needed not complain, ought not to meddle with what was already improved by another's labour: if he did, it is plain he desired the benefit of another's pains, which he had no right to, and not the ground which God had given him in common with others to labour on, and whereof there was as good left, as that
35 already possessed, and more than he knew what to do with, or his industry could reach to.

§. 35. It is true, in *land* that is *common* in *England,* or any other country, where there is plenty of people under government, who have money and commerce, no one can inclose or appropriate any part, without the consent of all
40 his fellow-commoners; because this is left common by compact, *i. e.* by the law

of the land, which is not to be violated. And though it be common, in respect of some men, it is not so to all mankind; but is the joint property of this country, or this parish. Besides, the remainder, after such inclosure, would not be as good to the rest of the commoners, as the whole was when they could all make use of the
5 whole; whereas in the beginning and first peopling of the great common of the world, it was quite otherwise. The law man was under, was rather for appropriating. God commanded, and his wants forced him to *labour.* That was his *property* which could not be taken from him where-ever he had fixed it. And hence subduing or cultivating the earth, and having dominion, we see are joined
10 together. The one gave title to the other. So that God, by commanding to subdue, gave authority so far to *appropriate:* and the condition of human life, which requires labour and materials to work on, necessarily introduces private possessions.

§. 36. The *measure of property* nature has well set by the extent of men's
15 *labour and the conveniencies of life:* no man's labour could subdue, or appropriate all; nor could his enjoyment consume more than a small part; so that it was impossible for any man, this way, to intrench upon the right of another, or acquire to himself a property, to the prejudice of his neighbour, who would still have room for as good, and as large a possession (after the other had taken out
20 his) as before it was appropriated. This *measure* did confine every man's *possession* to a very moderate proportion, and such as he might appropriate to himself, without injury to any body, in the first ages of the world, when men were more in danger to be lost, by wandering from their company, in the then vast wilderness of the earth, than to be straitened for want of room to plant in.
25 And the same *measure* may be allowed still without prejudice to any body, as full as the world seems: for supposing a man, or family, in the state they were at first peopling of the world by the children of *Adam,* or *Noah;* let him plant in some in-land, vacant places of *America,* we shall find that the *possessions* he could make himself, upon the *measures* we have given, would not be very large,
30 nor, even to this day, prejudice the rest of mankind, or give them reason to complain, or think themselves injured by this man's incroachment, though the race of men have now spread themselves to all the corners of the world, and do infinitely exceed the small number was at the beginning. Nay, the extent of *ground* is of so little value, *without labour,* that I have heard it affirmed, that in
35 *Spain* itself a man may be permitted to plough, sow and reap, without being disturbed, upon land he has no other title to, but only his making use of it. But, on the contrary, the inhabitants think themselves beholden to him, who, by his industry on neglected, and consequently waste land, has increased the stock of corn, which they wanted. But be this as it will, which I lay no stress on; this I
40 dare boldly affirm, that the same *rule of propriety,* (*viz.*) that every man should

324

have as much as he could make use of, would hold still in the world, without straitening any body; since there is land enough in the world to suffice double the inhabitants, had not the *invention of money,* and the tacit agreement of men to put a value on it, introduced (by consent) larger possessions, and a right to
5   them; which, how it has done, I shall by and by shew more at large.

§. *37.* This is certain, that in the beginning, before the desire of having more than man needed had altered the intrinsic value of things, which depends only on their usefulness to the life of man; or had *agreed, that a little piece of yellow metal,* which would keep without wasting or decay, should be worth a
10   great piece of flesh, or a whole heap of corn; though men had a right to appropriate, by their labour, each one to himself, as much of the things of nature, as he could use: yet this could not be much, nor to the prejudice of others, where the same plenty was still left to those who would use the same industry. To which let me add, that he who appropriates land to himself by his labour, does
15   not lessen, but increase the common stock of mankind: for the provisions serving to the support of human life, produced by one acre of inclosed and cultivated land, are (to speak much within compass) ten times more than those which are yielded by an acre of land of an equal richness lying waste in common. And therefore he that incloses land, and has a greater plenty of the
20   conveniencies of life from ten acres, than he could have from an hundred left to nature, may truly be said to give ninety acres to mankind: for his labour now supplies him with provisions out of ten acres, which were but the product of an hundred lying in common. I have here rated the improved land very low, in making its product but as ten to one, when it is much nearer an hundred to one:
25   for I ask, whether in the wild woods and uncultivated waste of *America,* left to nature, without any improvement, tillage or husbandry, a thousand acres yield the needy and wretched inhabitants as many conveniencies of life, as ten acres of equally fertile land do in *Devonshire,* where they are well cultivated?

Before the appropriation of land, he who gathered as much of the wild fruit,
30   killed, caught, or tamed, as many of the beasts, as he could; he that so imployed his pains about any of the spontaneous products of nature, as any way to alter them from the state which nature put them in, *by* placing any of his *labour* on them, did thereby *acquire a propriety in them:* but if they perished, in his possession, without their due use; if the fruits rotted, or the venison putrified,
35   before he could spend it, he offended against the common law of nature, and was liable to be punished; he invaded his neighbour's share, for he had *no right, farther than his use* called for any of them, and they might serve to afford him conveniencies of life.

§. *38.* The same *measures* governed the *possession of land* too: whatsoever
40   he tilled and reaped, laid up and made use of, before it spoiled, that was his

peculiar right; whatsoever he enclosed, and could feed, and make use of, the cattle and product was also his. But if either the grass of his inclosure rotted on the ground, or the fruit of his planting perished without gathering, and laying up, this part of the earth, notwithstanding his inclosure, was still to be looked on as
5 waste, and might be the possession of any other. Thus, at the beginning, *Cain* might take as much ground as he could till, and make it his own land, and yet leave enough to *Abel*'s sheep to feed on; a few acres would serve for both their possessions. But as families increased, and industry inlarged their stocks, their *possessions inlarged* with the need of them; but yet it was commonly *without*
10 *any fixed property in the ground* they made use of, till they incorporated, settled themselves together, and built cities; and then, by consent, they came in time, to set out the *bounds of their distinct territories,* and agree on limits between them and their neighbours; and by laws within themselves, settled the *properties* of those of the same society: for we see, that in that part of the world which was
15 first inhabited, and therefore like to be best peopled, even as low down as *Abraham*'s time, they wandered with their flocks, and their herds, which was their substance, freely up and down; and this *Abraham* did, in a country where he was a stranger. Whence it is plain, that at least a great part of the *land lay in common;* that the inhabitants valued it not, nor claimed property in any more
20 than they made use of. But when there was not room enough in the same place, for their herds to feed together, they by consent, as *Abraham* and *Lot* did, *Gen.* xiii. 5. separated and inlarged their pasture, where it best liked them. And for the same reason *Esau* went from his father, and his brother, and planted in *mount Seir, Gen.* xxxvi. 6.
25   *§. 39.* And thus, without supposing any private dominion, and property in *Adam,* over all the world, exclusive of all other men, which can no way be proved, nor any one's property be made out from it; but supposing the *world* given, as it was, to the children of men *in common,* we see how *labour* could make men distinct titles to several parcels of it, for their private uses; wherein
30 there could be no doubt of right, no room for quarrel.
   §. 40. Nor is it so strange, as perhaps before consideration it may appear, that the *property of labour* should be able to over-balance the community of land: for it is *labour* indeed that *puts the difference of value* on every thing; and let any one consider what the difference is between an acre of land planted with
35 tobacco or sugar, sown with wheat or barley, and an acre of the same land lying in common, without any husbandry upon it, and he will find, that the improvement of *labour makes* the far greater part of the value. I think it will be but a very modest computation to say, that of the *products* of the earth useful to the life of man nine tenths are the *effects of labour:* nay, if we will rightly
40 estimate things as they come to our use, and cast up the several expences about

326

them, what in them is purely owing to *nature,* and what to *labour,* we shall find, that in most of them ninety-nine hundredths are wholly to be put on the account of *labour.*

§. 41. There cannot be a clearer demonstration of any thing, than several
5   nations of the *Americans* are of this, who are rich in land, and poor in all the comforts of life; whom nature having furnished as liberally as any other people, with the materials of plenty, *i. e.* a fruitful soil, apt to produce in abundance, what might serve for food, raiment, and delight; yet for *want of improving it by labour,* have not one hundredth part of the conveniencies we enjoy: and a king
10 of a large and fruitful territory there, feeds, lodges, and is clad worse than a day-labourer in *England.*

§. 42. To make this a little clearer, let us but trace some of the ordinary provisions of life, through their several progresses, before they come to our use, and see how much they receive of their *value from human industry.* Bread, wine
15 and cloth, are things of daily use, and great plenty; yet notwithstanding, acorns, water and leaves, or skins, must be our bread, drink and cloathing, did not *labour* furnish us with these more useful commodities: for whatever *bread* is more worth than acorns, wine than water, and *cloth* or *silk,* than leaves, skins or moss, that is wholly *owing to labour* and *industry;* the one of these being the
20 food and raiment which unassisted nature furnishes us with; the other, provisions which our industry and pains prepare for us, which how much they exceed the other in value, when any one hath computed, he will then see how much *labour makes the far greatest part of the value* of things we enjoy in this world: and the ground which produces the materials, is scarce to be reckoned in,
25 as any, or at most, but a very small part of it; so little, that even amongst us, land that is left wholly to nature, that hath no improvement of pasturage, tillage, or planting, is called, as indeed it is, *waste;* and we shall find the benefit of it amount to little more than nothing.

This shews how much numbers of men are to be preferred to largeness of
30 dominions; and that the increase of lands, and the right employing of them, is the great art of government: and that prince, who shall be so wise and godlike, as by established laws of liberty to secure protection and encouragement to the honest industry of mankind, against the oppression of power and narrowness of party, will quickly be too hard for his neighbours: but this by the by. To return to
35 the argument in hand,

§. 43. An acre of land, that bears here twenty bushels of wheat, and another in *America,* which, with the same husbandry, would do the like, are, without doubt, of the same natural intrinsic value: but yet the benefit mankind receives from the one in a year, is worth 5 *l.* and from the other possibly not worth a
40 penny, if all the profit an *Indian* received from it were to be valued, and sold

here; at least, I may truly say, not one thousandth. It is *labour* then which *puts the greatest part of value upon land,* without which it would scarcely be worth any thing: it is to that we owe the greatest part of all its useful products; for all that the straw, bran, bread, of that acre of wheat, is more worth than the product
5 of an acre of as good land, which lies waste, is all the effect of labour: for it is not barely the plough-man's pains, the reaper's and thresher's toil, and the baker's sweat, is to be counted into the *bread* we eat; the labour of those who broke the oxen, who digged and wrought the iron and stones, who felled and framed the timber employed about the plough, mill, oven, or any other utensils,
10 which are a vast number, requisite to this corn, from its being seed to be sown to its being made bread, must all be *charged on* the account of *labour,* and received as an effect of that: nature and the earth furnished only the almost worthless materials, as in themselves. It would be a strange *catalogue of things, that industry provided and made use of, about every loaf of bread,* before it came to
15 our use, if we could trace them; iron, wood, leather, bark, timber, stone, bricks, coals, lime, cloth, dying drugs, pitch, tar, masts, ropes, and all the materials made use of in the ship, that brought any of the commodities made use of by any of the workmen, to any part of the work; all which it would be almost impossible, at least too long, to reckon up.
20   *§. 44.* From all which it is evident, that though the things of nature are given in common, yet man, by being master of himself, and *proprietor of his own person, and the actions or labour of it, had still in himself the great foundation of property;* and that, which made up the great part of what he applied to the support or comfort of his being, when invention and arts had
25 improved the conveniencies of life, was perfectly his own, and did not belong in common to others.
    §. 45. Thus *labour,* in the beginning, *gave a right of property,* wherever any one was pleased to employ it upon what was common, which remained a long while the far greater part, and is yet more than mankind makes use of. Men,
30 at first, for the most part, contented themselves with what unassisted nature offered to their necessities: and though afterwards, in some parts of the world, (where the increase of people and stock, with the *use of money,* had made land scarce, and so of some value) the several *communities* settled the bounds of their distinct territories, and by laws within themselves regulated the properties of the
35 private men of their society, and so, *by compact* and agreement, *settled the property* which labour and industry began; and the leagues that have been made between several states and kingdoms, either expresly or tacitly disowning all claim and right to the land in the others possession, have, by common consent, given up their pretences to their natural common right, which originally they had
40 to those countries, and so have, by *positive agreement, settled a property*

amongst themselves, in distinct parts and parcels of the earth; yet there are still *great tracts of ground* to be found, which (the inhabitants thereof not having joined with the rest of mankind, in the consent of the use of their common money) *lie waste,* and are more than the people who dwell on it do, or can make
5 use of, and so still lie in common; tho' this can scarce happen amongst that part of mankind that have consented to the use of money.

   §. 46. The greatest part of *things really useful* to the life of man, and such as the necessity of subsisting made the first commoners of the world look after, as it doth the *Americans* now, *are* generally things of *short duration;* such as, if
10 they are not consumed by use, will decay and perish of themselves: gold, silver and diamonds, are things that fancy or agreement hath put the value on, more than real use, and the necessary support of life. Now of those good things which nature hath provided in common, every one had a right (as hath been said) to as much as he could use, and *property* in all that he could effect with his labour; all
15 that his *industry* could extend to, to alter from the state nature had put it in, was his. He that *gathered* a hundred bushels of acorns or apples, had thereby a *property* in them, they were his goods as soon as gathered. He was only to look, that he used them before they spoiled, else he took more than his share, and robbed others. And indeed it was a foolish thing, as well as dishonest, to hoard
20 up more than he could make use of. If he gave away a part to any body else, so that it perished not uselesly in his possession, these he also made use of. And if he also bartered away plums, that would have rotted in a week, for nuts that would last good for his eating a whole year, he did no injury; he wasted not the common stock; destroyed no part of the portion of goods that belonged to others,
25 so long as nothing perished uselesly in his hands. Again, if he would give his nuts for a piece of metal, pleased with its colour; or exchange his sheep for shells, or wool for a sparkling pebble or a diamond, and keep those by him all his life, he invaded not the right of others, he might heap up as much of these durable things as he pleased; the *exceeding of the bounds of* his *just property* not
30 lying in the largeness of his possession, but the perishing of any thing uselesly in it.

   §. 47. And thus *came in the use of money,* some lasting thing that men might keep without spoiling, and that by mutual consent men would take in exchange for the truly useful, but perishable supports of life.
35 *§. 48.* And as different degrees of industry were apt to give men possessions in different proportions, so this *invention of money* gave them the opportunity to continue and enlarge them: for supposing an island, separate from all possible commerce with the rest of the world, wherein there were but an hundred families, but there were sheep, horses and cows, with other useful
40 animals, wholsome fruits, and land enough for corn for a hundred thousand

times as many, but nothing in the island, either because of its commonness, or perishableness, fit to supply the place of *money;* what reason could any one have there to enlarge his possessions beyond the use of his family, and a plentiful supply to its *consumption,* either in what their own industry produced, or they

5 could barter for like perishable, useful commodities, with others? Where there is not some thing, both lasting and scarce, and so valuable to be hoarded up, there men will be apt to enlarge their *possessions of land,* were it never so rich, never so free for them to take: for I ask, what would a man value ten thousand, or an hundred thousand acres of excellent *land,* ready cultivated, and well stocked too

10 with cattle, in the middle of the inland parts of *America,* where he had no hopes of commerce with other parts of the world, to draw *money* to him by the sale of the product? It would not be worth the inclosing, and we should see him give up again to the wild common of nature, whatever was more than would supply the conveniencies of life to be had there for him and his family.

15 *§. 49.* Thus in the beginning all the world was *America,* and more so than that is now; for no such thing as *money* was any where known. Find out something that hath the *use and value of money* amongst his neighbours, you shall see the same man will begin presently to enlarge his possessions.

§. 50. But since gold and silver, being little useful to the life of man in

20 proportion to food, raiment, and carriage, has its *value* only from the consent of men, whereof *labour* yet *makes,* in great part, *the measure,* it is plain, that men have agreed to a disproportionate and unequal *possession of the earth,* they having, by a tacit and voluntary consent, found out a way how a man may fairly possess more land than he himself can use the product of, by receiving in

25 exchange for the overplus gold and silver, which may be hoarded up without injury to any one; these metals not spoiling or decaying in the hands of the possessor. This partage of things in an inequality of private possessions, men have made practicable out of the bounds of society, and without compact, only by putting a value on gold and silver, and tacitly agreeing in the use of money:

30 for in governments, the laws regulate the right of property, and the possession of land is determined by positive constitutions.

§. 51. And thus, I think, it is very easy to conceive, without any difficulty, *how labour could at first begin a title of property* in the common things of nature, and how the spending it upon our uses bounded it. So that there could

35 then be no reason of quarrelling about title, nor any doubt about the largeness of possession it gave. Right and conveniency went together; for as a man had a right to all he could employ his labour upon, so he had no temptation to labour for more than he could make use of. This left no room for controversy about the title, nor for incroachment on the right of others; what portion a man carved to

himself, was easily seen; and it was useless, as well as dishonest, to carve himself too much, or take more than he needed.

CHAPTER VI.
Of Paternal Power.

§. *52.* IT may perhaps be censured as an impertinent criticism, in a
5   discourse of this nature, to find fault with words and names, that have obtained in the world: and yet possibly it may not be amiss to offer new ones, when the old are apt to lead men into mistakes, as this of *paternal power* probably has done, which seems so to place the power of parents over their children wholly in the *father,* as if the *mother* had no share in it; whereas, if we consult reason or
10   revelation, we shall find, she hath an equal title. This may give one reason to ask, whether this might not be more properly called *parental power?* for whatever obligation nature and the right of generation lays on children, it must certainly bind them equal to both the concurrent causes of it. And accordingly we see the positive law of God every where joins them together, without
15   distinction, when it commands the obedience of children, *Honour thy father and thy mother,* Exod. xx. 12. *Whosoever curseth his father or his mother,* Lev. xx. 9. *Ye shall fear every man his mother and his father,* Lev. xix. 3. *Children, obey your parents,* &c. Eph. vi. 1. is the stile of the Old and New Testament.

§. *53.* Had but this one thing been well considered, without looking any
20   deeper into the matter, it might perhaps have kept men from running into those gross mistakes, they have made, about this power of parents; which, however it might, without any great harshness, bear the name of absolute dominion, and regal authority, when under the title of *paternal power* it seemed appropriated to the father, would yet have sounded but oddly, and in the very name shewn the
25   absurdity, if this supposed absolute power over children had been called *parental;* and thereby have discovered, that it belonged to the *mother* too: for it will but very ill serve the turn of those men, who contend so much for the absolute power and authority of the *fatherhood,* as they call it, that the mother should have any share in it; and it would have but ill supported the *monarchy*
30   they contend for, when by the very name it appeared, that that fundamental authority, from whence they would derive their government of a single person only, was not placed in one, but two persons jointly. But to let this of names pass.

§. *54.* Though I have said above, *Chapter* II. *That all men by nature are*
35   *equal,* I cannot be supposed to understand all sorts of *equality: age* or *virtue* may give men a just precedency: *excellency of parts* and *merit* may place others above the common level: *birth* may subject some, and *alliance* or *benefits*

others, to pay an observance to those to whom nature, gratitude, or other respects, may have made it due: and yet all this consists with the *equality,* which all men are in, in respect of jurisdiction or dominion one over another; which was the *equality* I there spoke of, as proper to the business in hand, being that

5   *equal right,* that every man hath, *to his natural freedom,* without being subjected to the will or authority of any other man.

§. 55. *Children,* I confess, are not born in this full state of *equality,* though they are born to it. Their parents have a sort of rule and jurisdiction over them, when they come into the world, and for some time after; but it is but a temporary

10   one. The bonds of this subjection are like the swaddling clothes they art wrapt up in, and supported by, in the weakness of their infancy: age and reason as they grow up, loosen them, till at length they drop quite off, and leave a man at his own free disposal.

§. 56. *Adam* was created a perfect man, his body and mind in full

15   possession of their strength and reason, and so was capable, from the first instant of his being to provide for his own support and preservation, and govern his actions according to the dictates of the law of reason which God had implanted in him. From him the world is peopled with his descendants, who are all born infants, weak and helpless, without knowledge or understanding: but to supply

20   the defects of this imperfect state, till the improvement of growth and age hath removed them, *Adam* and *Eve,* and after them all *parents* were, by the law of nature, *under an obligation to preserve, nourish, and educate the children* they had begotten; not as their own workmanship, but the workmanship of their own maker, the Almighty, to whom they were to be accountable for them.

25   §. 57. The law, that was to govern *Adam,* was the same that was to govern all his posterity, the *law of reason.* But his offspring having another way of entrance into the world, different from him, by a natural birth, that produced them ignorant and without the use of *reason,* they were not presently *under that law;* for no body can be under a law, which is not promulgated to him; and this

30   law being promulgated or made known by *reason* only, he that is not come to the use of his *reason,* cannot be said to be *under this law;* and *Adam*'s children, being not presently as soon as born *under this law of reason,* were not presently *free:* for *law,* in its true notion, *is* not so much the limitation as *the direction of a free and intelligent agent* to his proper interest, and prescribes no farther than is

35   for the general good of those under that law: could they be happier without it, the *law,* as an useless thing, would of itself vanish; and that ill deserves the name of confinement which hedges us in only from bogs and precipices. So that, however it may be mistaken, *the end of law is* not to abolish or restrain, but *to preserve and enlarge freedom:* for in all the states of created beings capable of

40   laws, *where there is no law, there is no freedom:* for *liberty* is, to be free from

restraint and violence from others; which cannot be, where there is no law: but freedom is not, as we are told, *a liberty for every man to do what he lists:* (for who could be free, when every other man's humour might domineer over him?) but a *liberty* to dispose, and order as he lists, his person, actions, possessions,

5   and his whole property, within the allowance of those laws under which he is, and therein not to be subject to the arbitrary will of another, but freely follow his own.

    §. 58. The *power,* then, *that parents have* over their children, arises from that duty which is incumbent on them, to take care of their off-spring, during the

10   imperfect state of childhood. To inform the mind, and govern the actions of their yet ignorant non-age, till reason shall take its place, and ease them of that trouble, is what the children want, and the parents are bound to: for God having given man an understanding to direct his actions, has allowed him a freedom of will, and liberty of acting, as properly belonging thereunto, within the bounds of

15   that law he is under. But whilst he is in an estate, wherein he has not *understanding* of his own to direct his *will,* he is not to have any *will* of his own to follow: he that *understands* for him, must *will* for him too; he must prescribe to his will, and regulate his actions; but when he comes to the estate that made his *father a freeman,* the *son is a freeman* too.

20   *§. 59.* This holds in all the laws a man is under, whether natural or civil. Is a man under the law of nature? *What made him free* of that law? what gave him a free disposing of his property, according to his own will, within the compass of that law? I answer, a state of maturity wherein he might be supposed capable to know that law, that so he might keep his actions within the bounds of it.

25   When he has acquired that state, he is presumed to know how far that law is to be his guide, and how far he may make use of his *freedom,* and so comes to have it; till then, some body else must guide him, who is presumed to know how far the law allows a liberty. If such a state of reason, such an age of discretion *made him free,* the same shall make his son free too. Is a man under the law of

30   *England? What made him free* of that law? that is, to have the liberty to dispose of his actions and possessions according to his own will, within the permission of that law? A capacity of knowing that law; which is supposed by that law, at the age of one and twenty years, and in some cases sooner. If this *made* the father *free,* it shall *make* the son *free* too. Till then we see the law allows the son

35   to have no will, but he is to be guided by the will of his father or guardian, who is to understand for him. And if the father die, and fail to substitute a deputy in his trust; if he hath not provided a tutor, to govern his son, during his minority, during his want of understanding, the law takes care to do it; some other must govern him, and be a will to him, till he hath *attained to a state of freedom,* and

40   his understanding be fit to take the government of his will. But after that, the

father and son are equally *free* as much as tutor and pupil after nonage; equally subjects of the same law together, without any dominion left in the father over the life, liberty, or estate of his son, whether they be only in the state and under the law of nature, or under the positive laws of an established government.

5   *§. 60.* But if, through defects that may happen out of the ordinary course of nature, any one comes not to such a degree of reason, wherein he might be supposed capable of knowing the law, and so living within the rules of it, he is *never capable of being a free man,* he is never let loose to the disposure of his own will (because he knows no bounds to it, has not understanding, its proper
10   guide) but is continued under the tuition and government of others, all the time his own understanding is uncapable of that charge. And so *lunatics* and *ideots* are never set free from the government of their parents; *children, who are not as yet come unto those years whereat they may have; and innocents which are excluded by a natural defect from ever having;* thirdly, *madmen, which for the*
15 *present cannot possibly have the use of right reason to guide themselves, have for their guide, the reason that guideth other men which are tutors over them, to seek and procure their good for them, says* Hooker, Eccl. Pol. *lib. i. sect.* 7. All which seems no more than that duty, which God and nature has laid on man, as well as other creatures, to preserve their offspring, till they can be able to shift
20 for themselves, and will scarce amount to an instance or proof of *parents* regal authority.

    §. 61. Thus we are *born free,* as we are born rational; not that we have actually the exercise of either: age, that brings one, brings with it the other too. And thus we see how *natural freedom and subjection to parents* may consist
25 together, and are both founded on the same principle. A *child* is *free* by his father's title, by his father's understanding, which is to govern him till he hath it of his own. The *freedom of a man at years of discretion,* and the *subjection* of a child *to* his *parents,* whilst yet short of that age, are so consistent, and so distinguishable, that the most blinded contenders for monarchy, *by right of*
30 *fatherhood,* cannot miss this *difference;* the most obstinate cannot but allow their consistency: for were their doctrine all true, were the right heir of *Adam* now known, and by that title settled a monarch in his throne, invested with all the absolute unlimited power Sir *Robert Filmer* talks of; if he should die as soon as his heir were born, must not the *child,* notwithstanding he were never so free,
35 never so much sovereign, be in subjection to his mother and nurse, to tutors and governors, till age and education brought him reason and ability to govern himself and others? The necessities of his life, the health of his body, and the information of his mind, would require him to be directed by the will of others, and not his own; and yet will any one think, that this restraint and subjection
40 were inconsistent with, or spoiled him of that liberty or sovereignty he had a

right to, or gave away his empire to those who had the government of his nonage? This government over him only prepared him the better and sooner for it. If any body should ask me, when my son is *of age to be free?* I shall answer, just when his monarch is of age to govern. *But at what time,* says the judicious

5 *Hooker,* Eccl. Pol. l. i. sect. 6. *a man may be said to have attained so far forth the use of reason, as sufficeth to make him capable of those laws whereby he is then bound to guide his actions: this is a great deal more easy for sense to discern, than for any one by skill and learning to determine.*

§. 62. Common-wealths themselves take notice of, and allow, that there is a
10 *time when men* are to *begin to act like free men,* and therefore till that time require not oaths of fealty, or allegiance, or other public owning of, or submission to the government of their countries.

§. 63. The *freedom* then of man, and liberty of acting according to his own will, is *grounded on* his having *reason,* which is able to instruct him in that law
15 he is to govern himself by, and make him know how far he is left to the freedom of his own will. To turn him loose to an unrestrained liberty, before he has reason to guide him, is not the allowing him the privilege of his nature to be free; but to thrust him out amongst brutes, and abandon him to a state as wretched, and as much beneath that of a man, as their's. This is that which puts
20 the *authority* into the *parents* hands to govern the *minority* of their children. God hath made it their business to employ this care on their off-spring, and hath placed in them suitable inclinations of tenderness and concern to temper this power, to apply it, as his wisdom designed it, to the children's good, as long as they should need to be under it.

25 *§. 64.* But what reason can hence advance this care of the *parents* due to their off-spring into an *absolute arbitrary dominion* of the father, whose power reaches no farther, than by such a discipline, as he finds most effectual, to give such strength and health to their bodies, such vigour and rectitude to their minds, as may best fit his children to be most useful to themselves and others; and, if it
30 be necessary to his condition, to make them work, when they are able, for their own subsistence. But in this power the *mother* too has her share with the *father.*

§. 65. Nay, this *power* so little belongs to the *father* by any peculiar right of nature, but only as he is guardian of his children, that when he quits his care of them, he loses his power over them, which goes along with their nourishment
35 and education, to which it is inseparably annexed; and it belongs as much to the *foster-father* of an exposed child, as to the natural father of another. So little power does the bare *act of begetting* give a man over his issue; if all his care ends there, and this be all the title he hath to the name and authority of a father. And what will become of this *paternal power* in that part of the world, where
40 one woman hath more than one husband at a time? or in those parts of *America,*

where, when the husband and wife part, which happens frequently, the children are all left to the mother, follow her, and are wholly under her care and provision? If the father die whilst the children are young, do they not naturally every where owe the same obedience to their *mother,* during their minority, as to
5 their father were he alive? and will any one say, that the mother hath a legislative power over her children? that she can make standing rules, which shall be of perpetual obligation, by which they ought to regulate all the concerns of their property, and bound their liberty all the course of their lives? or can she inforce the observation of them with capital punishments? for this is the proper
10 *power of the magistrate,* of which the father hath not so much as the shadow. His command over his children is but temporary, and reaches not their life or property: it is but a help to the weakness and imperfection of their nonage, a discipline necessary to their education: and though a *father* may dispose of his own possessions as he pleases, when his children are out of danger of perishing
15 for want, yet *his power* extends not to the lives or goods, which either their own industry, or another's bounty has made their's; nor to their liberty neither, when they are once arrived to the infranchisement of the years of discretion. The *father*'s *empire* then ceases, and he can from thence forwards no more dispose of the liberty of his son, than that of any other man: and it must be far from an
20 absolute or perpetual jurisdiction, from which a man may withdraw himself, having licence from divine authority to *leave father and mother, and cleave to his wife.*

    §. 66. But though there be a time when a *child* comes to be as *free* from subjection to the will and command of his father, as the father himself is free
25 from subjection to the will of any body else, and they are each under no other restraint, but that which is common to them both, whether it be the law of nature, or municipal law of their country; yet this freedom exempts not a son from that *honour* which he ought, by the law of God and nature, *to* pay his *parents.* God having made the parents instruments in his great design of
30 continuing the race of mankind, and the occasions of life to their children; as he hath laid on them an obligation to nourish, preserve, and bring up their offspring; so he has laid on the children a perpetual obligation of *honouring their parents,* which containing in it an inward esteem and reverence to be shewn by all outward expressions, ties up the child from any thing that may ever
35 injure or affront, disturb or endanger, the happiness or life of those from whom he received his; and engages him in all actions of defence, relief, assistance and comfort of those, by whose means he entered into being, and has been made capable of any enjoyments of life: from this obligation no state, no freedom can absolve children. But this is very far from giving parents a power of command
40 over their children, or an authority to make laws and disposs as they please of

their lives or liberties. It is one thing to owe honour, respect, gratitude and assistance; another to require an absolute obedience and submission. The *honour due to parents,* a monarch in his throne owes his mother; and yet this lessens not his authority, nor subjects him to her government.

5   *§. 67.* The subjection of a minor places in the father a temporary government, which terminates with the minority of the child: and the *honour due from a child,* places in the parents a perpetual right to respect, reverence, support and compliance too, more or less, as the father's care, cost, and kindness in his education, has been more or less. This ends not with minority, but holds in
10 all parts and conditions of a man's life. The want of distinguishing these two powers, *viz.* that which the father hath in the right of *tuition,* during minority, and the right of *honour* all his life, may perhaps have caused a great part of the mistakes about this matter: for to speak properly of them, the first of these is rather the privilege of children, and duty of parents, than any prerogative of
15 paternal power. The nourishment and education of their children is a charge so incumbent on parents for their children's good, that nothing can absolve them from taking care of it: and though the *power of commanding and chastising* them go along with it, yet God hath woven into the principles of human nature such a tenderness for their off-spring, that there is little fear that parents should
20 use their power with too much rigour; the excess is seldom on the severe side, the strong byass of nature drawing the other way. And therefore God almighty when he would express his gentle dealing with the *Israelites,* he tells them, that though he chastened them, *he chastened them as a man chastens his son,* Deut. viii. 5. *i. e.* with tenderness and affection, and kept them under no severer
25 discipline than what was absolutely best for them, and had been less kindness to have slackened. This is that power to which *children* are commanded *obedience,* that the pains and care of their parents may not be increased, or ill rewarded.

    §. 68. On the other side, *honour* and *support,* all that which gratitude requires to return for the benefits received by and from them, is the indispensible
30 duty of the child, and the proper privilege of the parents. This is intended for the parents advantage, as the other is for the child's; though education, the parents duty, seems to have most power, because the ignorance and infirmities of childhood stand in need of restraint and correction; which is a visible exercise of rule, and a kind of dominion. And that duty which is comprehended in the word
35 *honour,* requires less obedience, though the obligation be stronger on grown, than younger children: for who can think the command, *Children obey your parents,* requires in a man, that has children of his own, the same submission to his father, as it does in his yet young children to him; and that by this precept he were bound to obey all his father's commands, if, out of a conceit of authority,
40 he should have the indiscretion to treat him still as a boy?

§. 69. The first part then of *paternal power,* or rather duty, which is *education,* belongs so to the father, that it terminates at a certain season; when the business of education is over, it ceases of itself, and is also alienable before: for a man may put the tuition of his son in other hands; and he that has made his

5 son an *apprentice* to another, has discharged him, during that time, of a great part of his obedience both to himself and to his mother. But all the *duty of honour,* the other part, remains never the less entire to them; nothing can cancel that: it is so inseparable from them both, that the father's authority cannot dispossess the mother of this right, nor can any man discharge his son from

10 *honouring* her that bore him. But both these are very far from a power to make laws, and inforcing them with penalties, that may reach estate, liberty, limbs and life. The power of commanding ends with nonage; and though, after that, *honour* and respect, support and defence, and whatsoever gratitude can oblige a man to, for the highest benefits he is naturally capable of, be always due from a

15 son to his parents; yet all this puts no scepter into the father's hand, no sovereign power of commanding. He has no dominion over his son's property, or actions; nor any right, that his will should prescribe to his son's in all things; however it may become his son in many things, not very inconvenient to him and his family, to pay a deference to it.

20 *§. 70.* A man may owe *honour* and respect to an ancient, or wise man; desence to his child or friend; relief and support to the distressed; and gratitude to a benefactor, to such a degree, that all he has, all he can do, cannot sufficiently pay it: but all these give no authority, no right to any one, of making laws over him from whom they are owing. And it is plain, all this is due not only

25 to the bare title of father; not only because, as has been said, it is owing to the mother too; but because these obligations to parents, and the degrees of what is required of children, may be varied by the different care and kindness, trouble and expence, which is often employed upon one child more than another.

§. 71. This shews the reason how it comes to pass, that *parents in societies,*

30 where they themselves are subjects, retain a *power over their children,* and have as much right to their subjection, as those who are in the state of nature. Which could not possibly be, if all political power were only paternal, and that in truth they were one and the same thing: for then, all paternal power being in the prince, the subject could naturally have none of it. But these two *powers,*

35 *political* and *paternal,* are so perfectly distinct and separate; are built upon so different foundations, and given to so different ends, that every subject that is a father, has as much a paternal power over his children, as the prince has over his: and every prince, that has parents, owes them as much filial duty and obedience, as the meanest of his subjects do to their's; and can therefore contain

338

not any part or degree of that kind of dominion, which a prince or magistrate has over his subject.

§. 72. Though the obligation on the parents to *bring up* their children, and the obligation on children to *honour* their parents, contain all the power on the
5 one hand, and submission on the other, which are proper to this relation, yet there is *another power* ordinarily *in the father,* whereby he has a tie on the obedience of his children; which tho' it be common to him with other men, yet the occasions of shewing it, almost constantly happening to fathers in their private families, and the instances of it elsewhere being rare, and less taken
10 notice of, it passes in the world for a part of *paternal jurisdiction.* And this is the power men generally have to *bestow their estates* on those who please them best; the possession of the father being the expectation and inheritance of the children, ordinarily in certain proportions, according to the law and custom of each country; yet it is commonly in the father's power to bestow it with a more
15 sparing or liberal hand, according as the behaviour of this or that child hath comported with his will and humour.

§. 73. This is no small tie on the obedience of children: and there being always annexed to the enjoyment of land, a submission to the government of the country, of which that land is a part; it has been commonly supposed, that a
20 *father* could *oblige his posterity to that government,* of which he himself was a subject, and that his compact held them; whereas, it being only a necessary condition annexed to the land, and the inheritance of an estate which is under that government, reaches only those who will take it on that condition, and so is no natural tie or engagement, but a voluntary submission: for *every man's*
25 *children* being by nature as *free* as himself, or any of his ancestors ever were, may, whilst they are in that freedom, choose what society they will join themselves to, what common-wealth they will put themselves under. But if they will enjoy the *inheritance* of their ancestors, they must take it on the same terms their ancestors had it, and submit to all the conditions annexed to such a
30 possession. By this power indeed fathers oblige their children to obedience to themselves, even when they are past minority, and most commonly too subject them to this or that political power: but neither of these by any peculiar right of *fatherhood,* but by the reward they have in their hands to inforce and recompence such a compliance; and is no more power than what a *French man*
35 has over an *English man,* who by the hopes of an estate he will leave him, will certainly have a strong tie on his obedience: and if, when it is left him, he will enjoy it, he must certainly take it upon the conditions annexed to the *possession of land* in that country where it lies, whether it be *France* or *England.*

§. 74. To conclude then, tho' the *father's power* of commanding extends no
40 farther than the minority of his children, and to a degree only fit for the

discipline and government of that age; and tho' that *honour* and *respect,* and all that which the *Latins* called *piety,* which they indispensibly owe to their parents all their life-time, and in all estates, with all that support and defence is due to them, gives the father no power of governing, *i. e.* making laws and enacting
5 penalties on his children; though by all this he has no dominion over the property or actions of his son: yet it is obvious to conceive how easy it was, in the first ages of the world, and in places still, where the thinness of people gives families leave to separate into unpossessed quarters, and they have room to remove or plant themselves in yet vacant habitations, for the *father of the family*
10 to become the prince of* it; he had been a ruler from the beginning of the infancy of his children: and since without some government it would be hard for them to live together, it was likeliest it should, by the express or tacit consent of the children when they were grown up, be in the father, where it seemed without any change barely to continue; when indeed nothing more was required to it,
15 than the permitting the *father* to exercise alone, in his family, that executive power of the law of nature, which every free man naturally hath, and by that permission resigning up to him a monarchical power, whilst they remained in it. But that this was not by any *paternal right,* but only by the consent of his children, is evident from hence, that no body doubts, but if a stranger, whom
20 chance or business had brought to his family, had there killed any of his children, or committed any other fact, he might condemn and put him to death, or otherwise have punished him, as well as any of his children; which it was impossible he should do by virtue of any paternal authority over one who was not his child, but by virtue of that executive power of the law of nature, which,
25 as a man, he had a right to: and he alone could punish him in his family, where the respect of his children had laid by the exercise of such a power, to give way to the dignity and authority they were willing should remain in him, above the rest of his family.

    §. 75. Thus it was easy, and almost natural for children, by a tacit, and
30 scarce avoidable consent, to make way for the *father's authority and government.* They had been accustomed in their childhood to follow his direction, and to refer their little differences to him; and when they were men, who fitter to rule them? Their little properties, and less covetousness, seldom afforded greater controversies; and when any should arise, where could they
35 have a fitter umpire than he, by whose care they had every one been sustained and brought up, and who had a tenderness for them all? It is no wonder that they made no distinction betwixt minority and full age; nor looked after one and twenty, or any other age that might make them the free disposers of themselves and fortunes, when they could have no desire to be out of their pupilage: the
40 government they had been under, during it, continued still to be more their

protection than restraint; and they could no where find a greater security to their peace, liberties, and fortunes, than in the *rule of a father.*

§. 76. Thus the natural *fathers of families,* by an insensible change, became the *politic monarchs* of them too: and as they chanced to live long, and leave
5   able and worthy heirs, for several successions, or otherwise; so they laid the foundations of hereditary, or elective kingdoms, under several constitutions and mannors, according as chance, contrivance, or occasions happened to mould them. But if princes have their titles in their fathers right, and it be a sufficient proof of the natural *right of fathers* to political authority, because they
10   commonly were those in whose hands we find, *de facto,* the exercise of government: I say, if this argument be good, it will as strongly prove, that all princes, nay princes only, ought to be priests, since it is as certain, that in the beginning, *the father of the family was priest, as that he was ruler n his own household.*

CHAPTER VII.
Of Political or Civil Society.

15   §. 77. GOD having made man such a creature, that in his own judgment, it was not good for him to be alone, put him under strong obligations of necessity, convenience, and inclination to drive him into *society,* as well as fitted him with understanding and language to continue and enjoy it. The *first society* was between man and wife, which gave beginning to that between parents and
20   children; to which, in time, that between master and servant came to be added: and though all these might, and commonly did meet together, and make up but one family, wherein the master or mistress of it had some sort of rule proper to a family; each of these, or all together, came short of *political society,* as we shall see, if we consider the different ends, ties, and bounds of each of these.

25   §. 78. *Conjugal society* is made by a voluntary compact between man and woman; and tho' it consist chiefly in such a communion and right in one another's bodies as is necessary to its chief end, procreation; yet it draws with it mutual support and assistance, and a communion of interests too, as necessary not only to unite their care and affection, but also necessary to their common
30   off-spring, who have a right to be nourished, and maintained by them, till they are able to provide for themselves.

§. 79. For the end of *conjunction, between male and female,* being not barely procreation, but the continuation of the species; this conjunction betwixt male and female ought to last, even after procreation, so long as is necessary to
35   the nourishment and support of the young ones, who are to be sustained by those that got them, till they are able to shift and provide for themselves. This rule,

which the infinite wise maker hath set to the works of his hands, we find the inferior creatures steadily obey. In those viviparous animals which feed on grass, the *conjunction between male and female* lasts no longer than the very act of copulation; because the teat of the dam being sufficient to nourish the young,
5   till it be able to feed on grass, the male only begets, but concerns not himself for the female or young, to whose sustenance he can contribute nothing. But in beasts of prey the *conjunction* lasts longer: because the dam not being able well to subsist herself, and nourish her numerous off-spring by her own prey alone, a more laborious, as well as more dangerous way of living, than by feeding on
10   grass, the assistance of the male is necessary to the maintenance of their common family, which cannot subsist till they are able to prey for themselves, but by the joint care of male and female. The same is to be observed in all birds, (except some domestic ones, where plenty of food excuses the cock from feeding, and taking care of the young brood) whose young needing food in the
15   nest, the cock and hen continue mates, till the young are able to use their wing, and provide for themselves.

     §. 80. And herein I think lies the chief, if not the only reason, *why the male and female in mankind are tied to a longer conjunction* than other creatures, *viz.* because the female is capable of conceiving, and *de facto* is commonly with
20   child again, and brings forth too a new birth, long before the former is out of a dependency for support on his parents help, and able to shift for himself, and has all the assistance is due to him from his parents: whereby the father, who is bound to take care for those he hath begot, is under an obligation to continue in conjugal society with the same woman longer than other creatures, whose young
25   being able to subsist of themselves, before the time of procreation returns again, the conjugal bond dissolves of itself, and they are at liberty, till *Hymen* at his usual anniversary season summons them again to chuse new mates. Wherein one cannot but admire the wisdom of the great Creator, who having given to man foresight, and an ability to lay up for the future, as well as to supply the present
30   necessity, hath made it necessary, that *society of man and wife should be more lasting,* than of male and female amongst other creatures; that so their industry might be encouraged, and their interest better united, to make provision and lay up goods for their common issue, which uncertain mixture, or easy and frequent solutions of conjugal society would mightily disturb.

35   *§. 81.* But tho' these are ties upon *mankind,* which make the *conjugal bonds* more firm and lasting in man, than the other species of animals; yet it would give one reason to enquire, why this *compact,* where procreation and education are secured, and inheritance taken care for, may not be made determinable, either by consent, or at a certain time, or upon certain conditions,
40   as well as any other voluntary compacts, there being no necessity in the nature

of the thing, nor to the ends of it, that it should always be for life; I mean, to such as are under no restraint of any positive law, which ordains all such contracts to be perpetual.

§. 82. But the husband and wife, though they have but one common
5 concern, yet having different understandings, will unavoidably sometimes have different wills too; it therefore being necessary that the last determination, *i. e.* the rule, should be placed somewhere; it naturally falls to the man's share, as the abler and the stronger. But this reaching but to the things of their common interest and property, leaves the wife in the full and free possession of what by
10 contract is her peculiar right, and gives the husband no more power over her life than she has over his; the *power of the husband* being so far from that of an absolute monarch, that the *wife* has in many cases a liberty to separate from him, where natural right, or their contract allows it; whether that contract be made by themselves in the state of nature, or by the customs or laws of the country they
15 live in; and the children upon such separation fall to the father or mother's lot, as such contract does determine.

§. 83. For all the ends of *marriage* being to be obtained under politic government, as well as in the state of nature, the civil magistrate doth not abridge the right or power of either naturally necessary to those ends, *viz.*
20 procreation and mutual support and assistance whilst they are together; but only decides any controversy that may arise between man and wife about them. If it were otherwise, and that absolute *sovereignty* and power of life and death naturally belonged to the husband, and were *necessary to the society between man and wife,* there could be no matrimony in any of those countries where the
25 husband is allowed no such absolute authority. But the ends of matrimony requiring no such power in the husband, the condition of *conjugal society* put it not in him, it being not at all necessary to that state. *Conjugal society* could subsist and attain its ends without it; nay, community of goods, and the power over them, mutual assistance and maintenance, and other things belonging to
30 *conjugal society,* might be varied and regulated by that contract which unites man and wife in that society, as far as may consist with procreation and the bringing up of children till they could shift for themselves; nothing being necessary to any society, that is not necessary to the ends for which it is made.

§. 84. The *society betwixt parents and children,* and the distinct rights and
35 powers belonging respectively to them, I have treated of so largely, in the foregoing chapter, that I shall not here need to say any thing of it. And I think it is plain, that it is far different from a politic society.

§. 85. *Master* and *servant* are names as old as history, but given to those of far different condition; for a freeman makes himself a servant to another, by
40 selling him, for a certain time, the service he undertakes to do, in exchange for

wages he is to receive: and though this commonly puts him into the family of his master, and under the ordinary discipline thereof; yet it gives the master but a temporary power over him, and no greater than what is contained in the *contract* between them. But there is another sort of servants, which by a peculiar name

5   we call *slaves,* who being captives taken in a just war, are by the right of nature subjected to the absolute dominion and arbitrary power of their masters. These men having, as I say, forfeited their lives, and with it their liberties, and lost their estates; and being in the *state of slavery,* not capable of any property, cannot in that state be considered as any part of *civil society;* the chief end

10   whereof is the preservation of property.

      §. 86. Let us therefore consider a *master of a family* with all these subordinate relations of *wife, children, servants,* and *slaves,* united under the domestic rule of a family; which, what resemblance soever it may have in its order, offices, and number too, with a little common-wealth, yet is very far from

15   it, both in its constitution, power and end: or if it must be thought a monarchy, and the *paterfamilias* the absolute monarch in it, absolute monarchy will have but a very shattered and short power, when it is plain, by what has been said before, that the *master of the family* has a very distinct and differently limited *power,* both as to time and extent, over those several persons that are in it; for

20   excepting the slave (and the family is as much a family, and his power as *paterfamilias* as great, whether there be any slaves in his family or no) he has no legislative power of life and death over any of them, and none too but what a *mistress of a family* may have as well as he. And he certainly can have no absolute power over the whole *family,* who has but a very limited one over every

25   individual in it. But how a *family,* or any other society of men, differ from that which is properly *political society,* we shall best see, by considering wherein *political society* itself consists.

      §. 87. Man being born, as has been proved, with a title to perfect freedom, and an uncontrouled enjoyment of all the rights and privileges of the law of

30   nature, equally with any other man, or number of men in the world, hath by nature a power, not only to preserve his property, that is, his life, liberty and estate, against the injuries and attempts of other men; but to judge of, and punish the breaches of that law in others, as he is persuaded the offence deserves, even with death itself, in crimes where the heinousness of the fact, in his opinion,

35   requires it. But because no *political society* can be, nor subsist, without having in itself the power to preserve the property, and in order thereunto, punish the offences of all those of that society; there, and there only is *political society,* where every one of the members hath quitted this natural power, resigned it up into the hands of the community in all cases that exclude him not from appealing

40   for protection to the law established by it. And thus all private judgment of

every particular member being excluded, the community comes to be umpire, by
settled standing rules, indifferent, and the same to all parties; and by men having
authority from the community, for the execution of those rules, decides all the
differences that may happen between any members of that society concerning
5 any matter of right; and punishes those offences which any member hath
committed against the society, with such penalties as the law has established:
whereby it is easy to discern, who are, and who are not, in *political society*
together. Those who are united into one body, and have a common established
law and judicature to appeal to, with authority to decide controversies between
10 them, and punish offenders, are in *civil society* one with another: but those who
have no such common people, I mean on earth, are still in the state of nature,
each being, where there is no other, judge for himself, and executioner; which is,
as I have before shewed it, the perfect *state of nature.*

§. 88. And thus the common-wealth comes by a power to set down what
15 punishment shall belong to the several transgressions which they think worthy
of it, committed amongst the members of that society, (which is the *power of
making laws)* as well as it has the power to punish any injury done unto any of
its members, by any one that is not of it, (which is the *power of war and peace;)*
and all this for the preservation of the property of all the members of that
20 society, as far as is possible. But though every man who has entered into civil
society, and is become a member of any common-wealth, has thereby quitted his
power to punish offences, against the law of *nature,* in prosecution of his own
private judgment, yet with the judgment of offences, which he has given up to
the legislative in all cases, where he can appeal to the magistrate, he has given a
25 right to the common-wealth to employ his force, for the execution of the
judgments of the common-wealth, whenever he shall be called to it; which
indeed are his own judgments, they being made by himself, or his
representative. And herein we have the original of the *legislative* and *executive
power* of civil society, which is to judge by standing laws, how far offences are
30 to be punished, when committed within the common-wealth; and also to
determine, by occasional judgments founded on the present circumstances of the
fact, how far injuries from without are to be vindicated; and in both these to
employ all the force of all the members, when there shall be need.

§. 89. Where-ever therefore any number of men are so united into one
35 society, as to quit every one his executive power of the law of nature, and to
resign it to the public, there and there only is a *political, or civil society.* And
this is done, where-ever any number of men, in the state of nature, enter into
society to make one people, one body politic, under one supreme government; or
else when any one joins himself to, and incorporates with any government
40 already made: for hereby he authorizes the society, or which is all one, the

legislative thereof, to make laws for him, as the public good of the society shall require; to the execution whereof, his own assistance (as to his own decrees) is due. And this *puts* *men* out of a state of nature *into* that of a *common-wealth,* by setting up a judge on earth, with authority to determine all the controversies, and

5 redress the injuries that may happen to any member of the common-wealth; which judge is the legislative, or magistrates appointed by it. And where-ever there are any number of men, however associated, that have no such decisive power to appeal to, there they are still in *the state of nature.*

§. 90. Hence it is evident, that *absolute monarchy,* which by some men is

10 counted the only government in the world, is indeed *inconsistent with civil society,* and so can be no form of civil-government at all: for the *end of civil society,* being to avoid, and remedy those inconveniencies of the state of nature, which necessarily follow from every man's being judge in his own case, by setting up a known authority, to which every one of that society may appeal

15 upon any injury received, or controversy that may arise, and which every one of the* society ought to obey; where-ever any persons are, who have not such an authority to appeal to, for the decision of any difference between them, there those persons are still *in the state of nature;* and so is every *absolute prince,* in respect of those who are under his *dominion.*

20 §. 91. For he being supposed to have all, both legislative and executive power in himself alone, there is no judge to be found, no appeal lies open to any one, who may fairly, and indifferently, and with authority decide, and from whose decision relief and redress may be expected of any injury or inconviency, that may be suffered from the prince, or by his order: so that such a man,

25 however intitled, *Czar,* or *Grand Seignior,* or how you please, is as much *in the state of nature,* with all under his dominion, as he is with the rest of mankind: for where-ever any two men are, who have no standing rule, and common judge to appeal to on earth, for the determination of controversies of right betwixt them, there they are still *in the state of* nature, and under all the

30 inconveniencies of it, with only this woful difference to the subject, or rather slave of an absolute prince: that whereas, in the ordinary state of nature, he has a liberty to judge of his right, and according to the best of his power, to maintain it; now, whenever his property is invaded by the will and order of his monarch, he has not only no appeal, as those in society ought to have, but as if he were

35 degraded from the common state of rational creatures, is denied a liberty to judge of, or to defend his right; and so is exposed to all the misery and inconveniencies, that a man can fear from one, who being in the unrestrained state of nature, is yet corrupted with flattery, and armed with power.

§. 92. For he that thinks *absolute power purifies men's blood,* and corrects

40 the baseness of human nature, need read but the history of this, or any other age,

to be convinced of the contrary. He that would have been insolent and injurious in the woods of *America,* would not probably be much better in a throne; where perhaps learning and religion shall be found out to justify all that he shall do to his subjects, and the sword presently silence all those that dare question it: for
5   what the *protection of absolute monarchy* is, what kind of fathers of their countries it makes princes to be, and to what a degree of happiness and security it carries civil society, where this sort of government is grown to perfection, he that will look into the late relation of *Ceylon,* may easily see.

    §. 93. In *absolute monarchies* indeed, as well as other governments of the
10 world, the subjects have an appeal to the law, and judges to decide any controversies, and restrain any violence that may happen betwixt the subjects themselves, one amongst another. This every one thinks necessary, and believes he deserves to be thought a declared enemy to society and mankind, who should go about to take it away. But whether this be from a true love of mankind and
15 society, and such a charity as we owe all one to another, there is reason to doubt: for this is no more than what every man, who loves his own power, profit, or greatness, may and naturally must do, keep those animals from hurting, or destroying one another, who labour and drudge only for his pleasure and advantage; and so are taken care of, not out of any love the master has for them,
20 but love of himself, and the profit they bring him: for if it be asked, what security, *what fence* is there, in such a state, *against the violence and oppression of this absolute ruler?* the very question can scarce be borne. They are ready to tell you, that it deserves death only to ask after safety. Betwixt subject and subject, they will grant, there must be measures, laws and judges, for their
25 mutual peace and security: but as for the *ruler,* he ought to be *absolute,* and is above all such circumstances; because he has power to do more hurt and wrong, it is right when he does it. To ask how you may be guarded from harm, or injury, on that side where the strongest hand is to do it, is presently the voice of faction and rebellion: as if when men quitting the state of nature entered into society,
30 they agreed that all of them but one, should be under the restraint of laws, but that he should still retain all the liberty of the state of nature, increased with power, and made licentious by impunity. This is to think, that men are so foolish, that they take care to avoid what mischiefs may be done them by *pole- cats,* or *foxes;* but are content, nay, think it safety, to be devoured by *lions.*
35   *§. 94.* But whatever flatterers may talk to amuse people's understandings, it hinders not men from feeling; and when they perceive, that any man, in what station soever, is out of the bounds of the civil society which they are of, and that they have no appeal on earth against any harm, they may receive from him, they are apt to think themselves in the state of nature, in respect of him whom
40 they find to be so; and to take care, as soon as they can, to have that *safety and*

security in civil society, for which it was first instituted, and for which only they entered into it. And therefore, though perhaps at first, (as shall be shewed more at large hereafter in the following part of this discourse) some one good and excellent man having got a pre-eminency amongst the rest, had this deference
5   paid to his goodness and virtue, as to a kind of natural authority, that the chief rule, with arbitration of their differences, by a tacit consent devolved into his hands, without any other caution, but the assurance they had of his uprightness and wisdom; yet when time, giving authority, and (as some men would persuade us) sacredness of customs, which the negligent, and unforeseeing innocence of
10   the first ages began, had brought in successors of another stamp, the people finding their properties not secure under the government, as then it was, (whereas government has no other end but the preservation of* property) could never be safe nor at rest, *nor think themselves in civil society,* till the legislature was placed in collective bodies of men, call them senate, parliament, or what
15   you please. By which means every single person became subject, equally with other the meanest men, to those laws, which he himself, as part of the legislative, had established; nor could any one, by his own authority, avoid the force of the law, when once made; nor by any pretence of superiority plead exemption, thereby to license his own, or the miscarriages of any of his
20   dependents. †*No man in civil society can be exempted from the laws of it:* for if any man may do what he thinks fit, and there be no appeal on earth, for redress or security against any harm he shall do; I ask, whether he be not perfectly still in the state of nature, and so can be *no part or member of that civil society;* unless any one will say, the state of nature and civil society are one and the same
25   thing, which I have never yet found any one so great a patron of anarchy as to affirm.

CHAPTER VIII.
Of the Beginning of Political Societies.

§. 95. MEN being, as has been said, by nature, all free, equal, and independent, no one can be put out of this estate, and subjected to the political
30   power of another, without his own consent. The only way whereby any one divests himself of his natural liberty, and puts on the *bonds of civil society,* is by agreeing with other men to join and unite into a community, for their comfortable, safe, and peaceable living one amongst another, in a secure enjoyment of their properties, and a greater security against any, that are not of
35   it. This any number of men may do, because it injures not the freedom of the rest; they are left as they were in the liberty of the state of nature. When any number of men have so *consented to make one community or government,* they

348

are thereby presently incorporated, and make *one body politic,* wherein the *majority* have a right to act and conclude the rest.

§. 96. For when any number of men have, by the consent of every individual, made a *community,* they have thereby made that *community* one
5 body, with a power to act as one body, which is only by the will and determination of the *majority:* for that which acts any community, being only the consent of the individuals of it, and it being necessary to that which is one body to move one way; it is necessary the body should move that way whither the greater force carries it, which is the *consent of the majority:* or else it is
10 impossible it should act or continue one body, *one community,* which the consent of every individual that united into it, agreed that it should; and so every one is bound by that consent to be concluded by the *majority.* And therefore we see, that in assemblies, impowered to act by positive laws, where no number is set by that positive law which impowers them, the *act of the majority* passes for
15 the act of the whole, and of course determines, as having, by the law of nature and reason, the power of the whole.

§. 97. And thus every man, by consenting with others to make one body politic under one government, puts himself under an obligation, to every one of that society, to submit to the determination of the *majority,* and to be concluded
20 by it; or else this *original compact,* whereby he with others incorporates into *one society,* would signify nothing, and be no compact, if he be left free, and under no other ties than he was in before in the state of nature. For what appearance would there be of any compact? what new engagement if he were no farther tied by any decrees of the society, than he himself thought fit, and did actually
25 consent to? This would be still as great a liberty, as he himself had before his compact, or any one else in the state of nature hath, who may submit himself, and consent to any acts of it if he thinks fit.

§. 98. For if *the consent of the majority* shall not, in reason, be received as *the act of the whole,* and conclude every individual; nothing but the consent of
30 every individual can make any thing to be the act of the whole: but such a consent is next to impossible ever to be had, if we consider the infirmities of health, and avocations of business, which in a number, though much less than that of a common-wealth, will necessarily keep many away from the public assembly. To which if we add the variety of opinions, and contrariety of
35 interests, which unavoidably happen in all collections of men, the coming into society upon such terms would be only like *Cato's* coming into the theatre, only to go out again. Such a constitution as this would make the mighty *Leviathan* of a shorter duration, than the feeblest creatures, and not let it outlast the day it was born in: which cannot be supposed, till we can think, that rational creatures
40 should desire and constitute societies only to be dissolved: for where the

majority cannot conclude the rest, there they cannot act as one body, and consequently will be immediately dissolved again.

§. 99. Whosoever therefore out of a state of nature unite into a *community,* must be understood to give up all the power, necessary to the ends for which they unite into society, to the *majority* of the community, unless they expresly agreed in any number greater than the majority. And this is done by barely agreeing to *unite into one political society,* which is *all the compact* that is, or needs be, between the individuals, that enter into, or make up a *common-wealth.* And thus that, which begins and actually *constitutes any political society,* is nothing but the consent of any number of freemen capable of a majority to unite and incorporate into such a society. And this is that, and that only, which did, or could give beginning to any *lawful government* in the world.

§. 100. To this I find two objections made.

First, That there are no instances to be found in story, of a company of men independent, and equal one amongst another, that met together, and in this way began and set up a government.

Secondly, It is impossible of right, that men should do so, because all men being born under government, they are to submit to that, and are not at liberty to begin a new one.

§. 101. To the first there is this to answer, That it is not at all to be wondered, that *history* gives us but a very little account of *men, that lived together in the state of nature.* The inconveniences of that condition, and the love and want of society, no sooner brought any number of them together, but they presently united and incorporated, if they designed to continue together. And if we may not suppose *men* ever to have been *in the state of nature,* because we hear not much of them in such a state, we may as well suppose the armies of *Salmanasser* or *Xerxes* were never children, because we hear little of them, till they were men, and imbodied in armies. Government is every where antecedent to records, and letters seldom come in amongst a people till a long continuation of civil society has, by other more necessary arts, provided for their safety, ease, and plenty: and then they begin to look after the history of their founders, and search into their *original,* when they have outlived the memory of it: for it is with *common-wealths* as with particular persons, they are commonly *ignorant of their own births and infancies:* and if they know any thing of their *original,* they are beholden for it, to the accidental records that others have kept of it. And those that we have, of the beginning of any polities in the world, excepting that of the *Jews,* where God himself immediately interposed, and which favours not at all paternal dominion, are all either plain instances of such a beginning as I have mentioned, or at least have manifest footsteps of it.

350

§. 102. He must shew a strange inclination to deny evident matter of fact, when it agrees not with his hypothesis, who will not allow, that the *beginning* of *Rome* and *Venice* were by the uniting together of several men free and independent one of another, amongst whom there was no natural superiority or
5   subjection. And if *Josephus Acosta*'s word may be taken, he tells us, that in many parts of *America* there was no government at all. *There are great and apparent conjectures,* says he, *that these men,* speaking of those of Peru, *for a long time had neither kings nor common-wealths, but lived in troops, as they do this day in* Florida, *the* Cheriquanas, *those of* Brasil, *and many other nations,*
10   *which have no certain kings, but as occasion is offered, in peace or war, they choose their captains as they please,* l. i. c. 25. If it be said, that every man there was born subject to his father, or the head of his family; that the subjection due from a child to a father took not away his freedom of uniting into what political society he thought fit, has been already proved. But be that as it will, these men,
15   it is evident, were actually *free;* and whatever superiority some politicians now would place in any of them, they themselves claimed it not, but by consent were all *equal,* till by the same consent they set rulers over themselves. So that their *politic societies* all *began* from a voluntary union, and the mutual agreement of men freely acting in the choice of their governors, and forms of government.
20   **§. 103.** And I hope those who went away from *Sparta* with *Palantus,* mentioned by *Justin,* l. iii. c. 4. will be allowed to have been *freemen independent* one of another, and to have set up a government over themselves, by their own consent. Thus I have given several examples, out of history, of *people free and in the state of nature,* that being met together incorporated and
25   *began a common-wealth.* And if the want of such instances be an argument to prove that *government* were not, nor could not be so *begun,* I suppose the contenders for paternal empire were better let it alone, than urge it against natural liberty: for if they can give so many instances, out of history, of *governments begun* upon paternal right, I think (though at best an argument
30   from what has been, to what should of right be, has no great force) one might, without any great danger, yield them the cause. But if I might advise them in the case, they would do well not to search too much into the *original of governments,* as they have begun *de facto,* lest they should find, at the foundation of most of them, something very little favourable to the design they
35   promote, and such a power as they contend for.
     §. 104. But to conclude, reason being plain on our side, that men are naturally free, and the examples of history shewing, that the *governments* of the world, that were begun in peace, had their beginning laid on that foundation, and were *made by the consent of the people;* there can be little room for doubt, either

where the right is, or what has been the opinion, or practice of mankind, about the *first erecting of governments.*

§. 105. I will not deny, that if we look back as far as history will direct us, towards the *original of common-wealths,* we shall generally find them under the
5   government and administration of one man. And I am also apt to believe, that where a family was numerous enough to subsist by itself, and continued entire together, without mixing with others, as it often happens, where there is much land, and few people, the government commonly began in the father: for the father having, by the law of nature, the same power with every man else to
10   punish, as he thought fit, any offences against that law, might thereby punish his transgressing children, even when they were men, and out of their pupilage; and they were very likely to submit to his punishment, and all join with him against the offender, in their turns, giving him thereby power to execute his sentence against any transgression, and so in effect make him the law-maker, and
15   governor over all that remained in conjunction with his family. He was fittest to be trusted; paternal affection secured their property and interest under his care; and the custom of obeying him, in their childhood, made it easier to submit to him, rather than to any other. If therefore they must have one to rule them, as government is hardly to be avoided amongst men that live together; who so
20   likely to be the man as he that was their common father; unless negligence, cruelty, or any other defect of mind or body made him unfit for it? But when either the father died, and left his next heir, for want of age, wisdom, courage, or any other qualities, less fit for rule; or where several families met, and consented to continue together; there, it is not to be doubted, but they used their natural
25   freedom, to set up him, whom they judged the ablest, and most likely, to rule well over them. Conformable hereunto we find the people of *America,* who (living out of the reach of the conquering swords, and spreading domination of the two great empires of *Peru* and *Mexico)* enjoyed their own natural freedom, though, *cæteris paribus,* they commonly prefer the heir of their deceased king;
30   yet if they find him any way weak, or uncapable, they pass him by, and set up the stoutest and bravest man for their ruler.

§. 106. Thus, though looking back as far as records give us any account of peopling the world, and the history of nations, we commonly find the *government* to be in one hand; yet it destroys not that which I affirm, *viz.* that the
35   *beginning of politic society* depends upon the consent of the individuals, to join into, and make one society; who, when they are thus incorporated, might set up what form of government they thought fit. But this having given occasion to men to mistake, and think, that by nature government was monarchical, and belonged to the father, it may not be amiss here to consider, why people in the
40   beginning generally pitched upon this form, which though perhaps the father's

pre-eminency might, in the first institution of some common-wealths, give a rise to, and place in the beginning, the power in one hand; yet it is plain that the reason, that continued the form of *government in a single person,* was not any regard, or respect to paternal authority; since all petty *monarchies,* that is,
5 almost all monarchies, near their original, have been commonly, at least upon occasion, *elective.*

    §. 107. First then, in the beginning of things, the father's government of the childhood of those sprung from him, having accustomed them to the *rule of one man,* and taught them that where it was exercised with care and skill, with
10 affection and love to those under it, it was sufficient to procure and preserve to men all the political happiness they sought for in society. It was no wonder that they should pitch upon, and naturally run into that form of government, which from their infancy they had been all accustomed to; and which, by experience, they had found both easy and safe. To which, if we add, that *monarchy* being
15 simple, and most obvious to men, whom neither experience had instructed in forms of government, nor the ambition or insolence of empire had taught to beware of the encroachments of prerogative, or the inconveniencies of absolute power, which monarchy in succession was apt to lay claim to, and bring upon them; it was not at all strange, that they should not much trouble themselves to
20 think of methods of restraining any exorbitances of those to whom they had given the authority over them, and of balancing the power of government, by placing several parts of it in different hands. They had neither felt the oppression of tyrannical dominion, nor did the fashion of the age, nor their possessions, or way of living, (which afforded little matter for covetousness or ambition) give
25 them any reason to apprehend or provide against it; and therefore it is no wonder they put themselves into such a *frame of government,* as was not only, as I said, most obvious and simple, but also best suited to their present state and condition; which stood more in need of defence against foreign invasions and injuries, than of multiplicity of laws. The equality of a simple poor way of
30 living, confining their desires within the narrow bounds of each man's small property, made few controversies, and so no need of many laws to decide them, or variety of officers to superintend the process, or look after the execution of justice, where there were but few trespasses, and few offenders. Since then those, who liked one another so well as to join into society, cannot but be
35 supposed to have some acquaintance and friendship together, and some trust one in another; they could not but have greater apprehensions of others, than of one another: and therefore their first care and thought cannot but be supposed to be, how to secure themselves against foreign force. It was natural for them to put themselves under a *frame of government* which might best serve to that end, and

chuse the wisest and bravest man to conduct them in their wars, and lead them out against their enemies, and in this chiefly be their *ruler.*

§. 108. Thus we see, that the *kings* of the *Indians* in *America,* which is still a pattern of the first ages in *Asia* and *Europe,* whilst the inhabitants were too few
5   for the country, and want of people and money gave men no temptation to enlarge their possessions of land, or contest for wider extent of ground, are little more than *generals of their armies;* and though they command absolutely in war, yet at home and in time of peace they exercise very little dominion, and have but a very moderate sovereignty, the resolutions of peace and war being
10 ordinarily either in the people, or in a council. Tho' the war itself, which admits not of plurality of governors, naturally devolves the command into the *king's sole authority.*

§. 109. And thus in *Israel* itself, the *chief business of their judges, and first kings,* seems to have been *to be captains in war,* and leaders of their armies;
15 which (besides what is signified by *going out and in before the people,* which was, to march forth to war, and home again in the heads of their forces) appears plainly in the story of *Jephtha.* The *Ammonites* making war upon *Israel,* the *Gileadites* in fear send to *Jephtha,* a bastard of their family whom they had cast off, and article with him, if he will assist them against the *Ammonites,* to make
20 him their ruler; which they do in these words, *And the people made him head and captain over them,* Judg. xi. 11. which was, as it seems, all one as to be *judge. And he judged Israel,* Judg. xii. 7. that is, was their *captain-general six years.* So when *Jotham* upbraids the *Shechemites* with the obligation they had to *Gideon,* who had been their *judge* and ruler, he tells them, *He fought for you,*
25 *and adventured his life far, and delivered you out of the hands of Midian,* Judg. ix. 17. Nothing mentioned of him, but what he did as a *general:* and indeed that is all is found in his history, or in any of the rest of the judges. And *Abimelech* particularly is called *king,* though at most he was but their *general.* And when, being weary of the ill conduct of *Samuel's* sons, the children of *Israel* desired a
30 *king, like all the nations to judge them, and to go out before them, and to fight their battles,* 1 Sam. viii. 20. God granting their desire, says to *Samuel, I will send thee a man, and thou shalt anoint him to be captain over my people Israel, that he may save my people out of the hands of the Philistines,* ix. 16. As if the only *business of a king* had been to lead out their armies, and fight in their
35 defence; and accordingly at his inauguration pouring a vial of oil upon him, declares to *Saul,* that *the Lord had anointed him to be captain over his inheritance,* x. 1. And therefore those, who after *Saul's* being solemnly chosen and saluted *king* by the *tribes* at *Mispah,* were unwilling to have him their king, made no other objection but this, *How shall this man save us?* v. 27. as if they
40 should have said, this man is unfit to be our *king,* not having skill and conduct

enough in war, to be able to defend us. And when God resolved to transfer the
government to *David,* it is in these words, *But now thy kingdom shall not
continue: the Lord hath sought him a man after his own heart, and the Lord hath
commanded him to be captain over his people,* xiii. 14. As if the whole *kingly*
5 *authority* were nothing else but to be their *general:* and therefore the *tribes* who
had stuck to *Saul*'s family, and opposed *David*'s reign, when they came to
Hebron with terms of submission to him, they tell him, amongst other arguments
they had to submit to him as to their king, that he was in effect their *king* in
Saul's time, and therefore they had no reason but to receive him as their *king*
10 now. *Also* (say they) *in time past, when Saul was king over us, thou wast he that
leddest out and broughtest in Israel, and the Lord said unto thee, Thou shalt
feed my people Israel, and thou shalt be a captain over Israel.*

    §. 110. Thus, whether *a family* by degrees *grew up into a common-wealth,*
and the fatherly authority being continued on to the elder son, every one in his
15 turn growing up under it, tacitly submitted to it, and the easiness and equality of
it not offending any one, every one acquiesced, till time seemed to have
confirmed it, and settled a right of succession by prescription: or whether several
families, or the descendants of several families, whom chance, neighbourhood,
or business brought together, uniting into society, the need of a general, whose
20 conduct might defend them against their enemies in war, and the great
confidence the innocence and sincerity of that poor but virtuous age, (such as are
almost all those which begin governments, that ever come to last in the world)
gave men one of another, made the first beginners of common-wealths generally
put the rule into one man's hand, without any other express limitation or
25 restraint, but what the nature of the thing, and the end of government required:
which ever of those it was that at first put the rule into the hands of a single
person, certain it is no body was intrusted with it but for the public good and
safety, and to those ends, in the infancies of common-wealths, those who had it
commonly used it. And unless they had done so, young societies could not have
30 subsisted; without such nursing fathers tender and careful of the public weal, all
governments would have sunk under the weakness and infirmities of their
infancy, and the prince and the people had soon perished together.

    §. 111. But though the *golden age* (before vain ambition, and *amor
scleratus habendi,* evil concupiscence, had corrupted men's minds into a
35 mistake of true power and honour) had more virtue, and consequently better
governors, as well as less vicious subjects; and there was then *no stretching
prerogative* on the one side, to oppress the people; *nor* consequently on the
other, any *dispute about privilege,* to lessen or restrain the power of the
magistrate, and so no contest betwixt rulers and people about governors or
40 government: yet, when ambition and luxury in future ages* would retain and

increase the power, without doing the business for which it was given; and aided by slattery, taught princes to have distinct and separate interests from their people, men found it necessary to examine more carefully *the original* and rights *of government;* and to find out ways to *restrain the exorbitances,* and *prevent*

5 *the abuses* of that power, which they having intrusted in another's hands only for their own good, they found was made use of to hurt them.

§. 112. Thus we may see how probable it is, that people that were naturally free, and by their own consent either submitted to the government of their father, or united together out of different families to make a government, should

10 generally put the *rule into one man's hands,* and chuse to be under the conduct of a *single person,* without so much as by express conditions limiting or regulating his power, which they thought safe enough in his honesty and prudence; though they never dreamed of monarchy being *Jure Divino,* which we never heard of among mankind, till it was revealed to us by the divinity of this

15 last age; nor ever allowed paternal power to have a right to dominion, or to be the foundation of all government. And thus much may suffice to shew, that as far as we have any light from history, we have reason to conclude, that all peaceful beginnings of *government* have been *laid in the consent of the people.* I say *peaceful,* because I shall have occasion in another place to speak of

20 conquest, which some esteem a way of beginning of governments.

The other objection I find urged against the beginning of polities, in the way I have mentioned, is this, viz.

§. 113. *That all men being born under government, some or other, it is impossible any of them should ever be free, and at liberty to unite together, and*

25 *begin a new one, or ever be able to erect a lawful government.*

If this argument be good; I ask, how came so many lawful monarchies into the world? for if any body, upon this supposition, can shew me any one man in any age of the world *free* to begin a lawful monarchy, I will be bound to shew him ten other *free men* at liberty, at the same time to unite and begin a new

30 government under a regal, or any other form; it being demonstration, that if any one, *born under the dominion* of another, may be so *free* as to have a right to command others in a new and distinct empire, every one that is *born under the dominion* of another may be so free too, and may become a ruler, or subject, of a distinct separate government. And so by this their own principle, either all men,

35 however *born,* are *free,* or else there is but one lawful prince, one lawful government in the world. And then they have nothing to do, but barely to shew us which that is; which when they have done, I doubt not but all mankind will easily agree to pay obedience to him.

§. 114. Though it be a sufficient answer to their objection, to shew that it involves them in the same difficulties that it doth those they use it against; yet I shall endeavour to discover the weakness of this argument a little farther.

All men, say they, *are born under government, and therefore they cannot be*
5   *at liberty to begin a new one. Every one is born a subject to his father, or his prince, and is therefore under the perpetual tie of subjection and allegiance.* It is plain mankind never owned nor considered any such natural *subjection that they were born in,* to one or to the other that tied them, without their own consents, to a subjection to them and their heirs.

10   *§. 115.* For there are no examples so frequent in history, both sacred and profane, as those of men withdrawing themselves, and their obedience, from the jurisdiction they were born under, and the family or community they were bred up in, and *setting up new governments* in other places; from whence sprang all that number of petty commonwealths in the beginning of ages, and which
15   always multiplied, as long as there was room enough, till the stronger, or more fortunate, swallowed the weaker; and those great ones again breaking to pieces, dissolved into lesser dominions. All which are so many testimonies against paternal sovereignty, and plainly prove, that it was not the natural right of the *father* descending to his heirs, that made governments in the beginning, since it
20   was impossible, upon that ground, there should have been so many little kingdoms; all must have been but only one universal monarchy, if men had not been at *liberty to separate* themselves from their families, and the government, be it what it will, that was set up in it, and go and make distinct common-wealths and other governments, as they thought fit.

25   *§. 116.* This has been the practice of the world from its first beginning to this day; nor is it now any more hindrance to the freedom of mankind, that they are *born under constituted and ancient polities,* that have established laws, and set forms of government, than if they were born in the woods, amongst the unconfined inhabitants, that run loose in them: for those, who would persuade
30   us, that *by being born under any government, we are naturally subjects to it,* and have no more any title or pretence to the freedom of the state of nature, have no other reason (bating that of paternal power, which we have already answered) to produce for it, but only, because our fathers or progenitors passed away their natural liberty, and thereby bound up themselves and their posterity to a
35   perpetual subjection to the government, which they themselves submitted to. It is true, that whatever engagements or promises any one has made for himself, he is under the obligation of them, but *cannot,* by any *compact* whatsoever, *bind his children or posterity:* for his son, when a man, being altogether as free as the father, any *act of the father can no more give away the liberty of the son,* than it
40   can of any body else: he may indeed annex such conditions to the land, he

enjoyed as a subject of any common-wealth, as may oblige his son to be of that community, if he will enjoy those possessions which were his father's; because that estate being his father's property, he may dispose, or settle it, as he pleases.

§. 117. And this has generally given the occasion to mistake in this matter;
5 because common-wealths not permitting any part of their dominions to be dismembered, nor to be enjoyed by any but those of their community, the son cannot ordinarily enjoy the possessions of his father, but under the same terms his father did, by becoming a member of the society; whereby he puts himself presently under the government he finds there established, as much as any other
10 subject of that common-wealth. And thus *the consent of freemen, born under government,* which only *makes them members of it,* being given separately in their turns, as each comes to be of age, and not in a multitude together; people take no notice of it, and thinking it not done at all, or not necessary, conclude they are naturally subjects as they are men.

15 §. 118. But, it is plain, *governments* themselves understand it otherwise; they claim *no power over the son, because of that they had over the father;* nor look on children as being their subjects, by their fathers being so. If a subject of *England* have a child, by an *English* woman in *France,* whose subject is he? Not the king of *England's;* for he must have leave to be admitted to the privileges of
20 it: nor the king of *France's;* for how then has his father a liberty to bring him away, and breed him as he pleases? and who ever was judged as a *traytor* or *deserter,* if he left, or warred against a country, for being barely born in it of parents that were aliens there? It is plain then, by the practice of governments themselves, as well as by the law of right reason, that *a child is born a subject of*
25 *no country or government.* He is under his father's tuition and authority, till he comes to age of discretion; and then he is a freeman, at liberty what government he will put himself under, what body politic he will unite himself to: for if an *Englishman's* son, born in *France,* be at liberty, and may do so, it is evident there is no tie upon him by his father's being a subject of this kingdom; nor is he
30 bound up by any compact of his ancestors. And why then hath not his son, by the same reason, the same liberty, though he be born any where else? Since the power that a father hath naturally over his children, is the same, where-ever they be born, and the ties of natural obligations, are not bounded by the positive limits of kingdoms and common-wealths.

35 §. 119. *Every man* being, as has been shewed, *naturally free,* and nothing being able to put him into subjection to any earthly power, but only his own *consent;* it is to be considered, what shall be understood to be a *sufficient declaration* of a man's *consent, to make him subject* to the laws of any government. There is a common distinction of an express and a tacit consent,
40 which will concern our present case. No body doubts but an express *consent,* of

any man entering into any society, makes him a perfect member of that society, a subject of that government. The difficulty is, what ought to be looked upon as a *tacit consent,* and how far it binds, *i. e.* how far any one shall be looked on to have consented, and thereby submitted to any government, where he has made
5   no expressions of it at all. And to this I say, that every man, that hath any possessions, or enjoyment, of any part of the dominions of any government, doth thereby give his *tacit consent,* and is as far forth obliged to obedience to the laws of that government, during such enjoyment, as any one under it; whether this his possession be of land, to him and his heirs for ever, or a lodging only for
10   a week; or whether it be barely travelling freely on the highway; and in effect, it reaches as far as the very being of any one within the territories of that government.

      §. 120. To understand this the better, it is fit to consider, that every man, when he at first incorporates himself into any common-wealth, he, by his uniting
15   himself thereunto, annexed also, and submits to the community, those possessions, which he has, or shall acquire, that do not already belong to any other government: for it would be a direct contradiction, for any one to enter into society with others for the securing and regulating of property; and yet to suppose his land, whose property is to be regulated by the laws of the society,
20   should be exempt from the jurisdiction of that government, to which he himself, the proprietor of the land, is a subject. By the same act therefore, whereby any one unites his person, which was before free, to any common-wealth; by the same he unites his possessions, which were before free, to it also; and they become, both of them, person and possession, subject to the government and
25   dominion of that common-wealth, as long as it hath a being. Whoever therefore, from thenceforth, by inheritance, purchase, permission, or otherways, *enjoys any part of the land,* so annexed to, and under the government *of that common-wealth, must take it with the condition* it is under; that is, *of submitting to the government of the common-wealth,* under whose jurisdiction it is, as far forth as
30   any subject of it.

      §. 121. But since the government has a direct jurisdiction only over the land, and reaches the possessor of it, (before he has actually incorporated himself in the society) only as he dwells upon, and enjoys that; the obligation any one is under, by virtue of such enjoyment, to *submit to the government,*
35   *begins and ends with the enjoyment;* so that whenever the owner, who has given nothing but such a *tacit consent* to the government, will, by donation, sale, or otherwise, quit the said possession, he is at liberty to go and incorporate himself into any other common-wealth; or to agree with others to begin a new one, *in vacuis locis,* in any part of the world, they can find free and unpossessed:
40   whereas he, that has once, by actual agreement, and any *express* declaration,

given his *consent* to be of any common-wealth, is, perpetually and indispensibly obliged to be, and remain unalterably a subject to it, and can never be again in the liberty of the state of nature; unless, by any calamity, the government he was under comes to be dissolved; or else by some public act cuts him off from being any longer a member of it.

5

§. *122.* But submitting to the laws of any country, living quietly, and enjoying privileges and protection under them, *makes not a man a member of that society:* this is only a local protection and homage due to and from all those, who, not being in a state of war, come within the territories belonging to any government, to all parts whereof the force of its laws extends. But this no more *makes a man a member of that society,* a perpetual subject of that common-wealth, than it would make a man a subject to another, in whose family he found it convenient to abide for some time; though, whilst he continued in it, he were obliged to comply with the laws, and submit to the government he found there. And thus we see, that *foreigners,* by living all their lives under another government, and enjoying the privileges and protection of it, though they are bound, even in conscience, to submit to its administration, as far forth as any denison; yet do not thereby come to be *subjects or members of that common-wealth.* Nothing can make any man so, but his actually entering into it by positive engagement, and express promise and compact. This is that, which I think, concerning the beginning of political societies, and that *consent which makes any one a member* of any common-wealth.

10

15

20

CHAPTER IX.
Of the Ends of Political Society and Government.

§. *123.* IF man in the state of nature be so free, as has been said; if he be absolute lord of his own person and possessions, equal to the greatest, and subject to no body, why will he part with his freedom? why will he give up this empire, and subject himself to the dominion and controul of any other power? To which it is obvious to answer, that though in the state of nature he hath such a right, yet the enjoyment of it is very uncertain, and constantly exposed to the invasion of others: for all being kings as much as he, every man his equal, and the greater part no strict observers of equity and justice, the enjoyment of the property he has in this state is very unsafe, very unsecure. This makes him willing to quit a condition, which, however free, is full of fears and continual dangers: and it is not without reason, that he seeks out, and is willing to join in society with others, who are already united, or have a mind to unite, for the mutual *preservation* of their lives, liberties and estates, which I call by the general name, *property.*

25

30

35

§. 124. The great and *chief end,* therefore, of men's uniting into common-wealths, and putting themselves under government, *is the preservation of their property.* To which in the state of nature there are many things wanting.

First, There wants an *established,* settled, known *law,* received and allowed
5   by common consent to be the standard of right and wrong, and the common measure to decide all controversies between them: for though the law of nature be plain and intelligible to all rational creatures; yet men being biassed by their interest, as well as ignorant for want of study of it, are not apt to allow of it as a law binding to them in the application of it to their particular cases.

10   *§. 125. Secondly,* In the state of nature there wants *a known and indifferent judge,* with authority to determine all differences according to the established law: for every one in that state being both judge and executioner of the law of nature, men being partial to themselves, passion and revenge is very apt to carry them too far, and with too much heat, in their own cases; as well as negligence,
15   and unconcernedness, to make them too remiss in other men's.

§. 126. Thirdly, In the state of nature there often wants *power* to back and support the sentence when right, and to *give* it due *execution.* They who by any injustice offended, will seldom fail, where they are able, by force to make good their injustice; such resistance many times makes the punishment dangerous,
20   and frequently destructive, to those who attempt it.

§. 127. Thus mankind, notwithstanding all the privileges of the state of nature, being but in an ill condition, while they remain in it, are quickly driven into society. Hence it comes to pass, that we seldom find any number of men live any time together in this state. The inconveniencies that they are therein
25   exposed to, by the irregular and uncertain exercise of the power every man has of punishing the transgressions of others, make them take sanctuary under the established laws of government, and therein seek *the preservation of their property.* It is this makes them so willingly give up every one his single power of punishing, to be exercised by such alone, as shall be appointed to it amongst
30   them; and by such rules as the community, or those authorized by them to that purpose, shall agree on. And in this we have the original *right and rise of both the legislative and executive power,* as well as of the governments and societies themselves.

§. 128. For in the state of nature, to omit the liberty he has of innocent
35   delights, a man has two powers.

The first is to do whatsoever he thinks fit for the preservation of himself, and others within the permission of the *law of nature:* by which law, common to them all, he and all the rest of *mankind are one community,* make up one society, distinct from all other creatures. And were it not for the corruption and
40   vitiousness of degenerate men, there would be no need of any other; no

necessity that men should separate from this great and natural community, and by positive agreements combine into smaller and divided associations.

The other power a man has in the state of nature, is the *power to punish the crimes* committed against that law. Both these he gives up, when he joins in a private, if I may so call it, or particular politic society, and incorporates into any common-wealth, separate from the rest of mankind.

5

§. 129. The first *power,* viz. *of doing whatsoever be thought for the preservation of himself,* and the rest of mankind, *he gives up* to be regulated by laws made by the society, so far forth as the preservation of himself, and the rest of that society shall require; which laws of the society in many things confine the liberty he had by the law of nature.

10

§. 130. Secondly, The *power of punishing he wholly gives up,* and engages his natural force, (which he might before employ in the execution of the law of nature, by his own single authority, as he thought fit) to assist the executive power of the society, as the law thereof shall require: for being now in a new state, wherein he is to enjoy many conveniencies, from the labour, assistance, and society of others in the same community, as well as protection from its whole strength; he is to part also with as much of his natural liberty, in providing for himself, as the good, prosperity, and safety of the society shall require; which is not only necessary, but just, since the other members of the society do the like.

15

20

§. 131. But though men, when they enter into society, give up the equality, liberty, and executive power they had in the state of nature, into the hands of the society, to be so far disposed of by the legislative, as the good of the society shall require; yet it being only with an intention in every one the better to preserve himself, his liberty and property; (for no rational creature can be supposed to change his condition with an intention to be worse) the power of the society, or *legislative* constituted by them, can *never be supposed to extend farther, than the common good;* but is obliged to secure every one's property, by providing against those three defects above mentioned, that made the state of nature so unsafe and uneasy. And so whoever has the legislative or supreme power of any common-wealth, is bound to govern by established *standing laws,* promulgated and known to the people, and not by extemporary decrees; by *indifferent* and upright *judges,* who are to decide controversies by those laws; and to employ the force of the community at home, *only in the execution of such laws,* or abroad to prevent or redress foreign injuries, and secure the community from inroads and invasion. And all this to be directed to no other *end,* but the *peace, safety,* and *public good* of the people.

25

30

35

CHAPTER X.
Of the Forms of a Common-wealth.

§. 132. THE majority having, as has been shewed, upon men's first uniting into society, the whole power of the community naturally in them, may employ all that power in making laws for the community from time to time, and executing those laws by officers of their own appointing; and then the *form* of
5   the government is a perfect *democracy:* or else may put the power of making laws into the hands of a few select men, and their heirs or successors; and then it is an *oligarchy:* or else into the hands of one man, and then it is a *monarchy:* if to him and his heirs, it is an *hereditary monarchy:* if to him only for life, but upon his death the power only of nominating a successor to return to them; an
10 *elective monarchy.* And so accordingly of these the community may make compounded and mixed forms of government, as they think good. And if the legislative power be at first given by the majority to one or more persons only for their lives, or any limited time, and then the supreme power to revert to them again; when it is so reverted, the community may dispose of it again anew into
15 what hands they please, and so constitute a new form of government: for the *form of government depending upon the placing the* supreme power, which is *the legislative,* it being impossible to conceive that an inferior power should prescribe to a superior, or any but the supreme make laws, according as the power of making laws is placed, such is the *form of the common-wealth.*
20 *§. 133.* By *common-wealth,* I must be understood all along to mean, not a democracy, or any form of government, but *any independent community,* which the *Latines* signified by the word *civitas,* to which the word which best answers in our language, is *common-wealth,* and most properly expresses such a society of men, which community or city in *English* does not; for there may be
25 subordinate communities in a government; and city amongst us has a quite different notion from common-wealth: and therefore, to avoid ambiguity, I crave leave to use the word *common-wealth* in that sense, in which I find it used by king *James the first;* and I take it to be its genuine signification; which if any body dislike, I consent with him to change it for a better.

CHAPTER XI.
Of the Extent of the Legislative Power.

30 *§. 134.* THE great end of men's entering into society, being the enjoyment of their properties in peace and safety, and the great instrument and means of that being the laws established in that society; the *first and fundamental positive law* of all common-wealths *is the establishing of the legislative* power; as the *first and fundamental natural law,* which is to govern even the legislative itself,

is the preservation of the society, and (as far as will consist with the public good) of every person in it. This *legislative* is not only *the supreme power* of the common-wealth, but sacred and unalterable in the hands where the community have once placed it; nor can any edict of any body else, in what form soever

5   conceived, or by what power soever backed, have the force and obligation of a *law,* which has not its *sanction from* that *legislative* which the public has chosen and appointed: for without this the law could not have that, which is absolutely necessary to its being a *law,** *the consent of the society,* over whom no body can have a power to make laws, but by their own consent, and by authority received

10   from them; and therefore all the *obedience,* which by the most solemn ties any one can be obliged *to* pay, ultimately terminates in this *supreme power,* and is directed by those laws which it enacts: nor can any oaths to any foreign power whatsoever, or any domestic subordinate power, discharge any member of the society from his *obedience to the legislative,* acting pursuant to their trust; nor

15   oblige him to any obedience contrary to the laws so enacted, or farther than they do allow; it being ridiculous to imagine one can be tied ultimately to *obey* any *power* in the society, which is not the *supreme.*

    §. 135. Though the *legislative,* whether placed in one or more, whether it be always in being, or only by intervals, though it be the *supreme* power in

20   every common-wealth; yet,

    First, It is *not,* nor can possibly be absolutely *arbitrary* over the lives and fortunes of the people: for it being but the joint power of every member of the society given up to that person, or assembly, which is legislator; it can be no more than those persons had in a state of nature before they entered into society,

25   and gave up to the community: for no body can transfer to another more power than he has in himself; and no body has an absolute arbitrary power over himself, or over any other, to destroy his own life, or take away the life or property of another. A man, as has been proved, cannot subject himself to the arbitrary power of another; and having in the state of nature no arbitrary power

30   over the life, liberty, or possession of another, but only so much as the law of nature gave him for the preservation of himself, and the rest of mankind; this is all he doth, or can give up to the common-wealth, and by it to the *legislative power,* so that the legislative can have no more than this. Their power, in the utmost bounds of it, is *limited to the public good* of the society. It is a power,

35   that hath no other end but preservation, and therefore can never* have a right to destroy, enslave, or designedly to impoverish the subjects. The obligations of the law of nature cease not in society, but only in many cases are drawn closer, and have by human laws known penalties annexed to them, to inforce their observation. Thus the law of nature stands as an eternal rule to all men,

40   *legislators* as well as others. The *rules* that they make for other men's actions,

must, as well as their own and other men's actions, be conformable to the law of nature, *i. e.* to the will of God, of which that is a declaration, and the *fundamental law of nature being the preservation of mankind,* no human sanction can be good, or valid against it.

5   *§. 136. Secondly,** The *legislative,* or supreme authority, cannot assume to its self a power to rule by extemporary arbitrary decrees, but *is bound to dispense justice,* and decide the rights of the subject *by promulgated standing laws, and known authorized judges:* for the law of nature being unwritten, and so no where to be found but in the minds of men, they who through passion or
10   interest shall miscite, or misapply it, cannot so easily be convinced of their mistake where there is no established judge: and so it serves not, as it ought, to determine the rights, and fence the properties of those that live under it, especially where every one is judge, interpreter, and executioner of it too, and that in his own case: and he that has right on his side, having ordinarily but his
15   own single strength, hath not force enough to defend himself from injuries, or to punish delinquents. To avoid these inconveniencies, which disorder men's properties in the state of nature, men unite into societies, that they may have the united strength of the whole society to secure and defend their properties, and may have *standing rules* to bound it, by which every one may know what is his.
20   To this end it is that men give up all their natural power to the society which they enter into, and the community put the legislative power into such hands as they think fit, with this trust, that they shall be governed by *declared laws,* or else their peace, quiet, and property will still be at the same uncertainty, as it was in the state of nature.

25   *§. 137.* Absolute arbitrary power, or governing without *settled standing laws,* can neither of them consist with the ends of society and government, which men would not quit the freedom of the state of nature for, and tie themselves up under, were it not to preserve their lives, liberties and fortunes, and by *stated rules* of right and property to secure their peace and quiet. It
30   cannot be supposed that they should intend, had they a power so to do, to give to any one, or more, an *absolute arbitrary power* over their persons and estates, and put a force into the magistrate's hand to execute his unlimited will arbitrarily upon them. This were to put themselves into a worse condition than the state of nature, wherein they had a liberty to defend their right against the
35   injuries of others, and were upon equal terms of force to maintain it, whether invaded by a single man, or many in combination. Whereas by supposing they have given up themselves to the *absolute arbitrary power* and will of a legislator, they have disarmed themselves, and armed him, to make a prey of them when he pleases; he being in a much worse condition, who is exposed to
40   the arbitrary power of one man, who has the command of 100,000, than he that

is exposed to the arbitrary power of 100,000 single men; no body being secure, that his will, who has such a command, is better than that of other men, though his force be 100,000 times stronger. And therefore, whatever form the commonwealth is under, the ruling power ought to govern by *declared* and
5   *received laws,* and nor by extemporary dictates and undetermined resolutions: for then mankind will be in a far worse condition than in the state of nature, if they shall have armed one, or a few men with the joint power of a multitude, to force them to obey at pleasure the exorbitant and unlimited decrees of their sudden thoughts, or unrestrained, and till that moment unknown wills, without
10 having any measures set down which may guide and justify their actions: for all the power the government has, being only for the good of the society, as it ought not to be *arbitrary* and at pleasure, so it ought to be exercised by *established and promulgated laws;* that both the people may know their duty, and be safe and secure within the limits of the law; and the rulers too kept within their bounds,
15 and not be tempted, by the power they have in their hands, to employ it to such purposes, and by such measures, as they would not have known, and own not willingly.

§. *138. Thirdly,* The *supreme power cannot take* from any man any part of his *property* without his own consent: for the preservation of property being the
20 end of government, and that for which men enter into society, it necessarily supposes and requires, that the people should *have property,* without which they must be supposed to lose that, by entering into society, which was the end for which they entered into it; too gross an absurdity for any man to own. *Men therefore in society having property,* they have such a right to the goods, which
25 by the law of the community are their's, that no body hath a right to take their substance or any part of it from them, without their own consent: without this they have no *property* at all; for I have truly no *property* in that, which another can by right take from me, when he pleases, against my consent. Hence it is a mistake to think, that the *supreme or legislative power* of any common-wealth,
30 can do what it will, and dispose of the estates of the subject *arbitrarily,* or take any part of them at pleasure. This is not much to be feared in governments where the *legislative* consists, wholly or in part, in assemblies which are variable, whose members, upon the dissolution of the assembly, are subjects under the common laws of their country, equally with the rest. But in
35 governments, where the *legislative* is in one lasting assembly always in being, or in one man, as in absolute monarchies, there is danger still, that they will think themselves to have a distinct interest from the rest of the community; and so will be apt to increase their own riches and power, by taking what they think fit from the people: for a man's *property* is not at all secure, tho' there be good and
40 equitable laws to set the bounds of it between him and his fellow subjects, if he

who commands those subjects have power to take from any private man, what part he pleases of his *property,* and use and dispose of it as he thinks good.

§. *139.* But *government,* into whatsoever hands it is put, being, as I have before shewed, intrusted with this condition, and *for this end,* that men might
5   have and secure their *properties;* the prince, or senate, however it may have power to make laws, for the regulating of *property* between the subjects one amongst another, yet can never have a power to take to themselves the whole, or any part of the subjects *property,* without their own consent: for this would be in effect to leave them no *property* at all. And to let us see, that even *absolute*
10 *power,* where it is necessary, is *not arbitrary* by being absolute, but is still limited by that reason, and confined to those ends, which required it in some cases to be absolute, we need look no farther than the common practice of martial discipline: for the preservation of the army, and in it of the whole common-wealth, requires an *absolute obedience* to the command of every
15 superior officer, and it is justly death to disobey or dispute the most dangerous or unreasonable of them; but yet we see, that neither the serjeant, that could command a soldier to march up to the mouth of a cannon, or stand in a breach, where he is almost sure to perish, can command that soldier to give him one penny of his money; nor the *general,* that can condemn him to death for
20 deserting his post, or for not obeying the most desperate orders, can yet, with all his *absolute power* of life and death, dispose of one farthing of that soldier's estate, or seize one jot of his goods; whom yet he can command any thing, and hang for the least disobedience; because such a blind obedience is necessary to that end, for which the commander has his power, *viz.* the preservation of the
25 rest; but the disposing of his goods has nothing to do with it.

§. *140.* It is true, governments cannot be supported without great charge, and it is fit every one who enjoys his share of the protection, should pay out of his estate his proportion for the maintenance of it. But still it must be with his own consent, *i. e.* the consent of the majority, giving it either by themselves, or
30 their representatives chosen by them: for if any one shall claim a *power to lay* and levy *taxes* on the people, by his own authority, and without such consent of the people, he thereby invades the *fundamental law of property,* and subverts the end of government: for what property have I in that, which another may by right take, when he pleases, to himself?

35 §. *141. Fourthly,* The *legislative cannot transfer the power of making laws* to any other hands: for it being but a delegated power from the people, they who have it cannot pass it over to others. The people alone can appoint the form of the common-wealth, which is by constituting the legislative, and appointing in whose hands that shall be. And when the people have said, We will submit to
40 rules, and be governed by *laws* made by such men, and in such forms, no body

else can say other men shall make *laws* for them; nor can the people be bound by any *laws*, but such as are enacted by those whom they have chosen, and authorized to make *laws* for them. The power of the *legislative*, being derived from the people by a positive voluntary grant and institution, can be no other
5 than what that positive grant conveyed, which being only to make *laws*, and not to make *legislators*, the *legislative* can have no power to transfer their authority of making laws, and place it in other hands.

§. 142. These are the *bounds* which the trust, that is put in them by the society, and the law of God and nature, have *set to the legislative* power of every
10 common-wealth, in all forms of government.

First, They are to govern by *promulgated established laws*, not to be varied in particular cases, but to have one rule for rich and poor, for the favourite at court, and the country man at plough.

Secondly, These *laws* also ought to be designed *for* no other end ultimately,
15 but *the good of the people.*

Thirdly, They must *not raise taxes* on the *property of the people, without the consent of the people,* given by themselves, or their deputies. And this properly concerns only such governments where the *legislative* is always in being, or at least where the people have not reserved any part of the legislative
20 to deputies, to be from time to time chosen by themselves.

Fourthly, The *legislative* neither must *nor can transfer the power of making laws* to any body else, or place it any where, but where the people have.

CHAPTER XII.
Of the Legislative, Executive, and Federative Power of the Common-wealth.

§. 143. THE *legislative* power is that, which has a right *to direct how the force of the common-wealth* shall be employed for preserving the community
25 and the members of it. But because those laws which are constantly to be executed, and whose force is always to continue, may be made in a little time; therefore there is no need, that the *legislative* should be always in being, not having always business to do. And because it may be too great a temptation to human frailty, apt to grasp at power, for the same persons, who have the power
30 of making laws, to have also in their hands the power to execute them, whereby they may exempt themselves from obedience to the laws they make, and suit the law, both in its making, and execution, to their own private advantage, and thereby come to have a distinct interest from the rest of the community, contrary to the end of society and government: therefore in well-ordered common-
35 wealths, where the good of the whole is so considered, as it ought, the *legislative* power is put into the hands of divers persons, who duly assembled, have by

themselves, or jointly with others, a power to make laws, which when they have done, being separated again, they are themselves subject to the laws they have made; which is a new and near tie upon them, to take care, that they make them for the public good.

5   *§. 144.* But because the laws, that are at once, and in a short time made, have a constant and lasting force, and need a *perpetual execution,* or an attendance thereunto; therefore it is necessary there should be a *power always in being,* which should see to the *execution* of the laws that are made, and remain in force. And thus the *legislative* and *executive power* come often to be

10 separated.

    §. 145. There is another *power* in every common-wealth, which one may call *natural,* because it is that which answers to the power every man naturally had before he entered into society: for though in a common-wealth the members of it are distinct persons still in reference to one another, and as such are

15 governed by the laws of the society; yet in reference to the rest of mankind, they make one body, which is, as every member of it before was, still in the state of nature with the rest of mankind. Hence it is, that the controversies that happen between any man of the society with those that are out of it, are managed by the public; and an injury done to a member of their body, engages the whole in the

20 reparation of it. So that under this consideration, the whole community is one body in the state of nature, in respect of all other states or persons out of its community.

    §. 146. This therefore contains the power of war and peace, leagues and alliances, and all the transactions, with all persons and communities without the

25 common-wealth, and may be called *federative,* if any one pleases. So the thing be understood, I am indifferent as to the name.

    §. 147. These two powers, *executive* and *federative,* though they be really distinct in themselves, yet one comprehending the *execution* of the municipal laws of the society *within* its self, upon all that are parts of it; the other the

30 management of the *security and interest of the public without,* with all those that it may receive benefit or damage from, yet they are always almost united. And though this *federative power* in the well or ill management of it be of great moment to the common-wealth, yet it is much less capable to be directed by antecedent, standing, positive laws, than the *executive;* and so must necessarily

35 be left to the prudence and wisdom of those, whose hands it is in, to be managed for the public good: for the *laws* that concern subjects one amongst another, being to direct their actions, may well enough *precede* them. But what is to be done in reference to *foreigners,* depending much upon their actions, and the variation of designs and interests, must be *left* in great part *to* the *prudence* of

those, who have this power committed to them, to be managed by the best of their skill, for the advantage of the common-wealth.

§. 148. Though, as I said, the *executive* and *federative power* of every community be really distinct in themselves, yet they are hardly to be separated, and placed at the same time, in the hands of distinct persons: for both of them requiring the force of the society for their exercise, it is almost impracticable to place the force of the common-wealth in distinct, and not subordinate hands; or that the *executive* and *federative power* should be *placed* in persons, that might act separately, whereby the force of the public would be under different commands: which would be apt some time or other to cause disorder and ruin.

CHAPTER XIII.
Of the Subordination of the Powers of the Common-wealth.

§. 149. THough in a constituted common-wealth, standing upon its own basis, and acting according to its own nature, that is, acting for the preservation of the community, there can be but *one supreme power,* which is *the legislative,* to which all the rest are and must be subordinate, yet the legislative being only a fiduciary power to act for certain ends, there remains still *in the people a supreme power to remove or alter the legislative,* when they find the *legislative* act contrary to the trust reposed in them: for all *power given with trust* for the attaining an *end,* being limited by that end, whenever that *end* is manifestly neglected, or opposed, the *trust* must necessarily be *forfeited,* and the power devolve into the hands of those that gave it, who may place it anew where they shall think best for their safety and security. And thus the *community* perpetually *retains a supreme power* of saving themselves from the attempts and designs of any body, even of their legislators, whenever they shall be so foolish, or so wicked, as to lay and carry on designs against the liberties and properties of the subject: for no man or society of men, having a power to deliver up their *preservation,* or consequently the means of it, to the absolute will and arbitrary dominion of another; when ever any one shall go about to bring them into such a slavish condition, they will always have a right to preserve, what they have not a power to part with; and to rid themselves of those, who invade this fundamental, sacred, and unalterable law of *self-preservation,* for which they entered into society. And thus the *community* may be said in this respect to be *always the supreme power,* but not as considered under any form of government, because this power of the people can never take place till the government be dissolved.

§. 150. In all cases, whilst the government subsists, the *legislative is the supreme power:* for what can give laws to another, must needs be superior to him; and since the legislative is no otherwise legislative of the society, but by the right it has to make laws for all the parts, and for every member of the society, prescribing rules to their actions, and giving power of execution, where they are transgressed, the *legislative* must needs be the *supreme,* and all other powers, in any members or parts of the society, derived from and subordinate to

5 it.

§. 151. In some common-wealths, where the *legislative* is not always in being, and the *executive* is vested in a single person, who has also a share in the legislative; there that single person in a very tolerable sense may also be called *supreme:* not that he has in himself all the supreme power, which is that of law-

10 making; but because he has in him the *supreme execution,* from whom all inferior magistrates derive all their several subordinate powers, or at least the greatest part of them: having also no legislative superior to him, there being no law to be made without his consent, which cannot be expected should ever subject him to the other part of the legislative, *be* is properly enough in this

15 sense *supreme.* But yet it is to be observed, that tho' *oaths of allegiance* and fealty are taken to him, it is not to him as supreme legislator, but as *supreme executor* of the law, made by a joint power of him with others; *allegiance* being nothing but an *obedience according to law,* which when he violates, he has no right to obedience, nor can claim it otherwise than as the public person vested

20 with the power of the law, and so is to be considered as the image, phantom, or representative of the common-wealth, acted by the will of the society, declared in its laws; and thus he has no will, no power, but that of the law. But when he quits this representation, this public will, and acts by his own private will, he degrades himself, and is but a single private person without power, and without

25 will, that has any right to *obedience;* the members owing no *obedience* but to the public will of the society.

§. 152. The *executive power,* placed any where but in a person that has also a share in the legislative, is visibly subordinate and accountable to it, and may be at pleasure changed and displaced; so that it is not the *supreme executive power,*

30 that is exempt from *subordination,* but the *supreme executive power* vested in one, who having a share in the legislative, has no distinct superior legislative to be subordinate and accountable to, farther than he himself shall join and consent; so that he is no more subordinate than he himself shall think fit, which one may certainly conclude will be but very little. Of other *ministerial and*

35 *subordinate powers* in a common-wealth, we need not speak, they being so multiplied with infinite variety, in the different customs and constitutions of distinct common-wealths, that it is impossible to give a particular account of them all. Only thus much, which is necessary to our present purpose, we may take notice of concerning them, that they have no manner of authority, any of

them, beyond what is by positive grant and commission delegated to them, and are all of them accountable to some other power in the common-wealth.

§. 153. It is not necessary, no, nor so much as convenient, that the *legislative* should be *always in being;* but absolutely necessary that the executive power should, because there is not always need of new laws to be made, but always need of execution of the laws that are made. When the *legislative* hath put the *execution* of the laws, they make, into other hands, they have a power still to resume it out of those hands, when they find cause, and to punish for any mal-administration against the laws. The same holds also in regard of the *federative* power, that and the *executive* being both *ministerial* and *subordinate to the legislative,* which, as has been shewed, in a constituted common-wealth is the supreme. The *legislative* also in this case being supposed to consist of several persons, (for if it be a single person, it cannot but be always in being, and so will, as supreme, naturally have the supreme executive power, together with the legislative) may *assemble, and exercise their legislature,* at the times that either their original constitution, or their own adjournment, appoints, or when they please; if neither of these hath appointed any time, or there be no other way prescribed to convoke them: for the supreme power being placed in them by the people, it is always in them, and they may exercise it when they please, unless by their original constitution they are limited to certain seasons, or by an act of their supreme power they have adjourned to a certain time; and when that time comes, they have a right to *assemble* and act again.

§. 154. If the *legislative,* or any part of it, be made up of *representatives* chosen for that time by the people, which afterwards return into the ordinary state of subjects, and have no share in the legislature but upon a new choice, this power of chusing must also be exercised by the people, either at certain appointed seasons, or else when they are summoned to it; and in this latter case, the power of convoking the legislative is ordinarily placed in the executive, and has one of these two limitations in respect of time: that either the original constitution requires their *assembling* and *acting* at certain intervals, and then the executive power does nothing but ministerially issue directions for their electing and assembling, according to due forms; or else it is left to his prudence to call them by new elections, when the occasions or exigencies of the public require the amendment of old, or making of new laws, or the redress or prevention of any inconveniencies, that lie on, or threaten the people.

§. 155. It may be demanded here, What if the executive power, being possessed of the force of the common-wealth, shall make use of that force to hinder the *meeting* and *acting of the legislative,* when the original constitution, or the public exigencies require it? I say, using force upon the people without authority, and contrary to the trust put in him that does so, is a state of war with

the people, who have a right to *reinstate* their *legislative in the exercise* of their power: for having erected a legislative, with an intent they should exercise the power of making laws, either at certain set times, or when there is need of it, when they are hindered by any force from what is so necessary to the society,

5   and wherein the safety and preservation of the people consists, the people have a right to remove it by force. In all states and conditions, the true remedy of *force* without authority, is to oppose *force* to it. The use of *force* without authority, always puts him that uses it into a *state of war,* as the aggressor, and renders him liable to be treated accordingly.

10   *§. 156.* The *power of assembling and dismissing the legislative,* placed in the executive, gives not the executive a superiority over it, but is a fiduciary trust placed in him, for the safety of the people, in a case where the uncertainty and variableness of human affairs could not bear a steady fixed rule: for it not being possible, that the first framers of the government should, by any foresight, be so

15   much masters of future events, as to be able to prefix so just periods of return and duration to the *assemblies of the legislative,* in all times to come, that might exactly answer all the exigencies of the common-wealth; the best remedy could be found for this defect, was to trust this to the prudence of one who was always to be present, and whose business it was to watch over the public good. Constant

20   *frequent meetings of the legislative,* and long continuations of their assemblies, without necessary occasion, could not but be burdensome to the people, and must necessarily in time produce more dangerous inconveniencies, and yet the quick turn of affairs might be sometimes such as to need their present help: any delay of their *convening* might endanger the public; and sometimes too their

25   business might be so great, that the limited time of their sitting might be too short for their work, and rob the public of that benefit which could be had only from their mature deliberation. What then could be done in this case to prevent the community from being exposed some time or other to eminent hazard, on one side or the other, by fixed intervals and periods, set to the *meeting and*

30   *acting of the legislative,* but to intrust it to the prudence of some, who being present, and acquainted with the state of public affairs, might make use of this prerogative for the public good? and where else could this be so well placed as in his hands, who was intrusted with the execution of the laws for the same end? Thus supposing the regulation of times for the *assembling and sitting of the*

35   *legislative,* not settled by the original constitution, it naturally fell into the hands of the executive, not as an arbitrary power depending on his good pleasure, but with this trust always to have it exercised only for the public weal, as the occurrences of times and change of affairs might require. Whether *settled periods of their convening,* or *a liberty* left to the prince for *convoking the*

40   *legislative,* or perhaps a mixture of both, hath the least inconvenience attending

it, it is not my business here to inquire, but only to shew, that though the executive power may have the prerogative of *convoking* and *dissolving* such *conventions of the legislative*, yet it is not thereby superior to it.

§. *157.* Things of this world are in so constant a flux, that nothing remains
5   long in the same state. Thus people, riches, trade, power, change their stations, flourishing mighty cities come to ruin, and prove in times neglected desolate corners, whilst other unfrequented places grow into populous countries, filled with wealth and inhabitants. But things not always changing equally, and private interest often keeping up customs and privileges, when the reasons of them are
10   ceased, it often comes to pass, that in governments, where part of the legislative consists of *representatives* chosen by the people, that in tract of time this *representation* becomes very *unequal* and disproportionate to the reasons it was at first established upon. To what gross absurdities the following of custom, when reason has left it, may lead, we may be satisfied, when we see the bare
15   name of a town, of which there remains not so much as the ruins, where scarce so much housing as a sheepcote, or more inhabitants than a shepherd is to be found, sends *as many representatives* to the grand assembly of law-makers, as a whole county numerous in people, and powerful in riches. This strangers stand amazed at, and every one must confess needs a remedy; tho' most think it hard
20   to find one, because the constitution of the legislative being the original and supreme act of the society, antecedent to all positive laws in it, and depending wholly on the people, no inferior power can alter it. And therefore the *people,* when the *legislative* is once constituted, *having,* in such a government as we have been speaking of, *no power* to act as long as the government stands; this
25   inconvenience is thought incapable of a remedy.

§. *158.* *Salus populi suprema lex,* is certainly so just and fundamental a rule, that he, who sincerely follows it, cannot dangerously err. If therefore the executive, who has the power of convoking the legislative, observing rather the true proportion, than fashion of *representation,* regulates, not by old custom, but
30   true reason, the *number of members,* in all places that have a right to be distinctly represented, which no part of the people however incorporated can pretend to, but in proportion to the assistance which it affords to the public, it cannot be judged to have set up a new legislative, but to have restored the old and true one, and to have rectified the disorders which succession of time had
35   insensibly, as well as inevitably introduced: For it being the interest as well as intention of the people, to have a fair and *equal representative;* whoever brings it nearest to that, is an undoubted friend to, and establisher of the government, and cannot miss the consent and approbation of the community; *prerogative* being nothing but a power, in the hands of the prince, to provide for the public
40   good, in such cases, which depending upon unforeseen and uncertain

occurrences, certain and unalterable laws could not safely direct; whatsoever shall be done manifestly for the good of the people, and the establishing the government upon its true foundations, is, and always will be, just *prerogative.* The power of erecting new corporations, and therewith *new representatives,*

5   carries with it a supposition, that in time the *measures of representation* might vary, and those places have a just right to be represented which before had none; and by the same reason, those cease to have a right, and be too inconsiderable for such a privilege, which before had it. 'Tis not a change from the present state, which perhaps corruption or decay has introduced, that makes an inroad

10   upon the government, but the tendency of it to injure or oppress the people, and to set up one part or party, with a distinction from, and an unequal subjection of the rest. Whatsoever cannot but be acknowledged to be of advantage to the society, and people in general, upon just and lasting measures, will always, when done, justify itself; and whenever the people shall chuse their

15   *representatives upon* just and undeniably *equal measures,* suitable to the original frame of the government, it cannot be doubted to be the will and act of the society, whoever permitted or caused them so to do.

CHAPTER XIV.
Of prerogative.

§. 159. WHERE the legislative and executive power are in distinct hands, (as they are in all moderated monarchies, and well-framed governments) there

20   the good of the society requires, that several things should be left to the discretion of him that has the executive power: for the legislators not being able to foresee, and provide by laws, for all that may be useful to the community, the executor of the laws, having the power in his hands, has by the common law of nature a right to make use of it for the good of the society, in many cases, where

25   the municipal law has given no direction, till the legislative can conveniently be assembled to provide for it. Many things there are, which the law can by no means provide for; and those must necessarily be left to the discretion of him that has the executive power in his hands, to be ordered by him as the public good and advantage shall require: nay, it is fit that the laws themselves should in

30   some cases give way to the executive power, or rather to this fundamental law of nature and government, *viz.* That as much as may be, *all* the members of the society are to be preserved: for since many accidents may happen, wherein a strict and rigid observation of the laws may do harm; (as not to pull down an innocent man's house to stop the fire, when the next to it is burning) and a man

35   may come somtimes within the reach of the law, which makes no distinction of persons, by an action that may deserve reward and pardon; 'tis fit the ruler

should have a power, in many cases, to mitigate the severity of the law, and pardon some offenders: for the *end of government* being *the preservation of all,* as much as may be, even the guilty are to be spared, where it can prove no prejudice to the innocent.

5   *§. 160.* This power to act according to discretion, for the public good, without the prescription of the law, and sometimes even against it, *is* that which is called *prerogative:* for since in some governments the lawmaking power is not always in being, and is usually too numerous, and so too slow, for the dispatch requisite to execution; and because also it is impossible to foresee, and
10   so by laws to provide for, all accidents and necessities that may concern the public, or to make such laws as will do no harm, if they are executed with an inflexible rigour, on all occasions, and upon all persons that may come in their way; therefore there is a latitude left to the executive power, to do many things of choice which the laws do not prescribe.

15   *§. 161.* This power, whilst employed for the benefit of the community, and suitably to the trust and ends of the government, *is undoubted prerogative,* and never is questioned: for the people are very seldom or never scrupulous or nice in the point; they are far from examining *prerogative,* whilst it is in any tolerable degree employed for the use it was meant, that is, for the good of the people, and
20   not manifestly against it: but if there comes to be a *question* between the executive power and the people, about a thing claimed as a *prerogative;* the tendency of the exercise of such *prerogative* to the good or hurt of the people, will easily decide that question.

    §. 162. It is easy to conceive, that in the infancy of governments, when
25   commonwealths differed little from families in number of people, they differed from them too but little in number of laws: and the governors, being as the fathers of them, watching over them for their good, the government was almost all *prerogative.* A few established laws served the turn, and the discretion and care of the ruler supplied the rest. But when mistake or flattery prevailed with
30   weak princes to make use of this power for private ends of their own, and not for the public good, the people were fain by express laws to get prerogative determined in those points wherein they found disadvantage from it: and thus declared *limitations of prerogative* were by the people found necessary in cases which they and their ancestors had left, in the utmost latitude, to the wisdom of
35   those princes who made no other but a right use of it, that is, for the good of their people.

    §. 163. And therefore they have a very wrong notion of government, who say, that the people have *incroached upon the prerogative,* when they have got any part of it to be defined by positive laws: for in so doing they have not pulled
40   from the prince any thing that of right belonged to him, but only declared, that

that power which they indefinitely left in his or his ancestors hands, to be exercised for their good, was not a thing which they intended him when he used it otherwise: for the end of government being the good of the community, whatsoever alterations are made in it, tending to that end, cannot be an
5 *incroachment* upon any body, since no body in government can have a right tending to any other end: and those only are *incroachments* which prejudice or hinder the public good. Those who say otherwise, speak as if the prince had a distinct and separate interest from the good of the community, and was not made for it; the root and source from which spring almost all those evils and disorders
10 which happen in kingly governments. And indeed, if that be so, the people under his government are not a society of rational creatures, entered into a community for their mutual good; they are not such as have set rulers over themselves, to guard, and promote that good; but are to be looked on as an herd of inferior creatures under the dominion of a master, who keeps them and works them for
15 his own pleasure or profit. If men were so void of reason, and brutish, as to enter into society upon such terms, *prerogative* might indeed be, what some men would have it, an arbitrary power to do things hurtful to the people.

§. 164. But since a rational creature cannot be supposed, when free, to put himself into subjection to another, for his own harm; (though, where he finds a
20 good and wise ruler, he may not perhaps think it either necessary or useful to set precise bounds to his power in all things) *prerogative* can be nothing but the people's permitting their rulers to do several things, of their own free choice, where the law was silent, and sometimes too against the direct letter of the law, for the public good; and their acquiescing in it when so done: for as a good
25 prince, who is mindful of the trust put into his hands, and careful of the good of his people, cannot have too much *prerogative,* that is, power to do good; so a weak and ill prince, who would claim that power which his predecessors exercised without the direction of the law, as a prerogative belonging to him by right of his office, which he may exercise at his pleasure, to make or promote an
30 interest distinct from that of the public, gives the people an occasion to claim their right, and limit that power, which, whilst it was exercised for their good, they were content should be tacitly allowed.

§. 165. And therefore he that will look into the *history of England,* will find, that *prerogative* was always *largest* in the hands of our wisest and best
35 princes; because the people, observing the whole tendency of their actions to be the public good, contested not what was done without law to that end: or, if any human frailty or mistake (for princes are but men, made as others) appeared in some small declinations from that end; yet 'twas visible, the main of their conduct tended to nothing but the care of the public. The people therefore,
40 finding reason to be satisfied with these princes, whenever they acted without, or

contrary to the letter of the law, acquiesced in what they did, and, without the least complaint, let them inlarge their *prerogative* as they pleased, judging rightly, that they did nothing herein to the prejudice of their laws, since they acted conformable to the foundation and end of all laws, the public good.

5   *§. 166.* Such god-like princes indeed had some title to arbitrary power by that argument, that would prove absolute monarchy the best government, as that which God himself governs the universe by; because such kings partake of his wisdom and goodness. Upon this is founded that saying, That the reigns of good princes have been always most dangerous to the liberties of their people: for
10   when their successors, managing the government with different thoughts, would draw the actions of those good rulers into precedent, and make them the standard of their *prerogative,* as if what had been done only for the good of the people was a right in them to do, for the harm of the people, if they so pleased; it has often occasioned contest, and sometimes public disorders, before the people
15   could recover their original right, and get that to be declared not to be *prerogative,* which truly was never so; since it is impossible that any body in the society should ever have a right to do the people harm; though it be very possible, and reasonable, that the people should not go about to set any bounds to the *prerogative* of those kings, or rulers, who themselves transgressed not the
20   bounds of the public good: for *prerogative is nothing but the power of doing public good without a rule.*

    §. 167. The power of *calling parliaments* in *England,* as to precise time, place, and duration, is certainly a *prerogative* of the king, but still with this trust, that it shall be made use of for the good of the nation, as the exigencies of the
25   times, and variety of occasions, shall require: for it being impossible to foresee which should always be the fittest place for them to assemble in, and what the best season; the choice of these was left with the executive power, as might be most subservient to the public good, and best suit the ends of parliaments.

    §. 168. The old question will be asked in this matter of *prerogative,* But
30   *who shall be judge* when this power is made a right use of? I answer: between an executive power in being, with such a prerogative, and a legislative that depends upon his will for their convening, there can be no *judge on earth;* as there can be none between the legislative and the people, should either the executive, or the legislative, when they have got the power in their hands, design, or go about to
35   enslave or destroy them. The people have no other remedy in this, as in all other cases where they have no judge on earth, but to *appeal to heaven:* for the rulers, in such attempts, exercising a power the people never put into their hands, (who can never be supposed to consent that any body should rule over them for their harm) do that which they have not a right to do. And where the body of the
40   people, or any single man, is deprived of their right, or is under the exercise of a

power without right, and have no appeal on earth, then they have a liberty to appeal to heaven, whenever they judge the cause of sufficient moment. And therefore, though the *people cannot* be *judge,* so as to have, by the constitution of that society, any superior power, to determine and give effective sentence in

5 the case; yet they have, by a law antecedent and paramount to all positive laws of men, reserved that ultimate determination to themselves which belongs to all mankind, where there lies no appeal on earth, *viz.* to judge, whether they have just cause to make their appeal to heaven. And this judgment they cannot part with, it being out of a man's power so to submit himself to another, as to give

10 him a liberty to destroy him; God and nature never allowing a man so to abandon himself, as to neglect his own preservation: and since he cannot take away his own life, neither can he give another power to take it. Nor let any one think, this lays a perpetual foundation for disorder; for this operates not, till the inconveniency is so great, that the majority feel it, and are weary of it, and find a

15 necessity to have it amended. But this the executive power, or wise princes, never need come in the danger of: and it is the thing, of all others, they have most need to avoid, as of all others the most perilous.

CHAPTER XV.
Of Paternal, Political, and Despotical Power, considered together.

§. 169. THOUGH I have had occasion to speak of these separately before, yet the great mistakes of late about government, having, as I suppose, arisen

20 from confounding these distinct powers one with another, it may not, perhaps, be amiss to consider them here together.

§. 170. First, then, *Paternal* or *parental power* is nothing but that which parents have over their children, to govern them for the children's good, till they come to the use of reason, or a state of knowledge, wherein they may be

25 supposed capable to understand that rule, whether it be the law of nature, or the municipal law of their country, they are to govern themselves by: capable, I say, to know it, as well as several others, who live as freemen under that law. The affection and tenderness which God hath planted in the breast of parents towards their children, makes it evident, that this is not intended to be a severe arbitrary

30 government, but only for the help, instruction, and preservation of their offspring. But happen it as it will, there is, as I have proved, no reason why it should be thought to extend to life and death, at any time, over their children, more than over any body else; neither can there be any pretence why this *parental power* should keep the child, when grown to a man, in subjection to the

35 will of his parents, any farther than having received life and education from his parents, obliges him to respect, honour, gratitude, assistance and support, all his

life, to both father and mother. And thus, 'tis true, the *paternal* is a natural *government,* but not at all extending itself to the ends and jurisdictions of that which is political. The *power of the father doth not reach* at all to the *property* of the child, which is only in his own disposing.

5   *§. 171. Secondly, Political power* is that power, which every man having in the state of nature, has given up into the hands of the society, and therein to the governors, whom the society hath set over itself, with this express or tacit trust, that it shall be employed for their good, and the preservation of their property: now this *power,* which every man has *in the state of nature,* and which he parts
10   with to the society in all such cases where the society can secure him, is to use such means, for the preserving of his own property, as he thinks good, and nature allows him; and to punish the breach of the law of nature in others, so as (according to the best of his reason) may most conduce to the preservation of himself, and the rest of mankind. So that the *end and measure of this power,*
15   when in every man's hands in the state of nature, being the preservation of all of his society, that is, all mankind in general, it can have no other *end or measure,* when in the hands of the magistrate, but to preserve the members of that society in their lives, liberties, and possessions; and so cannot be an absolute, arbitrary power over their lives and fortunes, which are as much as possible to be
20   preserved; but a *power to make laws,* and annex such *penalties* to them, as may tend to the preservation of the whole, by cutting off those parts, and those only, which are so corrupt, that they threaten the sound and healthy, without which no severity is lawful. And this *power has its original only from compact* and agreement, and the mutual consent of those who make up the community.

25   *§. 172. Thirdly, Despotical power* is an absolute, arbitrary power one man has over another, to take away his life, whenever he pleases. This is a power, which neither nature gives, for it has made no such distinction between one man and another; nor compact can convey: for man not having such an arbitrary power over his own life, cannot give another man such a power over it; but it is
30   the *effect only of forfeiture,* which the aggressor makes of his own life, when he puts himself into the state of war with another: for having quitted reason, which God hath given to be the rule betwixt man and man, and the common bond whereby human kind is united into one fellowship and society; and having renounced the way of peace which that teaches, and made use of the force of
35   war, to compass his unjust ends upon another, where he has no right; and so revolting from his own kind to that of beasts, by making force, which is their's, to be his rule of right, he renders himself liable to be destroyed by the injured person, and the rest of mankind, that will join with him in the execution of justice, as any other wild beast, or noxious brute, with whom mankind can have
40   neither society nor security*. And thus *captives,* taken in a just and lawful war,

and such only, are *subject to a despotical power,* which, as it arises not from compact, so neither is it capable of any, but is the state of war continued: for what compact can be made with a man that is not master of his own life? what condition can he perform? and if he be once allowed to be master of his own

5   life, the *despotical, arbitrary power* of his master ceases. He that is master of himself, and his own life, has a right too to the means of preserving it; so that *as soon as compact enters, slavery ceases,* and he so far quits his absolute power, and puts an end to the state of war, who enters into conditions with his captive.

    §. 173. Nature gives the first of these, *viz. paternal power to parents* for the

10   benefit of their children during their minority, to supply their want of ability, and understanding how to manage their property. (By *property* I must be understood here, as in other places, to mean that property which men have in their persons as well as goods.) *Voluntary agreement gives* the second, *viz. political power to governors* for the benefit of their subjects, to secure them in

15   the possession and use of their properties. And *forfeiture gives* the third *despotical power to lords* for their own benefit, over those who are stripped of all property.

    §. 174. He, that shall consider the distinct rise and extent, and the different ends of these several powers, will plainly see, that *paternal power* comes as far

20   short of that of the *magistrate,* as *despotical* exceeds it; and that *absolute dominion,* however placed, is so far from being one kind of civil society, that it is as inconsistent with it, as slavery is with property. *Paternal power* is only where minority makes the child incapable to manage his property; *political,* where men have property in their own disposal; and *despotical,* over such as

25   have no property at all.

CHAPTER XVI.
Of conquest.

    §. 175. THough governments can originally have no other rise than that before mentioned, nor *polities* be *founded on* any thing but *the consent of the people;* yet such have been the disorders ambition has filled the world with, that in the noise of war, which makes so great a part of the history of mankind, *this*

30   *consent* is little taken notice of: and therefore many have mistaken the force of arms for the consent of the people, and reckon conquest as one of the originals of government. But *conquest* is as far from setting up any government, as demolishing an house is from building a new one in the place. Indeed, it often makes way for a new frame of a common-wealth, by destroying the former; but,

35   without the consent of the people, can never erect a new one.

§. 176. That the *aggressor,* who puts himself into the state of war with another, and *unjustly invades* another man's right, *can,* by such an unjust war, *never* come to *have a right over the conquered,* will be easily agreed by all men, who will not think, that robbers and pyrates have a right of empire over

5   whomsoever they have force enough to master; or that men are bound by promises, which unlawful force extorts from them. Should a robber break into my house, and with a dagger at my throat make me seal deeds to convey my estate to him, would this give him any title? Just such a title, by his sword, has an *unjust conqueror,* who forces me into submission. The injury and the crime is

10   equal, whether committed by the wearer of a crown, or some petty villain. The title of the offender, and the number of his followers, make no difference in the offence, unless it be to aggravate it. The only difference is, great robbers punish little ones, to keep them in their obedience; but the great ones are rewarded with laurels and triumphs, because they are too big for the weak hands of justice in

15   this world, and have the power in their own possession, which should punish offenders. What is my remedy against a robber, that so broke into my house? *Appeal* to the law for justice. But perhaps justice is denied, or I am crippled and cannot stir, robbed and have not the means to do it. If God has taken away all means of seeking remedy, there is nothing left but patience. But my son, when

20   able, may seek the relief of the law, which I am denied: he or his son may renew his *appeal,* till he recover his right. But the conquered, or their children, have no court, no arbitrator on earth to appeal to. Then they may *appeal,* as *Jephtha* did, *to heaven,* and repeat their *appeal* till they have recovered the native right of their ancestors, which was, to have such a legislative over them, as the majority

25   should approve, and freely acquiesce in. If it be objected, This would cause endless trouble; I answer, no more than justice does, where she lies open to all that appeal to her. He that troubles his neighbour without a cause, is punished for it by the justice of the court he appeals to: and he that *appeals to heaven* must be sure he has right on his side; and a right too that is worth the trouble and

30   cost of the appeal, as he will answer at a tribunal that cannot be deceived, and will be sure to retribute to every one according to the mischiefs he hath created to his fellow subjects; that is, any part of mankind: from whence it is plain, that he that *conquers in an unjust war can thereby have no title to the subjection and obedience of the conquered.*

35   *§. 177.* But supposing victory favours the right side, let us consider a *conqueror in a lawful war,* and see what power he gets, and over whom.

First, It is plain he *gets no power by his conquest over those that conquered with him.* They that fought on his side cannot suffer by the conquest, but must at least be as much freemen as they were before. And most commonly they serve

40   upon terms, and on condition to share with their leader, and enjoy a part of the

382

spoil, and other advantages that attend the conquering sword; or at least have a part of the subdued country bestowed upon them. And *the conquering people are not, I hope, to be slaves by conquest,* and wear their laurels only to shew they are sacrifices to their leaders triumph. They that found absolute monarchy

5 upon the title of the sword, make their heroes, who are the founders of such monarchies, arrant *Draw-can-sirs,* and forget they had any officers and soldiers that fought on their side in the battles they won, or assisted them in the subduing, or shared in possessing, the countries they mastered. We are told by some, that the *English* monarchy is founded in the *Norman* conquest, and that

10 our princes have thereby a title to absolute dominion: which if it were true, (as by the history it appears otherwise) and that *William* had a right to make war on this island; yet his dominion by conquest could reach no farther than to the *Saxons* and *Britons,* that were then inhabitants of this country. The *Normans* that came with him, and helped to conquer, and all descended from them, are

15 freemen, and no subjects by conquest; let that give what dominion it will. And if I, or any body else, shall claim freedom, as derived from them, it will be very hard to prove the contrary: and it is plain, the law, that has made no distinction between the one and the other, intends not there should be any difference in their freedom or privileges.

20 *§. 178.* But supposing, which seldom happens, that the conquerors and conquered never incorporate into one people, under the same laws and freedom; let us see next *what power a lawful conqueror has over the subdued:* and that I say is purely despotical. He has an absolute power over the lives of those who by an unjust war have forfeited them; but not over the lives or fortunes of those

25 who engaged not in the war, nor over the possessions even of those who were actually engaged in it.

§. 179. Secondly, I say then the *conqueror* gets no power but only over those who have actually assisted, concurred, or consented to that unjust force that is used against him: for the people having given to their governors no power

30 to do an unjust thing, such as is to make an unjust war, (for they never had such a power in themselves) they ought not to be charged as guilty of the violence and unjustice that is committed in an unjust war, any farther than they actually abet it; no more than they are to be thought guilty of any violence or oppression their governors should use upon the people themselves, or any part of their

35 fellow subjects, they having impowered them no more to the one than to the other. Conquerors, it is true, seldom trouble themselves to make the distinction, but they willingly permit the confusion of war to sweep all together: but yet this alters not the right; for the conquerors power over the lives of the conquered, being only because they have used force to do, or maintain an injustice, he can

40 have that power only over those who have concurred in that force; all the rest

are innocent; and he has no more title over the people of that country, who have done him no injury, and so have made no forfeiture of their lives, than he has over any other, who, without any injuries or provocations, have lived upon fair terms with him.

5   *§. 180. Thirdly,* The *power a conqueror gets* over those he overcomes *in a just war, is perfectly despotical:* he has an absolute power over the lives of those, who, by putting themselves in a state of war, have forfeited them; but he has not thereby a right and title to their possessions. This I doubt not, but at first sight will seem a strange doctrine, it being so quite contrary to the practice of the
10   world; there being nothing more familiar in speaking of the dominion of countries, than to say such an one conquered it; as if conquest, without any more ado, conveyed a right of possession. But when we consider, that the practice of the strong and powerful, how universal soever it may be, is seldom the rule of right, however it be one part of the subjection of the conquered, not to argue
15   against the conditions cut out to them by the conquering sword.

     §. 181. Though in all war there be usually a complication of force and damage, and the aggressor seldom fails to harm the estate, when he uses force against the persons of those he makes war upon; yet it is the use of force only that puts a man into the state of war: for whether by force he begins the injury,
20   or else having quietly, and by fraud, done the injury, he refuses to make reparation, and by force maintains it, (which is the same thing, as at first to have done it by force) it is the unjust use of force that makes the war: for he that breaks open my house, and violently turns me out of doors; or having peaceably got in, by force keeps me out, does in effect the same thing; supposing we are in
25   such a state, that we have no common judge on earth, whom I may appeal to, and to whom we are both obliged to submit: for of such I am now speaking. It is the *unjust use of force* then, that *puts a man into the state of war* with another; and thereby he that is guilty of it makes a forfeiture of his life: for quitting reason, which is the rule given between man and man, and using force, the way
30   of beasts, he becomes liable to be destroyed by him he uses force against, as any savage ravenous beast, that is dangerous to his being.

     §. 182. But because the miscarriages of the father are no faults of the children, and they may be rational and peaceable, notwithstanding the brutishness and injustice of the father; the father, by his miscarriages and
35   violence, can forfeit but his own life, but involves not his children in his guilt or destruction. His goods, which nature, that willeth the preservation of all mankind as much as is possible, hath made to belong to the children to keep them from perishing, do still continue to belong to his children: for supposing them not to have joined in the war, either thro' infancy, absence, or choice, they
40   have done nothing to forfeit them: *nor has the conqueror any right* to take them

away, by the bare title of having subdued him that by force attempted his destruction; though perhaps he may have some right to them, to repair the damages he has sustained by the war, and the defence of his own right; which how far it reaches to the possessions of the conquered, we shall see by and by.

5   So that he that *by conquest has a right over a man's person* to destroy him if he pleases, has *not* thereby a right over *his estate* to possess and enjoy it: for it is the brutal force the aggressor has used, that gives his adversary a right to take away his life, and destroy him if he pleases, as a noxious creature; but it is damage sustained that alone gives him title to another man's goods: for though I

10   may kill a thief that sets on me in the high-way, yet I may not (which seems less) take away his money, and let him go: this would be robbery on my side. His force, and the state of war he put himself in, made him forfeit his life, but gave me no title to his goods. The *right* then of *conquest extends only to the lives* of those who joined in the war, *not to their estates,* but only in order to

15   make reparation for the damages received, and the charges of the war, and that too with reservation of the right of the innocent wife and children.

     §. 183. Let the *conqueror* have as much justice on his side, as could be supposed, he *has* no *right* to seize more than the vanquished could forfeit: his life is at the victor's mercy; and his service and goods he may appropriate, to

20   make himself reparation; but he cannot take the goods of his wife and children; they too had a title to the goods he enjoyed, and their shares in the estate he possessed: for example, I in the state of nature (and all common-wealths are in the state of nature one with another) have injured another man, and refusing to give satisfaction, it comes to a state of war, wherein my defending by force what

25   I had gotten unjustly, makes me the aggressor. I am conquered: my life, it is true, as forfeit, is at mercy, but not my wife's and children's. They made not the war, nor assisted in it. I could not forfeit their lives; they were not mine to forfeit. My wife had a share in my estate; that neither could I forfeit. And my children also, being born of me, had a right to be maintained out of my labour or

30   substance. Here then is the case: the conqueror has a title to reparation for damages received, and the children have a title to their father's estate for their subsistence: for as to the wife's share, whether her own labour, or compact, gave her a title to it, it is plain, her husband could not forfeit what was her's. What must be done in the case? I answer; the fundamental law of nature being, that

35   all, as much as may be, should be preserved, it follows, that if there be not enough fully to *satisfy* both, *viz.* for the *conqueror's losses,* and children's maintenance, he that hath, and to spare, must remit something of his full satisfaction, and give way to the pressing and preferable title of those who are in danger to perish without it.

§. 184. But supposing the *charge* and *damages of the war* are to be made up to the conqueror, to the utmost farthing; and that the children of the vanquished, spoiled of all their father's goods, are to be left to starve and perish; yet the satisfying of what shall, on this score, be due to the conqueror, will
5 scarce give him a *title to any country be shall conquer:* for the damages of war can scarce amount to the value of any considerable tract of land, in any part of the world, where all the land is possessed, and none lies waste. And if I have not taken away the conqueror's land, which, being vanquished, it is impossible I should; scarce any other spoil I have done him can amount to the value of mine,
10 supposing it equally cultivated, and of an extent any way coming near what I had over-run of his. The destruction of a year's product or two (for it seldom reaches four or five) is the utmost spoil that usually can be done: for as to money, and such riches and treasure taken away, these are none of nature's goods, they have but a fantastical imaginary value: nature has put no such upon
15 them: they are of no more account by her standard, than the wampompeke of the *Americans* to an *European* prince, or the silver money of *Europe* would have been formerly to an *American.* And five years product is not worth the perpetual inheritance of land, where all is possessed, and none remains waste, to be taken up by him that is disseized: which will be easily granted, if one do but take away
20 the imaginary value of money, the disproportion being more than between five and five hundred; though, at the same time, half a year's product is more worth than the inheritance, where there being more land than the inhabitants possess and make use of, any one has liberty to make use of the waste: but there conquerors take little care to possess themselves of the *lands of the vanquished.*
25 No damage therefore, that men in the state of nature (as all princes and governments are in reference to one another) suffer from one another, can give a conqueror power to dispossess the posterity of the vanquished, and turn them out of that inheritance, which ought to be the possession of them and their descendants to all generations. The conqueror indeed will be apt to think himself
30 master: and it is the very condition of the subdued not to be able to dispute their right. But if that be all, it gives no other title than what bare force gives to the stronger over the weaker: and, by this reason, he that is strongest will have a right to whatever he pleases to seize on.

    §. 185. Over those then that joined with him in the war, and over those of
35 the subdued country that opposed him not, and the posterity even of those that did, the conqueror, even in a just war, hath, by his conquest, no *right of dominion:* they are free from any subjection to him, and if their former government be dissolved, they are at liberty to begin and erect another to themselves.

§. 186. The conqueror, it is true, usually, by the force he has over them, compels them, with a sword at their breasts, to stoop to his conditions, and submit to such a government as he pleases to afford them; but the enquiry is, what right he has to do so? If it be said, they submit by their own consent, then
5   this allows their own *consent* to be *necessary to give the conqueror a title to rule over them.* It remains only to be considered, whether *promises extorted by force, without right,* can be thought consent, and *how far they bind.* To which I shall say, they *bind not at all;* because whatsoever another gets from me by force, I still retain the right of, and he is obliged presently to restore. He that forces my
10   horse from me, ought presently to restore him, and I have still a right to retake him. By the same reason, he that *forced a promise* from me, ought presently to restore it, *i. e.* quit me of the obligation of it; or I may resume it myself, *i. e.* chuse whether I will perform it: for the law of nature laying an obligation on me only by the rules the prescribes, cannot oblige me by the violation of her rules:
15   such is the extorting any thing from me by force. Nor does it at all alter the case to say, *I gave my promise,* no more than it excuses the force, and passes the right, when I put my hand in my pocket, and deliver my purse myself to a thief, who demands it with a pistol at my breast.
 §. 187. From all which it follows, that the *government of a conqueror,*
20   imposed by force on the subdued, against whom he had no right of war, or who joined not in the war against him, where he had right, *has no obligation* upon them.
 §. 188. But let us suppose, that all the men of that community, being all members of the same body politic, may be taken to have joined in that unjust
25   war wherein they are subdued, and so their lives are at the mercy of the conqueror.
 §. 189. I say, this concerns not their children who are in their minority: for since a father hath not, in himself, a power over the life or liberty of his child, no act of his can possibly forfeit it. So that the children, whatever may have
30   happened to the fathers, are freemen, and the absolute power of the *conqueror* reaches no farther than the persons of the men that were subdued by him, and dies with them: and should he govern them as slaves, subjected to his absolute arbitrary power, he *has* no *such right of dominion over their children.* He can have no power over them but by their own consent, whatever he may drive them
35   to say or do; and he has no lawfull authority, whilst force, and not choice, compels them to submission.
 §. 190. Every man is born with a double right: *first,* a *right of freedom to his person,* which no other man has a power over, but the free disposal of it lies in himself. *Secondly,* a *right,* before any other man, *to inherit* with his brethren
40   his *father's goods.*

§. 191. By the first of these, a man is *naturally free* from subjection to any government, tho' he be born in a place under its jurisdiction; but if he disclaim the lawful government of the country he was born in, he must also quit the right that belonged to him by the laws of it, and the possessions there descending to
5   him from his ancestors, if it were a government made by their consent.

    §. 192. By the second, the *inhabitants* of any country, who are descended, and derive a title to their estates from those who are subdued, and had a government forced upon them against their free consents, *retain a right to the possession of their ancestors,* though they consent not freely to the government,
10   whose hard conditions were by force imposed on the possessors of that country: for the first *conqueror never having had a title to the land* of that country, the people who are the descendants of, or claim under those who were forced to submit to the yoke of a government by constraint, have always a right to shake it off, and free themselves from the usurpation or tyranny which the sword hath
15   brought in upon them, till their rulers put them under such a frame of government as they willingly and of choice consent to. Who doubts but the Grecian christians, descendants of the ancient possessors of that country, may justly cast off the Turkish yoke, which they have so long groaned under, whenever they have an opportunity to do it? For no government can have a right
20   to obedience from a people who have not freely consented to it; which they can never be supposed to do, till either they are put in a full state of liberty to chuse their government and governors, or at least till they have such standing laws, to which they have by themselves or their representatives given their free consent, and also till they are allowed their due property, which is so to be proprietors of
25   what they have, that no body can take away any part of it without their own consent, without which, men under any government are not in the state of freemen, but are direct slaves under the force of war.

    §. 193. But granting that the *conqueror* in a just war has a right to the estates, as well as power over the persons, of the conquered; which, it is plain,
30   he *hath* not: nothing of *absolute power* will follow from hence, in the continuance of the government; because the descendants of these being all freemen, if he grants them estates and possessions to inhabit his country, (without which it would be worth nothing) whatsoever he grants them, they have, so far as it is granted, *property* in. The nature whereof is, that *without a*
35   *man's own consent* it *cannot be taken from him.*

    §. 194. Their *persons* are *free* by a native right, and their *properties,* be they more or less, are *their own, and at their own dispose,* and not at his; or else it is no *property.* Supposing the conqueror gives to one man a thousand acres, to him and his heirs for ever, to another he lets a thousand acres for his life, under
40   the rent of 50l. or 500l. *per ann.* has not the one of these a right to his thousand

acres for ever, and the other, during his life, paying the said rent? and hath not the tenant for life a *property* in all that he gets over and above his rent, by his labour and industry during the said term, supposing it be double the rent? Can any one say, the king, or conqueror, after his grant, may by his power of
5   conqueror take away all, or part of the land from the heirs of one, or from the other during his life, he paying the rent? or can he take away from either the goods or money they have got upon the said land, at his pleasure? If he can, then all free and voluntary *contracts* cease, and are void in the world; there needs nothing to dissolve them at any time, but power enough: and all the *grants* and
10 *promises* of *men in power* are but mockery and collusion: for can there be any thing more ridiculous than to say, I give you and your's this for ever, and that in the surest and most solemn way of conveyance can be devised; and yet it is to be understood, that I have right, if I please, to take it away from you again to morrow?

15   *§. 195.* I will not dispute now whether princes are exempt from the laws of their country; but this I am sure, they owe subjection to the laws of God and nature, No body, no power, can exempt them from the obligations of that eternal law. Those are so great, and so strong, in the case of *promises,* that omnipotency itself can be tied by them. *Grants, promises,* and *oaths,* are *bonds* that *hold the*
20 *Almighty:* whatever some flatterers say to princes of the world, who all together, with all their people joined to them, are, in comparison of the great God, but as a drop of the bucket, or a dust on the balance, inconsiderable, nothing!

     §. 196. The short of the *case in conquest* is this: the conqueror, if he have a just cause, has a despotical right over the persons of all, that actually aided, and
25 concurred in the war against him, and a right to make up his damage and cost out of their labour and estates, so he injure not the right of any other. Over the rest of the people, if there were any that consented not to the war, and over the children of the captives themselves, or the possessions of either, he has no power; and so can have, *by virtue of conquest, no lawful title* himself *to*
30 *dominion* over them, or derive it to his posterity; but is an aggressor, if he attempts upon their properties, and thereby puts himself in a state of war against them, and has no better a right of principality, he, nor any of his successors, than *Hingar,* or *Hubba,* the Danes, had here in *England;* or *Spartacus,* had he conquered *Italy,* would have had; which is to have their yoke cast off, as soon as
35 God shall give those under their subjection courage and opportunity to do it. Thus, notwithstanding whatever title the kings of *Assyria* had over *Judah,* by the sword, God assisted *Hezekiah* to throw off the dominion of that conquering empire. *And the lord was with Hezekiah, and he prospered; wherefore he went forth, and he rebelled against the king of Assyria, and served him not,* 2 Kings
40 xviii. 7. Whence it is plain, that shaking off a power, which force, and not right,

hath set over any one, though it hath the name of *rebellion,* yet is no offence before God, but is that which he allows and countenances, though even promises and covenants, when obtained by force, have intervened: for it is very probable, to any one that reads the story of *Ahaz* and *Hezekiah* attentively, that the

5   *Assyrians* subdued *Ahaz,* and deposed him, and made *Hezekiah* king in his father's lifetime; and that *Hezekiah* by agreement had done him homage, and paid him tribute all this time.

CHAPTER XVII.
Of usurpation.

§. 197. AS conquest may be called a foreign usurpation, so usurpation is a kind of domestic conquest, with this difference, that an usurper can never have

10   right on his side, it being no *usurpation,* but where one is got into the *possession of what another has right to.* This, so far as it is *usurpation,* is a change only of persons, but not of the forms and rules of the government: for if the usurper extend his power beyond what of right belonged to the lawful princes, or governors of the commonwealth, it is *tyranny* added to *usurpation.*

15   *§. 198.* In all lawful governments, the designation of the persons, who are to bear rule, is as natural and necessary a part as the form of the government itself, and is that which had its establishment originally from the people; the anarchy being much alike, to have no form of government at all; or to agree, that it shall be monarchical, but to appoint no way to design the person that shall

20   have the power, and be the monarch. Hence all commonwealths, with the form of government established, have rules also of appointing those who are to have any share in the public authority, and settled methods of conveying the right to them: for the anarchy is much alike, to have no form of government at all; or to agree that it shall be monarchical, but to appoint no way to know or design the

25   person that shall have the power, and be the monarch. Whoever gets into the exercise of any part of the power, by other ways than what the laws of the community have prescribed, hath no right to be obeyed, though the form of the commonwealth be still preserved; since he is not the person the laws have appointed, and consequently not the person the people have consented to. Nor

30   can such an *usurper,* or any deriving from him, ever have a title, till the people are both at liberty to consent, and have actually consented to allow, and confirm in him the power he hath till then usurped.

CHAPTER XVIII.
Of tyranny.

§. 199. AS usurpation is the exercise of power, which another hath a right
to; so *tyranny is the exercise of power beyond right,* which no body can have a
right to. And this is making use of the power any one has in his hands, not for
the good of those who are under it, but for his own private separate advantage.
5 When the governor, however intitled, makes not the law, but his will, the rule;
and his commands and actions are not directed to the preservation of the
properties of his people, but the satisfaction of his own ambition, revenge,
covetousness, or any other irregular passion.

§. 200. If one can doubt this to be truth, or reason, because it comes from
10 the obscure hand of a subject, I hope the authority of a king will make it pass
with him. King *James* the first, in his speech to the parliament, 1603, tells them
thus, *I will ever prefer the weal of the public, and of the whole commonwealth,
in making of good laws and constitutions, to any particular and private ends of
mine; thinking ever the wealth and weal of the commonwealth to be my greatest*
15 *weal and worldly felicity; a point wherein a lawful king doth directly differ from
a tyrant: for I do acknowledge, that the special and greatest point of difference
that is between a rightful king and an usurping tyrant, is this, that whereas the
proud and ambitious tyrant doth think his kingdom and people are only
ordained for satisfaction of his desires and unreasonable appetites, the*
20 *righteous and just king doth by the contrary acknowledge himself to be ordained
for the procuring of the wealth and property of his people.* And again, in his
speech to the parliament, 1609, he hath these words, *The king binds himself by a
double oath, to the observation of the fundamental laws of his kingdom; tacitly,
as by being a king, and so bound to protect as well the people, as the laws of his*
25 *kingdom; and expresly, by his oath at his coronation; so as every just king, in a
settled kingdom, is bound to observe that paction made to his people, by his
laws, in framing his government agreeable thereunto, according to that paction
which God made with* Noah *after the deluge. Hereafter, seed-time and harvest,
and cold and heat, and summer and winter, and day and night, shall not cease*
30 *while the earth remaineth. And therefore a king governing in a settled kingdom,
leaves to be a king, and degenerates into a tyrant, as soon as he leaves off to
rule according to his laws.* And a little after, *Therefore all kings that are not
tyrants, or perjured, will be glad to bound themselves within the limits of their
laws; and they that persuade them the contrary, are vipers, and pests both*
35 *against them and the commonwealth.* Thus that learned king, who well
understood the notion of things, makes the difference betwixt a *king* and a *tyrant*
to consist only in this, that one makes the laws the bounds of his power, and the

good of the public, the end of his government; the other makes all give way to his own will and appetite.

§. 201. It is a mistake, to think this fault is proper only to monarchies; other forms of government are liable to it, as well as that: for wherever the power, that
5   is put in any hands for the government of the people, and the preservation of their properties, is applied to other ends, and made use of to impoverish, harass, or subdue them to the arbitrary and irregular commands of those that have it; there it presently becomes *tyranny,* whether those that thus use it are one or many. Thus we read of the thirty tyrants at *Athens,* as well as one at *Syracuse;*
10   and the intolerable dominion of the *Decemviri* at *Rome* was nothing better.

§. 202. *Where-ever law ends, tyranny begins,* if the law be transgressed to another's harm; and whosoever in authority exceeds the power given him by the law, and makes use of the force he has under his command, to compass that upon the subject, which the law allows not, ceases in that to be a magistrate;
15   and, acting without authority, may be opposed, as any other man, who by force invades the right of another. This is acknowledged in subordinate magistrates. He that hath authority to seize my person in the street, may be opposed as a thief and a robber, if he endeavours to break into my house to execute a writ, notwithstanding that I know he has such a warrant, and such a legal authority, as
20   will impower him to arrest me abroad. And why this should not hold in the highest, as well as in the most inferior magistrate, I would gladly be informed. Is it reasonable, that the eldest brother, because he has the greatest part of his father's estate, should thereby have a right to take away any of his younger brothers portions? or that a rich man, who possessed a whole country, should
25   from thence have a right to seize, when he pleased, the cottage and garden of his poor neighbour? The being rightfully possessed of great power and riches, exceedingly beyond the greatest part of the sons of *Adam,* is so far from being an excuse, much less a reason, for rapine and oppression, which the endamaging another without authority is, that it is a great aggravation of it: for the exceeding
30   the bounds of authority is no more a right in a great, than in a petty officer; no more justifiable in a king than a constable; but is so much the worse in him, in that he has more trust put in him, has already a much greater share than the rest of his brethren, and is supposed, from the advantages of his education, employment, and counsellors, to be more knowing in the measures of right and
35   wrong.

§. 203. May the *commands* then *of a prince be opposed?* may he be resisted as often as any one shall find himself aggrieved, and but imagine he has not right done him? This will unhinge and overturn all polities, and, instead of government and order, leave nothing but anarchy and confusion.

§. 204. To this I answer, that *force* is to be *opposed* to nothing, but to unjust and unlawful *force;* whoever makes any opposition in any other case, draws on himself a just condemnation both from God and man; and so no such danger or confusion will follow, as is often suggested: for,

5   *§. 205. First,* As, in some countries, the person of the prince by the law is sacred; and so, whatever he commands or does, his person is still free from all question or violence, not liable to force, or any judicial censure or condemnation. But yet opposition may be made to the illegal acts of any inferior officer, or other commissioned by him; unless he will, by actually putting

10   himself into a state of war with his people, dissolve the government, and leave them to that defence which belongs to every one in the state of nature: for of such things who can tell what the end will be? and a neighbour kingdom has shewed the world an odd example. In all other cases the *sacredness* of the *person exempts him from all inconveniencies,* whereby he is secure, whilst the

15   government stands, from all violence and harm whatsoever; than which there cannot be a wiser constitution: for the harm he can do in his own person not being likely to happen often, nor to extend itself far; nor being able by his single strength to subvert the laws, nor oppress the body of the people, should any prince have so much weakness, and ill nature as to be willing to do it, the

20   inconveniency of some particular mischiefs, that may happen sometimes, when a heady prince comes to the throne, are well recompensed by the peace of the public, and security of the government, in the person of the chief magistrate, thus set out of the reach of danger: it being safer for the body, that some few private men should be sometimes in danger to suffer, than that the head of the

25   republic should be easily, and upon slight occasions, exposed.

    §. 206. Secondly, But this privilege, belonging only to the king's person, hinders not, but they may be questioned, opposed, and resisted, who use unjust force, though they pretend a commission from him, which the law authorizes not; as is plain in the case of him that has the king's writ to arrest a man, which

30   is a full commission from the king; and yet he that has it cannot break open a man's house to do it, nor execute this command of the king upon certain days, nor in certain places, though this commission have no such exception in it; but they are the limitations of the law, which if any one transgress, the king's commission excuses him not: for the king's authority being given him only by

35   the law, he cannot impower any one to act against the law, or justify him, by his commission, in so doing; the *commission,* or *command of any magistrate, where he has no authority,* being as *void* and insignificant, as that of any private man; the difference between the one and the other, being that the magistrate has some authority so far, and to such ends, and the private man has none at all: for it is

40   not the *commission,* but the *authority,* that gives the right of acting; and *against*

the laws there can be no authority. But, notwithstanding such resistance, the king's person and authority are still both secured, and so *no danger to governor or government.*

§. 207. *Thirdly,* Supposing a government wherein the person of the chief magistrate is not thus sacred; yet this *doctrine* of the lawfulness of *resisting* all unlawful exercises of his power, *will not* upon every slight occasion indanger him, or *imbroil the government:* for where the injured party may be relieved, and his damages repaired by appeal to the law, there can be no pretence for force, which is only to be used where a man is intercepted from appealing to the law: for nothing is to be accounted hostile force, but where it leaves not the remedy of such an appeal; and it is such *force* alone, that *puts* him that uses it *into a state of war,* and makes it lawful to resist him. A man with a sword in his hand demands my purse in the high-way, when perhaps I have not twelve pence in my pocket: this man I may lawfully kill. To another I deliver 100 l. to hold only whilst I alight, which he refuses to restore me, when I am got up again, but draws his sword to defend the possession of it by force, if I endeavour to retake it. The mischief this man does me is a hundred, or possibly a thousand times more than the other perhaps intended me (whom I killed before he really did me any); and yet I might lawfully kill the one, and cannot so much as hurt the other lawfully. The reason whereof is plain; because the one using *force,* which threatened my life, I could not have *time to appeal* to the law to secure it: and when it was gone, it was too late to appeal. The law could not restore life to my dead carcass: the loss was irreparable; which to prevent, the law of nature gave me a right to *destroy* him, who had put himself into a state of war with me, and threatened my destruction. But in the other case, my life not being in danger, I may have the *benefit of appealing* to the law, and have reparation for my 100 l. that way.

§. 208. *Fourthly,* But if the unlawful acts done by the magistrate be maintained (by the power he has got), and the remedy which is due by law, be by the same power obstructed; yet the *right of resisting,* even in such manifest acts of tyranny, *will not* suddenly, or on slight occasions, *disturb the government:* for if it reach no farther than some private men's cases, though they have a right to defend themselves, and to recover by force what by unlawful force is taken from them; yet the right to do so will not easily engage them in a contest, wherein they are sure to perish; it being as impossible for one, or a few oppressed men to *disturb the government,* where the body of the people do not think themselves concerned in it, as for a raving mad-man, or heady mal-content to overturn a well-settled state; the people being as little apt to follow the one, as the other.

§. 209. But if either these illegal acts have extended to the majority of the people; or if the mischief and oppression has lighted only on some few, but in such cases, as the precedent, and consequences seem to threaten all; and they are persuaded in their consciences, that their laws, and with them their estates,
5 liberties, and lives are in danger, and perhaps their religion too; how they will be hindered from resisting illegal force, used against them, I cannot tell. This is an *inconvenience,* I confess, *that attends all governments* whatsoever, when the governors have brought it to this pass, to be generally suspected of their people; the most dangerous state which they can possibly put themselves in; wherein
10 they are the less to be pitied, because it is so easy to be avoided; it being as impossible for a governor, if he really means the good of his people, and the preservation of them, and their laws together, not to make them see and feel it, as it is for the father of a family, not to let his children see he loves, and takes care of them.
15 *§. 210.* But if all the world shall observe pretences of one kind, and actions of another; arts used to elude the law, and the trust of prerogative (which is an arbitrary power in some things left in the prince's hand to do good, not harm to the people) employed contrary to the end for which it was given: if the people shall find the ministers and subordinate magistrates chosen suitable to such ends,
20 and favoured, or laid by, proportionably as they promote or oppose them: if they see several experiments made of arbitrary power, and that religion underhand favoured, (tho' publicly proclaimed against) which is readiest to introduce it; and the operators in it supported, as much as may be; and when that cannot be done, yet approved still, and liked the better: if a *long train of actions shew the*
25 *councils* all tending that way; how can a man any more hinder himself from being persuaded in his own mind, which way things are going; or from casting about how to save himself, than he could from believing the captain of the ship he was in, was carrying him, and the rest of the company, to *Algiers,* when he found him always steering that course, though cross winds, leaks in his ship, and
30 want of men and provisions did often force him to turn his course another way for some time, which he steadily returned to again, as soon as the wind, weather, and other circumstances would let him?

CHAPTER XIX.
Of the Dissolution of Government.

§. 211. HE that will with any clearness speak of the *dissolution of government,* ought in the first place to distinguish between the *dissolution of the*
35 *society* and the *dissolution of the government.* That which makes the community, and brings men out of the loose state of nature, into *one politic*

society, is the agreement which every one has with the rest to incorporate, and act as one body, and so be one distinct common-wealth. The usual, and almost only way whereby *this union is dissolved,* is the inroad of foreign force making a conquest upon them: for in that case, (not being able to maintain and support
5   themselves, as *one intire* and *independent body)* the union belonging to that body which consisted therein, must necessarily cease, and so every one return to the state he was in before, with a liberty to shift for himself, and provide for his own safety, as he thinks fit, in some other society. Whenever the *society is dissolved,* it is certain the government of that society cannot remain. Thus
10 conquerors swords often cut up governments by the roots, and mangle societies to pieces, separating the subdued or scattered multitude from the protection of, and dependence on, that society which ought to have preserved them from violence. The world is too well instructed in, and too forward to allow of, this way of dissolving of governments, to need any more to be said of it; and there
15 wants not much argument to prove, that where the *society is dissolved,* the government cannot remain; that being as impossible, as for the frame of an house to subsist when the materials of it are scattered and dissipated by a whirl-wind, or jumbled into a confused heap by an earthquake.

§. 212. Besides this over-turning from without, *governments are dissolved*
20 *from within,*

First, When the *legislative* is *altered.* Civil society being a state of peace, amongst those who are of it, from whom the state of war is excluded by the umpirage, which they have provided in their legislative, for the ending all differences that may arise amongst any of them, it is in their *legislative,* that the
25 members of a common-wealth are united, and combined together into one coherent living body. This *is the soul that gives form, life, and unity,* to the common-wealth: from hence the several members have their mutual influence, sympathy, and connexion: and therefore, when the *legislative* is broken, or *dissolved,* dissolution and death follows: for the *essence and union of the society*
30 consisting in having one will, the legislative, when once established by the majority, has the declaring, and as it were keeping of that will. The *constitution of the legislative* is the first and fundamental act of society, whereby provision is made for the *continuation of their union,* under the direction of persons, and bonds of laws, made by persons authorized thereunto, by the consent and
35 appointment of the people, without which no one man, or number of men, amongst them, can have authority of making laws that shall be binding to the rest. When any one, or more, shall take upon them to make laws, whom the people have not appointed so to do, they make laws without authority, which the people are not therefore bound to obey; by which means they come again to be
40 out of subjection, and may constitute to themselves a *new legislative,* as they

think best, being in full liberty to resist the force of those, who without authority would impose any thing upon them. Every one is at the disposure of his own will, when those who had, by the delegation of the society, the declaring of the public will, are excluded from it, and others usurp the place, who have no such
5   authority or delegation.

§. 213. This being usually brought about by such in the common-wealth who misuse the power they have; it is hard to consider it aright, and know at whose door to lay it, without knowing the form of government in which it happens. Let us suppose then the legislative placed in the concurrence of three
10 distinct persons.

1. A single hereditary person, having the constant, supreme, executive power, and with it the power of convoking and dissolving the other two within certain periods of time.

2. An assembly of hereditary nobility.
15 3. An assembly of representatives chosen, *pro tempore,* by the people. Such a form of government supposed, it is evident,

§. 214. First, That when such a single person, or prince, sets up his own arbitrary will in place of the laws, which are the will of the society, declared by the legislative, then the *legislative is changed:* for that being in effect the
20 legislative, whose rules and laws are put in execution, and required to be obeyed; when other laws are set up, and other rules pretended, and inforced, than what the legislative, constituted by the society, have enacted, it is plain that the *legislative is changed.* Whoever introduces new laws, not being thereunto authorized by the fundamental appointment of the society, or subverts the old,
25 disowns and overturns the power by which they were made, and so sets up a *new legislative.*

§. 215. Secondly, When the prince hinders the legislative from assembling in its due time, or from acting freely, pursuant to those ends for which it was constituted, the *legislative is altered:* for it is not a certain number of men, no,
30 nor their meeting, unless they have also freedom of debating, and leisure of perfecting, what is for the good of the society, wherein the legislative consists: when these are taken away or altered, so as to deprive the society of the due exercise of their power, the *legislative* is truly altered; for it is not names that constitute governments, but the use and exercise of those powers that were
35 intended to accompany them; so that he, who takes away the freedom, or hinders the acting of the legislative in its due seasons, in effect takes *away the legislative,* and *puts an end to the government.*

§. 216. Thirdly, When, by the arbitrary power of the prince, the electors, or ways of election, are altered, without the consent, and contrary to the common
40 interest of the people, there also the *legislative is altered:* for, if others than

those whom the society hath authorized thereunto, do chuse, or in another way than what the society hath prescribed, those chosen are not the legislative appointed by the people.

§. 217. Fourthly, The delivery also of the people into the subjection of a foreign power, either by the prince, or by the legislative, is certainly a *change of the legislative,* and so a *dissolution of the government:* for the end why people entered into society being to be preserved one intire, free, independent society, to be governed by its own laws; this is lost, whenever they are given up into the power of another.

§. 218. Why, in such a constitution as this, the *dissolution of the government* in these cases is to be imputed to the prince, is evident; because he, having the force, treasure and offices of the state to employ, and often persuading himself, or being flattered by others, that as supreme magistrate he is uncapable of controul; he alone is in a condition to make great advances toward such changes, under pretence of lawful authority, and has it in his hands to terrify or suppress opposers, as factious, seditious, and enemies to the government: whereas no other part of the legislative, or people, is capable by themselves to attempt any alteration of the legislative, without open and visible rebellion, apt enough to be taken notice of, which, when it prevails, produces effects very little different from foreign conquest. Besides, the prince in such a form of government, having the power of dissolving the other parts of the legislative, and thereby rendering them private persons, they can never in opposition to him, or without his concurrence, alter the legislative by a law, his consent being necessary to give any of their decrees that sanction. But yet, so far as the other parts of the legislative any way contribute to any attempt upon the government, and do either promote, or not, what lies in them, hinder such designs, they are guilty, and partake in this, which is certainly the greatest crime men can be guilty of one towards another.

§. 219. There is one way more whereby such a government may be dissolved, and that is, when he who has the supreme executive power, neglects and abandons that charge, so that the laws already made can no longer be put in execution. This is demonstratively to reduce all to anarchy, and so effectually *to dissolve the government:* for laws not being made for themselves, but to be, by their execution, the bonds of the society, to keep every part of the body politic in its due place and function; when that totally ceases, the *government* visibly *ceases,* and the people become a confused multitude, without order or connexion. Where there is no longer the administration of justice, for the securing of men's rights, nor any remaining power within the community to direct the force, or provide for the necessities of the public, there certainly is *no government left.* Where the laws cannot be executed, it is all one as if there were

no laws; and a government without laws is, I suppose, a mystery in politics, unconceivable to human capacity, and inconsistent with human society.

§. *220.* In these and the like cases, *when the government is dissolved,* the people are at liberty to provide for themselves, by erecting a new legislative,
5 differing from the other, by the change of persons, or form, or both, as they shall find it most for their safety and good: for the *society* can never, by the fault of another, lose the native and original right it has to preserve itself, which can only be done by a settled legislative, and a fair and impartial execution of the laws made by it. But the state of mankind is not so miserable that they are not capable
10 of using this remedy, till it be too late to look for any. To tell *people* they *may provide for themselves,* by erecting a new legislative, when by oppression, artifice, or being delivered over to a foreign power, their old one is gone, is only to tell them, they may expect relief when it is too late, and the evil is past cure. This is in effect no more than to bid them first be slaves, and then to take care of
15 their liberty; and when their chains are on, tell them, they may act like freemen. This, if barely so, is rather mockery than relief; and men can never be secure from tyranny, if there be no means to escape it till they are perfectly under it: and therefore it is, that they have not only a right to get out of it, but to prevent it.
20 §. *221.* There is therefore, secondly, another way whereby *governments are dissolved,* and that is, when the legislative, or the prince, either of them, act contrary to their trust.

First, The *legislative acts against the trust* reposed in them, when they endeavour to invade the property of the subject, and to make themselves, or any
25 part of the community, masters, or arbitrary disposers of the lives, liberties, or fortunes of the people.

§. *222.* The reason why men enter into society, is the preservation of their property; and the end why they chuse and authorize a legislative, is, that there may be laws made, and rules set, as guards and fences to the properties of all the
30 members of the society, to limit the power, and moderate the dominion, of every part and member of the society: for since it can never be supposed to be the will of the society, that the legislative should have a power to destroy that which every one designs to secure, by entering into society, and for which the people submitted themselves to legislators of their own making; whenever the
35 *legislators endeavour to take away, and destroy the property of the people,* or to reduce them to slavery under arbitrary power, they put themselves into a state of war with the people, who are thereupon absolved from any farther obedience, and are left to the common refuge, which God hath provided for all men, against force and violence. Whensoever therefore the *legislative* shall transgress this
40 fundamental rule of society; and either by ambition, fear, folly or corruption,

endeavour to grasp themselves, *or put into the hands of any other, an absolute power* over the lives, liberties, and estates of the people; by this breach of trust they forfeit *the power* the people had put into their hands for quite contrary ends, and it devolves to the people, who have a right to resume their original liberty,

5 and, by the establishment of a new legislative, (such as they shall think fit) provide for their own safety and security, which is the end for which they are in society. What I have said here, concerning the legislative in general, holds true also concerning the supreme executor, who having a double trust put in him, both to have a part in the legislative, and the supreme execution of the law, acts

10 against both, when he goes about to set up his own arbitrary will as the law of the society. He *acts* also *contrary to his trust,* when he either employs the force, treasure, and offices of the society, to corrupt the *representatives,* and gain them to his purposes; or openly pre-engages the *electors,* and prescribes to their choice, such, whom he has, by sollicitations, threats, promises, or otherwise,

15 won to his designs; and employs them to bring in such, who have promised before-hand what to vote, and what to enact. Thus to regulate candidates and electors, and new-model the ways of election, what is it but to cut up the government by the roots, and poison the very fountain of public security? for the people having reserved to themselves the choice of their *representatives,* as the

20 fence to their properties, could do it for no other end, but that they might always be freely chosen, and so chosen, freely act, and advise, as the necessity of the common-wealth, and the public good should, upon examination, and mature debate, be judged to require. This, those who give their votes before they hear the debate, and have weighed the reasons on all sides, are not capable of doing.

25 To prepare such an assembly as this, and endeavour to set up the declared abettors of his own will, for the true *representatives* of the people, and the law-makers of the society, is certainly as great a *breach of trust,* and as perfect a declaration of a design to subvert the government, as is possible to be met with. To which, if one shall add rewards and punishments visibly employed to the

30 same end, and all the arts of perverted law made use of, to take off and destroy all that stand in the way of such a design, and will not comply and consent to betray the liberties of their country, it will be past doubt what is doing. What power they ought to have in the society, who thus employ it contrary to the trust went along with it in its first institution, is easy to determine; and one cannot but

35 see, that he, who has once attempted any such thing as this, cannot any longer be trusted.

§. 223. To this perhaps it will be said, that the people being ignorant, and always discontented, to lay the foundation of government in the unsteady opinion and uncertain humour of the people, is to expose it to certain ruin; and

40 *no government will be able long to subsist,* if the people may set up a new

legislative, whenever they take offence at the old one. To this I answer, Quite the contrary. People are not so easily got out of their old forms, as some are apt to suggest. They are hardly to be prevailed with to amend the acknowledged faults in the frame they have been accustomed to. And if there be any original
5   defects, or adventitious ones introduced by time, or corruption; it is not an easy thing to get them changed, even when all the world sees there is an opportunity for it. This slowness and aversion in the people to quite their old constitutions, has, in the many revolutions which have been seen in this kingdom, in this and former ages, still kept us to, or, after some interval of fruitless attempts, still
10 brought us back again to our old legislative of king, lords and commons: and whatever provocations have made the crown be taken from some of our princes heads, they never carried the people so far as to place it in another line.

     §. 224. But it will be said, this *hypothesis* lays a *ferment for* frequent *rebellion.* To which I answer,
15   *First,* No more than any other *hypothesis:* for when the people are made miserable, and find themselves *exposed to the ill usage of arbitrary power,* cry up their governors, as much as you will, for sons of *Jupiter;* let them be sacred and divine, descended, or authorized from heaven; give them out for whom or what you please, the same will happen. *The people generally ill treated,* and
20 contrary to right, will be ready upon any occasion to ease themselves of a burden that sits heavy upon them. They will wish, and seek for the opportunity, which in the change, weakness and accidents of human affairs, seldom delays long to offer itself. He must have lived but a little while in the world, who has not seen examples of this in his time; and he must have read very little, who
25 cannot produce examples of it in all sorts of governments in the world.

     §. 225. Secondly, I answer, such *revolutions happen* not upon every little mismanagement in public affairs. *Great mistakes* in the ruling part, many wrong and inconvenient laws, and all the *slips* of human frailty, will be *born by the people* without mutiny or murmur. But if a long train of abuses, prevarications
30 and artifices, all tending the same way, make the design visible to the people, and they cannot but feel what they lie under, and see whither they are going; it is not to be wondered, that they should then rouze themselves, and endeavour to put the rule into such hands which may secure to them the ends for which government was at first erected; and without which, ancient names, and specious
35 forms, are so far from being better, that they are much worse, than the state of nature, or pure anarchy; the inconveniencies being all as great and as near, but the remedy farther off and more difficult.

     §. 226. Thirdly, I answer, that *this doctrine* of a power in the people of providing for their safety a-new, by a new legislative, when their legislators
40 have acted contrary to their trust, by invading their property, is *the best fence*

against rebellion, and the probablest means to hinder it: for *rebellion* being an
opposition, not to persons, but authority, which is founded only in the
constitutions and laws of the government; those, whoever they be, who by force
break through, and by force justify their violation of them, are truly and properly
5 *rebels:* for when men, by entering into society and civil-government, have
excluded force, and introduced laws for the preservation of property, peace, and
unity amongst themselves, those who set up force again in opposition to the
laws, do *rebellare,* that is, bring back again the state of war, and are properly
rebels: which they who are in power, (by the pretence they have to authority, the
10 temptation of force they have in their hands, and the flattery of those about
them) being likeliest to do; the properest way to prevent the evil, is to shew them
the danger and injustice of it, who are under the greatest temptation to run into
it.

§. 227. In both the fore-mentioned cases, when either the legislative is
15 changed, or the legislators act contrary to the end for which they were
constituted; those who are guilty are *guilty of rebeliion:* for if any one by force
takes away the established legislative of any society, and the laws by them
made, pursuant to their trust, he thereby takes away the umpirage, which every
one had consented to, for a peaceable decision of all their controversies, and a
20 bar to the state of war amongst them. They, who remove, or change the
legislative, take away this decisive power, which no body can have, but by the
appointment and consent of the people; and so destroying the authority which
the people did, and no body else can set up, and introducing a power which the
people hath not authorized, they actually *introduce a state of war,* which is that
25 of force without authority: and thus, by removing the legislative established by
the society, (in whose decisions the people acquiesced and united, as to that of
their own will) they untie the knot, and *expose the people a-new to the state of
war.* And if those, who by force take away the legislative, are *rebels,* the
legislators themselves, as has been shewn, can be no less esteemed so; when
30 they, who were set up for the protection, and preservation of the people, their
liberties and properties, shall by force invade and endeavour to take them away;
and so they putting themselves into a state of war with those who made them the
protectors and guardians of their peace, are properly, and with the greatest
aggravation, *rebellantes,* rebels.
35 §. 228. But if they, who say *it lays a foundation for rebellion,* mean that it
may occasion civil wars, or intestine broils, to tell the people they are absolved
from obedience when illegal attempts are made upon their liberties or properties,
and may oppose the unlawful violence of those who were their magistrates,
when they invade their properties contrary to the trust put in them; and that
40 therefore this doctrine is not to be allowed, being so destructive to the peace of

the world: they may as well say, upon the same ground, that honest men may not oppose robbers or pirates, because this may occasion disorder or bloodshed. If any *mischief* come in such cases, it is not to be charged upon him who defends his own right, but *on him that invades* his neighbours. If the innocent honest

5   man must quietly quit all he has, for peace sake, to him who will lay violent hands upon it, I desire it may be considered, what a kind of peace there will be in the world, which consists only in violence and rapine; and which is to be maintained only for the benefit of robbers and oppressors. Who would not think it an admirable peace betwixt the mighty and the mean, when the lamb, without

10   resistance, yielded his throat to be torn by the imperious wolf? *Polyphemus*'s den gives us a perfect pattern of such a peace, and such a government, wherein *Ulysses* and his companions had nothing to do, but quietly to suffer themselves to be devoured. And no doubt *Ulysses,* who was a prudent man, preached up *passive obedience,* and exhorted them to a quiet submission, by representing to

15   them of what concernment peace was to mankind; and by shewing the inconveniences might happen, if they should offer to resist *Polyphemus,* who had now the power over them.

    §. 229. The end of government is the good of mankind; and which is *best for mankind,* that the people should be always exposed to the boundless will of

20   tyranny, or that the rulers should be sometimes liable to be opposed, when they grow exorbitant in the use of their power, and employ it for the destruction, and not the preservation of the properties of their people?

    §. 230. Nor let any one say, that mischief can arise from hence, as often as it shall please a busy head, or turbulent spirit, to desire the alteration of the

25   government. It is true, such men may stir, whenever they please; but it will be only to their own just ruin and perdition: for till the mischief be grown general, and the ill designs of the rulers become visible, or their attempts sensible to the greater part, the people, who are more disposed to suffer than right themselves by resistance, are not apt to stir. The examples of particular injustice, or

30   oppression of here and there an unfortunate man, moves them not. But if they universally have a persuasion, grounded upon manifest evidence, that designs are carrying on against their liberties, and the general course and tendency of things cannot but give them strong suspicions of the evil intention of their governors, who is to be blamed for it? Who can help it, if they, who might avoid

35   it, bring themselves into this suspicion? Are the people to be blamed, if they have the sense of rational creatures, and can think of things no otherwise than as they find and feel them? And is it not rather *their fault,* who put things into such a posture, that they would not have them thought to be as they are? I grant, that the pride, ambition, and turbulency of private men have sometimes caused great

40   disorders in common-wealths, and factions have been fatal to states and

kingdoms. But whether *the mischief* hath *oftener* begun *in the peoples wantonness,* and a desire to cast off the lawful authority of their rulers, or *in the rulers insolence,* and endeavours to get and exercise an arbitrary power over their people; whether oppression, or disobedience, gave the first rise to the
5   disorder, I leave it to impartial history to determine. This I am sure, whoever, either ruler or subject, by force goes about to invade the rights of either prince or people, and lays the foundation for *overturning* the constitution and frame of *any just government,* is highly guilty of the greatest crime, I think, a man is capable of, being to answer for all those mischiefs of blood, rapine, and
10   desolation, which the breaking to pieces of governments bring on a country. And he who does it, is justly to be esteemed the common enemy and pest of mankind, and is to be treated accordingly.

       §. 231. That *subjects* or *foreigners,* attempting by force on the properties of any people, may be *resisted* with force, is agreed on all hands. But that
15   *magistrates,* doing the same thing, may be *resisted,* hath of late been denied: as if those who had the greatest privileges and advantages by the law, had thereby a power to break those laws, by which alone they were set in a better place than their brethren: whereas their offence is thereby the greater, both as being ungrateful for the greater share they have by the law, and breaking also that
20   trust, which is put into their hands by their brethren.

       §. 232. Whosoever uses *force without right,* as every one does in society, who does it without law, puts himself into a *state of war* with those against whom he so uses it; and in that state all former ties are cancelled, all other rights cease, and every one has a right to defend himself, and *to resist the aggressor.*
25   This is so evident, that *Barclay* himself, that great assertor of the power and sacredness of kings, is forced to confess, That it is lawful for the people, in some cases, to *resist* their king; and that too in a chapter, wherein he pretends to shew, that the divine law shuts up the people from all manner of rebellion. Whereby it is evident, even by his own doctrine, that, since they may in some cases *resist,*
30   all resisting of *princes* is not rebellion. His words are these. *Quod siquis dicat, Ergone populus tyrannicæ crudelitati & furori jugulum semper præbehit? Ergone multitudo civitates suas fame, ferro, & flammâ vastari, seque, conjuges, & liberos fortunæ ludibrio & tyranni libidini exponi, inque omnia vitæ pericula omnesque miserias & molestias á rege deduci patientur? Num illis quod omni*
35   *animantium generi est á naturâ tributum, denegari debet, ut sc. vim vi repellant, seseq; ab injuriâ tueantur? Huic breviter responsum sit, Populo universo negari defensionem, quæ juris naturalis est, neque ultionem quæ præter naturam est adversus regem concedi debere. Quapropter si rex non in singulares tantum personas aliquot privatum odium exerceat, sed corpus etiam reipublicæ, cujus*
40   *ipse caput est,* i. e. *totum populum, vel insignem aliquam ejus partem immani &*

intolerandâ seu tyrannide divexet; populo, quidem hoc casu resistendi ac tuendi
se ab injuriâ potestas competit, sed tuendi se tantum, non enim in principem
invadendi: & restituendœ injuriœ illatœ, non recedendi à debitâ reverentiâ
propter acceptam injuriam. Prœsentem denique impetum propulsandi non vim
5 *prœteritam ulciscenti jus habet. Horum enim alterum à naturâ est, ut vitam*
scilicet corpusque tueamur. Alterum vero contra naturam, ut inferior de
superiori supplicium sumat. Quod itaque populus malum, antequam factum sit,
impedire potest, ne fiat, id postquam factum est, in regem authorem sceleris
vindicare non potest: populus igitur hoc ampliùs quam privatus quispiam habet:
10 *quod huic, vel ipsis adversariis judicibus, excepto Buchanano, nullum nisi in*
patientia remedium superest. Cùm ille si intolerabilis tyrannus est (modicum
enim ferre omnino debet) resistere cum reverentiâ possit, Barclay contra
Monarchom. l. iii. c. 8.

In *English* thus.

15 *§. 233. But if any one should ask, Must the people then always lay*
themselves open to the cruelty and rage of tyranny? Must they see their cities
pillaged, and laid in ashes, their wives and children exposed to the tyrant's lust
and fury, and themselves and families reduced by their king to ruin, and all the
miseries of want and oppression, and yet sit still? Must men alone be debarred
20 *the common privilege of opposing force with force, which nature allows so*
freely to all other creatures for their preservation from injury? I answer: Self-
defence is a part of the law of nature; nor can it be denied the community, even
against the king himself: but to revenge themselves upon him, must by no means
be allowed them: it being not agreeable to that law. Wherefore if the king shall
25 *shew an hatred, not only to some particular persons, but sets himself against the*
body of the common-wealth, whereof he is the head, and shall, with intolerable
ill usage, cruelly tyrannize over the whole, or a considerable part of the people,
in this case the people have a right to resist and defend themselves from injury:
but it must be with this caution, that they only defend themselves, but do not
30 *attack their prince: they may repair the damages received, but must not for any*
provocation exceed the bounds of due reverence and respect. They may repulse
the present attempt, but must not revenge past violences: for it is natural for us
to defend life and limb, but that an inferior should punish a superior, is against
nature. The mischief which is designed them, the people may prevent before it be
35 *done; but when it is done, they must not revenge it on the king, though author of*
the villany. This therefore is the privilege of the people in general, above what
any private person hath; that particular men are allowed by our adversaries
themselves (Buchanan only excepted) to have no other remedy but patience; but
the body of the people may with respect resist intolerable tyranny; for when it is
40 *but moderate, they ought to endure it.*

§. 234. Thus far that great advocate of monarchical power allows of *resistance.*

§. 235. It is true, he has annexed two limitations to it, to no purpose:

First, He says, it must be with reverence.

5   *Secondly,* It must be without retribution, or punishment; and the reason he gives is, *because an inferior cannot punish a superior.*

First, How to *resist force without striking again,* or how to *strike with reverence,* will need some skill to make intelligible. He that shall oppose an assault only with a shield to receive the blows, or in any more respectful posture,

10   without a sword in his hand, to abate the confidence and force of the assailant, will quickly be at an end of his *resistance,* and will find such a defence serve only to draw on himself the worse usage. This is as ridiculous a way of *resisting,* as *Juvenal* thought it of fighting; *ubi tu pulsas, ego vapulo tantum.* And the success of the combat will be unavoidably the same he there describes it:

15   —Libertas pauperis hæc est:

Pulsatus rogat, & pugnis concisus, adorat,

Ut liceat paucis cum dentibus inde reverti.

This will always be the event of such an imaginary *resistance,* where men may not strike again. He therefore *who may resist, must be allowed to strike.*

20   And then let our author, or any body else, join a knock on the head, or a cut on the face, with as much *reverence* and *respect* as he thinks fit. He that can reconcile blows and reverence, may, for aught I know, desire for his pains, a civil, respectful cudgeling where-ever he can meet with it.

Secondly, As to his second, *An inferior cannot punish a superior;* that is

25   true, generally speaking, whilst he is his superior. But to resist force with force, being *the state of war* that *levels the parties,* cancels all former relation of reverence, respect, and *superiority:* and then the odds that remains, is, that he, who opposes the unjust aggressor, has this *superiority* over him, that he has a right, when he prevails, to punish the offender, both for the breach of the peace,

30   and all the evils that followed upon it. *Barclay* therefore, in another place, more coherently to himself, denies it to be lawful to *resist* a king in any case. But he there assigns two cases, whereby a king may un-king himself. His words are,

Quid ergo, nulline casus incidere possunt quibus populo sese erigere atque in regem impotentius dominantem arma capere & invadere jure suo suâque

35   *authoritate liceat? Nulli certe quamdiu rex manet. Semper enim ex divinis id obstat, Regem honorificato; & qui potestati resistit, Dei ordinationi resistit: non aliàs igitur in eum populo potestas est quam si id committat propter quod ipso jure rex esse desinat. Tunc enim se ipse principatu exuit atque in privatis constituit liber: hoc modo populus & superior efficitur, reverso ad eum sc. jure*

40   *illo quod ante regem inauguratum in interregno habuit. At sunt paucorum*

generum commissa ejusmodi quæ hunc effectum pariunt. At ego cum plurima animo perlustrem, duo tantum invenio, duos, inquam, casus quibus rex ipso facto ex rege non regem se facit & omni honore & dignitate regali atque in subditos potestate destituit; quorum etiam meminit Winzerus. Horum unus est, Si
5   *regnum disperdat, quemadmodum de Nerone fertur, quod is nempe senatum populumque Romanum, atque adeo urbem ipsam ferro flammaque vastare, ac novas sibi sedes quærere decrevisset. Et de Caligula, quod palam denunciarit se neque civem neque principem senatui amplius fore, inque animo habuerit interempto utriusque ordinis electissimo quoque Alexandriam commigrare, ac ut*
10   *populum uno ictu interimeret, unam ei cervicem optavit. Talia cum rex aliquis meditatur & molitur serio, omnem regnandi curam & animum ilico abjicit, ac proinde imperium in subditos amittit, ut dominus servi pro derelicto habiti dominium.*

    §. 236. Alter casus est, Si rex in alicujus clientelam se contulit; ac regnum
15   *quod liberum à majoribus & populo traditum accepit, alienæ ditioni mancipavit. Nam tunc quamvis forte non eâ mente id agit populo plane ut incommodet: tamen quia quod præcipuum est regiæ dignitatis amisit, ut summus scilicet in regno secundum Deum sit, & solo Deo inferior, atque populum etiam totum ignorantem vel invitum, cujus libertatem sartam & tectam conservare debuit, in*
20   *alterius gentis ditionem & potestatem dedidit; hâc velut quadam regni ab alienatione effecit, ut nec quod ipse in regno imperium habuit retineat, nec in eum cui collatum voluit, juris quicquam transferat; atque ita eo facto liberum jam & suæ potestatis populum relinquit, cujus rei exemplum unum annales Scotici suppeditant. Barclay contra Monarchom. l. iii. c. 16.*
25   Which in *English* runs thus.

    §. 237. What then, can there no case happen wherein the people may of right, and by their own authority, help themselves, take arms, and set upon their king, imperiously domineering over them? None at all, whilst he remains a king. Honour the king, and he that resists the power, resists the ordinance of God; are
30   *divine oracles that will never permit it. The people therefore can never come by a power over him, unless he does something that makes him cease to be a king: for then he divests himself of his crown and dignity, and returns to the state of a private man, and the people become free and superior, the power which they had in the interregnum, before they crowned him king, devolving to them again.*
35   *But there are but few miscarriages which bring the matter to this state. After considering it well on all sides, I can find but two. Two cases there are, I say, whereby a king, ipso facto, becomes no king, and loses all power and regal authority over his people; which are also taken notice of by Winzerus.*

    The first is, If he endeavour to overturn the government, that is, if he have a
40   *purpose and design to ruin the kingdom and common-wealth, as it is recorded of*

Nero, that he resolved to cut off the senate and people of Rome, lay the city waste with fire and sword, and then remove to some other place. And of Caligula, that he openly declared, that he would be no longer a head to the people or senate, and that he had it in his thoughts to cut off the worthiest men
5   of both ranks, and then retire to Alexandria: and he wisht that the people had but one neck, that he might dispatch them all at a blow. Such designs as these, when any king harbours in his thoughts, and seriously promotes, he immediately gives up all care and thought of the common-wealth; and consequently forfeits the power of governing his subjects, as a master does the dominion over his
10 slaves whom he hath abandoned.

    §. 238. *The other case is, When a king makes himself the dependent of another, and subjects his kingdom which his ancestors left him, and the people put free into his hands, to the dominion of another: for however perhaps it may not be his intention to prejudice the people; yet because he has hereby lost the*
15 *principal part of regal dignity, viz. to be next and immediately under God, supreme in his kingdom; and also because he betrayed or forced his people, whose liberty he ought to have carefully preserved, into the power and dominion of a foreign nation. By this, as it were, alienation of his kingdom, he himself loses the power he had in it before, without transferring any the least right to*
20 *those on whom he would have bestowed it; and so by this act sets the people free, and leaves them at their own disposal. One example of this is to be found in the Scotch Annals.*

    §. 239. In these cases *Barclay,* the great champion of absolute monarchy, is forced to allow, that a king may be *resisted,* and *ceases to be a king.* That is, in
25 short, not to multiply cases, in whatsoever he has *no authority,* there he is *no king,* and may be *resisted:* for wheresoever the *authority ceases, the king ceases too,* and becomes like other men who have no authority. And these two cases he instances in, differ little from those above mentioned, to be destructive to governments, only that he has omitted the principle from which his doctrine
30 flows; and that is, the breach of trust, in not preserving the form of government agreed on, and in not intending the end of government itself, which is the public good and preservation of property. When a king has dethroned himself, and put himself in a state of war with his people, what shall hinder them from prosecuting him who is no king, as they would any other man, who has put
35 himself into a state of war with them; *Barclay,* and those of his opinion, would do well to tell us. This farther I desire may be taken notice of out of *Barclay,* that he says, *The mischief that is designed them, the people may prevent before it be done:* whereby he allows *resistance* when tyranny is but in design. *Such designs as these* (says he) *when any king harbours in his thoughts and seriously*
40 *promotes, he immediately gives up all care and thought of the common-wealth;*

so that, according to him, the neglect of the public good is to be taken as an evidence of such *design,* or at least for a sufficient cause of *resistance.* And the reason of all, he gives in these words, *Because he betrayed or forced his people, whose liberty he ought carefully to have preserved.* What he adds, *into the*

5   *power and dominion of a foreign nation,* signifies nothing, the fault and forfeiture lying in the loss of their *liberty,* which he *ought to have preserved,* and not in any distinction of the persons to whose dominion they were subjected. The peoples right is equally invaded, and their liberty lost, whether they are made slaves to any of their own, or a *foreign nation;* and in this lies the injury,

10   and against this only have they the right of defence. And there are instances to be found in all countries, which shew, that it is not the change of nations in the persons of their governors, but the change of government, that gives the offence. *Bilson,* a bishop of our church, and a great stickler for the power and prerogative of princes, does, if I mistake not, in his treatise of *Christian subjection,*

15   acknowledge, that *princes may forfeit their power,* and their title to the obedience of their subjects; and if there needed authority in a case where reason is so plain, I could send my reader to *Bracton, Fortescue,* and the author of *the Mirrour,* and others, writers that cannot be suspected to be ignorant of our government, or enemies to it. But I thought *Hooker* alone might be enough to

20   satisfy those men, who relying on him for their ecclesiastical polity, are by a strange fate carried to deny those principles upon which he builds it. Whether they are herein made the tools of cunninger workmen, to pull down their own fabric, they were best look. This I am sure, their civil policy is so new, so dangerous, and so destructive to both rulers and people, that as former ages

25   never could bear the broaching of it; so it may be hoped, those to come, redeemed from the impositions of these *Egyptian* under-task-masters, will abhor the memory of such servile flatterers, who, whilst it seemed to serve their turn, resolved all government into absolute tyranny, and would have all men born to, what their mean souls fitted them for, slavery.

30   *§. 240.* Here, it is like, the common question will be made, *Who shall be judge,* whether the prince or legislative act contrary to their trust? This, perhaps, ill-affected and factious men may spread amongst the people, when the prince only makes use of his due prerogative. To this I reply, *The people shall be judge;* for who shall be *judge* whether his trustee or deputy acts well, and

35   according to the trust reposed in him, but he who deputes him, and must, by having deputed him, have still a power to discard him, when he fails in his trust? If this be reasonable in particular cases of private men, why should it be otherwise in that of the greatest moment, where the welfare of millions is concerned, and also where the evil, if not prevented, is greater, and the redress

40   very difficult, dear, and dangerous?

§. 141. But farther, this question, *(Who shall be judge?)* cannot mean, that there is no judge at all: for where there is no judicature on earth, to decide controversies amongst men, *God* in heaven is *judge.* He alone, it is true, is judge of the right. But *every man* is *judge* for himself, as in all other cases, so in this,
5 whether another hath put himself into a state of war with him, and whether he should appeal to the Supreme Judge, as *Jeptha* did.

§. 242. If a controversy arise betwixt a prince and some of the people, in a matter where the law is silent, or doubtful, and the thing be of great consequence, I should think the proper *umpire,* in such a case, should be the
10 body of the *people:* for in cases where the prince hath a trust reposed in him, and is dispensed from the common ordinary rules of the law; there, if any men find themselves aggrieved, and think the prince acts contrary to, or beyond that trust, who so proper to *judge* as the body of the *people,* (who, at first, lodged that trust in him) how far they meant it should extend? But if the prince, or whoever they
15 be in the administration, decline that way of determination, the appeal then lies no where but to heaven; force between either persons, who have no known superior on earth, or which permits no appeal to a judge on earth, being properly a state of war, wherein the appeal lies only to heaven; and in that state the *injured party must judge* for himself, when he will think fit to make use of that
20 appeal, and put himself upon it.

§. 243. To conclude, The *power that every individual gave the society,* when he entered into it, can never revert to the individuals again, as long as the society lasts, but will always remain in the community; because without this there can be no community, no common-wealth, which is contrary to the
25 original agreement: so also when the society hath placed the legislative in any assembly of men, to continue in them and their successors, with direction and authority for providing such successors, *the legislative can never revert to the people* whilst that government lasts; because having provided a legislative with power to continue for ever, they have given up their political power to the
30 legislative, and cannot resume it. But if they have set limits to the duration of their legislative, and made this supreme power in any person, or assembly, only temporary; or else, when by the miscarriages of those in authority, it is forfeited; upon the forfeiture, or at the determination of the time set, *it reverts to the society,* and the people have a right to act as supreme, and continue the
35 legislative in themselves; or erect a new form, or under the old form place it in new hands, as they think good.

FINIS.

---

[*] It is no improbable opinion therefore, which the archphilosopher was of, that the chief person in every houshold was always, as it were, a king: so when numbers of
40 housholds joined themselves in civil societies together, kings were the first kind of

governors amongst them, which is also, as it seemeth, the reason why the name of fathers continued still in them, who, of fathers, were made rulers; as also the ancient custom of governors to do as *Melchizedec,* and being kings, to exercise the office of priests, which fathers did at the first, grew perhaps by the same occasion. Howbeit, this is not the only
5   kind of regiment that has been received in the world. The inconveniences of one kind have caused sundry others to be devised; so that in a word, all public regiment, of what kind soever, seemeth evidently to have risen from the deliberate advice, consultation and composition between men, judging it convenient and behoveful; there being no impossibility in nature considered by itself, but that man might have lived without: any
10   public regiment, *Hooker's Eccl. P. lib.* i. *sect.* 10.

      [*] The public power of all society is above every soul contained in the same society; and the principal use of that power is, to give laws unto all that are under it, which laws in such cases we must obey, unless there be reason shewed which may necessarily inforce, that the law of reason, or of God, doth enjoin the contrary, *Hook.*
15   *Eccl. Pol. l.* i. *sect.* 16.

      [*] To take away all such mutual grievances, injuries and wrongs, *i. e.* such as attend men in the state of nature, there was no way but only by growing into composition and agreement amongst themselves, by ordaining some kind of government public, and by yielding themselves subject thereunto, that unto whom they granted authority to rule
20   and govern, by them the peace, tranquillity and happy estate of the rest might be procured. Men always knew that where force and injury was offered, they might be defenders of themselves; they knew that however men may seek their own commodity, yet if this were done with injury unto others, it was not to be suffered, but by all men, and all good means to be withstood. Finally, they knew that no man might in reason take
25   upon him to determine his own right, and according to his own determination proceed in maintenance thereof, in as much as every man is towards himself, and them whom he greatly affects, partial; and therefore that strifes and troubles would be endless, except they gave their common consent, all to be ordered by some, whom they should agree upon, without which consent there would be no reason that one man should take upon
30   him to be lord or judge over another, *Hooker's Eccl. Pol. l.* i. *sect.* 10.

      [*] At the first, when some certain kind of regiment was once appointed, it may be that nothing was then farther thought upon for the manner of governing, but all permitted unto their wisdom and discretion, which were to rule, till by experience they found this for all parts very inconvenient, so as the thing which they had devised for a remedy, did
35   indeed but increase the sore, which it should have cured. They saw, that *to live by one man's will, became the cause of all men's misery.* This constrained them to come unto laws, wherein all men might see their duty beforehand, and know the penalties of transgressing them. *Hooker's Eccl. Pol. l.* i. *sect.* 10.

      [†] Civil law being the act of the whole body politic, doth therefore over-rule each
40   several part of the same body. *Hooker ibid.*

      [*] At first, when some certain kind of regiment was once approved, it may be nothing was then farther thought upon for the manner of governing, but all permitted unto their wisdom and discretion which were to rule, till by experience they found this for all parts very inconvenient, so as the thing which they had devised for a remedy, did indeed
45   but increase the sore which it should have cured. They saw, that to live by one man's will, became the cause of all men's misery. This constrained them to come unto laws wherein all men might see their duty before hand, and know the penalties of transgressing them. *Hooker's Eccl. Pol. l.* i. *sect.* 10.

      [*] The lawful power of making laws to command whole politic societies of men,
50   belonging so properly unto the same intire societies, that for any prince or potentate of

what kind soever upon earth, to exercise the same of himself, and not by express commission immediately and personally received from God, or else by authority derived at the first from their consent, upon whose persons they impose laws, it is no better than mere tyranny. Laws they are not therefore which public approbation hath not made so. *Hooker's Eccl. Pol. l. i. sect.* 10. Of this point therefore we are to note, that sith men naturally have no full and perfect power to command whole politic multitudes of men, therefore utterly without our consent, we could in such sort be at no man's commandment living. And to be commanded we do consent, when that society, whereof we be a part, hath at any time before consented, without revoking the same after by the like universal agreement. Laws therefore human, of what kind so ever, are available by consent. *Ibid.*

[*] Two foundations there are which bear up public societies; the one a natural inclination, whereby all men desire sociable life and fellowship; the other an order, expresly or secretly agreed upon, touching the manner of their union in living together: the latter is that which we call the law of a common-weal, the very soul of a politic body, the parts whereof are by law animated, held together, and set on work in such actions as the common good requireth. Laws politic, ordained for external order and regiment amongst men, are never framed as they should be, unless presuming the will of man to be inwardly obstinate, rebellious, and averse from all obedience to the sacred laws of his nature; in a word, unless presuming man to be, in regard of his depraved mind, little better than a wild beast, they do accordingly provide, notwithstanding, so to frame his outward actions, that they be no hindrance unto the common good, for which societies are instituted. Unless they do this, they are not perfect. *Hooker's Eccl. Pol. l. i. sect.* 10.

[*] Human laws are measures in respect of men whose actions they must direct, howbeit such measures they are as have also their higher rules to be measured by, which rules are two, the law of God, and the law of nature; so that laws human must be made according to the general laws of nature, and without contradiction to any positive law of scripture, otherwise they are ill made. *Hooker's Eccl. Pol. l. iii. sect.* 9. To constrain men to any thing inconvenient doth seem unreasonable. *Ibid. l. i. sect.* 10.